Entire contents copyright © 2012, 2018 by Ancco. Translation copyright © 2018 by Janet Hong. All rights reserved. No part of this book (except small portions for review purposes) may be reproduced in any form without written permission from Ancco or Drawn & Quarterly. Originally published in Korean by Changbi Publishers, Inc.

drawnandquarterly.com

978-1-77046-329-5 | First edition: September 2018 | Printed in Canada | 10 9 8 7 6 5 4 3 2 1

Cataloguing data available from Library and Archives Canada.

Published in the USA by Drawn & Quarterly, a client publisher of Farrar, Straus and Giroux. Orders: 888.330.8477 | Published in Canada by Drawn & Quarterly, a client publisher of Raincoast Books. Orders: 800.663.5714 | Published in the United Kingdom by Drawn & Quarterly, a client publisher of Publishers Group UK. Orders: info@pguk.co.uk

Bad Friends is published under the support of Literature Translation Institute of Korea (LTI Korea).

Canada Drawn & Quarterly acknowledges the support of the Government of Canada and the Canada Council for the Arts for our publishing program.

bad friends / ancco

translated by janet hong

drawn & quarterly

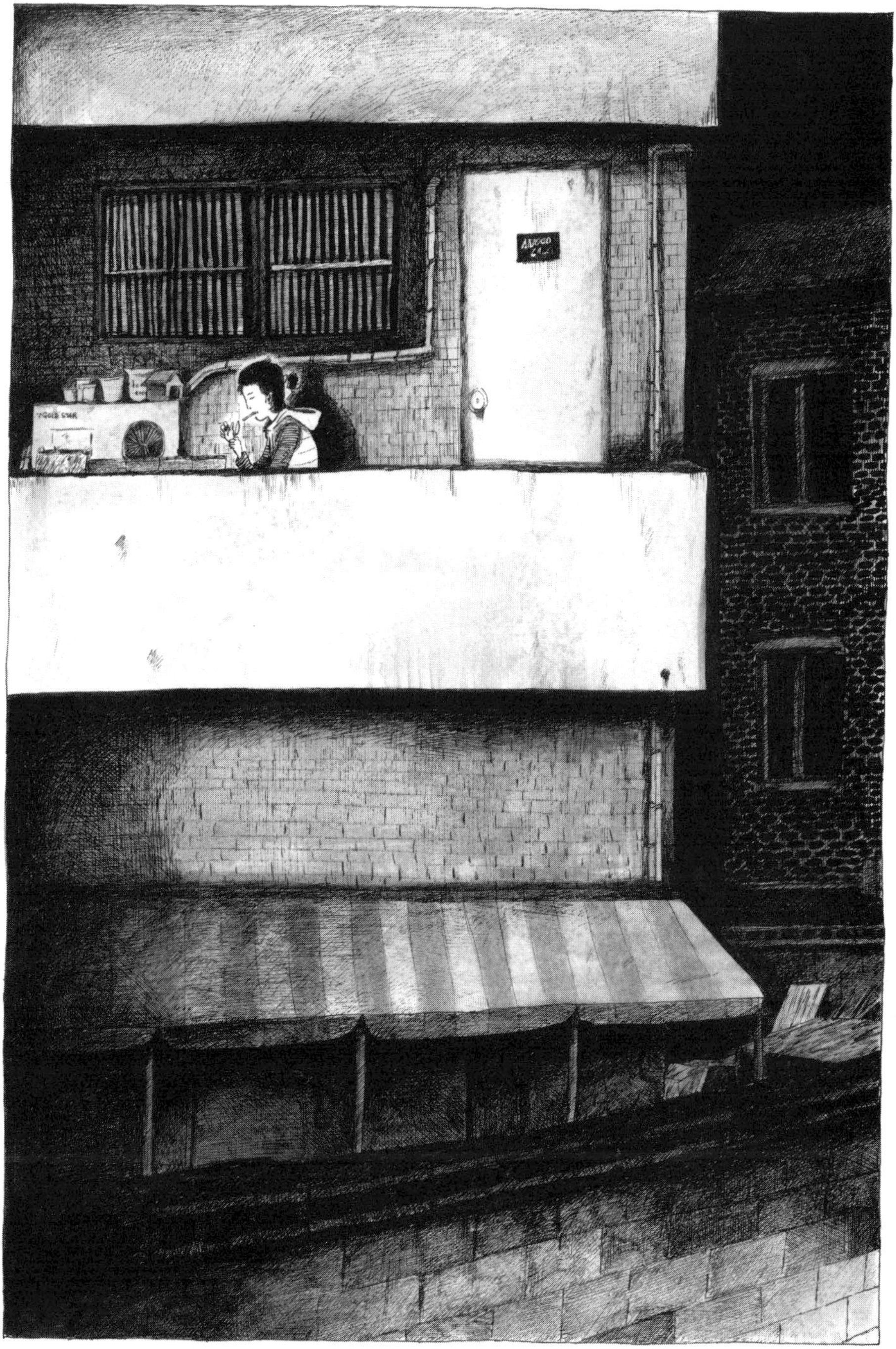

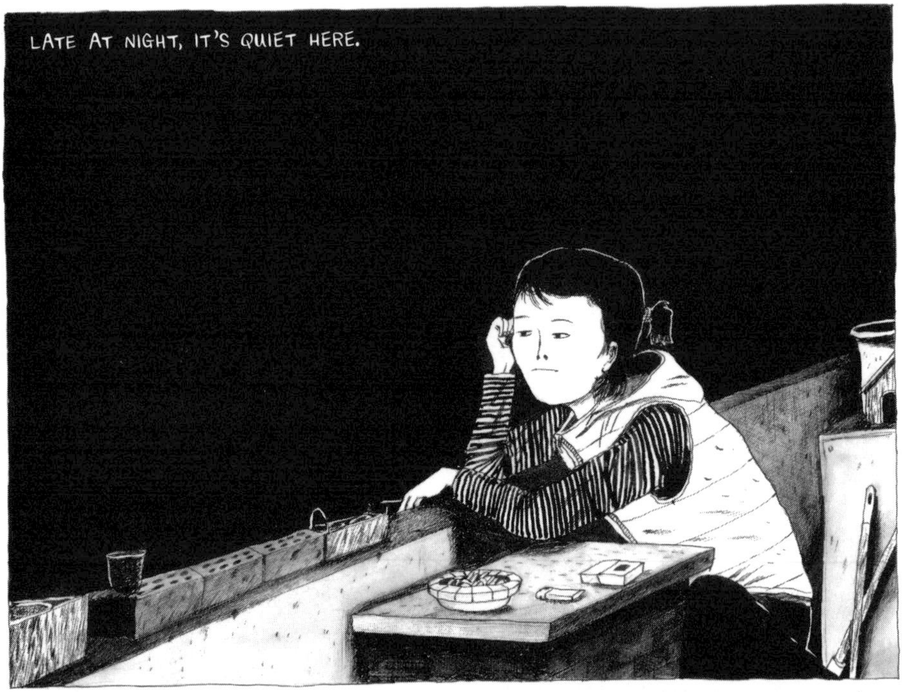
LATE AT NIGHT, IT'S QUIET HERE.

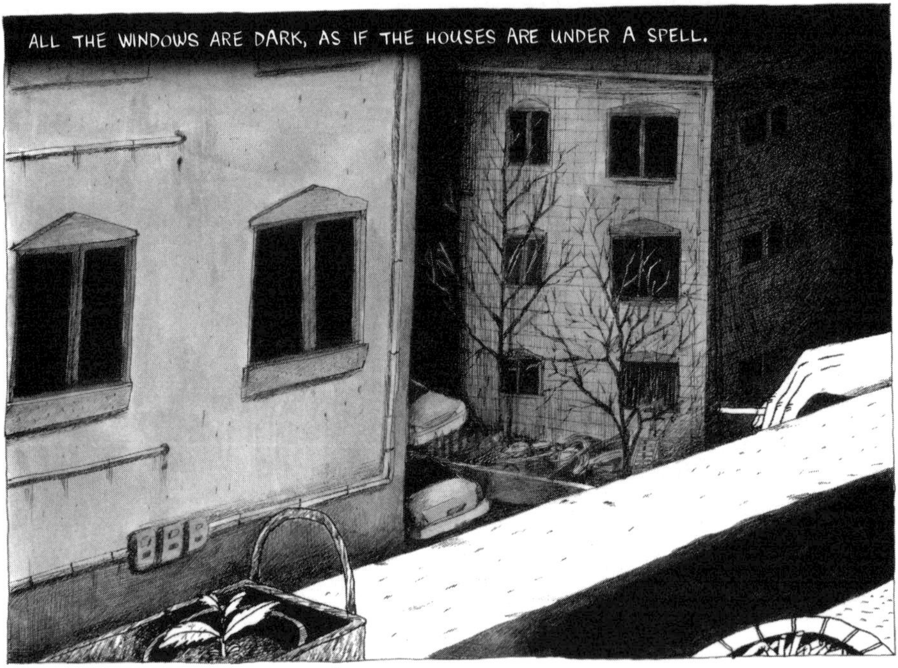
ALL THE WINDOWS ARE DARK, AS IF THE HOUSES ARE UNDER A SPELL.

I'VE BEEN HEARING DUCKS FOR THE PAST SEVERAL YEARS.
QUACK
QUACK
QUACK
QUACK
I DON'T KNOW EXACTLY WHERE...
BUT A BUNCH OF THEM LIVE SOMEWHERE OVER THERE.
QUACK
QUACK
QUACK
QUACK
QUACK
QUACK

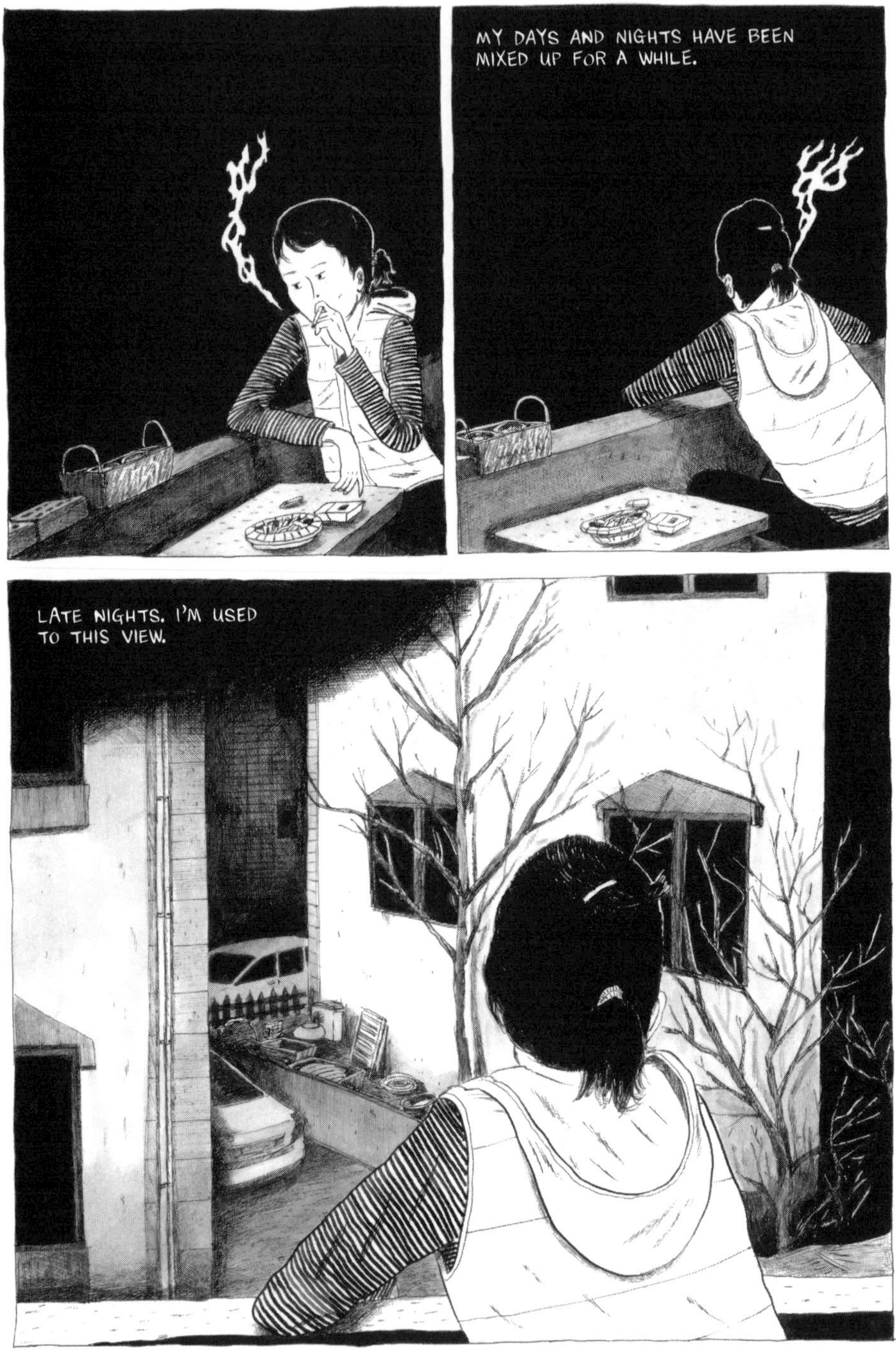
MY DAYS AND NIGHTS HAVE BEEN MIXED UP FOR A WHILE.
LATE NIGHTS. I'M USED TO THIS VIEW.

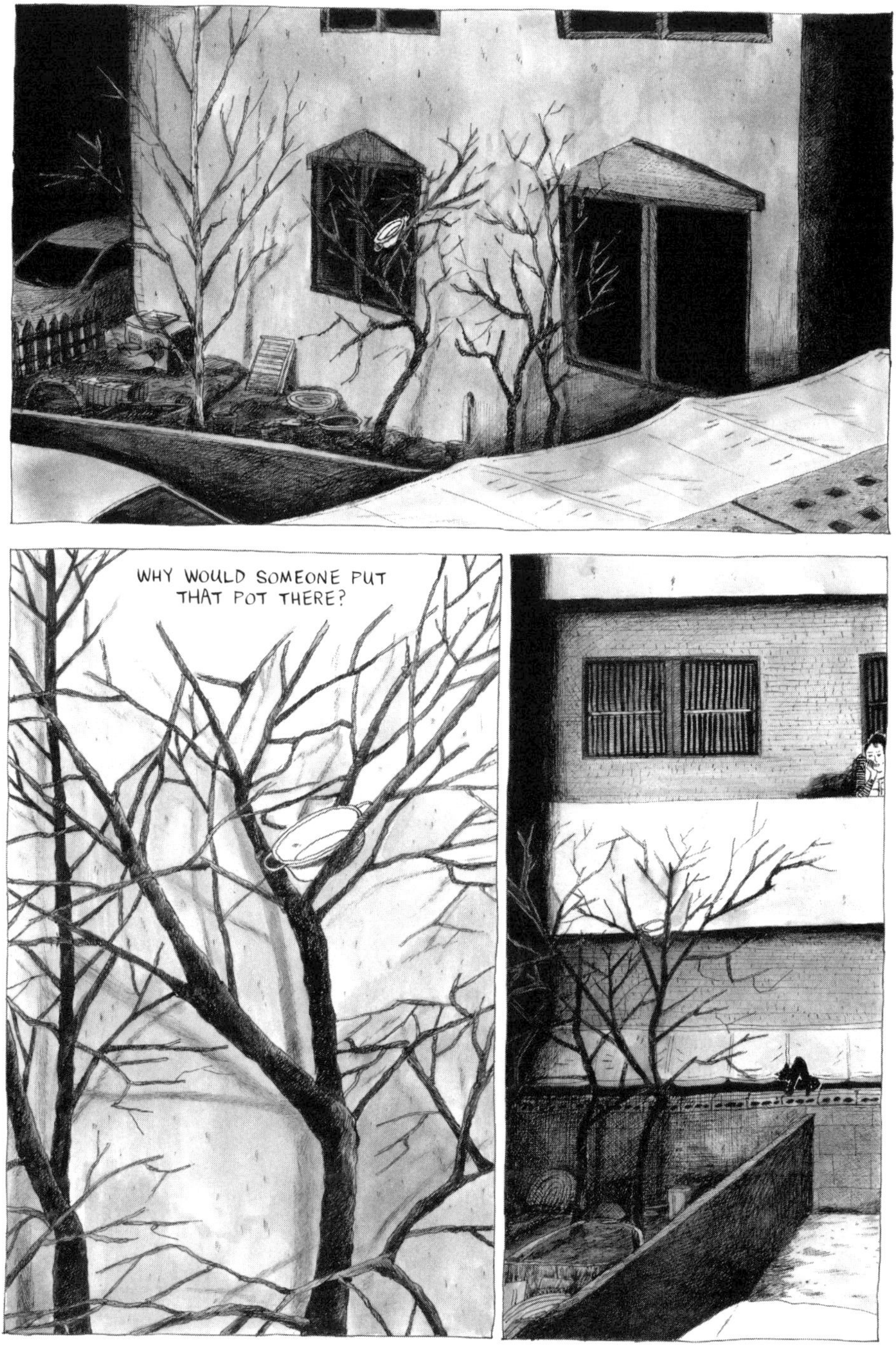
WHY WOULD SOMEONE PUT THAT POT THERE?

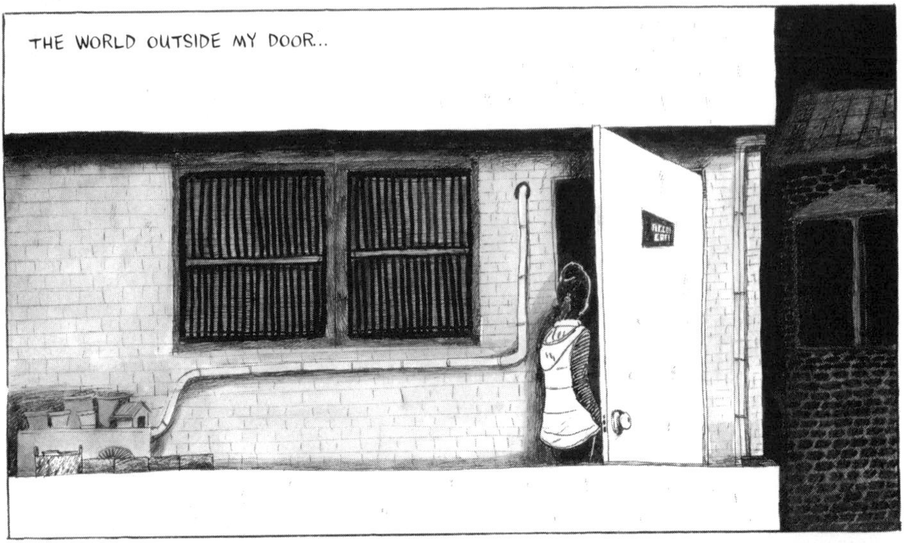
THE WORLD OUTSIDE MY DOOR...

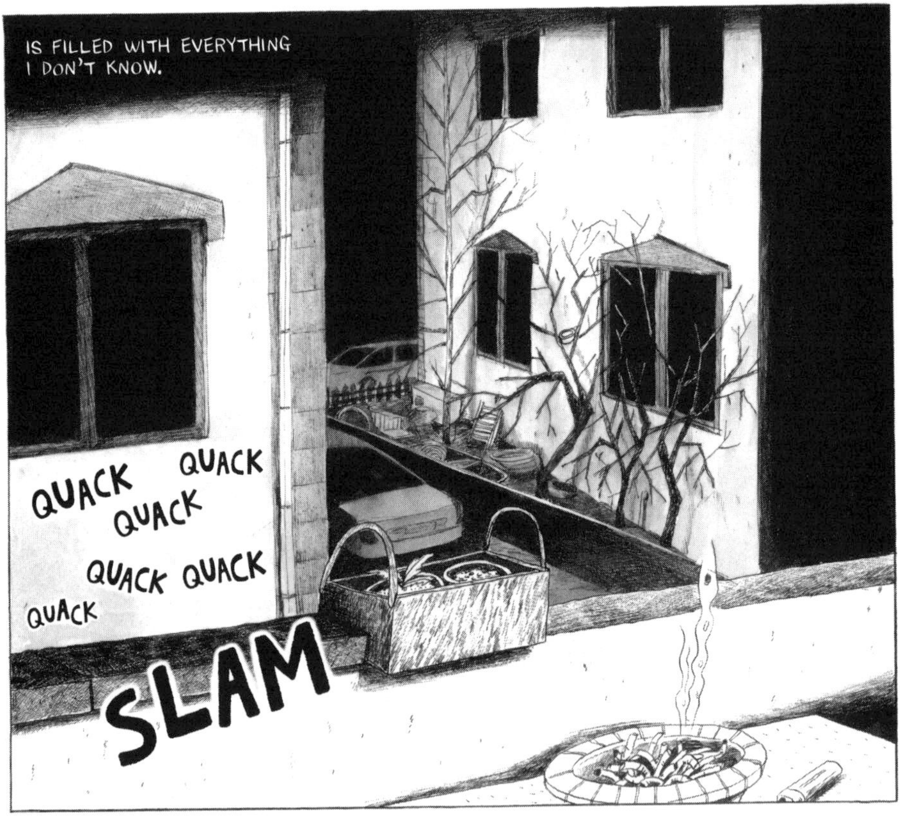
IS FILLED WITH EVERYTHING
I DON'T KNOW.
QUACK QUACK
QUACK
QUACK QUACK
QUACK
QUACK
SLAM

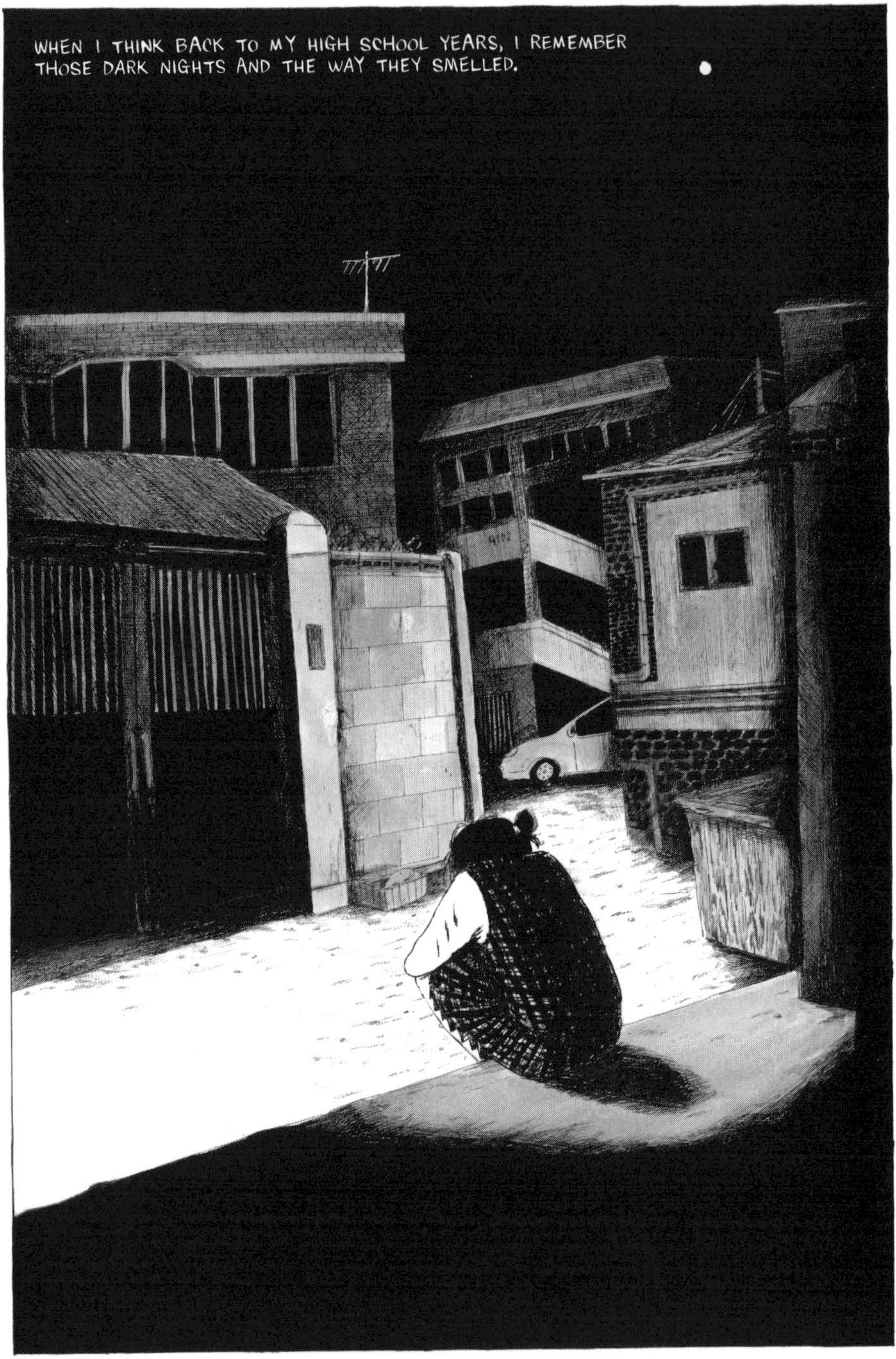
WHEN I THINK BACK TO MY HIGH SCHOOL YEARS, I REMEMBER THOSE DARK NIGHTS AND THE WAY THEY SMELLED.

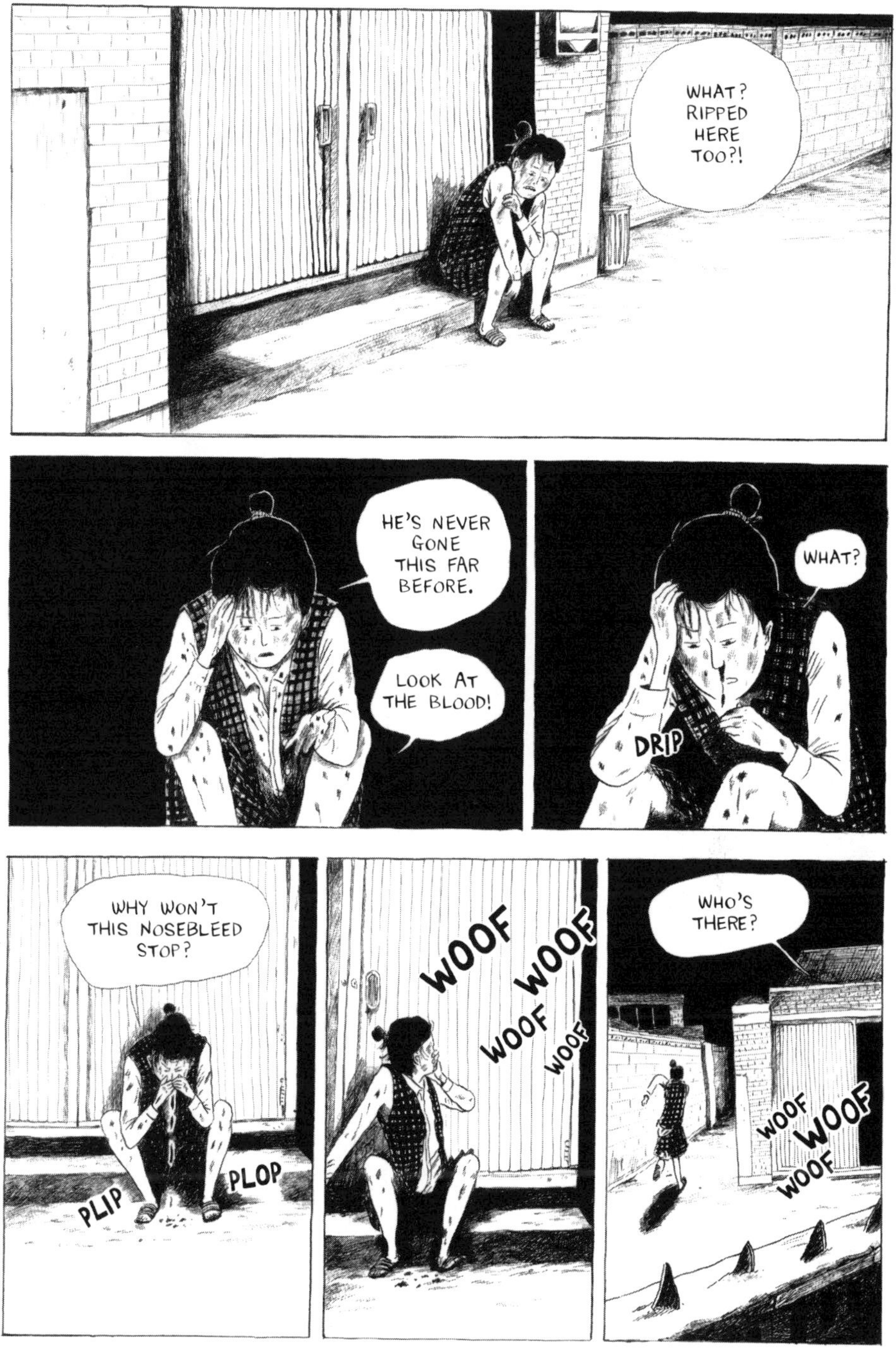
WHAT? RIPPED HERE TOO?!
HE'S NEVER GONE THIS FAR BEFORE.
LOOK AT THE BLOOD!
WHAT?
DRIP
WHY WON'T THIS NOSEBLEED STOP?
PLIP
PLOP
WOOF
WOOF
WOOF
WOOF
WHO'S THERE?
WOOF
WOOF
WOOF

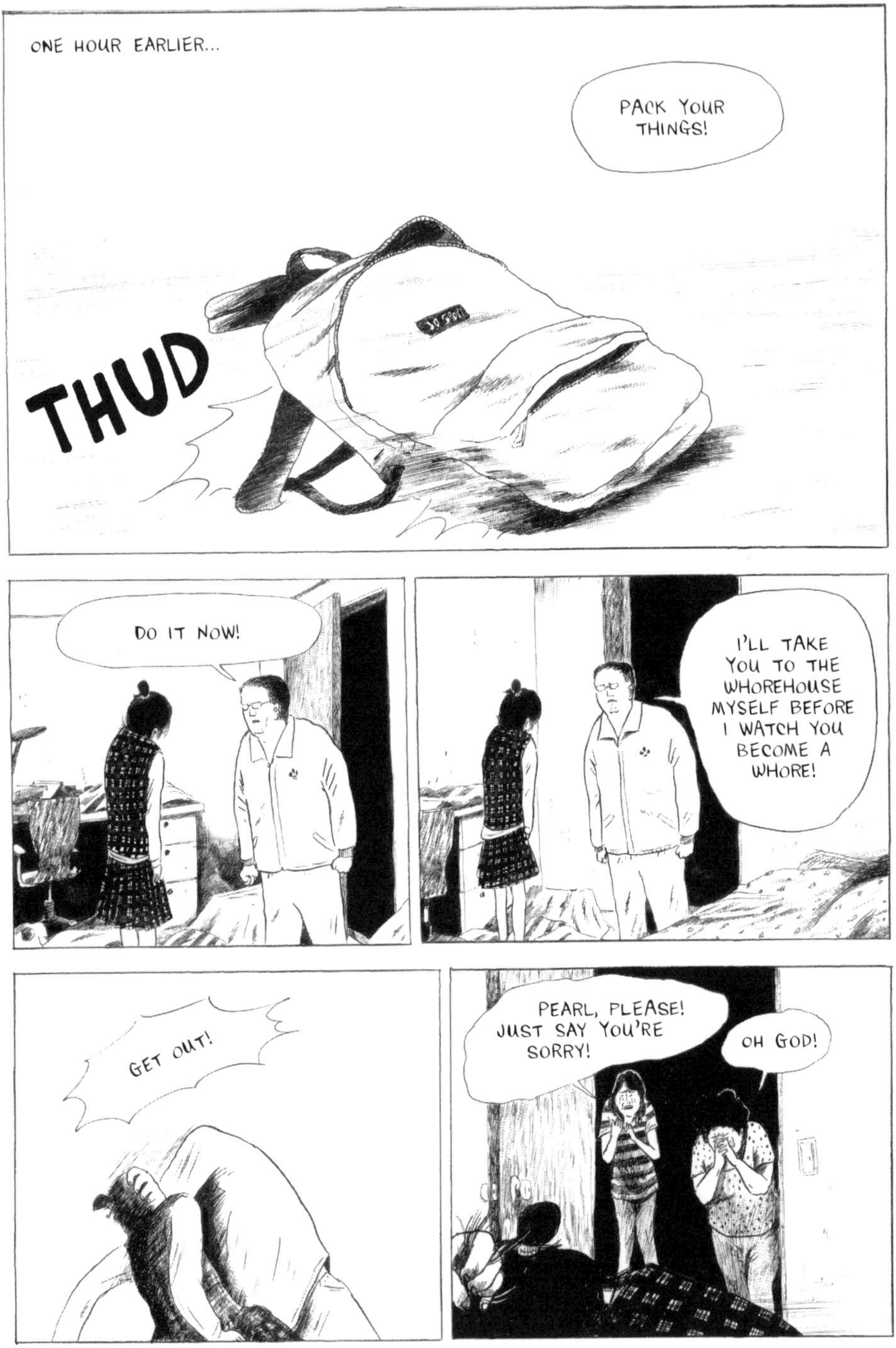
ONE HOUR EARLIER...
PACK YOUR THINGS!
THUD
DO IT NOW!
I'LL TAKE YOU TO THE WHOREHOUSE MYSELF BEFORE I WATCH YOU BECOME A WHORE!
GET OUT!
PEARL, PLEASE! JUST SAY YOU'RE SORRY!
OH GOD!

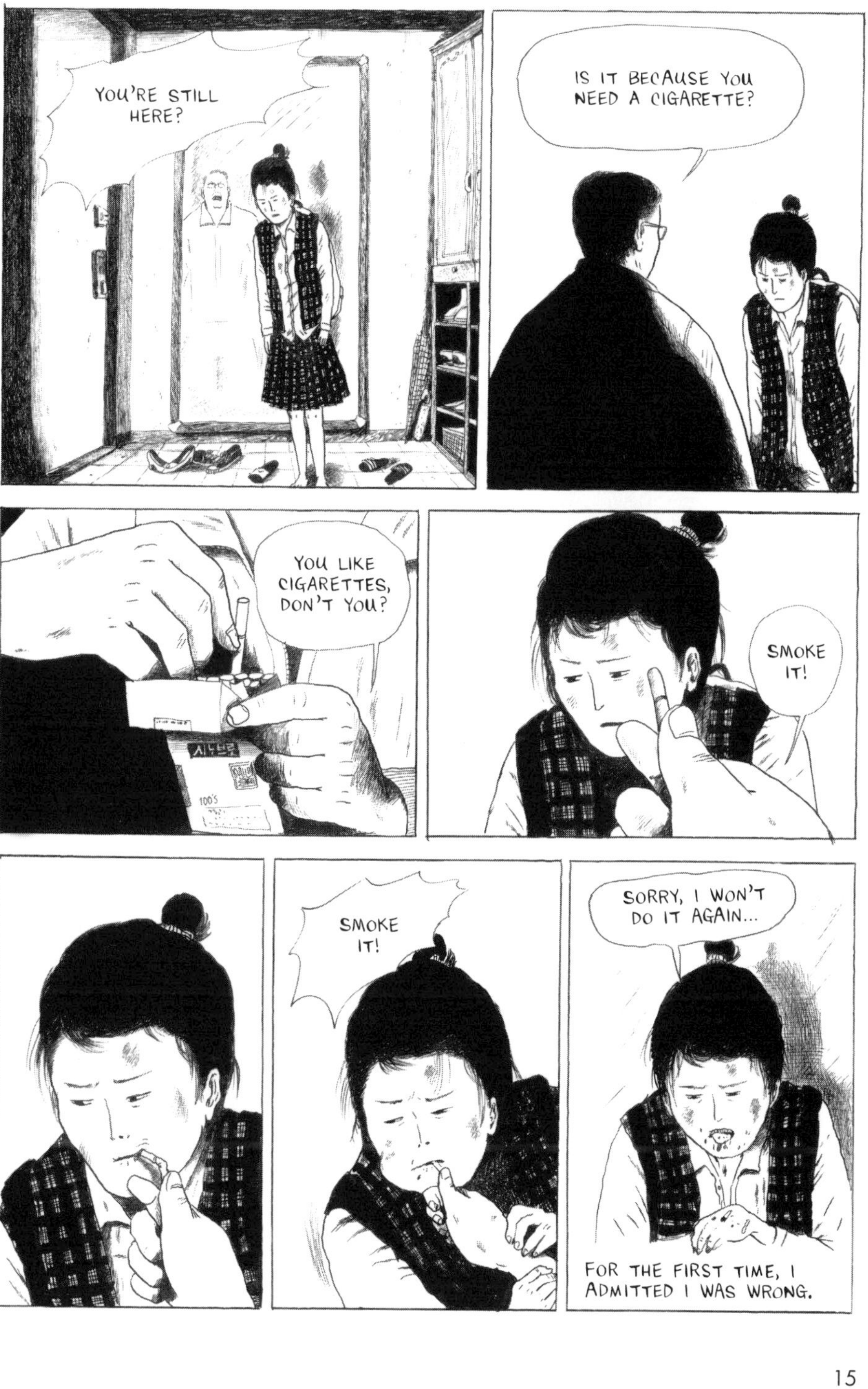
YOU'RE STILL HERE?
IS IT BECAUSE YOU NEED A CIGARETTE?
YOU LIKE CIGARETTES, DON'T YOU?
SMOKE IT!
SMOKE IT!
SORRY, I WON'T DO IT AGAIN...
FOR THE FIRST TIME, I ADMITTED I WAS WRONG.

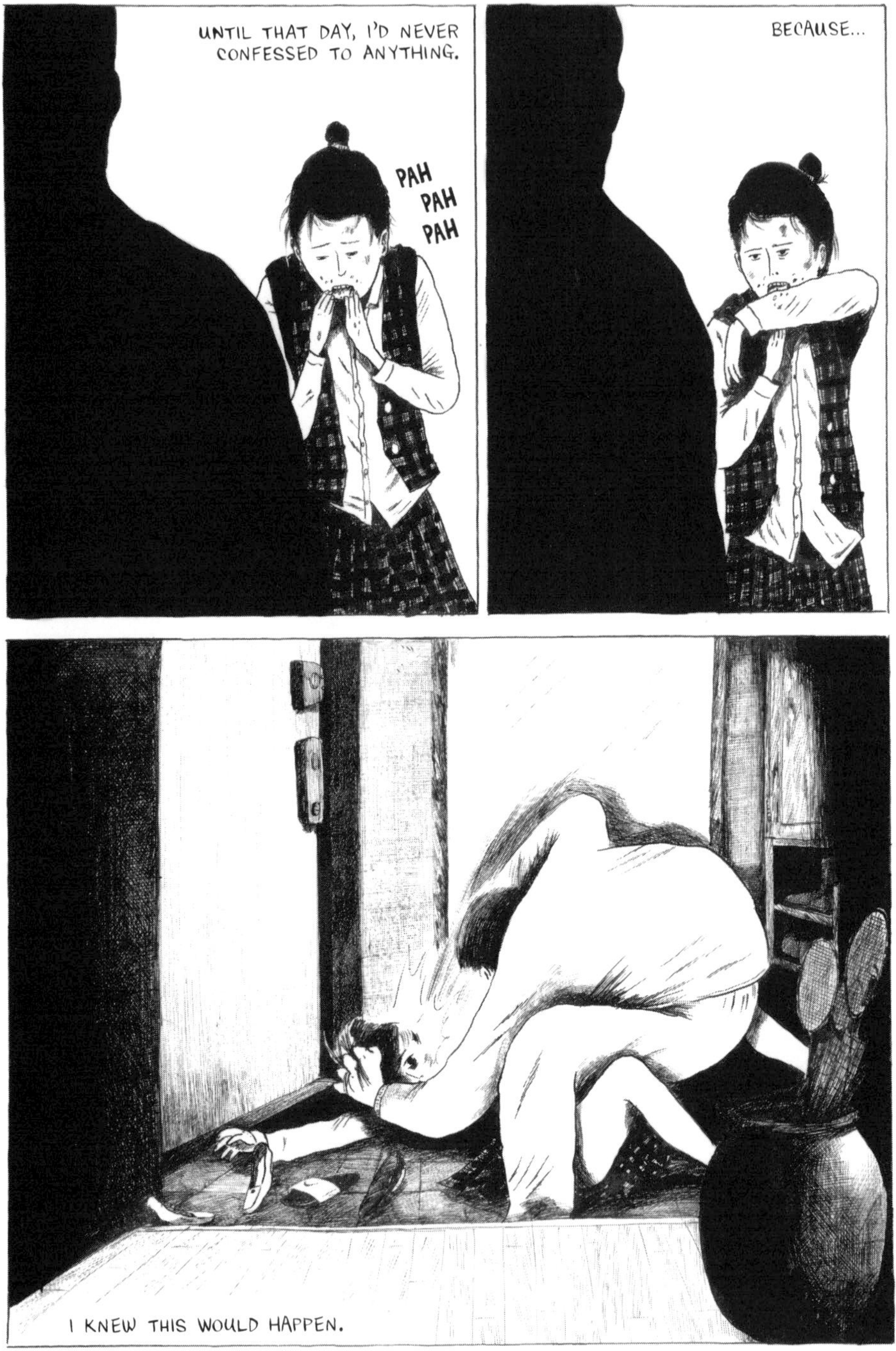
UNTIL THAT DAY, I'D NEVER CONFESSED TO ANYTHING.
PAH PAH PAH
BECAUSE...
I KNEW THIS WOULD HAPPEN.

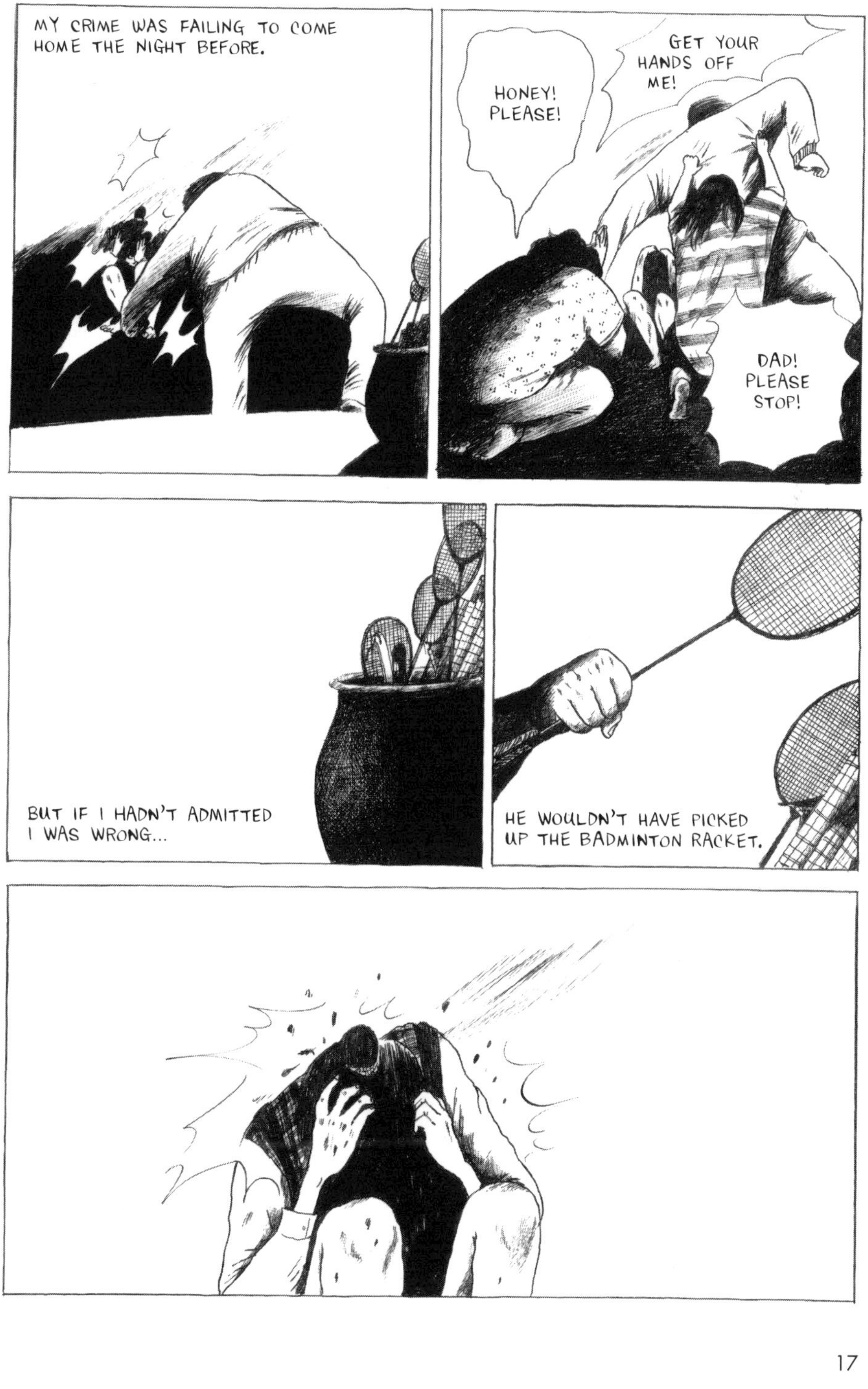
MY CRIME WAS FAILING TO COME HOME THE NIGHT BEFORE.
GET YOUR HANDS OFF ME!
HONEY! PLEASE!
DAD! PLEASE STOP!
BUT IF I HADN'T ADMITTED I WAS WRONG...
HE WOULDN'T HAVE PICKED UP THE BADMINTON RACKET.

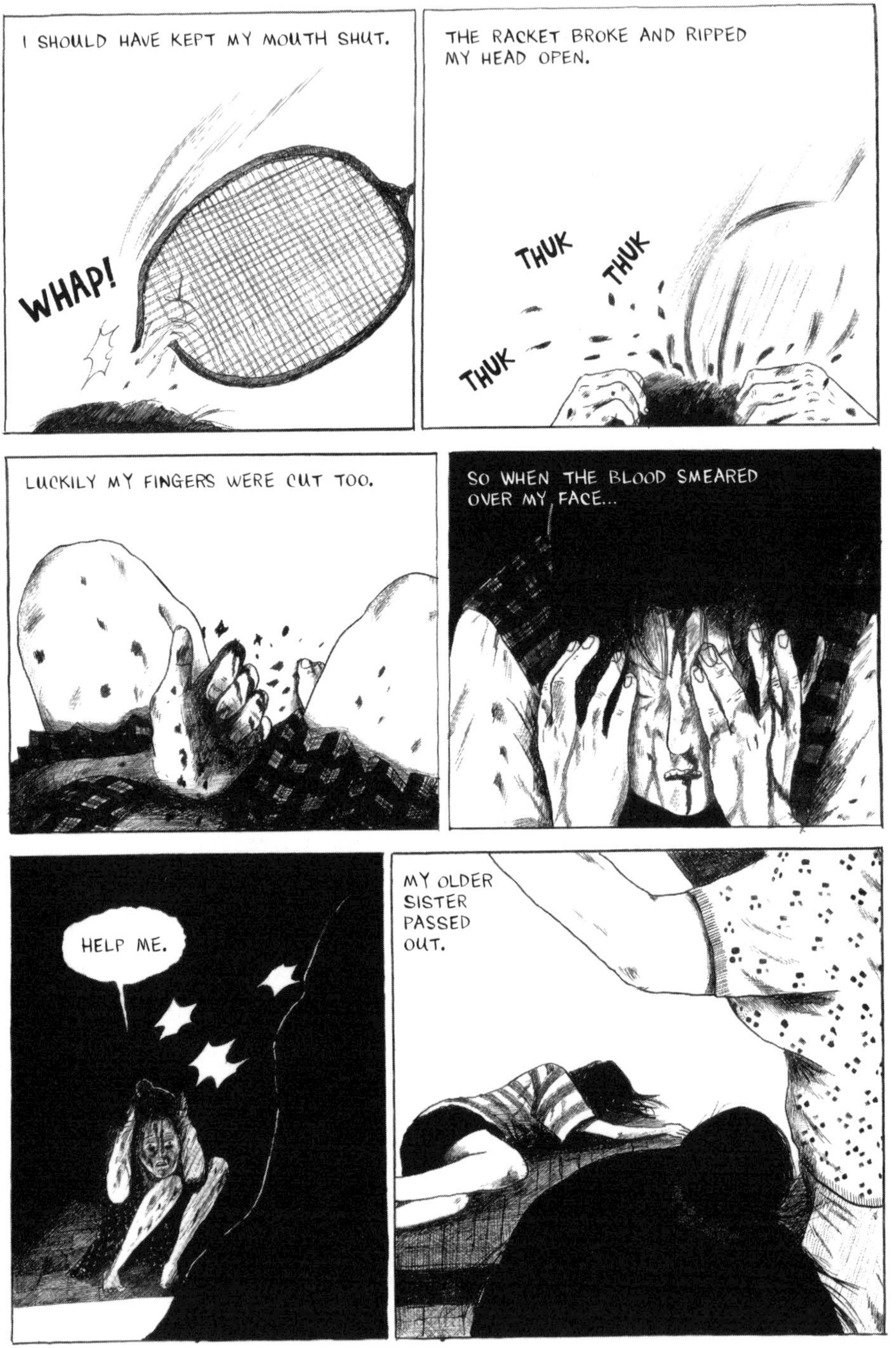
I SHOULD HAVE KEPT MY MOUTH SHUT.
WHAP!
THE RACKET BROKE AND RIPPED MY HEAD OPEN.
THUK
THUK
THUK
LUCKILY MY FINGERS WERE CUT TOO.
SO WHEN THE BLOOD SMEARED OVER MY FACE...
HELP ME.
MY OLDER SISTER PASSED OUT.

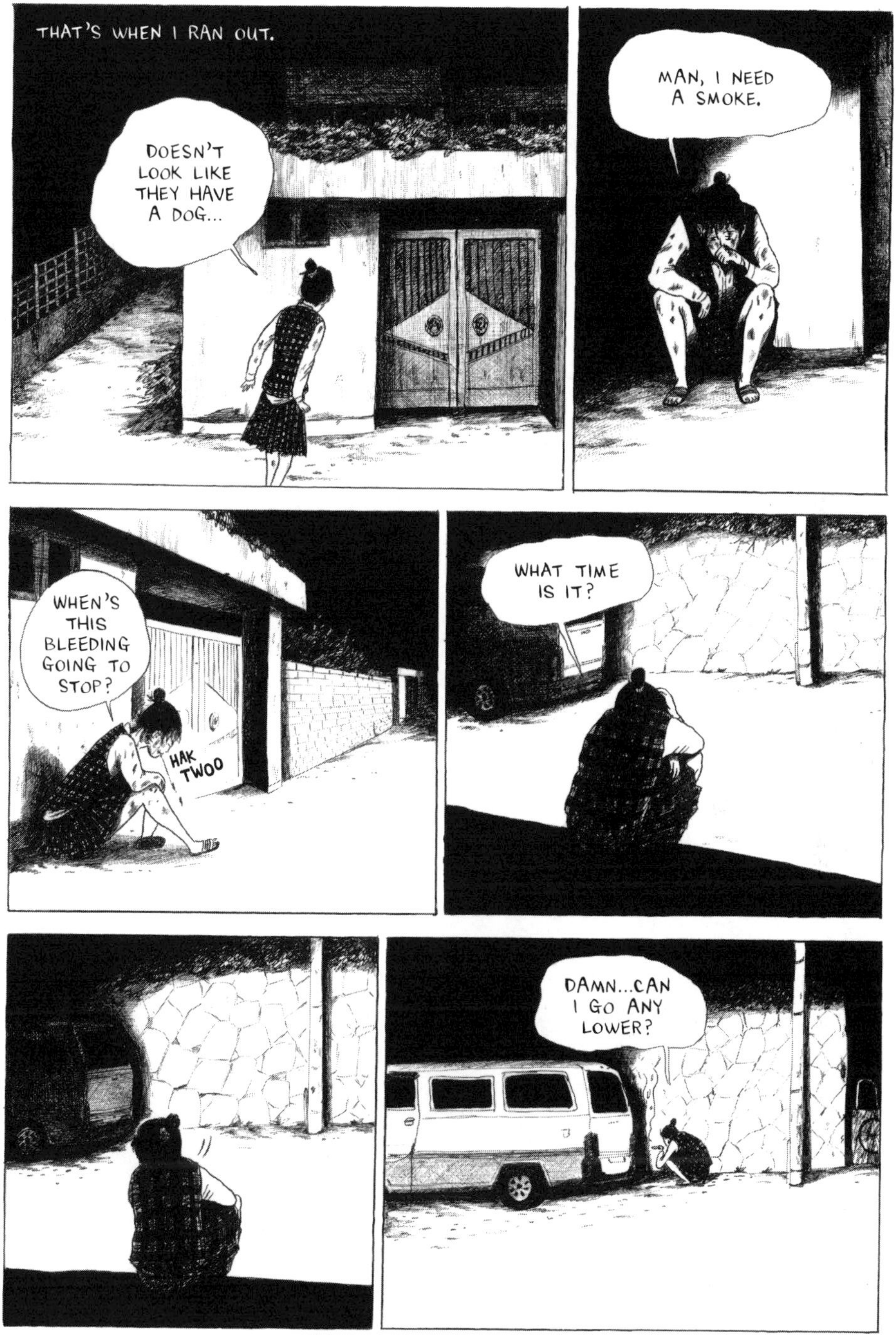
THAT'S WHEN I RAN OUT.
DOESN'T LOOK LIKE THEY HAVE A DOG...
MAN, I NEED A SMOKE.
WHEN'S THIS BLEEDING GOING TO STOP?
HAK TWOO
WHAT TIME IS IT?
DAMN...CAN I GO ANY LOWER?

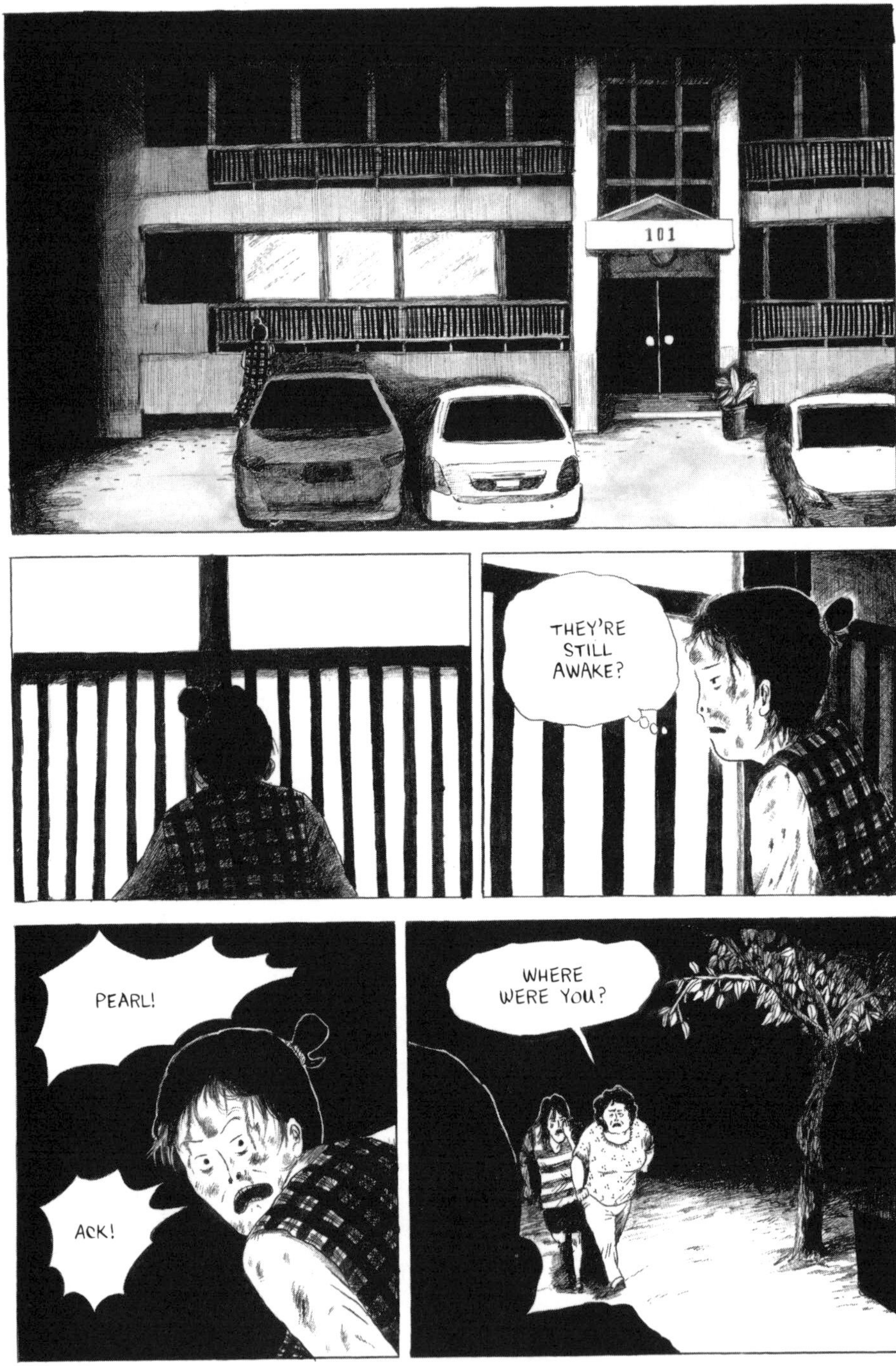
101
THEY'RE STILL AWAKE?
PEARL!
ACK!
WHERE WERE YOU?

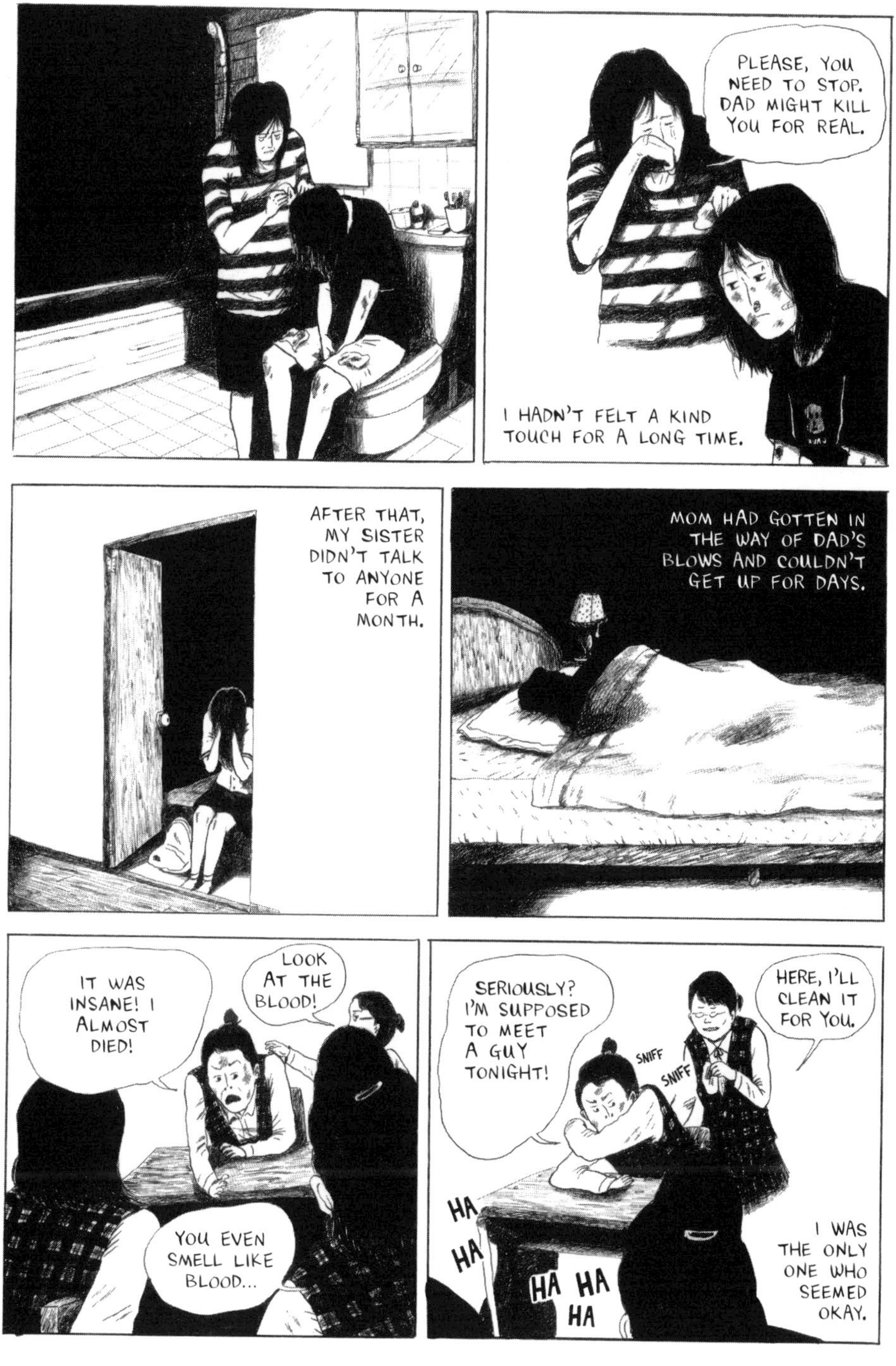
PLEASE, YOU NEED TO STOP. DAD MIGHT KILL YOU FOR REAL.
I HADN'T FELT A KIND TOUCH FOR A LONG TIME.
AFTER THAT, MY SISTER DIDN'T TALK TO ANYONE FOR A MONTH.
MOM HAD GOTTEN IN THE WAY OF DAD'S BLOWS AND COULDN'T GET UP FOR DAYS.
IT WAS INSANE! I ALMOST DIED!
LOOK AT THE BLOOD!
YOU EVEN SMELL LIKE BLOOD...
SERIOUSLY? I'M SUPPOSED TO MEET A GUY TONIGHT!
SNIFF
SNIFF
HERE, I'LL CLEAN IT FOR YOU.
HA
HA
HA HA
HA
I WAS THE ONLY ONE WHO SEEMED OKAY.

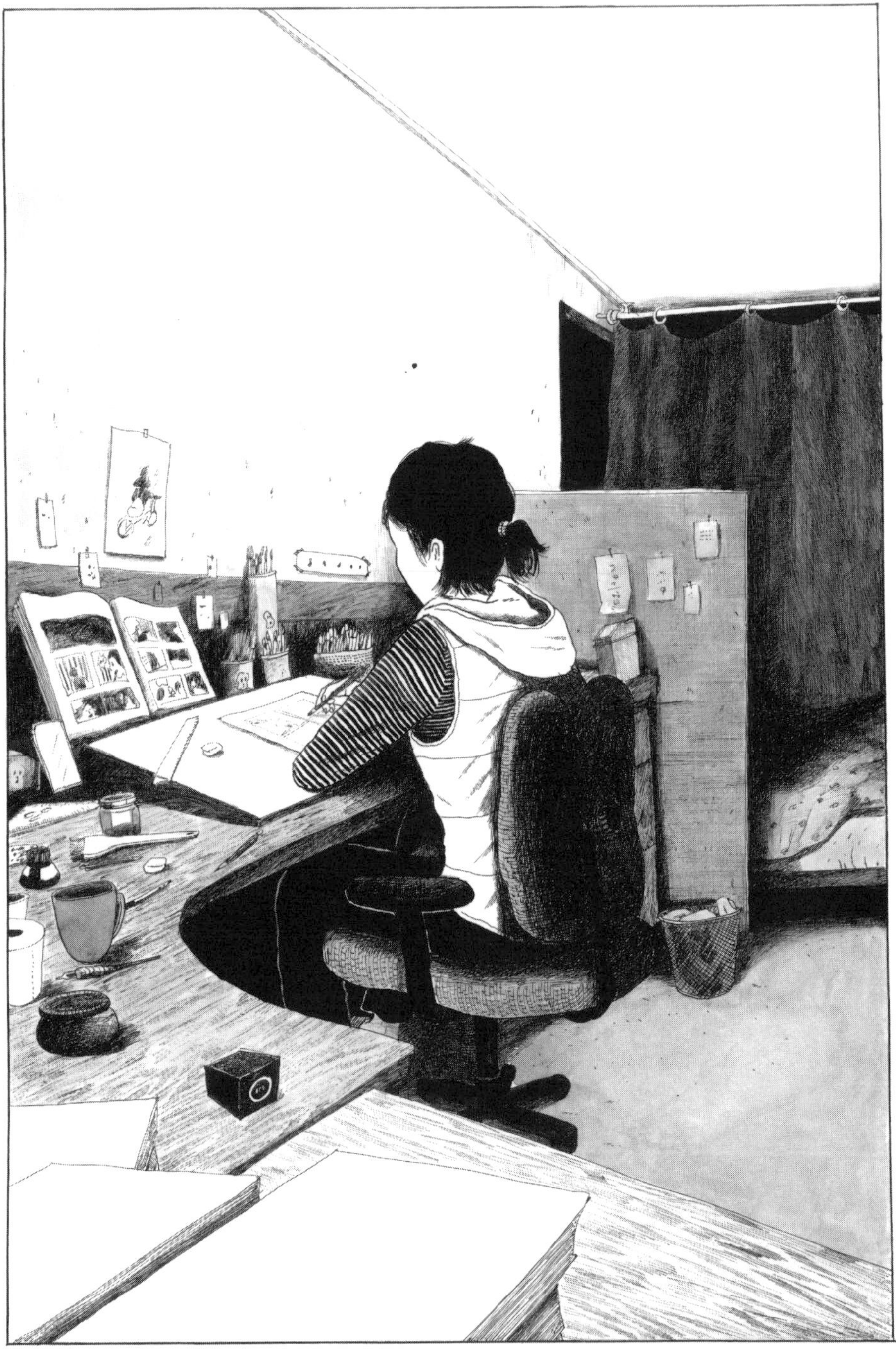

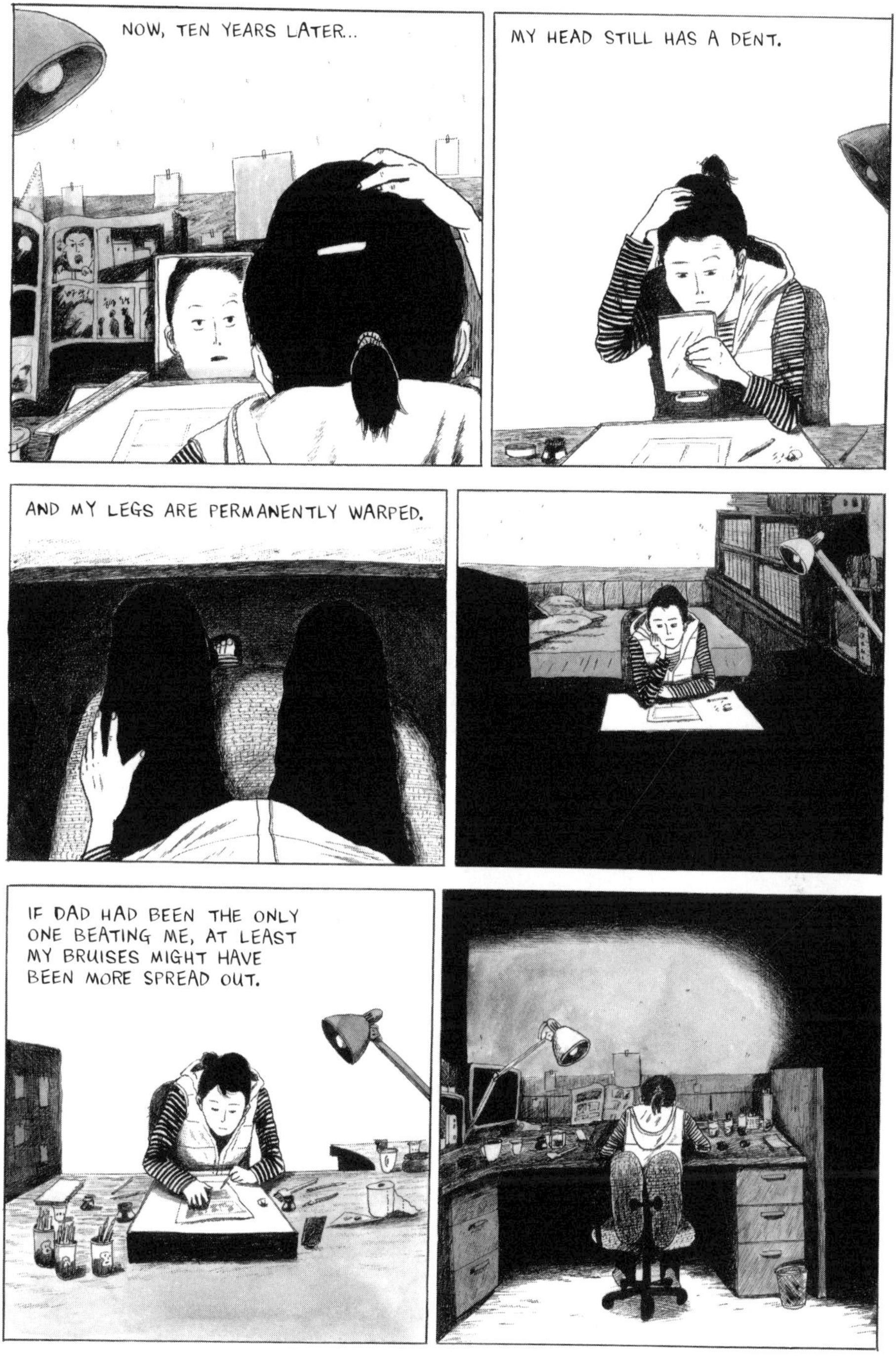
NOW, TEN YEARS LATER...
MY HEAD STILL HAS A DENT.
AND MY LEGS ARE PERMANENTLY WARPED.
IF DAD HAD BEEN THE ONLY ONE BEATING ME, AT LEAST MY BRUISES MIGHT HAVE BEEN MORE SPREAD OUT.

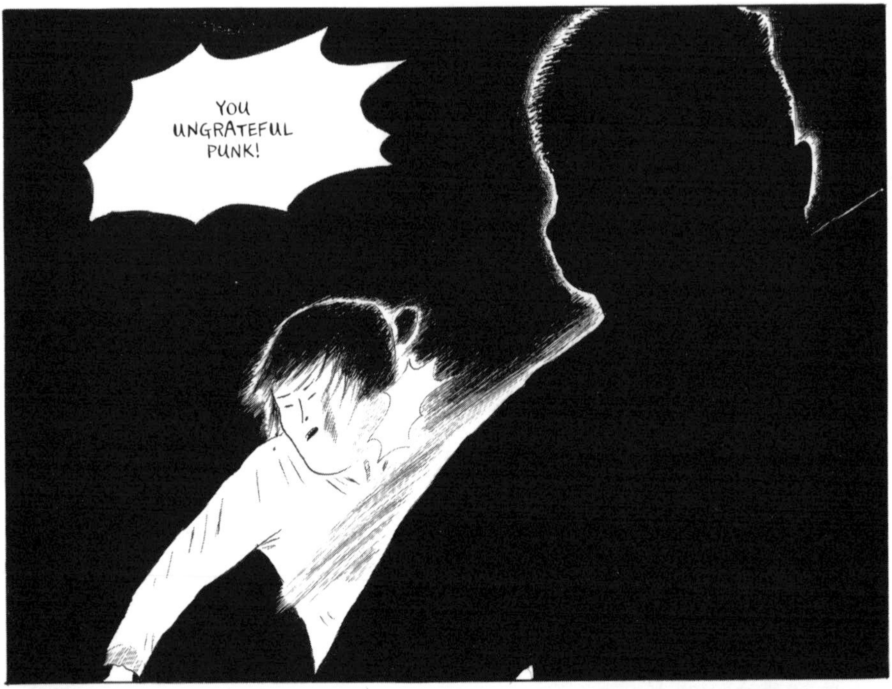
YOU UNGRATEFUL PUNK!

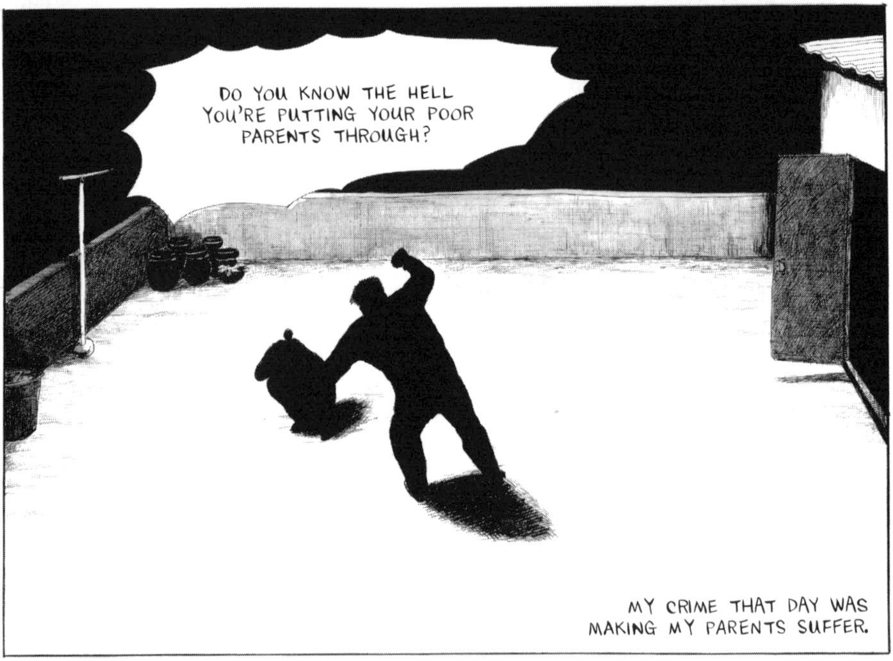
DO YOU KNOW THE HELL YOU'RE PUTTING YOUR POOR PARENTS THROUGH?
MY CRIME THAT DAY WAS MAKING MY PARENTS SUFFER.

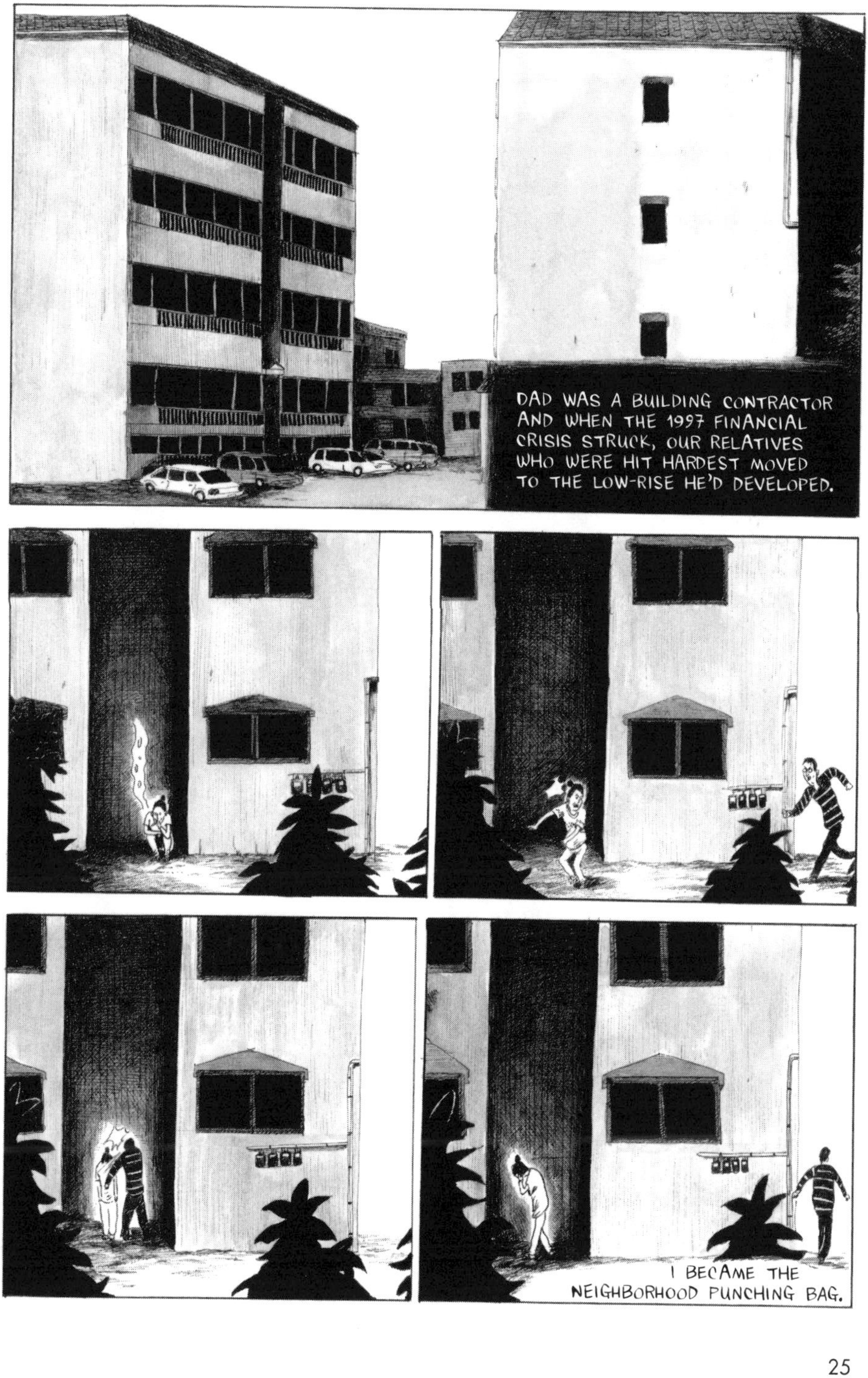
DAD WAS A BUILDING CONTRACTOR AND WHEN THE 1997 FINANCIAL CRISIS STRUCK, OUR RELATIVES WHO WERE HIT HARDEST MOVED TO THE LOW-RISE HE'D DEVELOPED.
I BECAME THE NEIGHBORHOOD PUNCHING BAG.

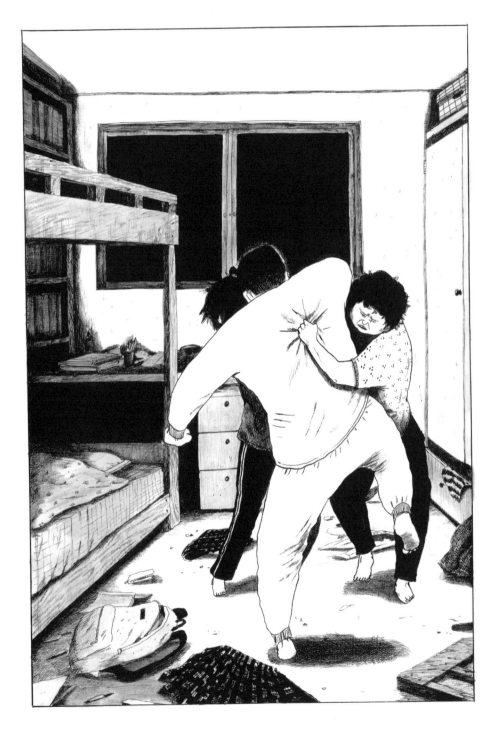

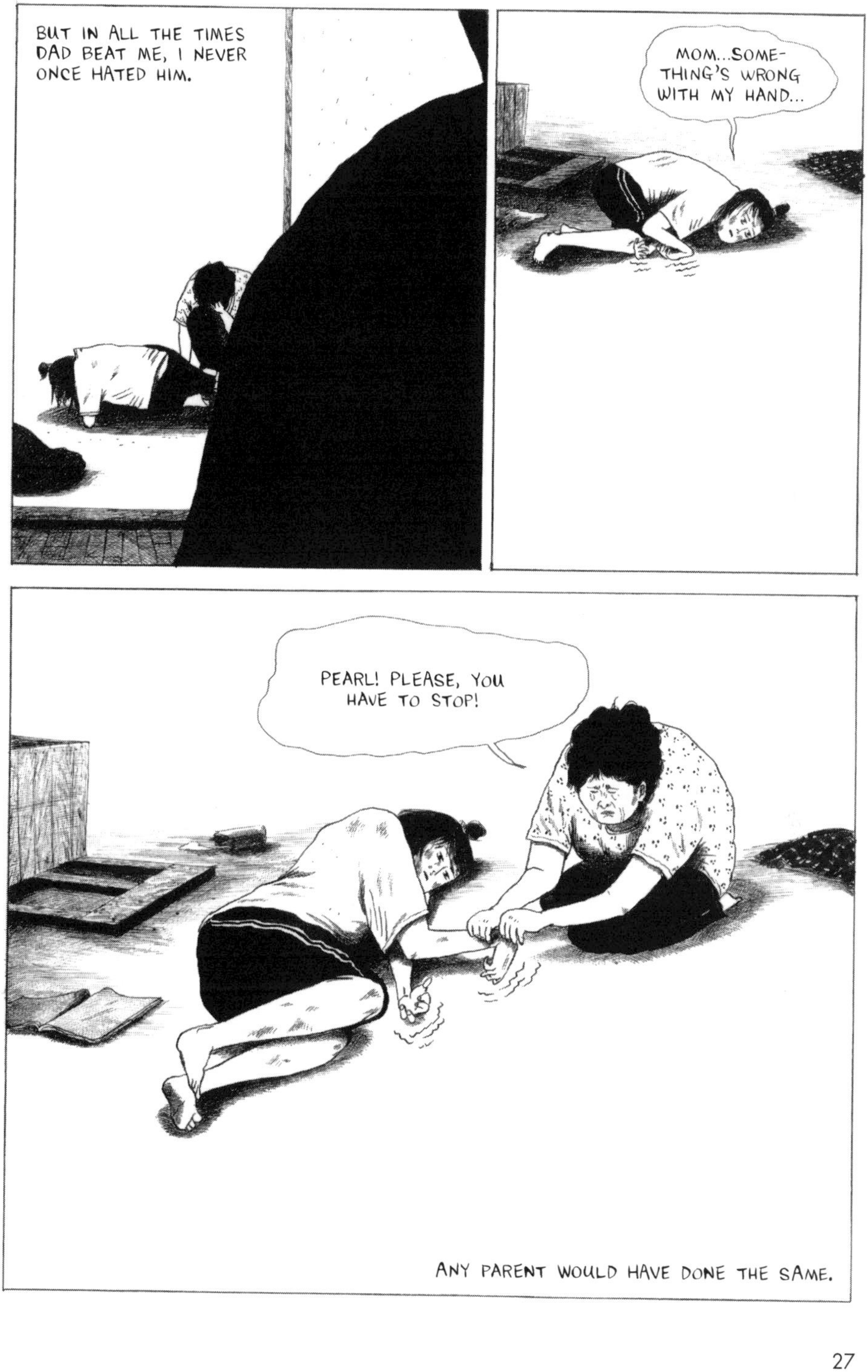
BUT IN ALL THE TIMES DAD BEAT ME, I NEVER ONCE HATED HIM.
MOM...SOME-THING'S WRONG WITH MY HAND...
PEARL! PLEASE, YOU HAVE TO STOP!
ANY PARENT WOULD HAVE DONE THE SAME.

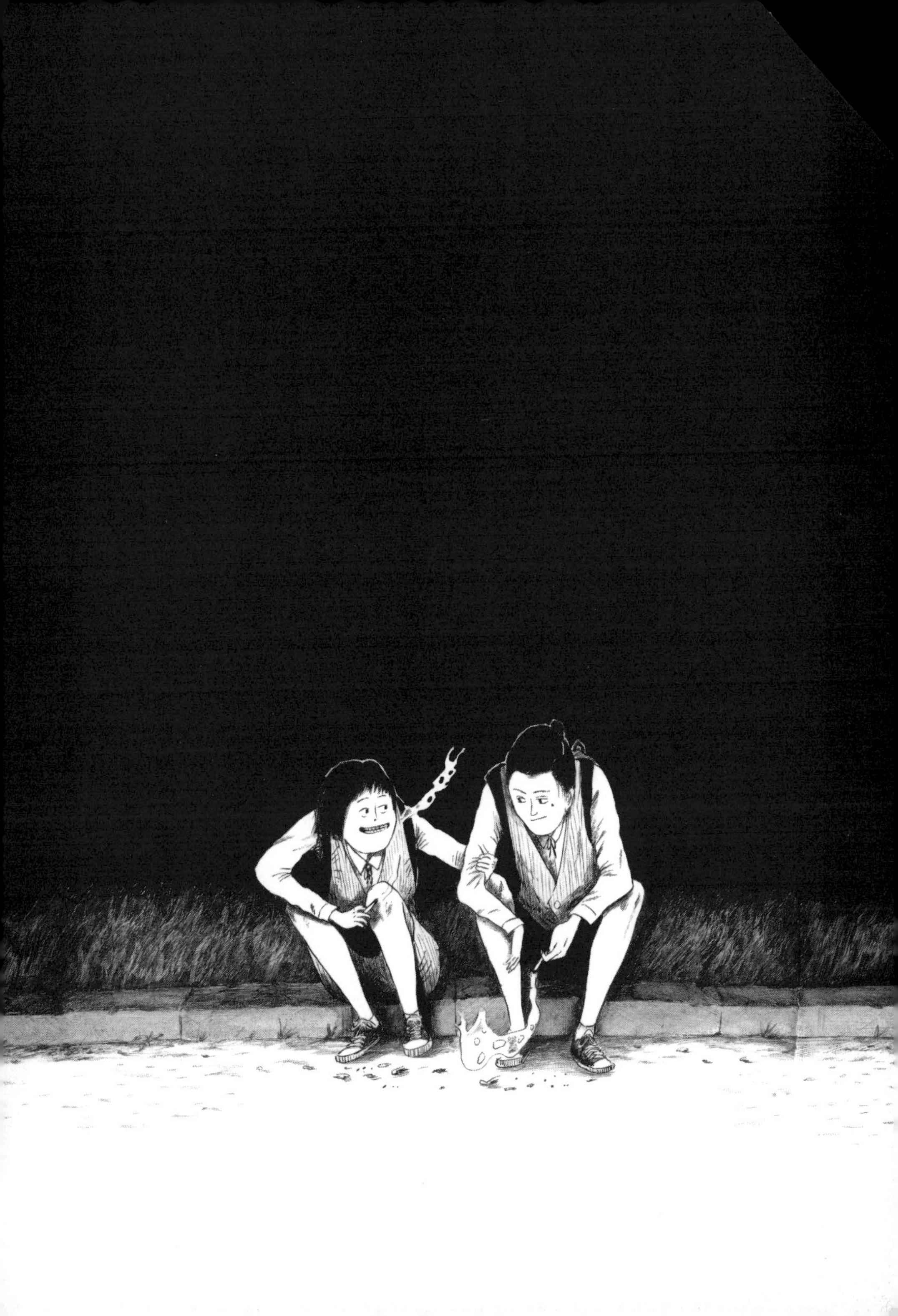

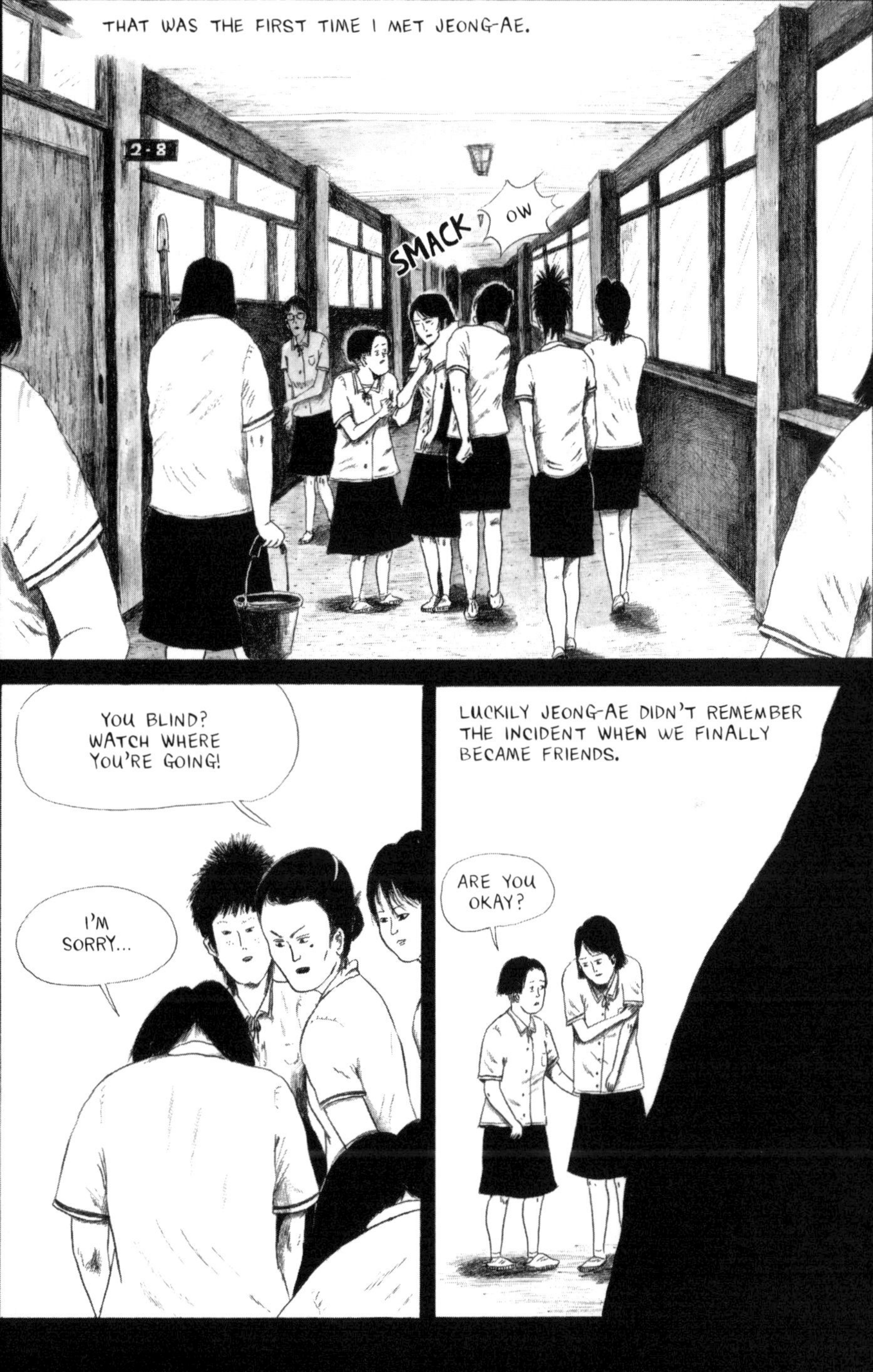
THAT WAS THE FIRST TIME I MET JEONG-AE.
2-8
SMACK
OW
YOU BLIND? WATCH WHERE YOU'RE GOING!
I'M SORRY...
LUCKILY JEONG-AE DIDN'T REMEMBER THE INCIDENT WHEN WE FINALLY BECAME FRIENDS.
ARE YOU OKAY?

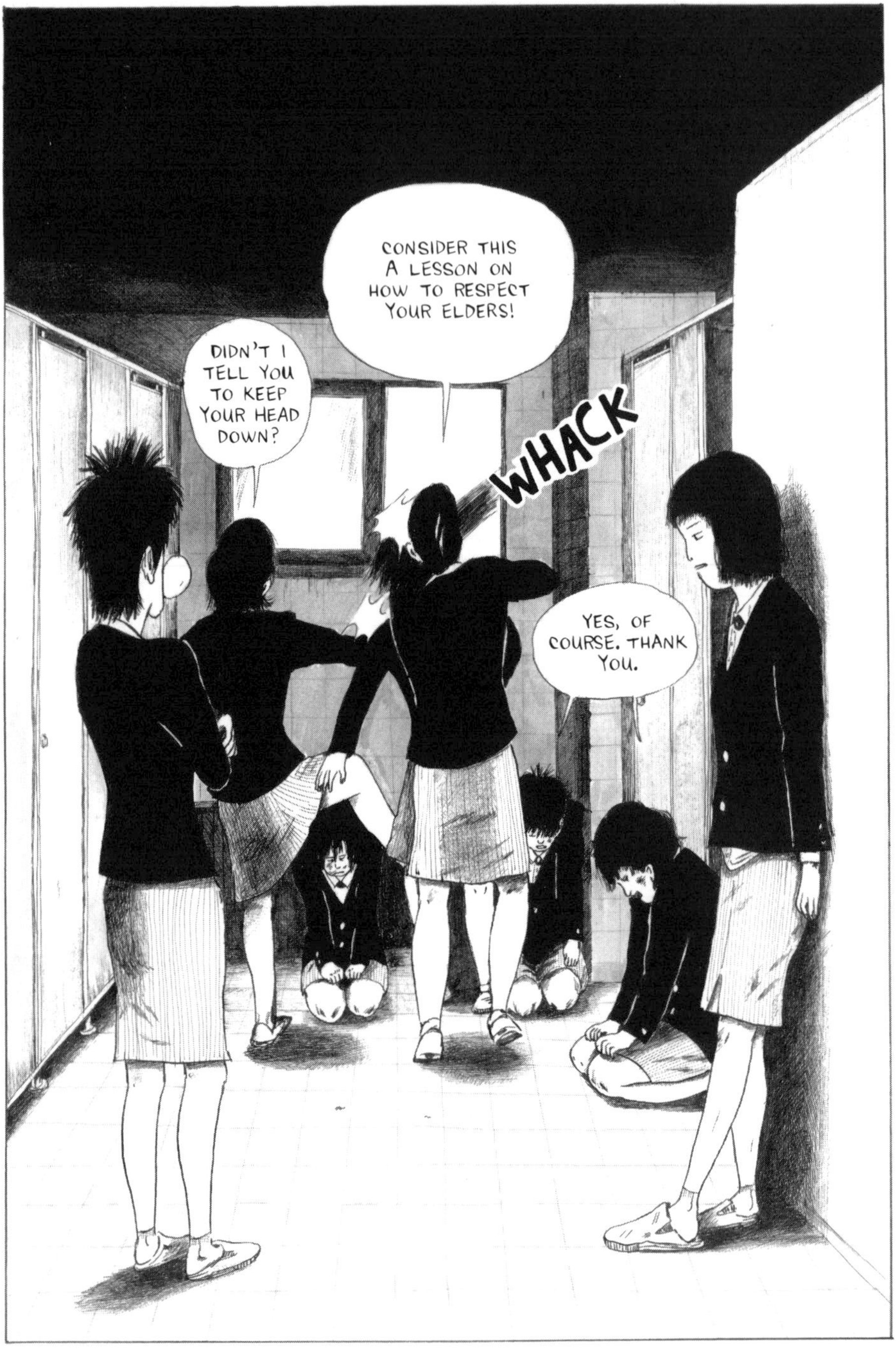
CONSIDER THIS A LESSON ON HOW TO RESPECT YOUR ELDERS!
DIDN'T I TELL YOU TO KEEP YOUR HEAD DOWN?
WHACK
YES, OF COURSE. THANK YOU.

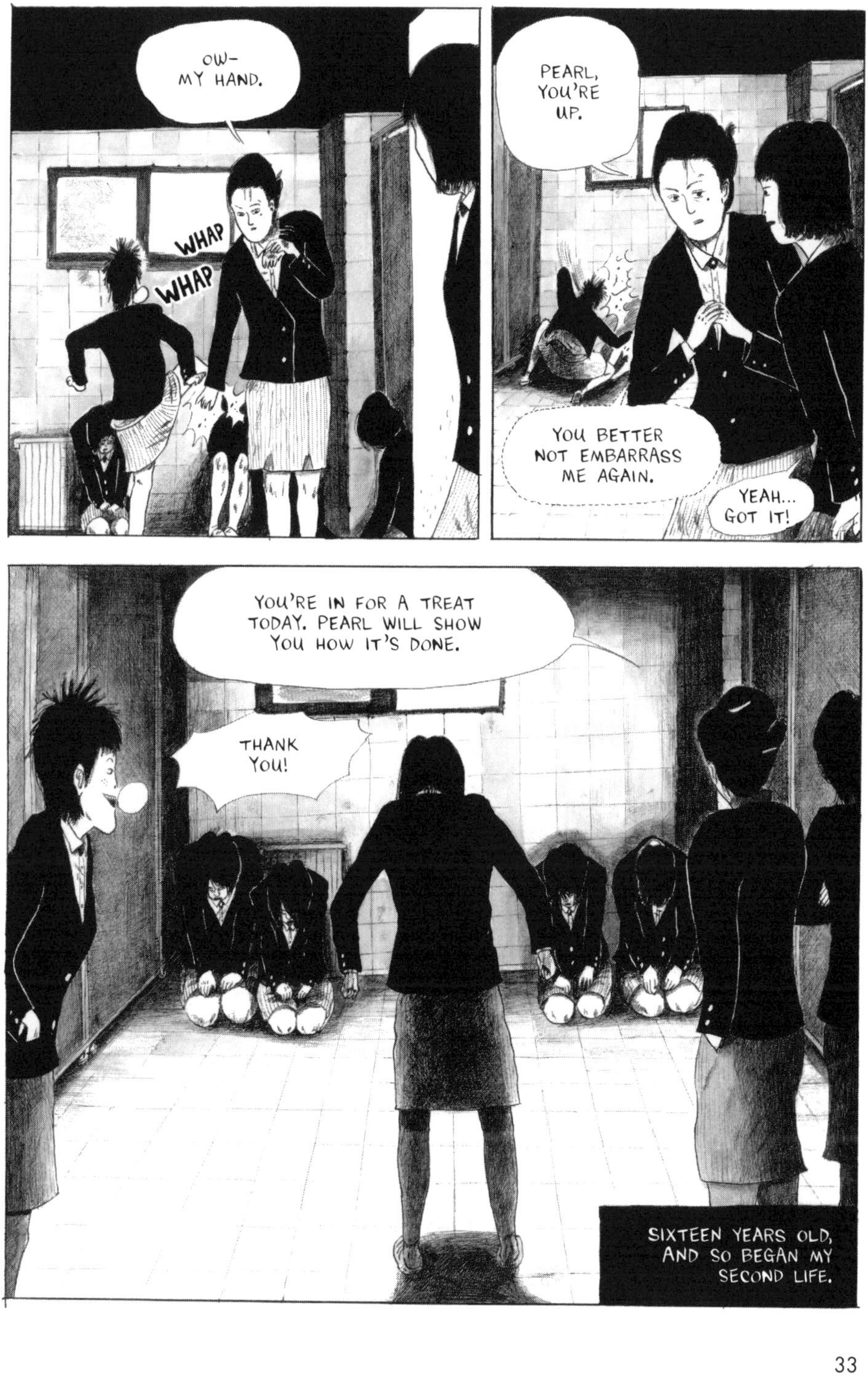
OW—
MY HAND.
WHAP
WHAP
PEARL, YOU'RE UP.
YOU BETTER NOT EMBARRASS ME AGAIN.
YEAH... GOT IT!
YOU'RE IN FOR A TREAT TODAY. PEARL WILL SHOW YOU HOW IT'S DONE.
THANK YOU!
SIXTEEN YEARS OLD, AND SO BEGAN MY SECOND LIFE.

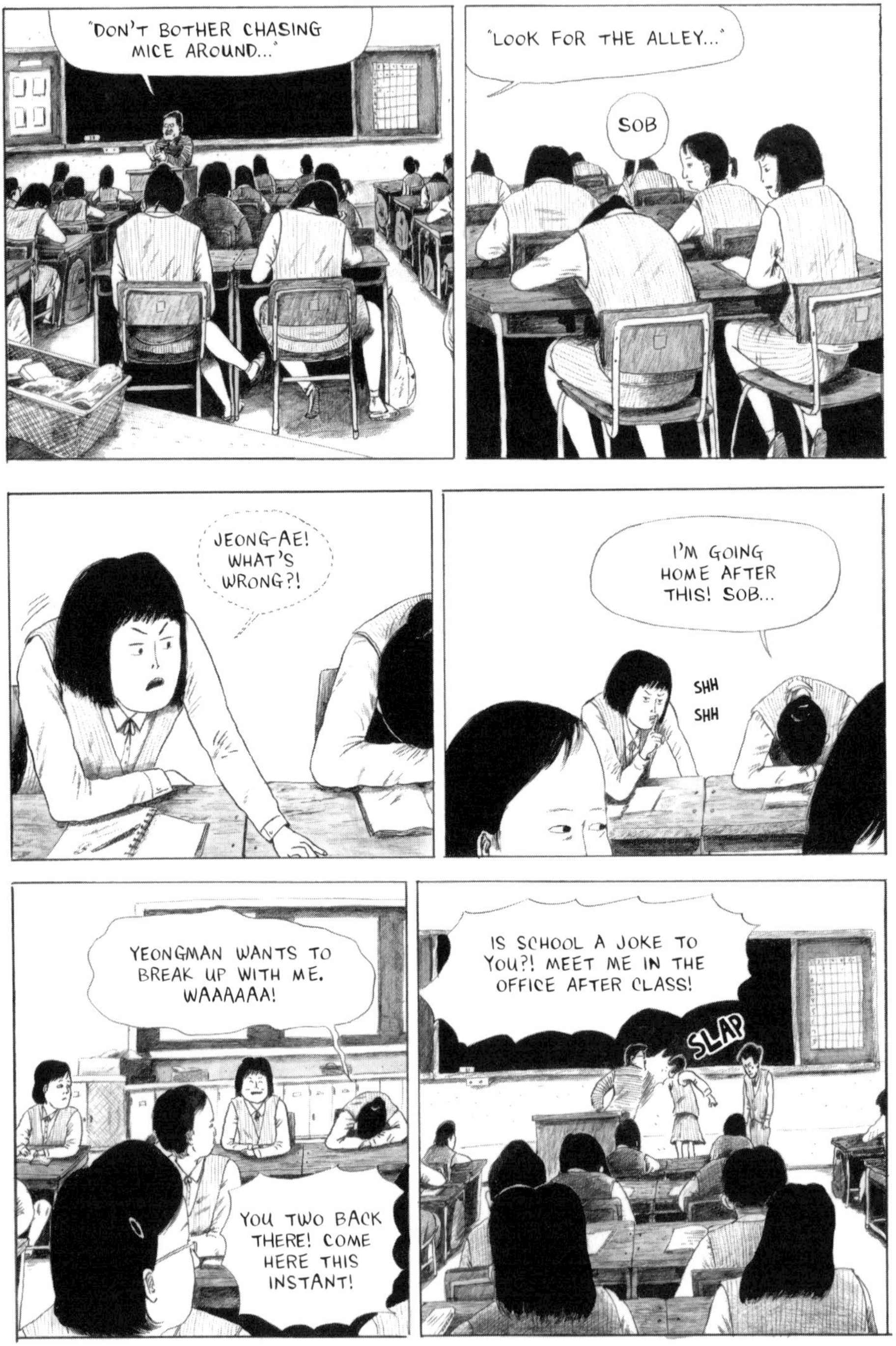
"DON'T BOTHER CHASING MICE AROUND..."
"LOOK FOR THE ALLEY..."
SOB
JEONG-AE! WHAT'S WRONG?!
I'M GOING HOME AFTER THIS! SOB...
SHH
SHH
YEONGMAN WANTS TO BREAK UP WITH ME. WAAAAAA!
YOU TWO BACK THERE! COME HERE THIS INSTANT!
IS SCHOOL A JOKE TO YOU?! MEET ME IN THE OFFICE AFTER CLASS!
SLAP

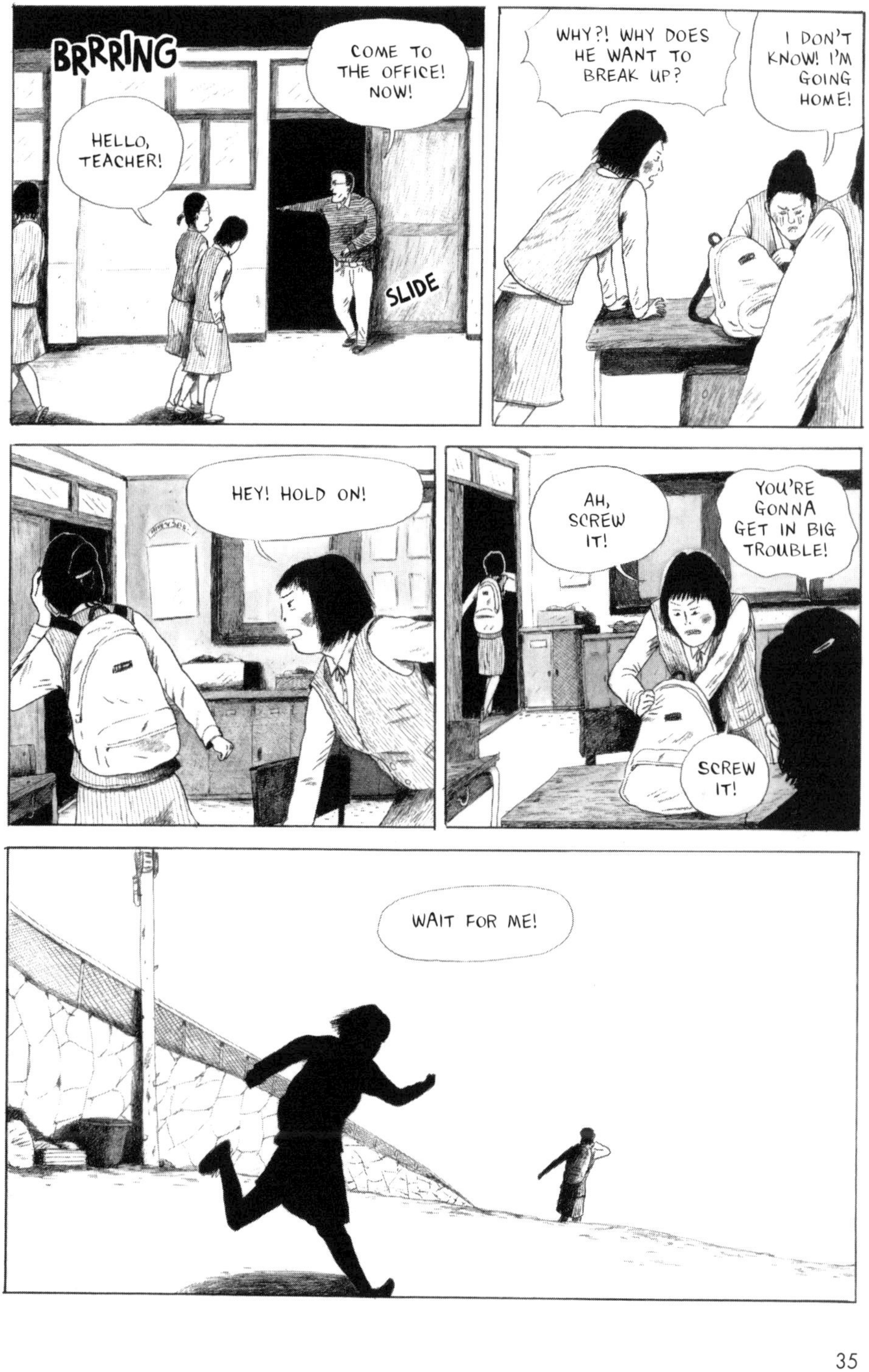
BRRRING
HELLO, TEACHER!
COME TO THE OFFICE! NOW!
SLIDE
WHY?! WHY DOES HE WANT TO BREAK UP?
I DON'T KNOW! I'M GOING HOME!
HEY! HOLD ON!
AH, SCREW IT!
YOU'RE GONNA GET IN BIG TROUBLE!
SCREW IT!
WAIT FOR ME!

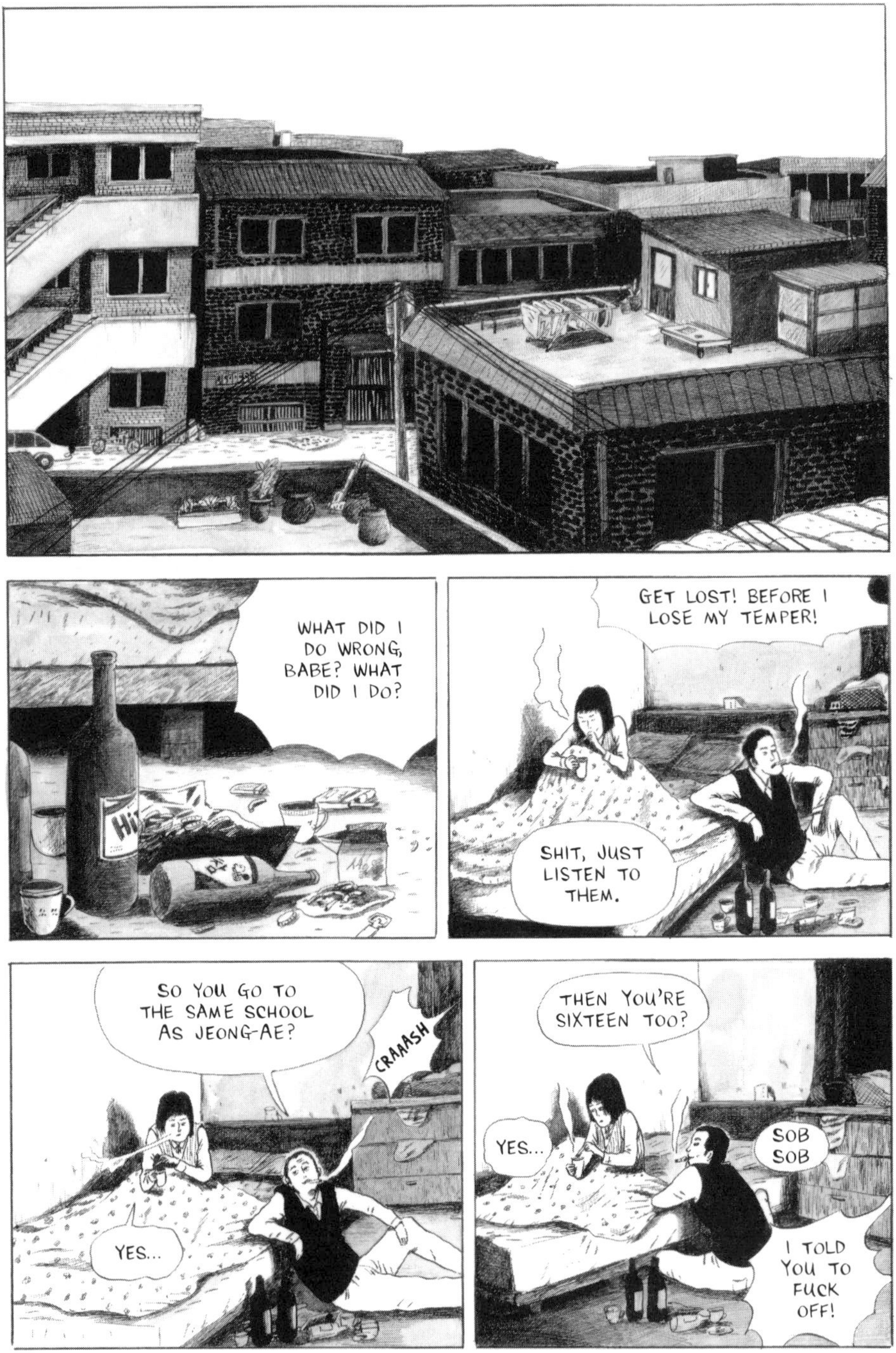
WHAT DID I DO WRONG, BABE? WHAT DID I DO?
GET LOST! BEFORE I LOSE MY TEMPER!
SHIT, JUST LISTEN TO THEM.
SO YOU GO TO THE SAME SCHOOL AS JEONG-AE?
CRAAASH
YES...
THEN YOU'RE SIXTEEN TOO?
YES...
SOB SOB
I TOLD YOU TO FUCK OFF!

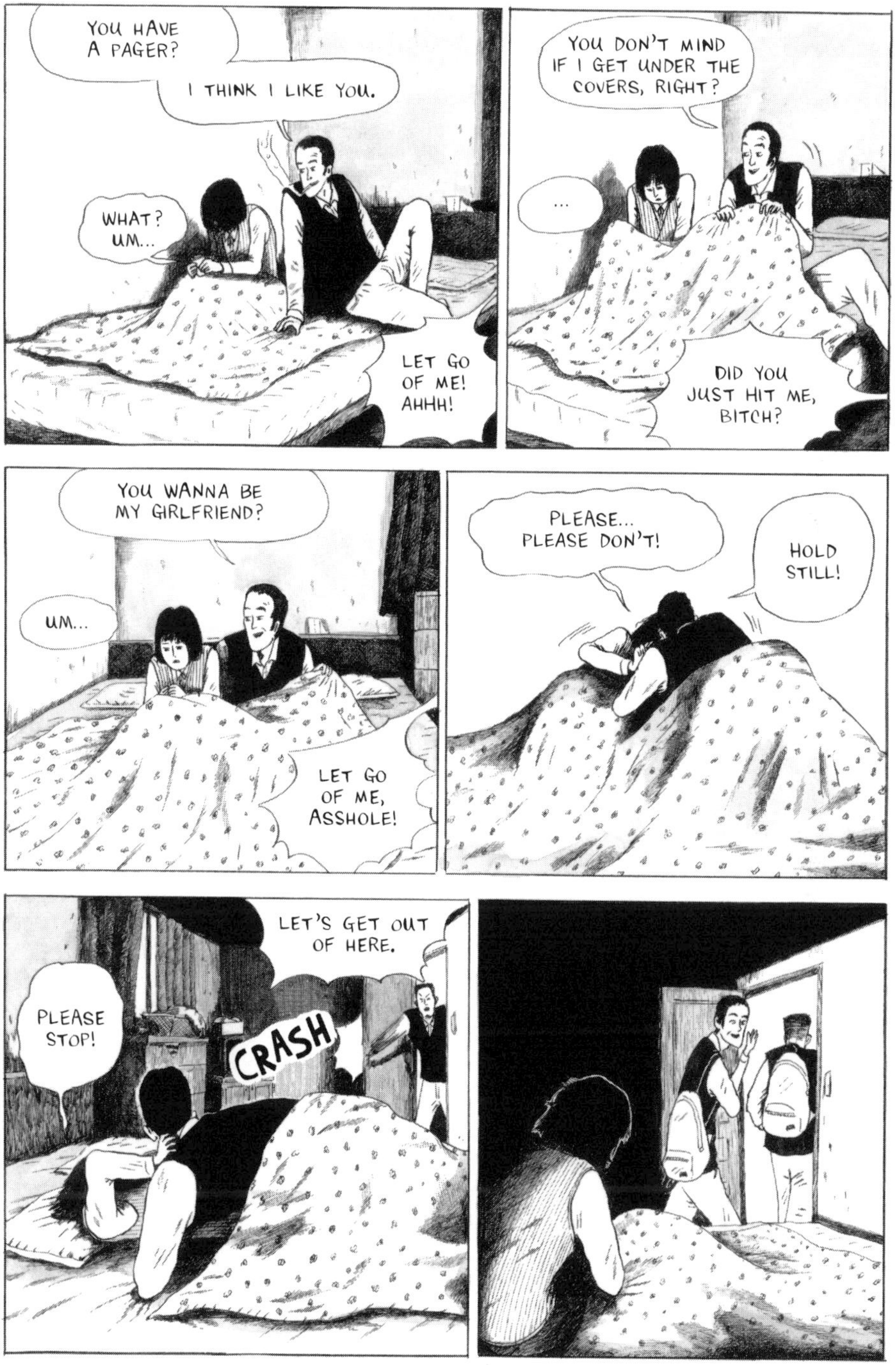
YOU HAVE A PAGER?
I THINK I LIKE YOU.
WHAT? UM...
LET GO OF ME! AHHH!
YOU DON'T MIND IF I GET UNDER THE COVERS, RIGHT?
...
DID YOU JUST HIT ME, BITCH?
YOU WANNA BE MY GIRLFRIEND?
UM...
LET GO OF ME, ASSHOLE!
PLEASE... PLEASE DON'T!
HOLD STILL!
LET'S GET OUT OF HERE.
PLEASE STOP!
CRASH

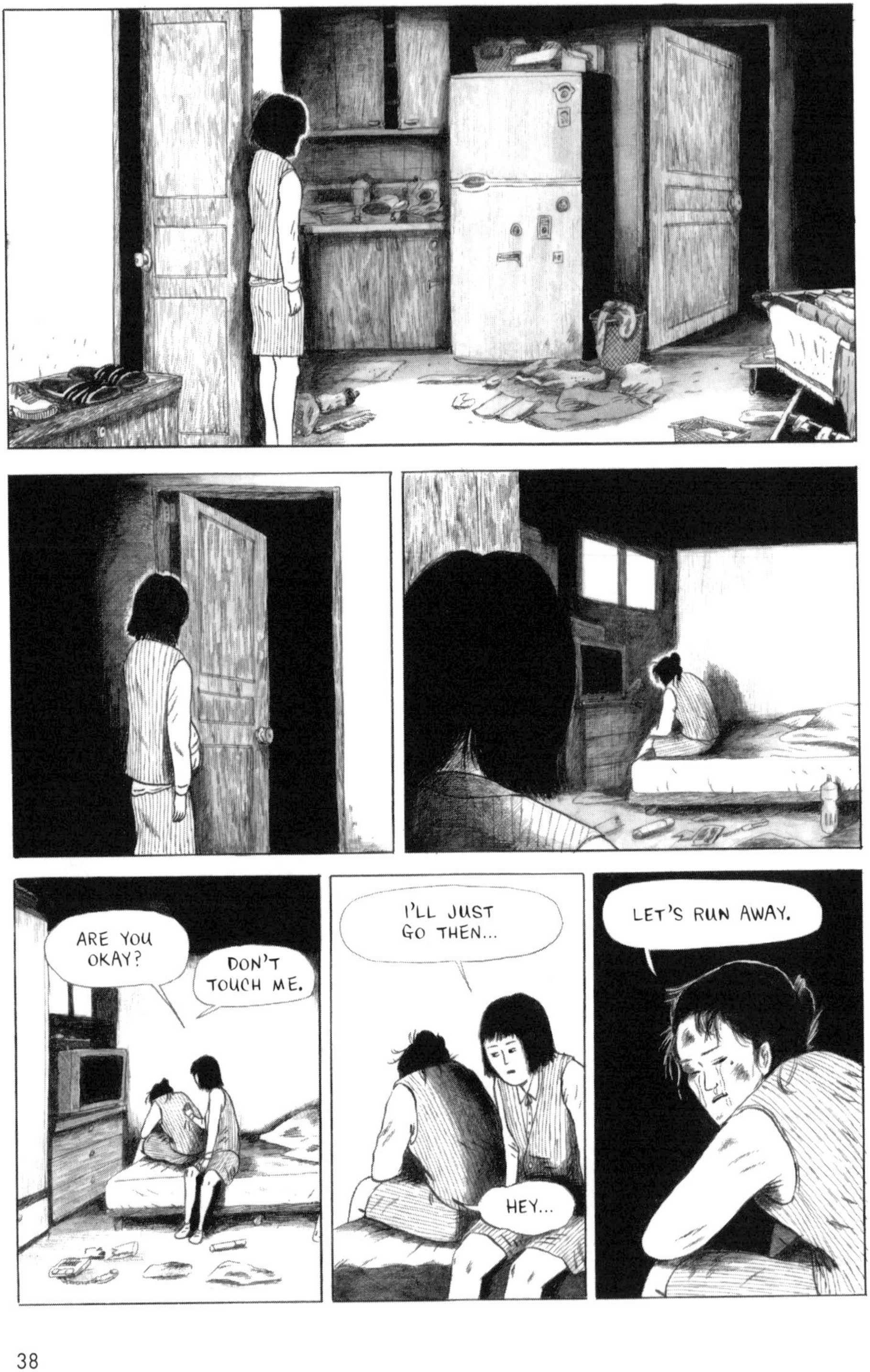
ARE YOU OKAY?
DON'T TOUCH ME.
I'LL JUST GO THEN...
HEY...
LET'S RUN AWAY.

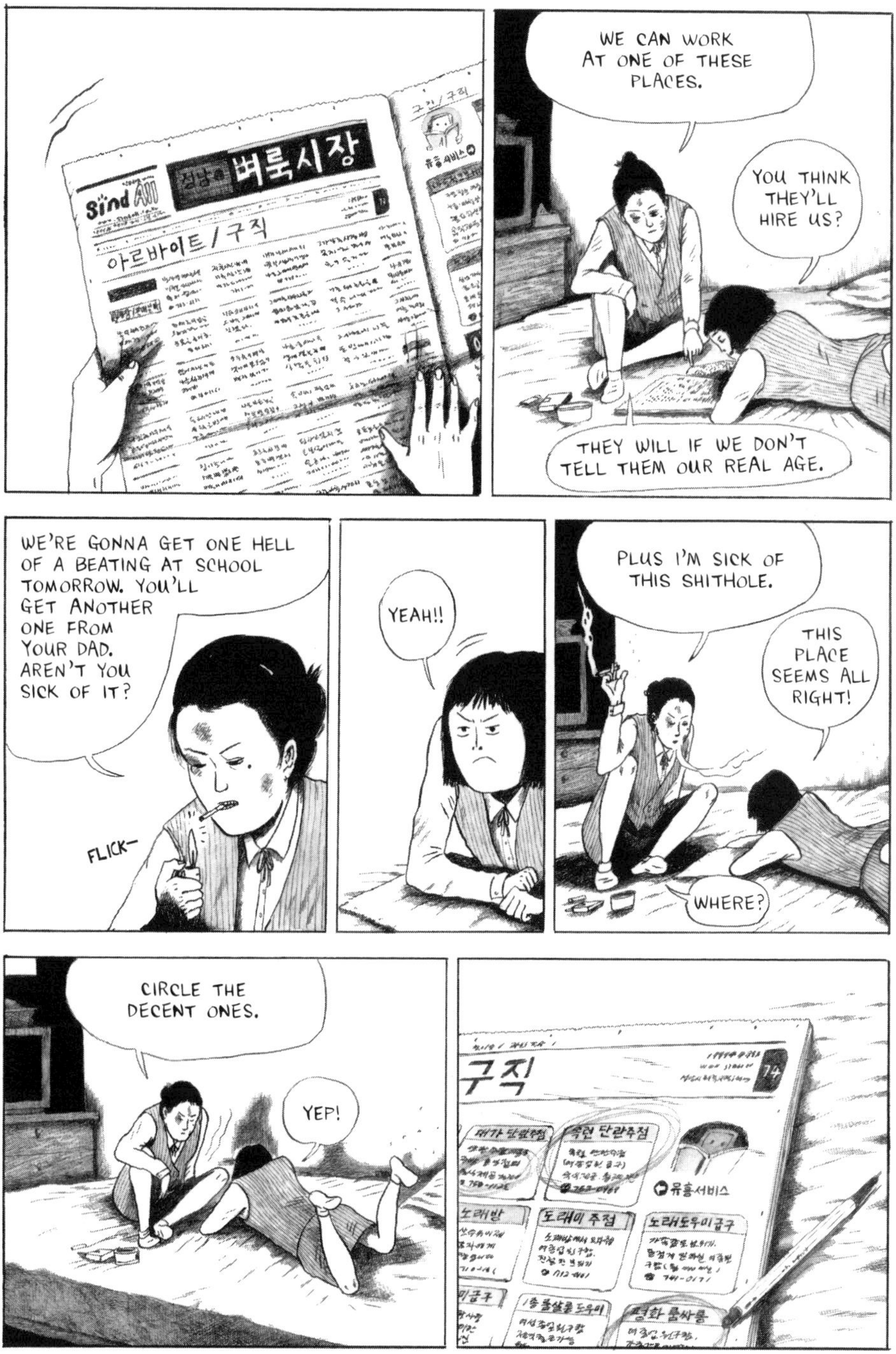
벼룩시장
아르바이트/구직
WE CAN WORK AT ONE OF THESE PLACES.
YOU THINK THEY'LL HIRE US?
THEY WILL IF WE DON'T TELL THEM OUR REAL AGE.
WE'RE GONNA GET ONE HELL OF A BEATING AT SCHOOL TOMORROW. YOU'LL GET ANOTHER ONE FROM YOUR DAD. AREN'T YOU SICK OF IT?
FLICK—
YEAH!!
PLUS I'M SICK OF THIS SHITHOLE.
THIS PLACE SEEMS ALL RIGHT!
WHERE?
CIRCLE THE DECENT ONES.
YEP!
구직
유흥서비스

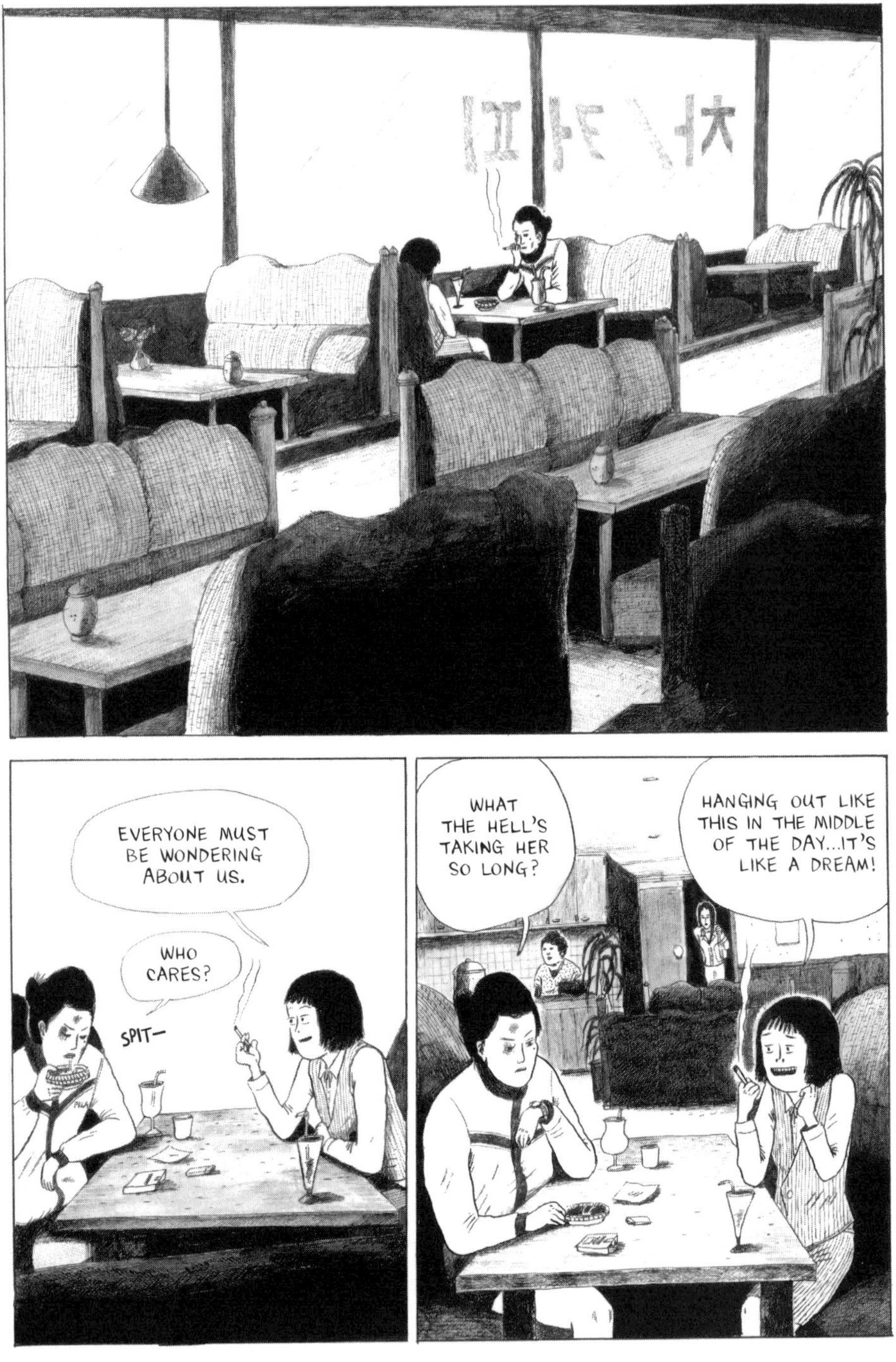
EVERYONE MUST BE WONDERING ABOUT US.
WHO CARES?
SPIT—
WHAT THE HELL'S TAKING HER SO LONG?
HANGING OUT LIKE THIS IN THE MIDDLE OF THE DAY...IT'S LIKE A DREAM!

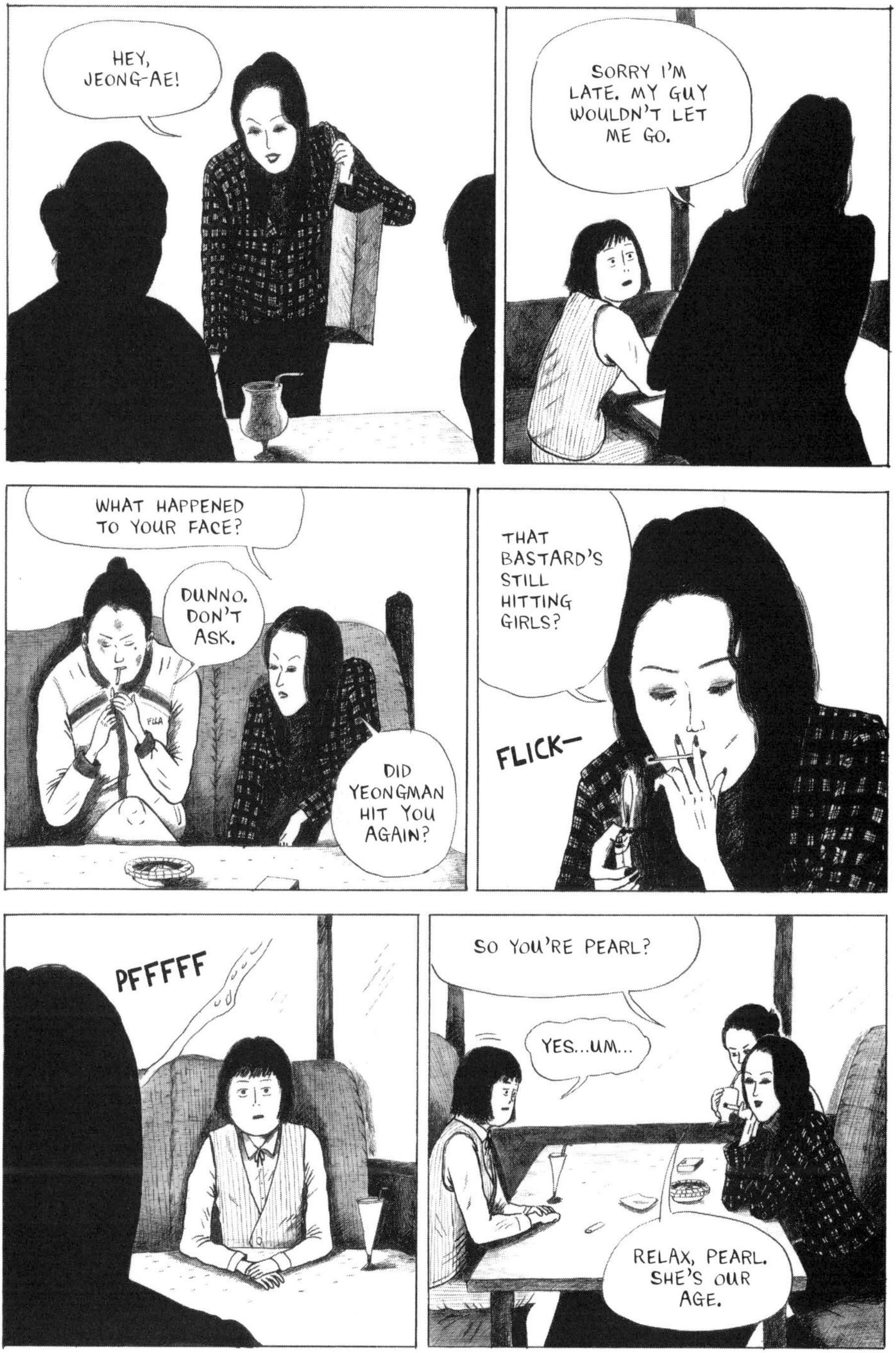
HEY, JEONG-AE!
SORRY I'M LATE. MY GUY WOULDN'T LET ME GO.
WHAT HAPPENED TO YOUR FACE?
DUNNO. DON'T ASK.
DID YEONGMAN HIT YOU AGAIN?
THAT BASTARD'S STILL HITTING GIRLS?
FLICK—
PFFFFF
SO YOU'RE PEARL?
YES...UM...
RELAX, PEARL. SHE'S OUR AGE.

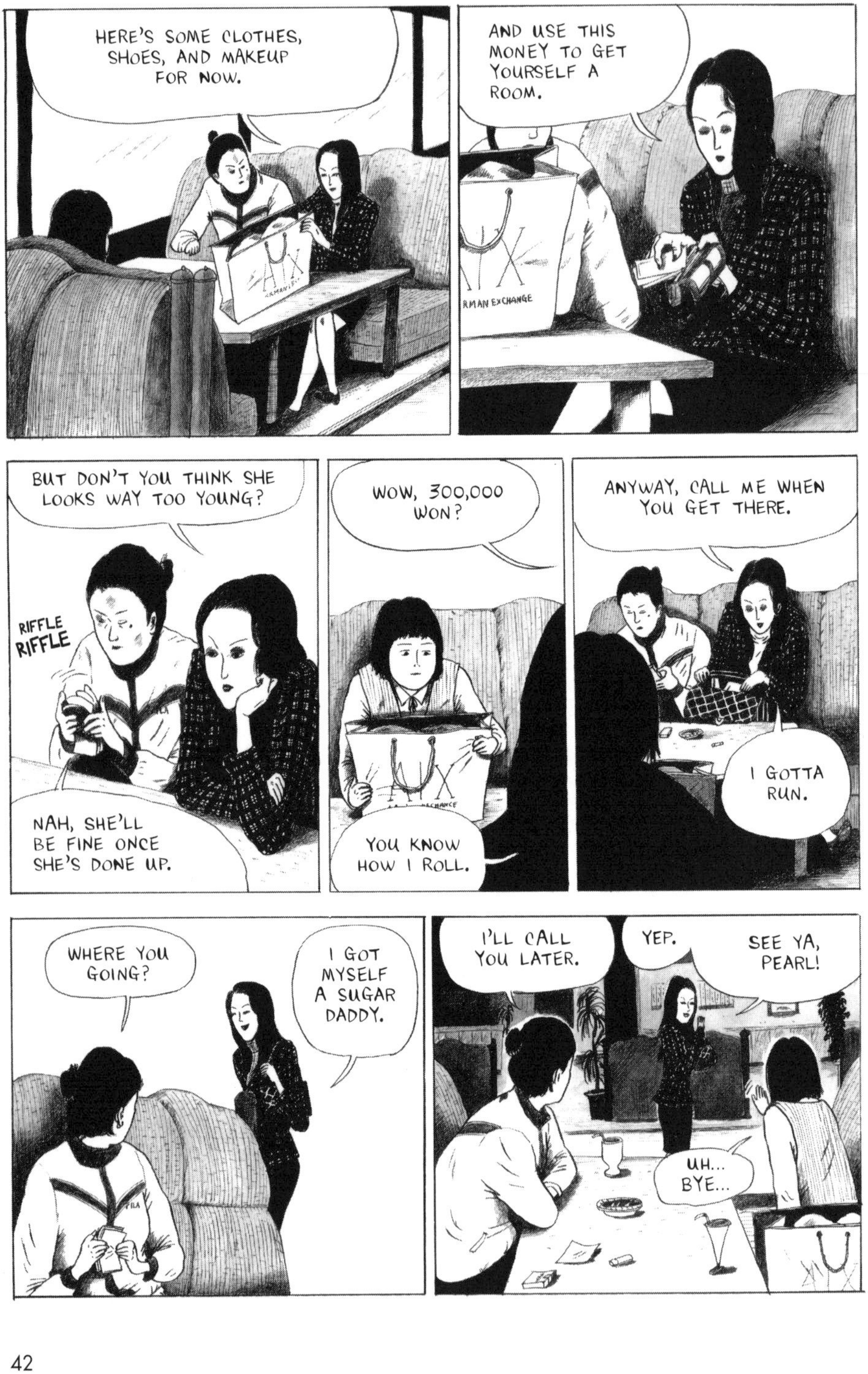
HERE'S SOME CLOTHES, SHOES, AND MAKEUP FOR NOW.
AND USE THIS MONEY TO GET YOURSELF A ROOM.
BUT DON'T YOU THINK SHE LOOKS WAY TOO YOUNG?
RIFFLE RIFFLE
NAH, SHE'LL BE FINE ONCE SHE'S DONE UP.
WOW, 300,000 WON?
YOU KNOW HOW I ROLL.
ANYWAY, CALL ME WHEN YOU GET THERE.
I GOTTA RUN.
WHERE YOU GOING?
I GOT MYSELF A SUGAR DADDY.
I'LL CALL YOU LATER.
YEP.
SEE YA, PEARL!
UH... BYE...

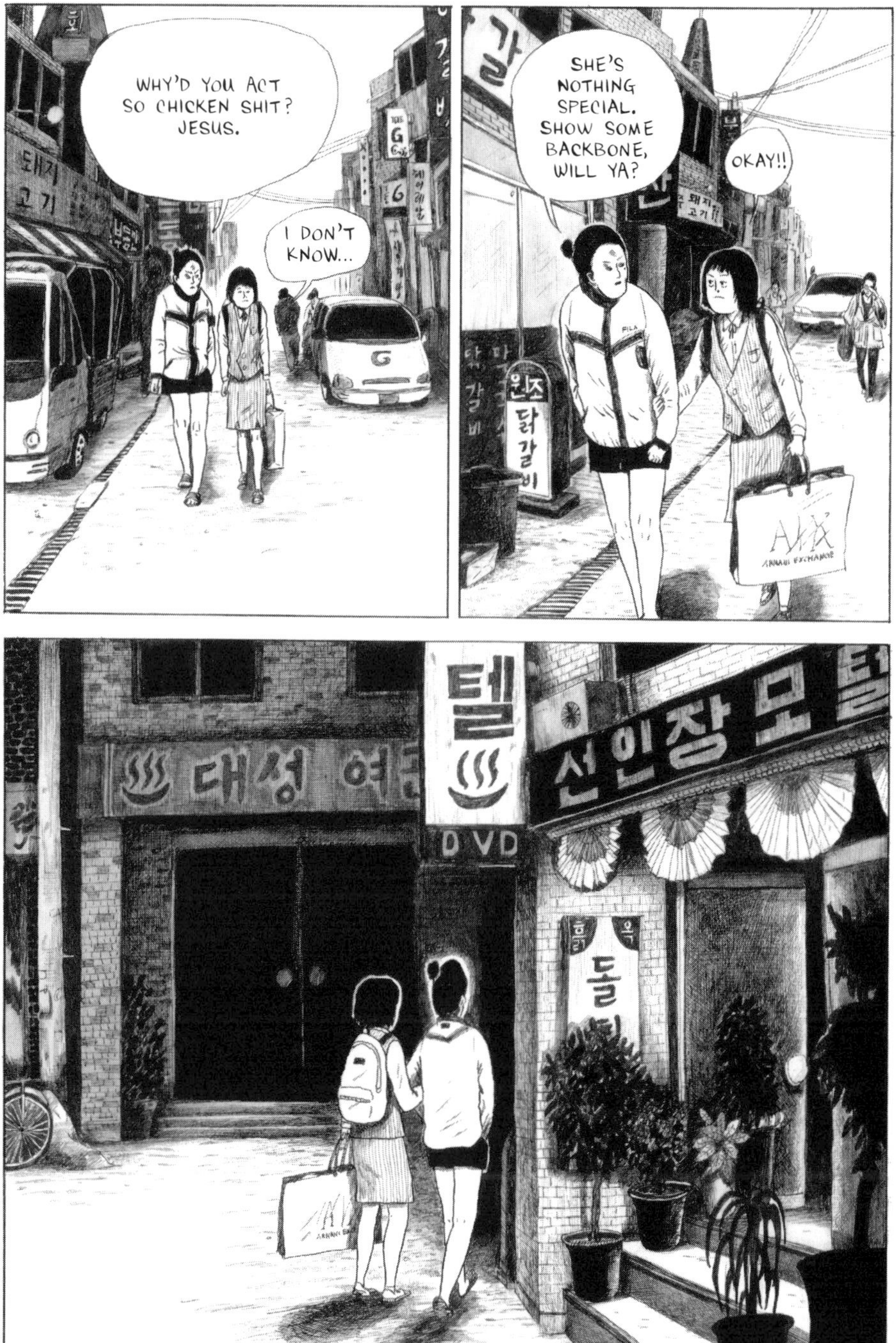
WHY'D YOU ACT SO CHICKEN SHIT? JESUS.
I DON'T KNOW...
SHE'S NOTHING SPECIAL. SHOW SOME BACKBONE, WILL YA?
OKAY!!
닭갈비
DVD

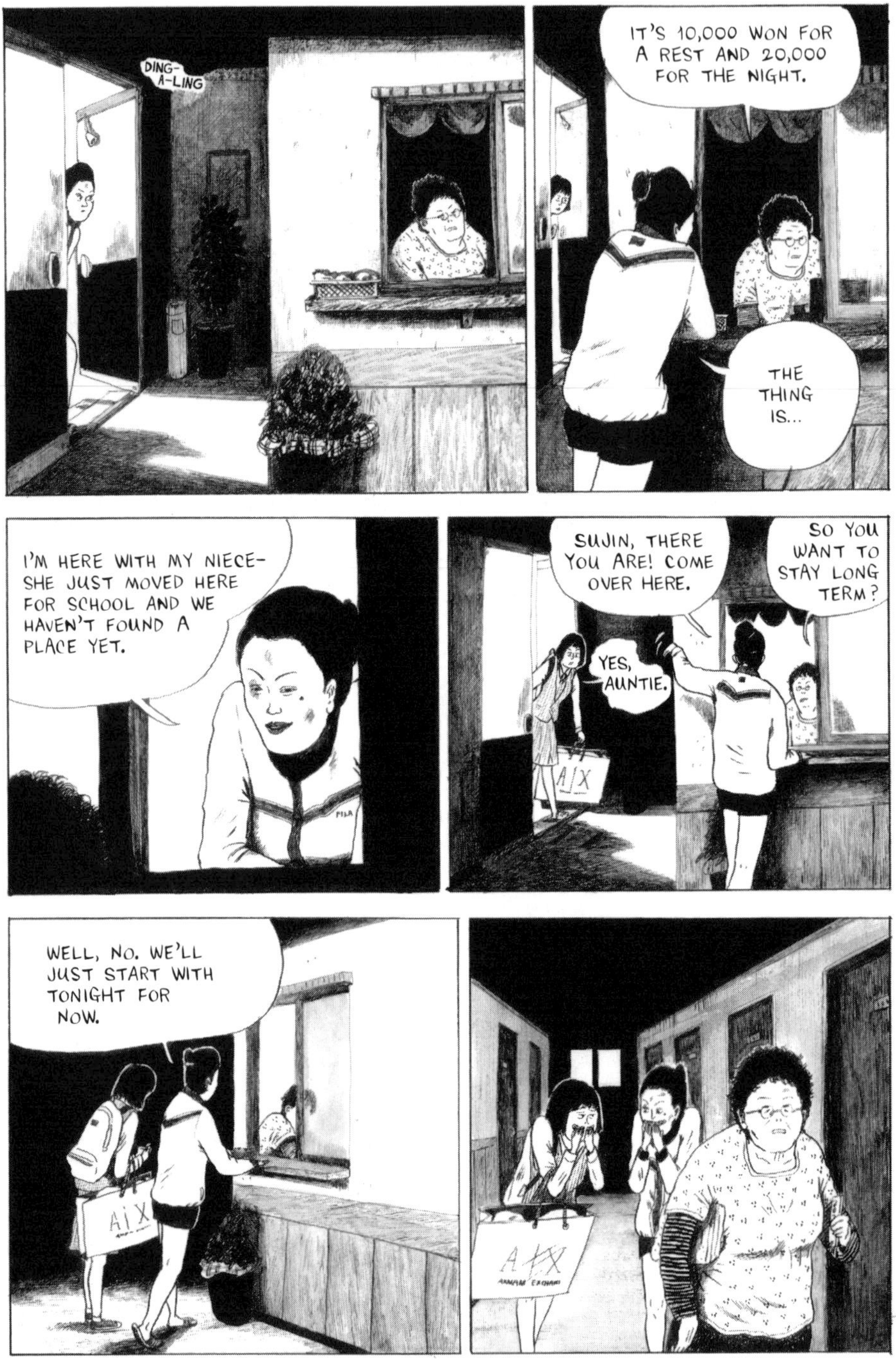
DING-A-LING
IT'S 10,000 WON FOR A REST AND 20,000 FOR THE NIGHT.
THE THING IS...
I'M HERE WITH MY NIECE- SHE JUST MOVED HERE FOR SCHOOL AND WE HAVEN'T FOUND A PLACE YET.
SUJIN, THERE YOU ARE! COME OVER HERE.
YES, AUNTIE.
SO YOU WANT TO STAY LONG TERM?
WELL, NO. WE'LL JUST START WITH TONIGHT FOR NOW.

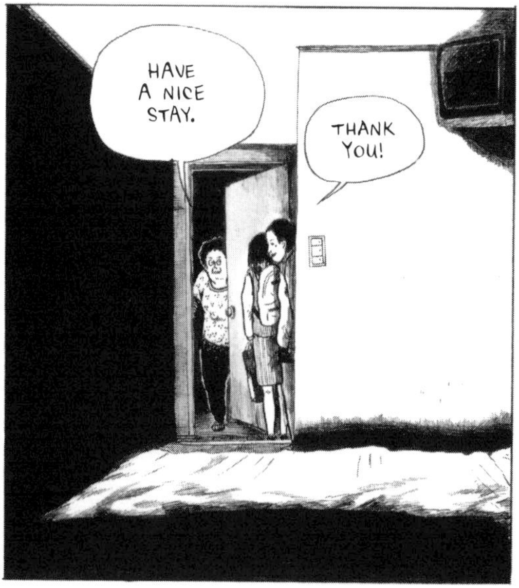
HAVE A NICE STAY.
THANK YOU!

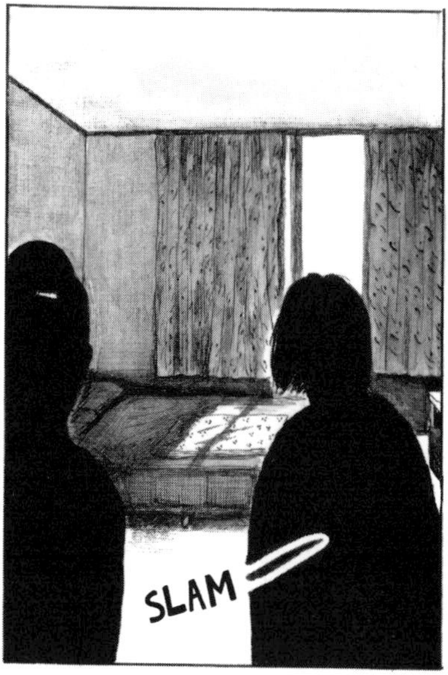
SLAM

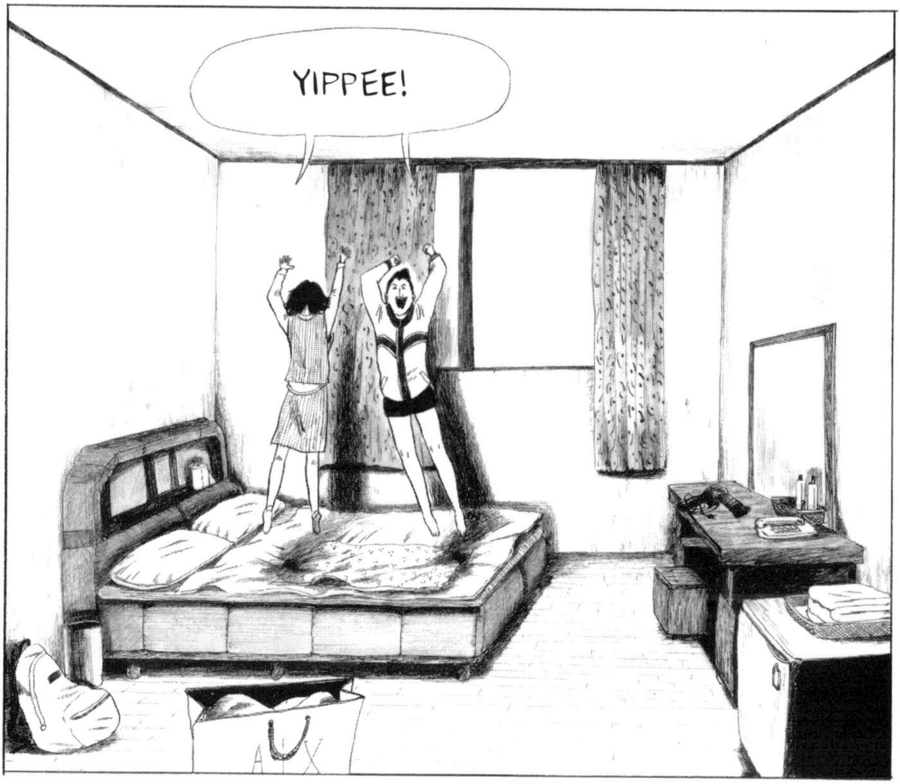
YIPPEE!

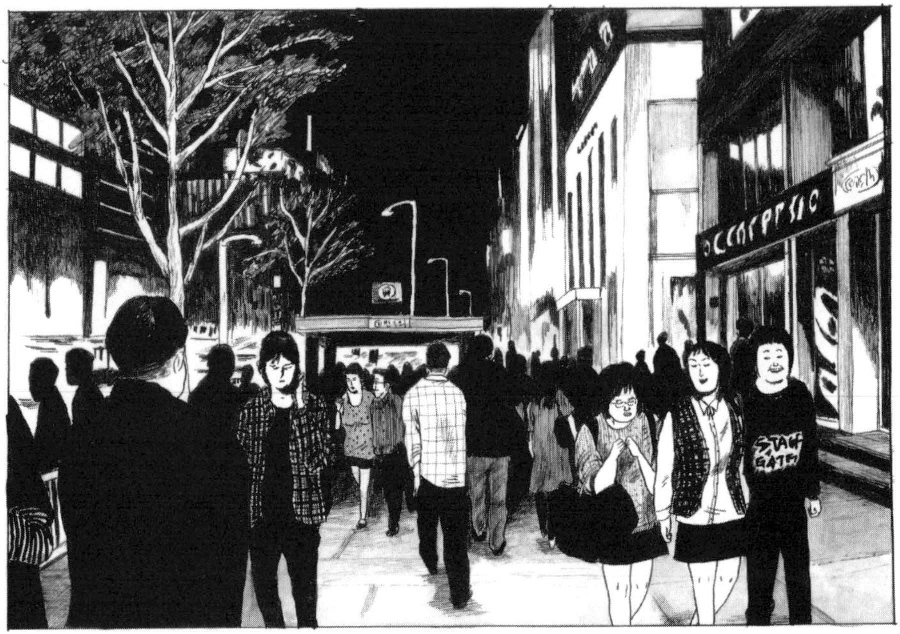

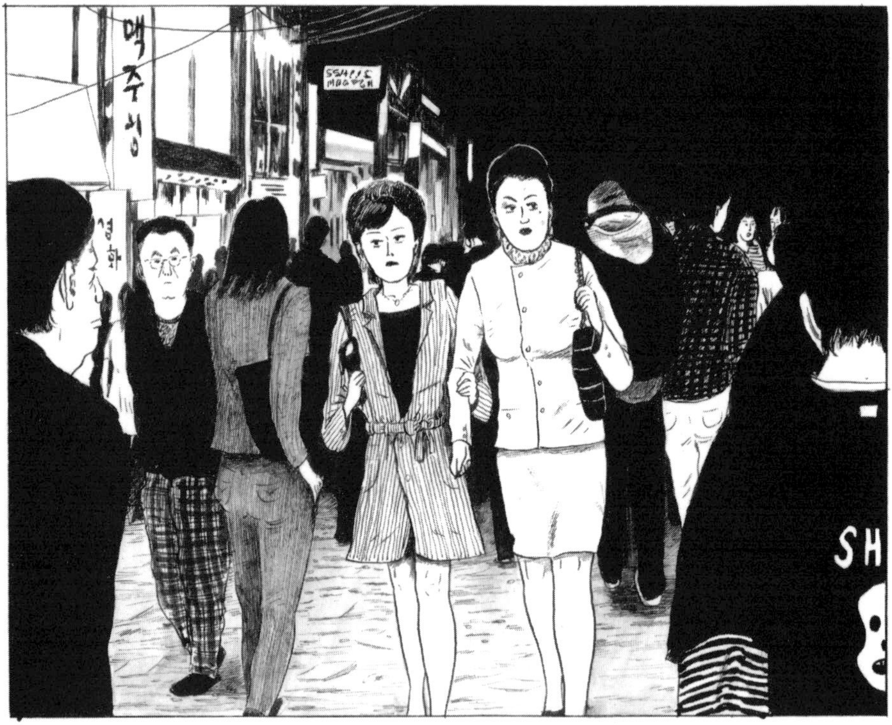
영화
SH

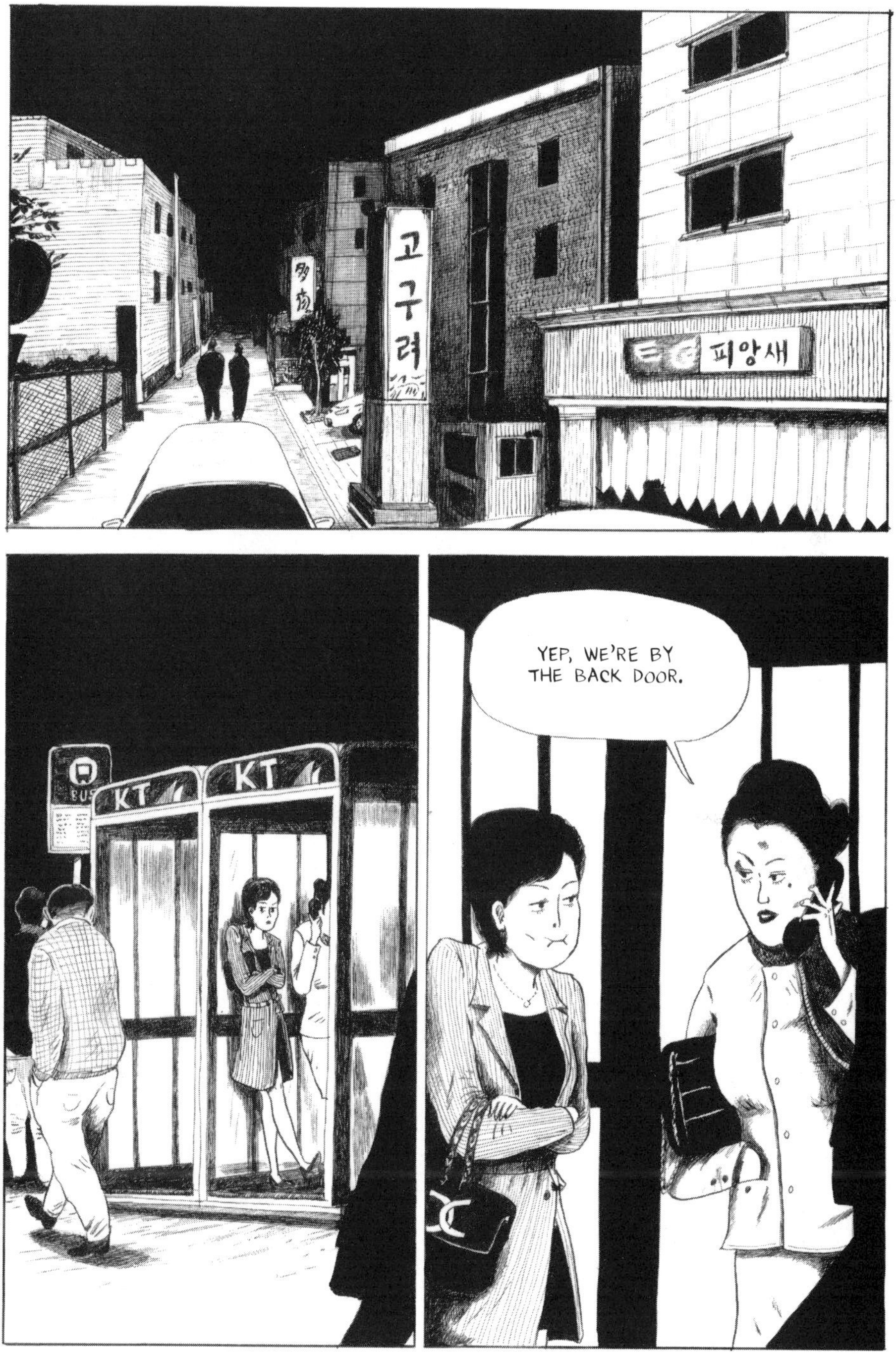

고구려
피앙새
KT
KT
YEP, WE'RE BY THE BACK DOOR.

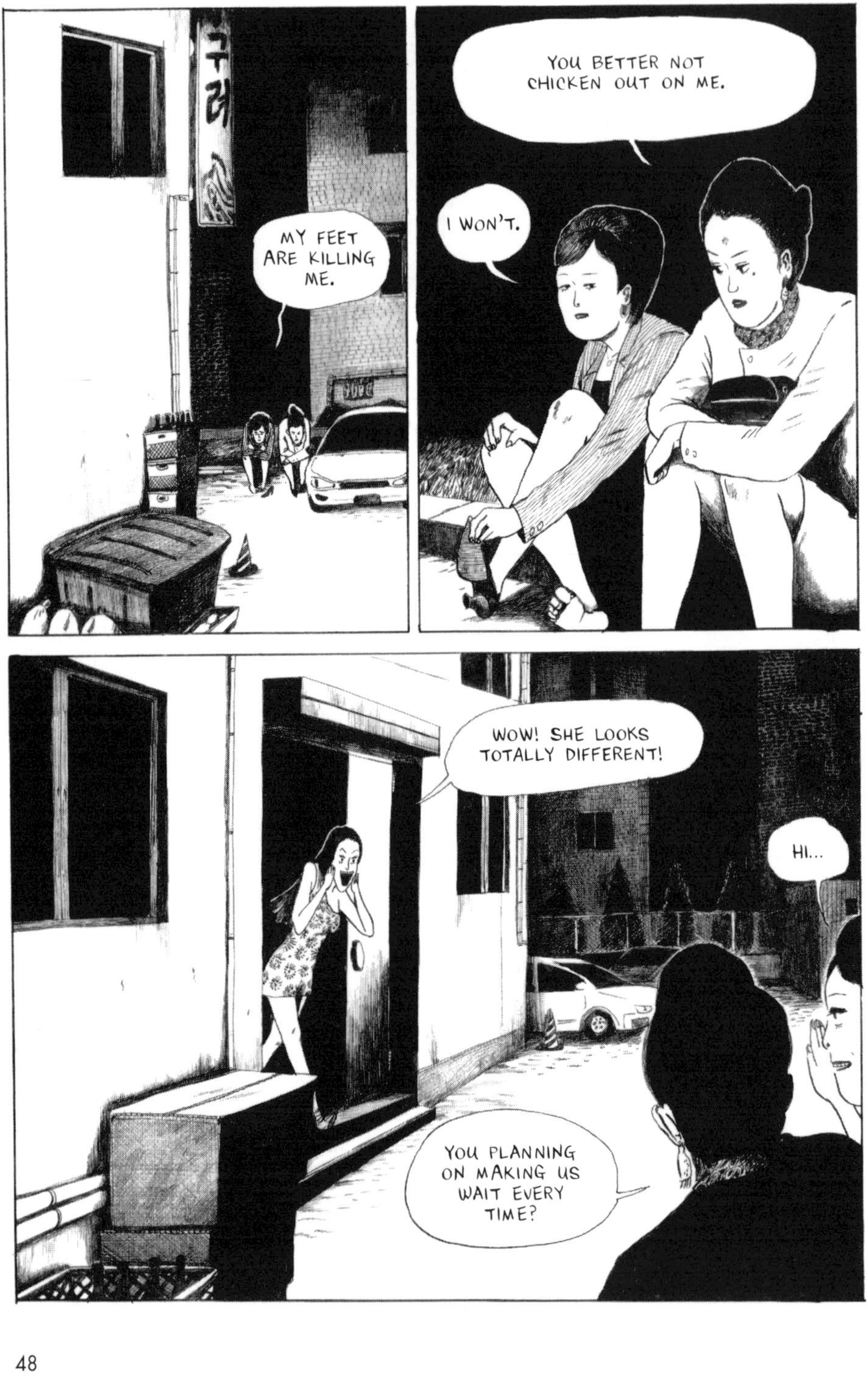
MY FEET ARE KILLING ME.
YOU BETTER NOT CHICKEN OUT ON ME.
I WON'T.
WOW! SHE LOOKS TOTALLY DIFFERENT!
HI...
YOU PLANNING ON MAKING US WAIT EVERY TIME?

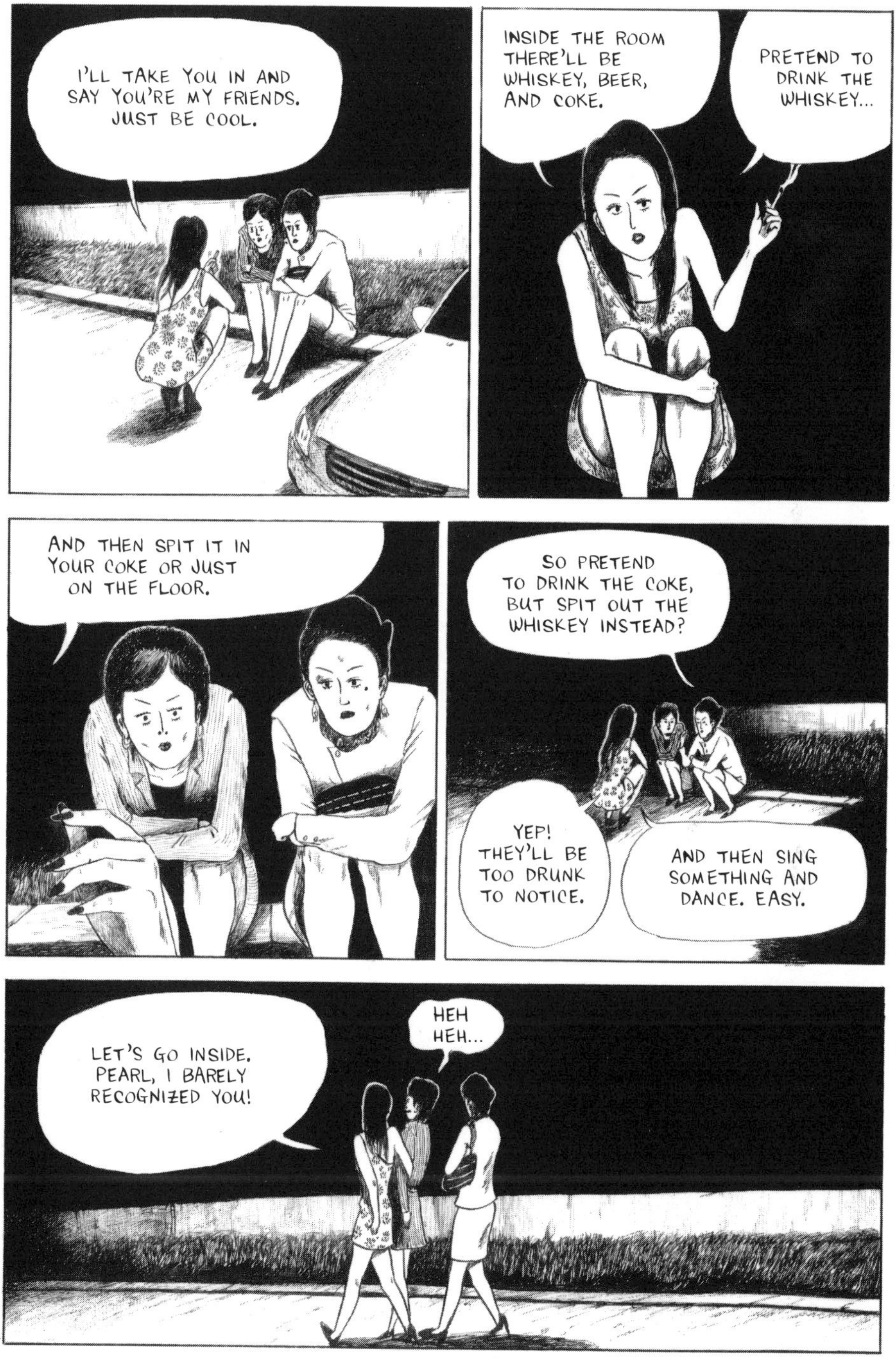

I'LL TAKE YOU IN AND SAY YOU'RE MY FRIENDS. JUST BE COOL.
INSIDE THE ROOM THERE'LL BE WHISKEY, BEER, AND COKE.
PRETEND TO DRINK THE WHISKEY...
AND THEN SPIT IT IN YOUR COKE OR JUST ON THE FLOOR.
SO PRETEND TO DRINK THE COKE, BUT SPIT OUT THE WHISKEY INSTEAD?
YEP! THEY'LL BE TOO DRUNK TO NOTICE.
AND THEN SING SOMETHING AND DANCE. EASY.
LET'S GO INSIDE. PEARL, I BARELY RECOGNIZED YOU!
HEH HEH...

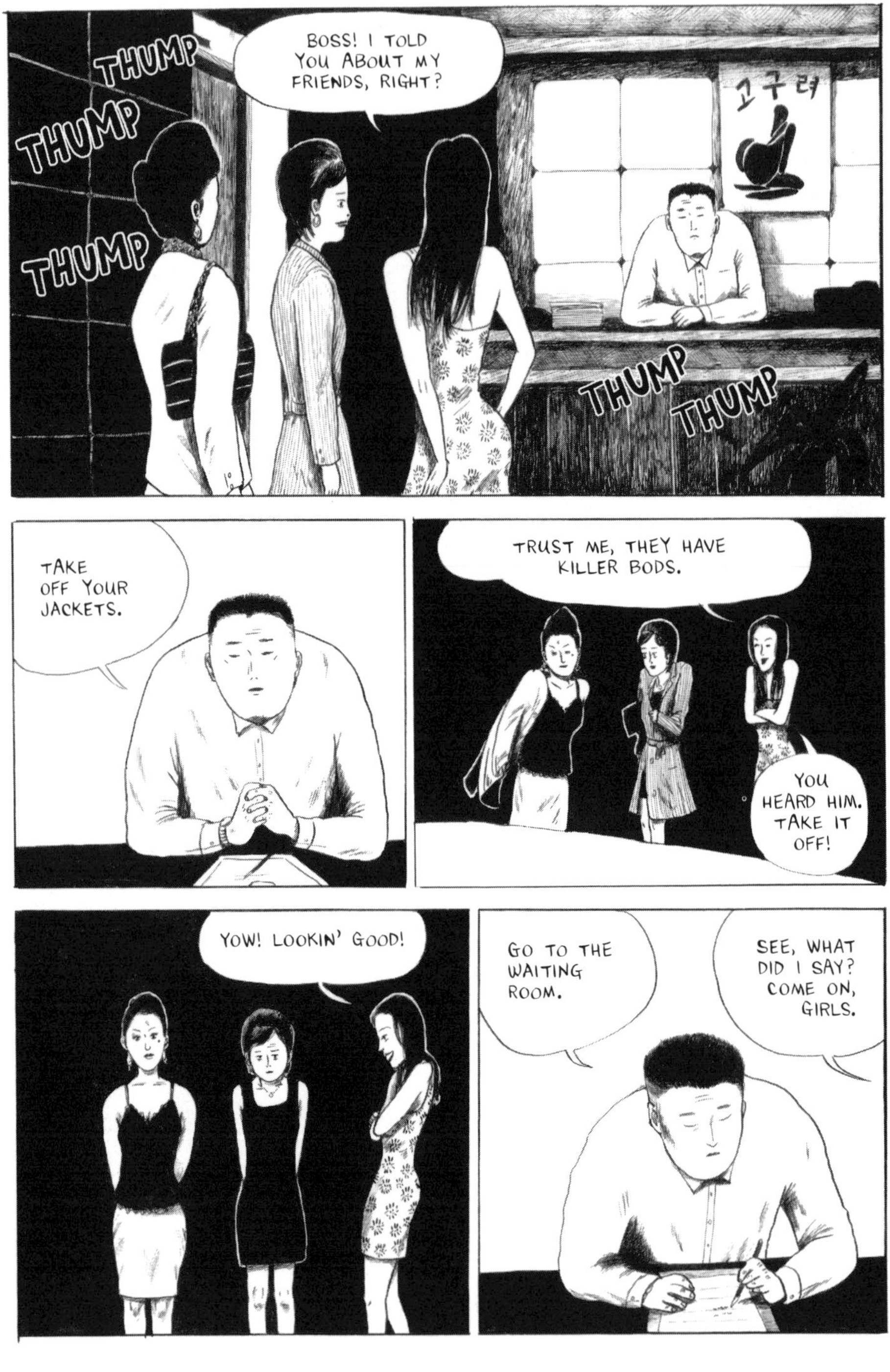
THUMP
THUMP
THUMP
BOSS! I TOLD YOU ABOUT MY FRIENDS, RIGHT?
고구려
THUMP
THUMP
TAKE OFF YOUR JACKETS.
TRUST ME, THEY HAVE KILLER BODS.
YOU HEARD HIM. TAKE IT OFF!
YOW! LOOKIN' GOOD!
GO TO THE WAITING ROOM.
SEE, WHAT DID I SAY? COME ON, GIRLS.

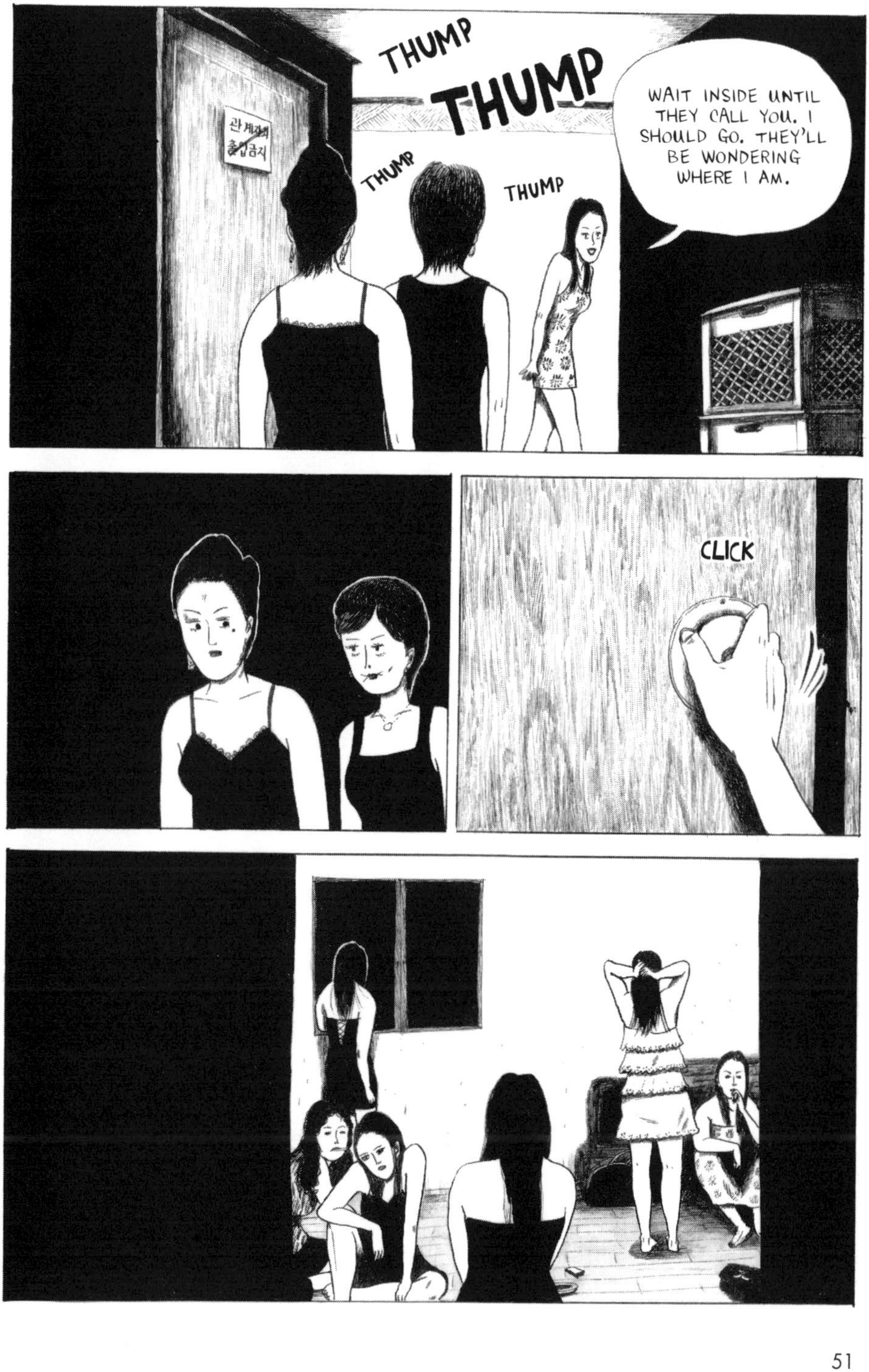
THUMP
THUMP
THUMP
THUMP
WAIT INSIDE UNTIL THEY CALL YOU. I SHOULD GO. THEY'LL BE WONDERING WHERE I AM.
CLICK

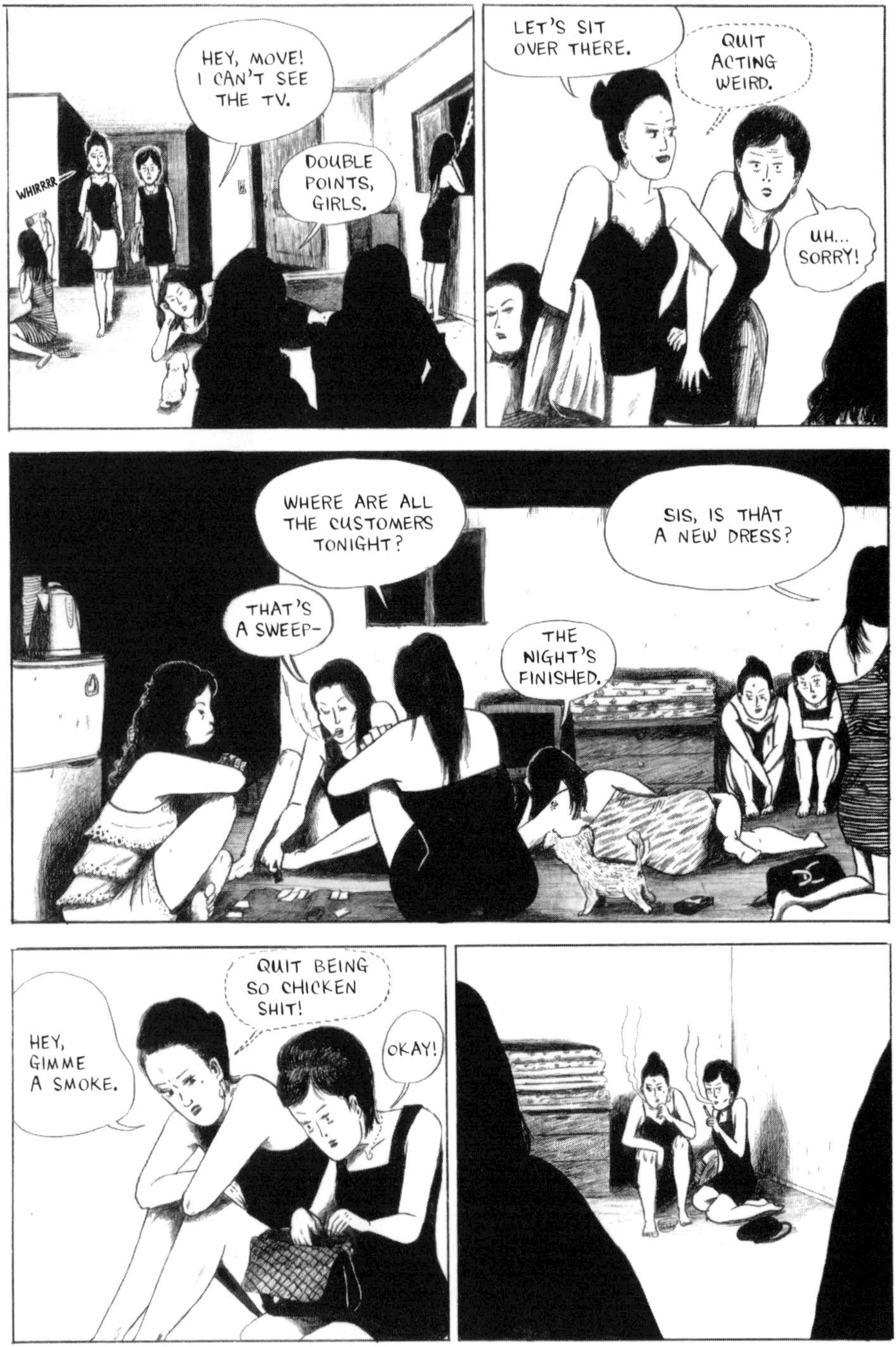
HEY, MOVE! I CAN'T SEE THE TV.
WHIRRRR
DOUBLE POINTS, GIRLS.
LET'S SIT OVER THERE.
QUIT ACTING WEIRD.
UH... SORRY!
WHERE ARE ALL THE CUSTOMERS TONIGHT?
SIS, IS THAT A NEW DRESS?
THAT'S A SWEEP-
THE NIGHT'S FINISHED.
HEY, GIMME A SMOKE.
QUIT BEING SO CHICKEN SHIT!
OKAY!

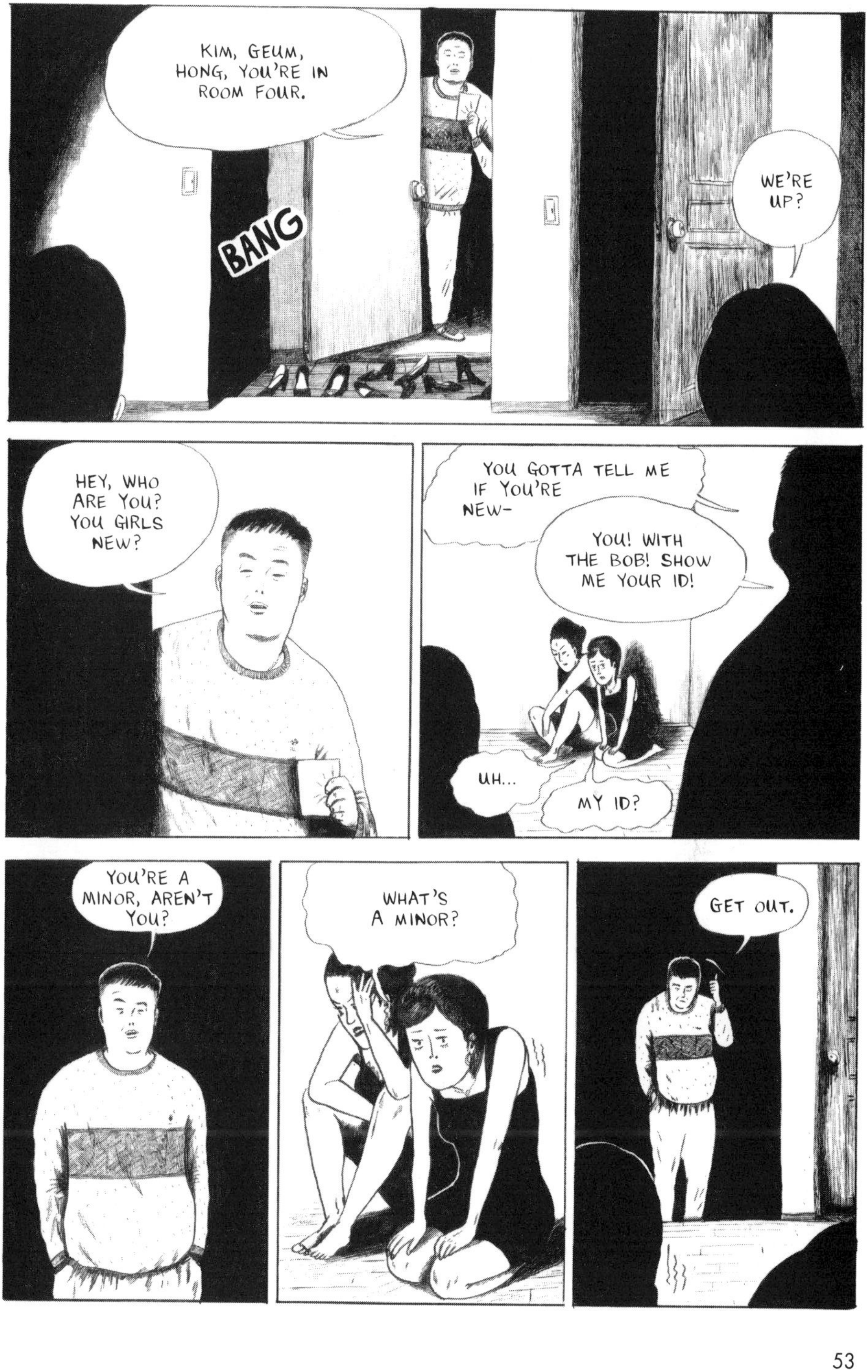
KIM, GEUM, HONG, YOU'RE IN ROOM FOUR.
BANG
WE'RE UP?
HEY, WHO ARE YOU? YOU GIRLS NEW?
YOU GOTTA TELL ME IF YOU'RE NEW-
YOU! WITH THE BOB! SHOW ME YOUR ID!
UH...
MY ID?
YOU'RE A MINOR, AREN'T YOU?
WHAT'S A MINOR?
GET OUT.

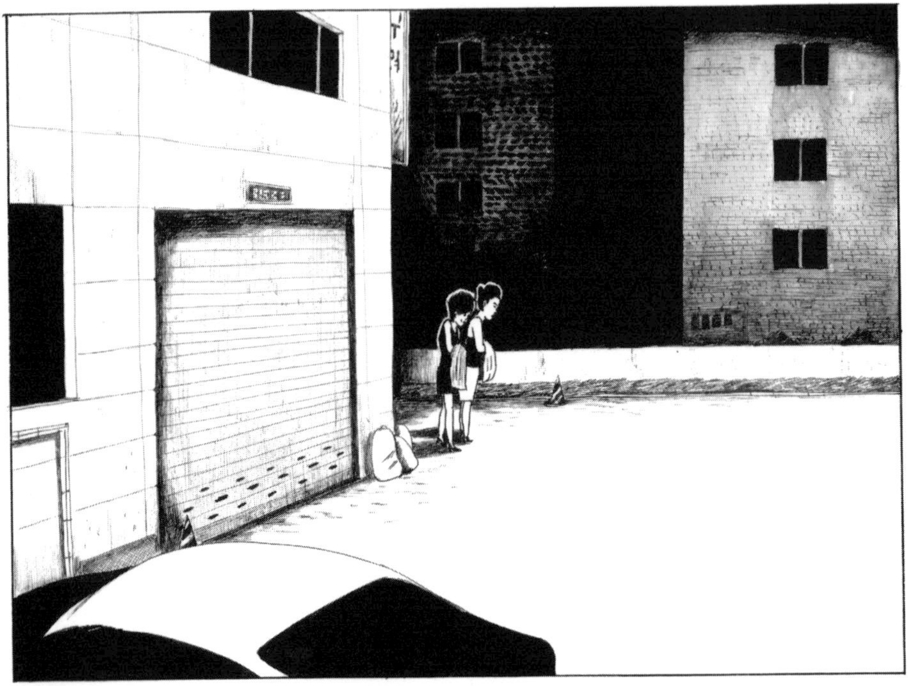

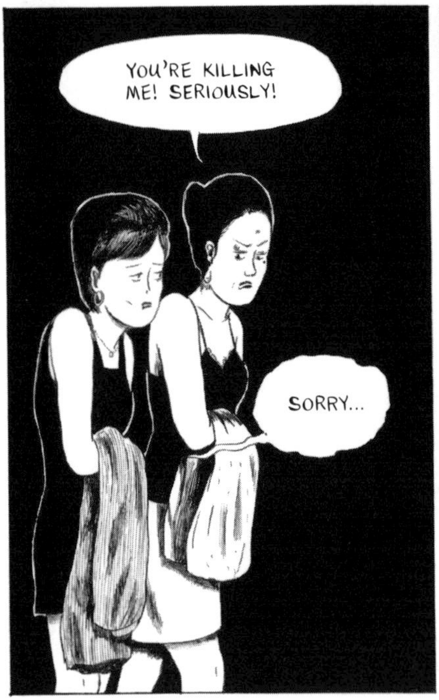
YOU'RE KILLING ME! SERIOUSLY!
SORRY...

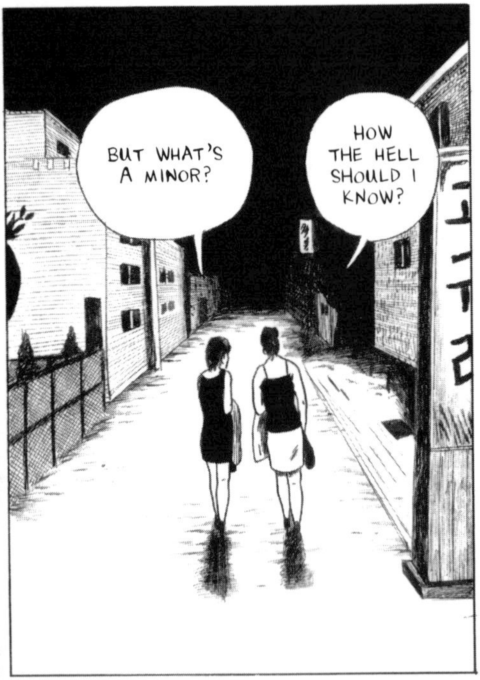
BUT WHAT'S A MINOR?
HOW THE HELL SHOULD I KNOW?

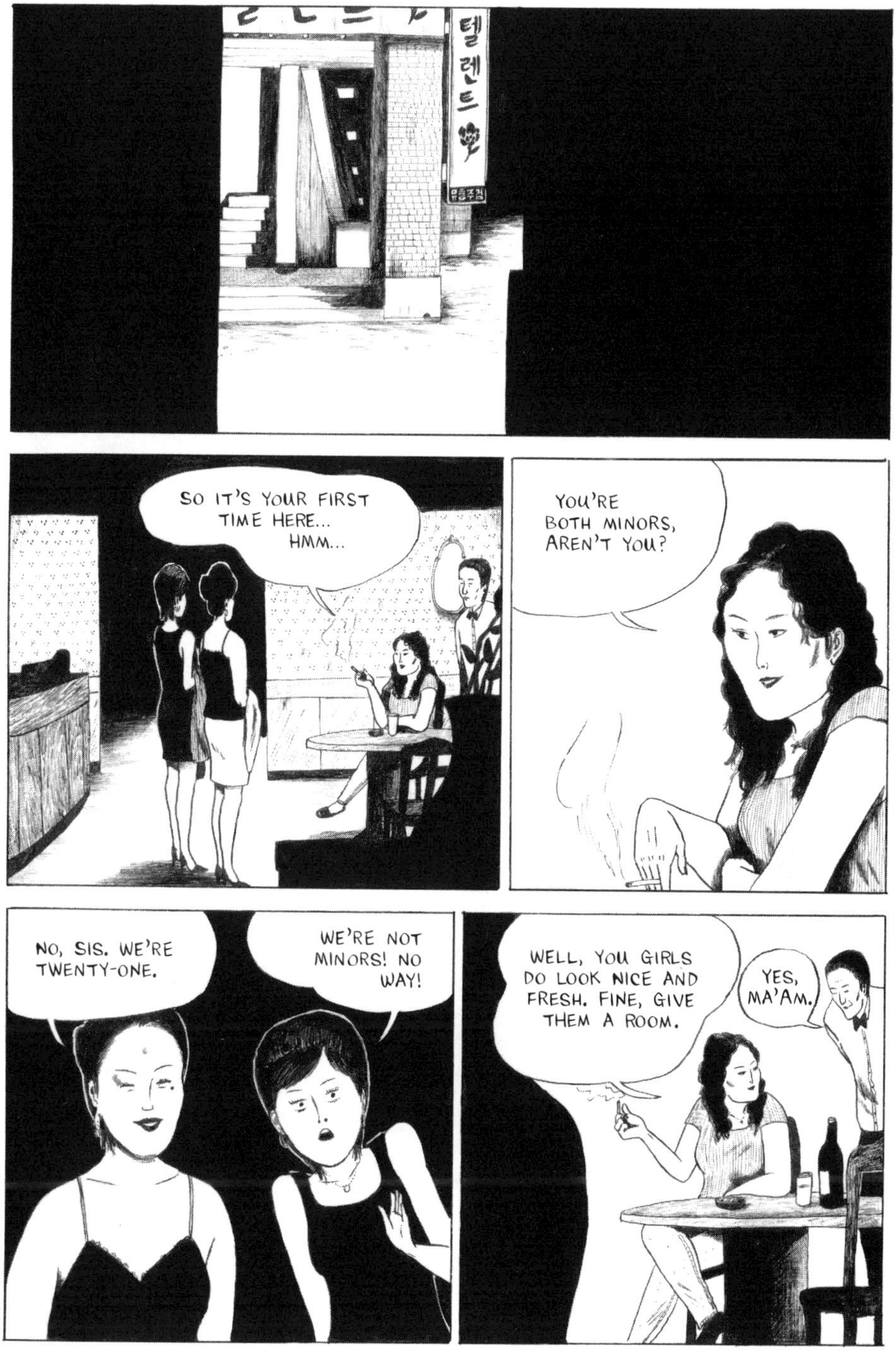

텔렌트
유흥주점
SO IT'S YOUR FIRST TIME HERE... HMM...
YOU'RE BOTH MINORS, AREN'T YOU?
NO, SIS. WE'RE TWENTY-ONE.
WE'RE NOT MINORS! NO WAY!
WELL, YOU GIRLS DO LOOK NICE AND FRESH. FINE, GIVE THEM A ROOM.
YES, MA'AM.

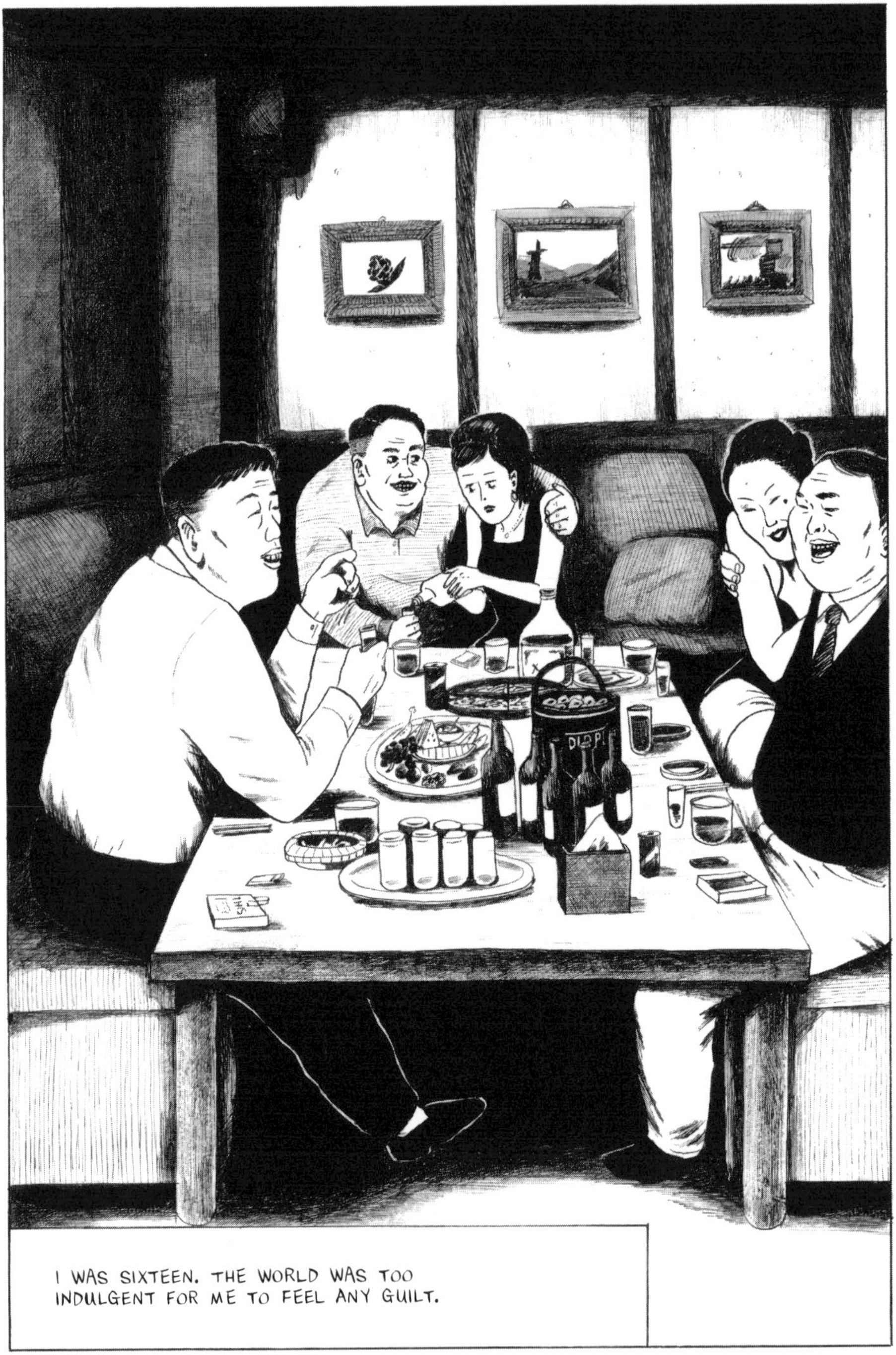
I WAS SIXTEEN. THE WORLD WAS TOO INDULGENT FOR ME TO FEEL ANY GUILT.

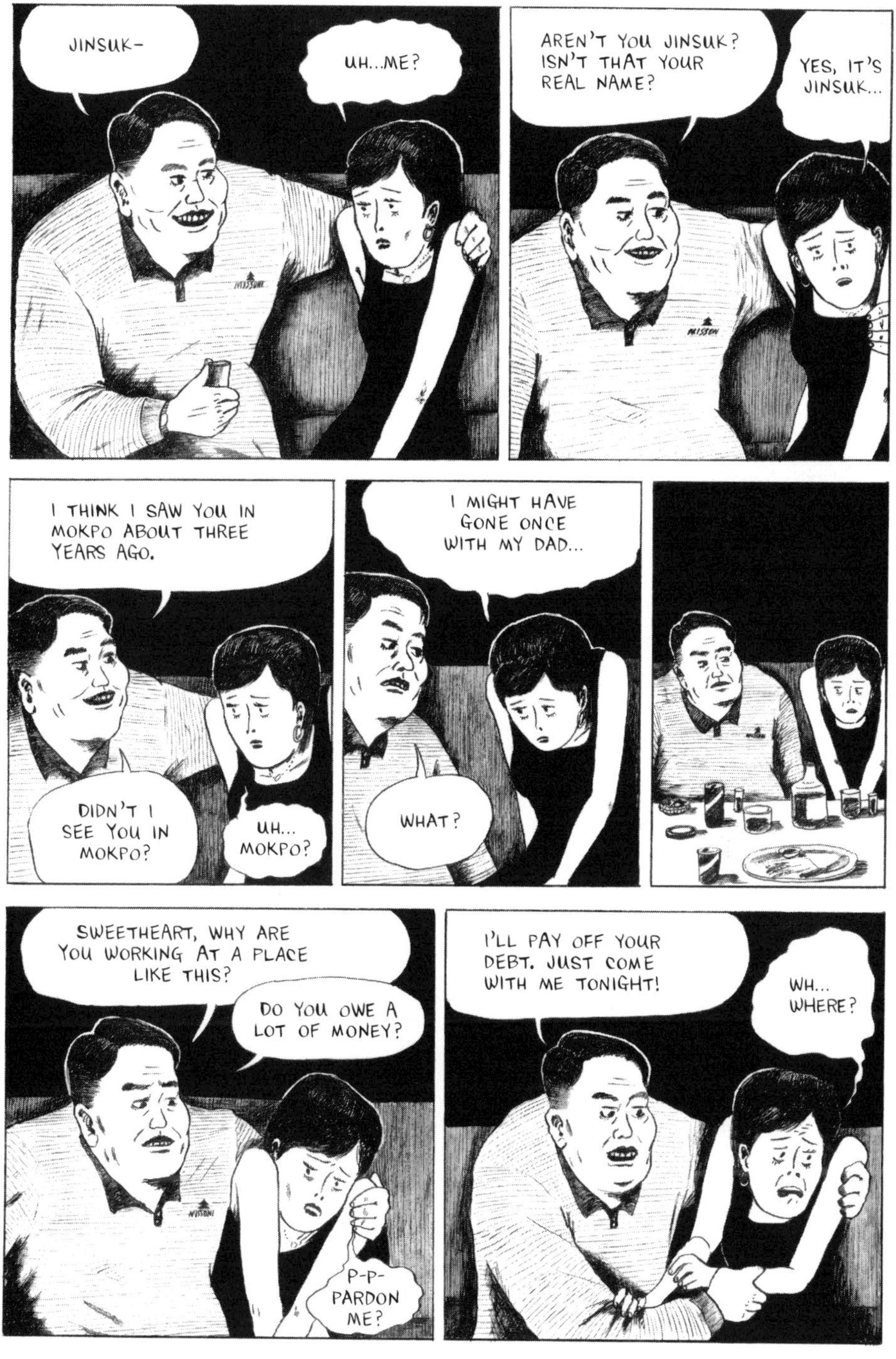

JINSUK-
UH...ME?
AREN'T YOU JINSUK? ISN'T THAT YOUR REAL NAME?
YES, IT'S JINSUK...
I THINK I SAW YOU IN MOKPO ABOUT THREE YEARS AGO.
DIDN'T I SEE YOU IN MOKPO?
UH... MOKPO?
I MIGHT HAVE GONE ONCE WITH MY DAD...
WHAT?
SWEETHEART, WHY ARE YOU WORKING AT A PLACE LIKE THIS?
DO YOU OWE A LOT OF MONEY?
P-P-PARDON ME?
I'LL PAY OFF YOUR DEBT. JUST COME WITH ME TONIGHT!
WH... WHERE?

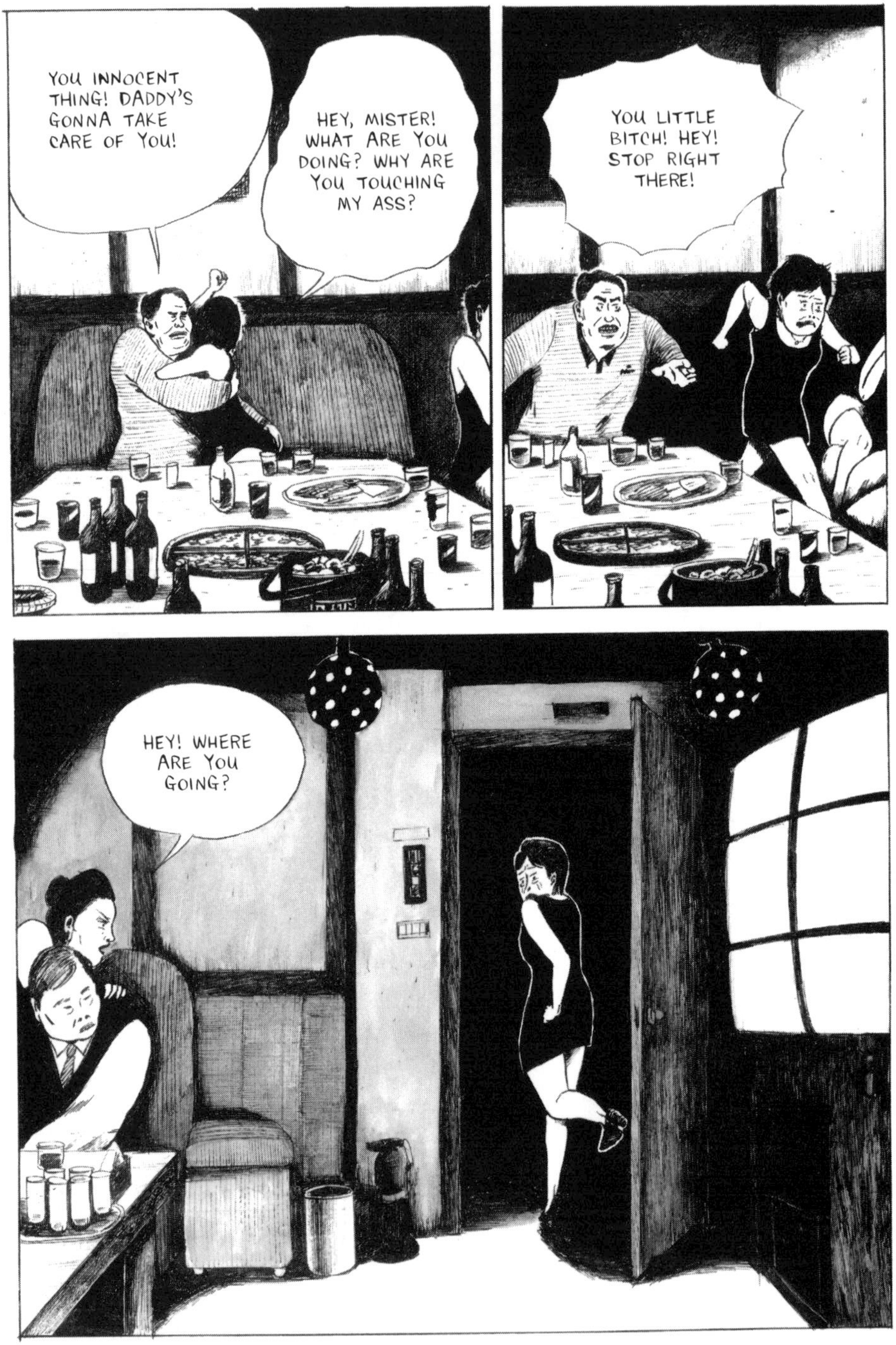
YOU INNOCENT THING! DADDY'S GONNA TAKE CARE OF YOU!
HEY, MISTER! WHAT ARE YOU DOING? WHY ARE YOU TOUCHING MY ASS?
YOU LITTLE BITCH! HEY! STOP RIGHT THERE!
HEY! WHERE ARE YOU GOING?

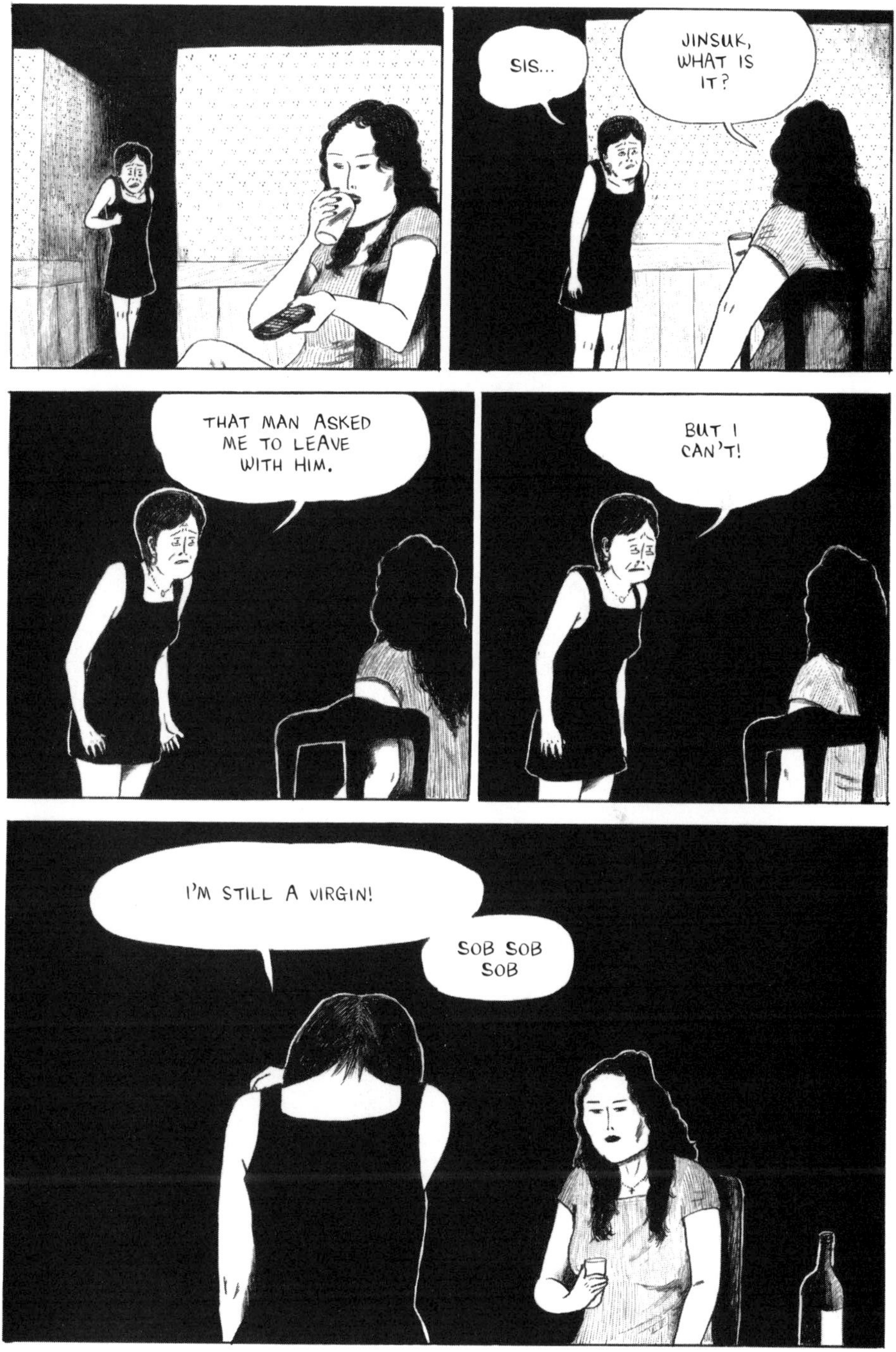
SIS...
JINSUK, WHAT IS IT?
THAT MAN ASKED ME TO LEAVE WITH HIM.
BUT I CAN'T!
I'M STILL A VIRGIN!
SOB SOB SOB

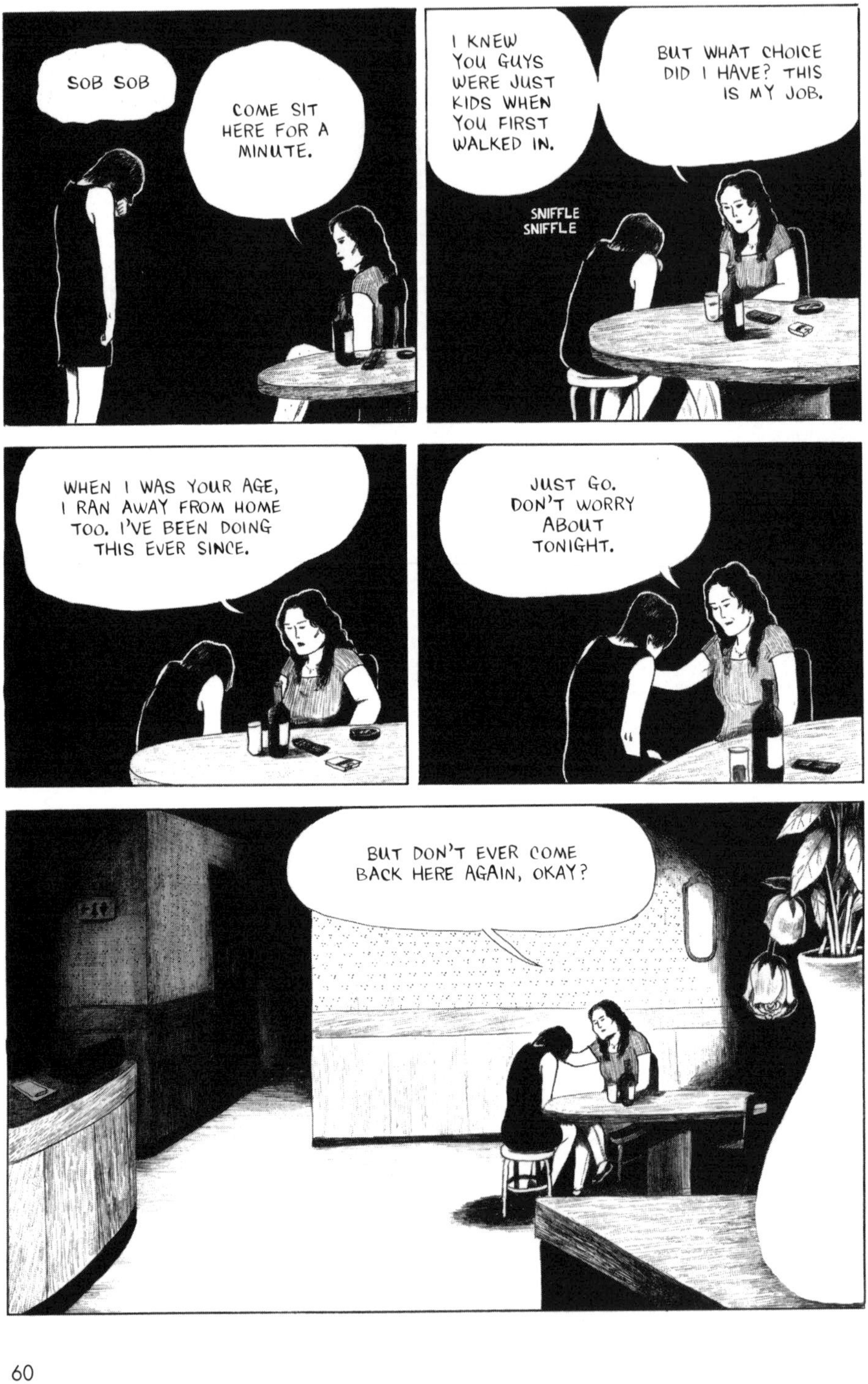
SOB SOB
COME SIT HERE FOR A MINUTE.
I KNEW YOU GUYS WERE JUST KIDS WHEN YOU FIRST WALKED IN.
BUT WHAT CHOICE DID I HAVE? THIS IS MY JOB.
SNIFFLE SNIFFLE
WHEN I WAS YOUR AGE, I RAN AWAY FROM HOME TOO. I'VE BEEN DOING THIS EVER SINCE.
JUST GO. DON'T WORRY ABOUT TONIGHT.
BUT DON'T EVER COME BACK HERE AGAIN, OKAY?

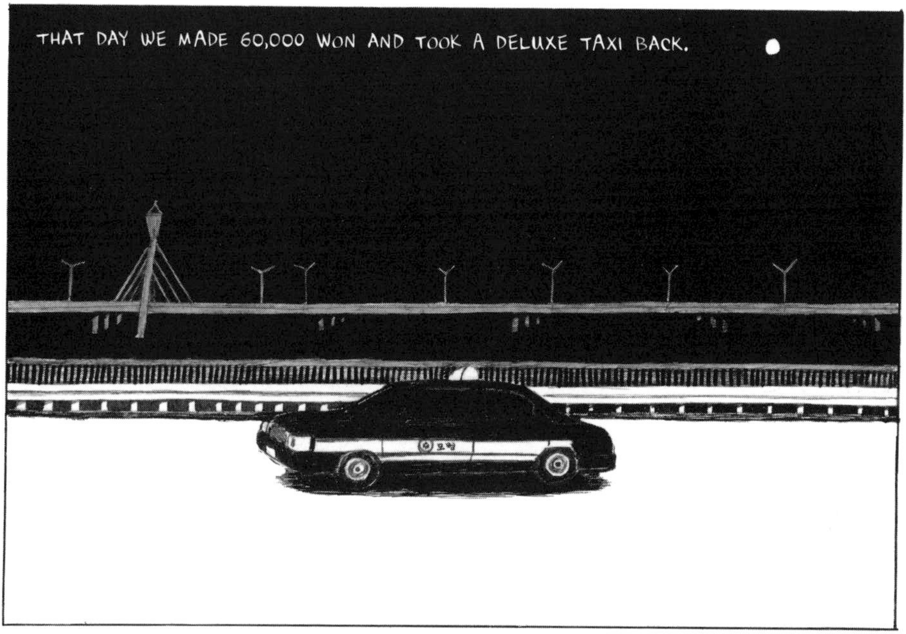
THAT DAY WE MADE 60,000 WON AND TOOK A DELUXE TAXI BACK.

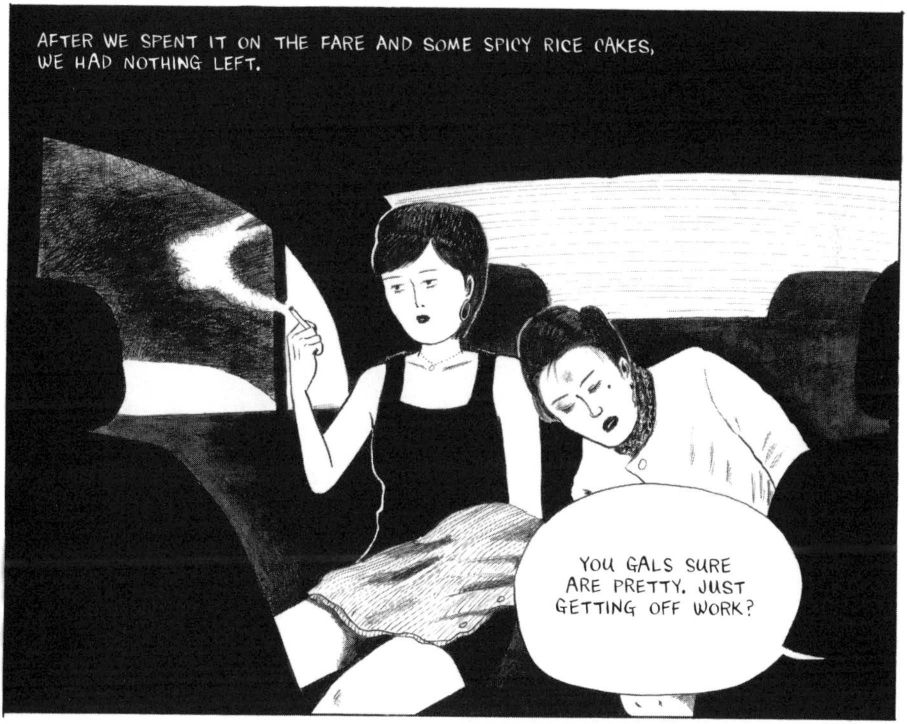
AFTER WE SPENT IT ON THE FARE AND SOME SPICY RICE CAKES, WE HAD NOTHING LEFT.
YOU GALS SURE ARE PRETTY. JUST GETTING OFF WORK?

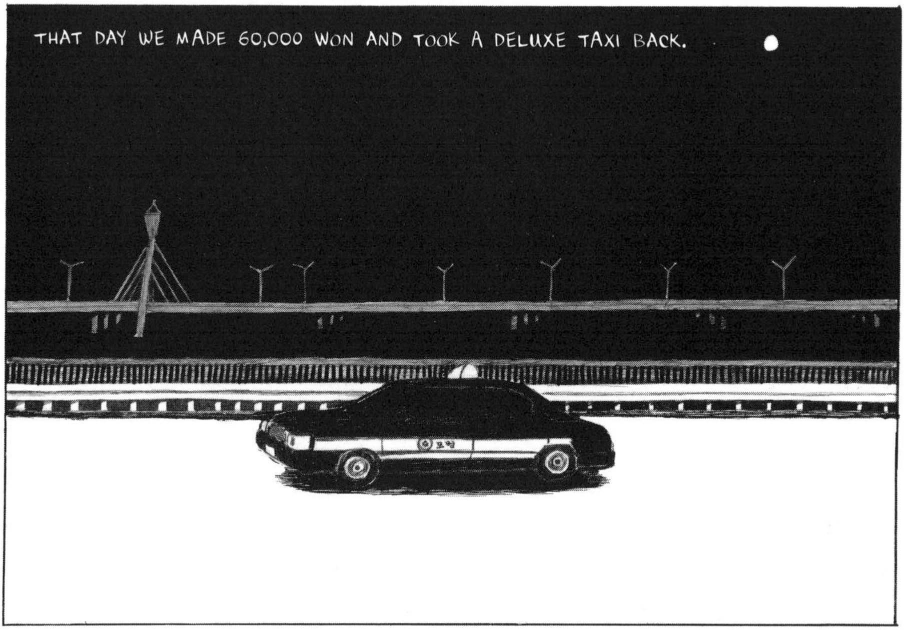
THAT DAY WE MADE 60,000 WON AND TOOK A DELUXE TAXI BACK.

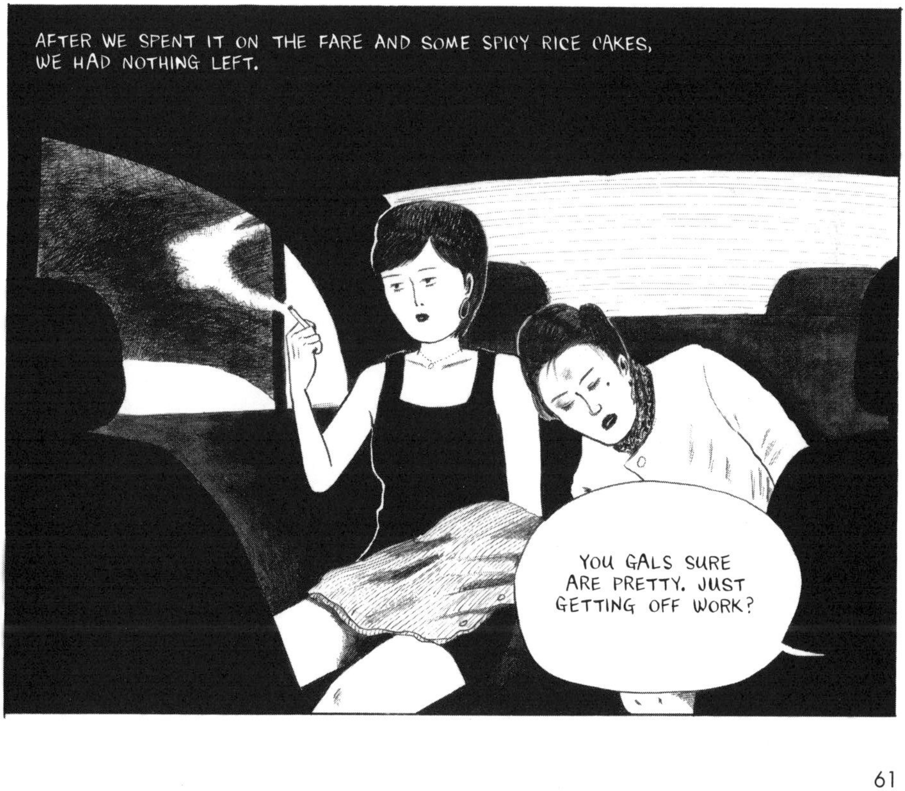
AFTER WE SPENT IT ON THE FARE AND SOME SPICY RICE CAKES, WE HAD NOTHING LEFT.
YOU GALS SURE ARE PRETTY. JUST GETTING OFF WORK?

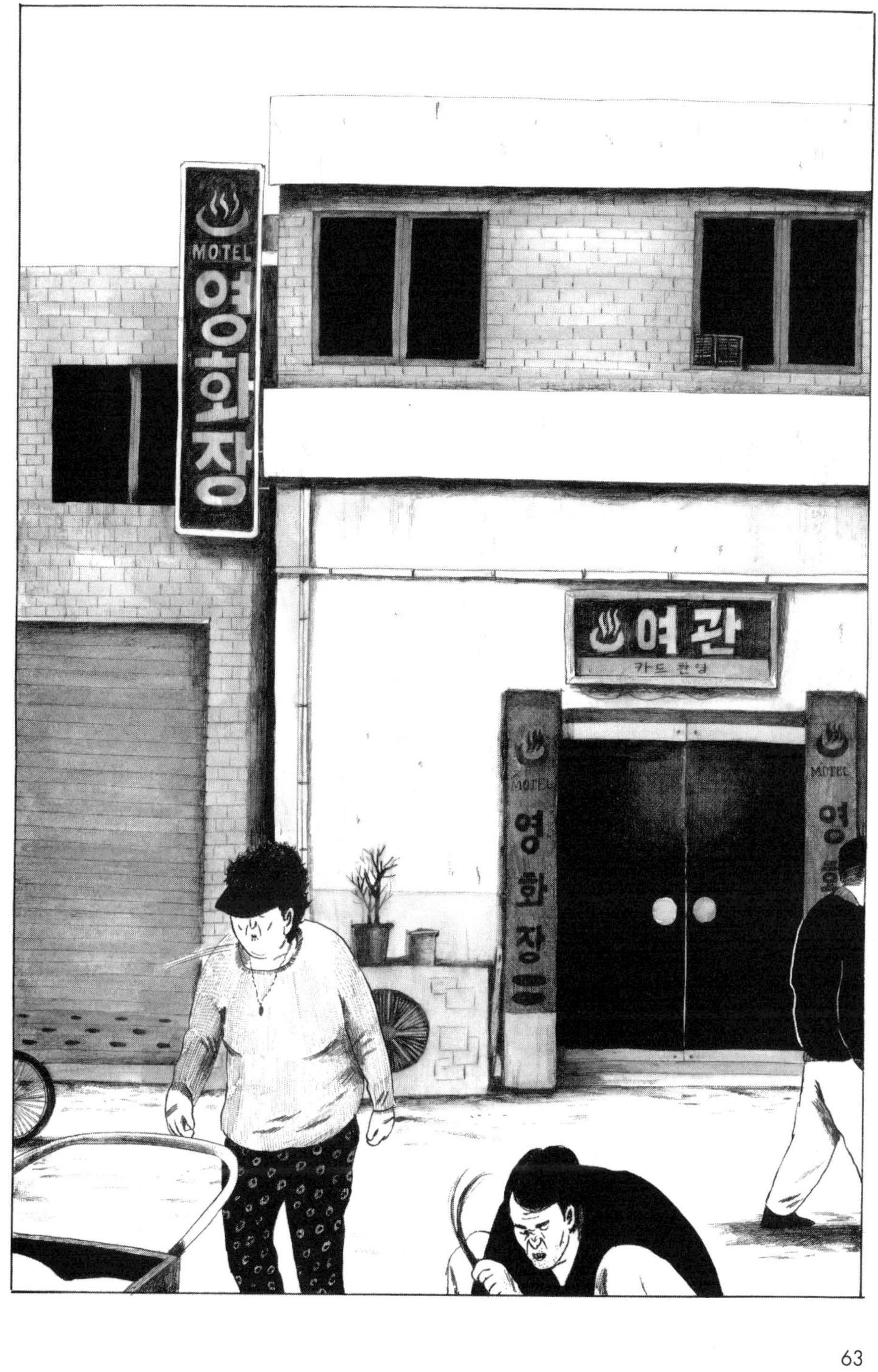
MOTEL
영화장
여관
MOTEL
영화장

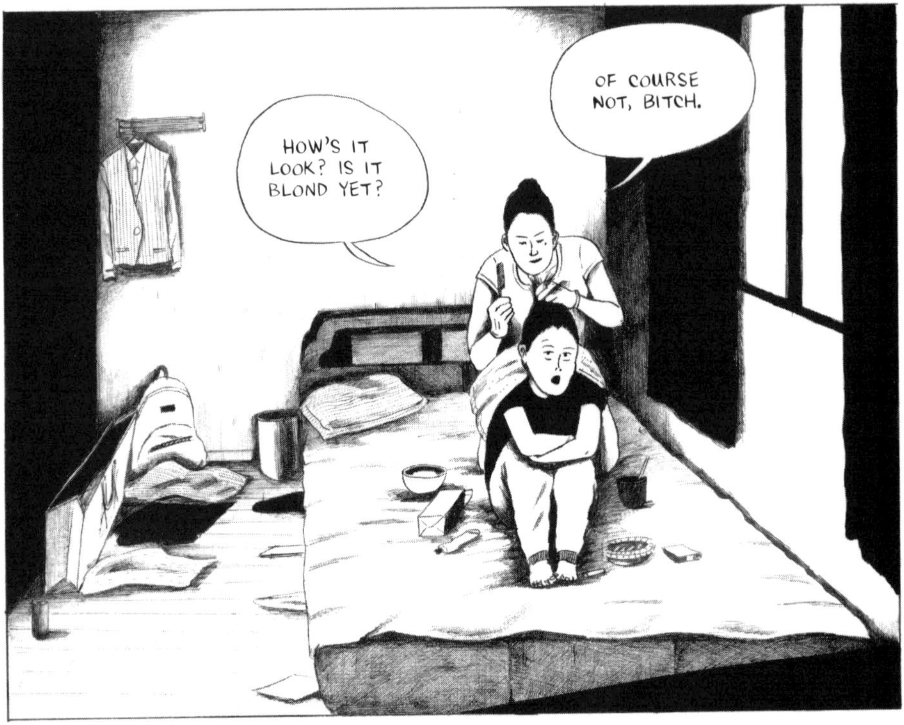
HOW'S IT LOOK? IS IT BLOND YET?
OF COURSE NOT, BITCH.

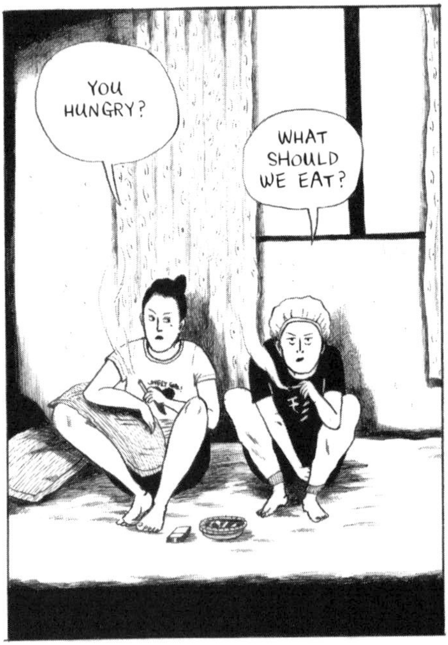
YOU HUNGRY?
WHAT SHOULD WE EAT?

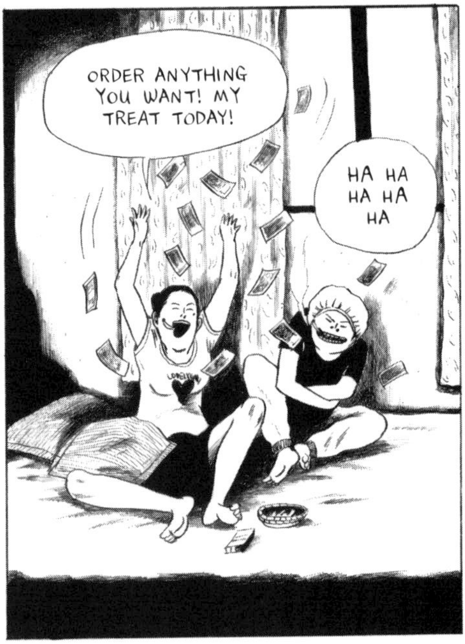
ORDER ANYTHING YOU WANT! MY TREAT TODAY!
HA HA HA HA HA

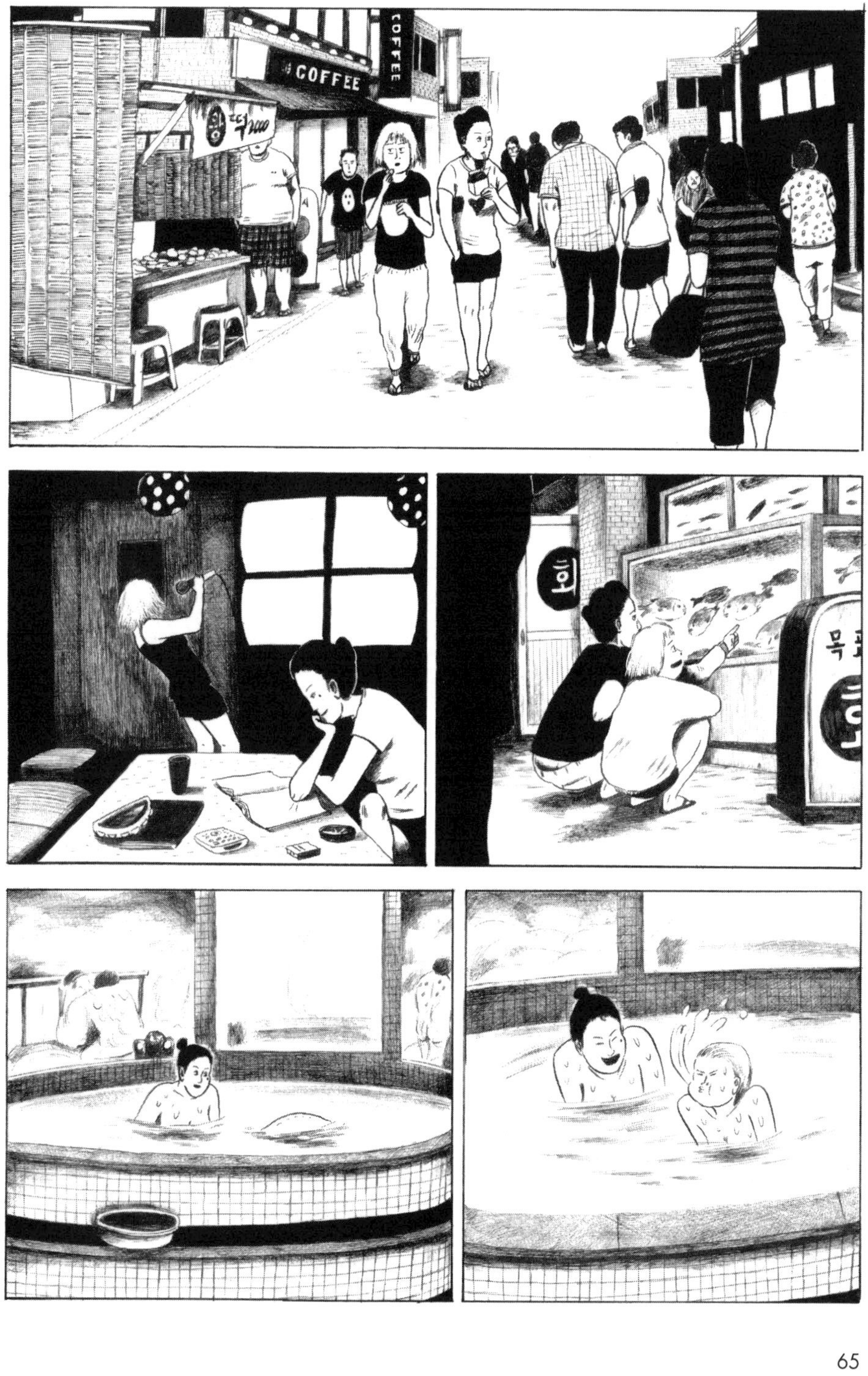
COFFEE
COFFEE
떡2000
회

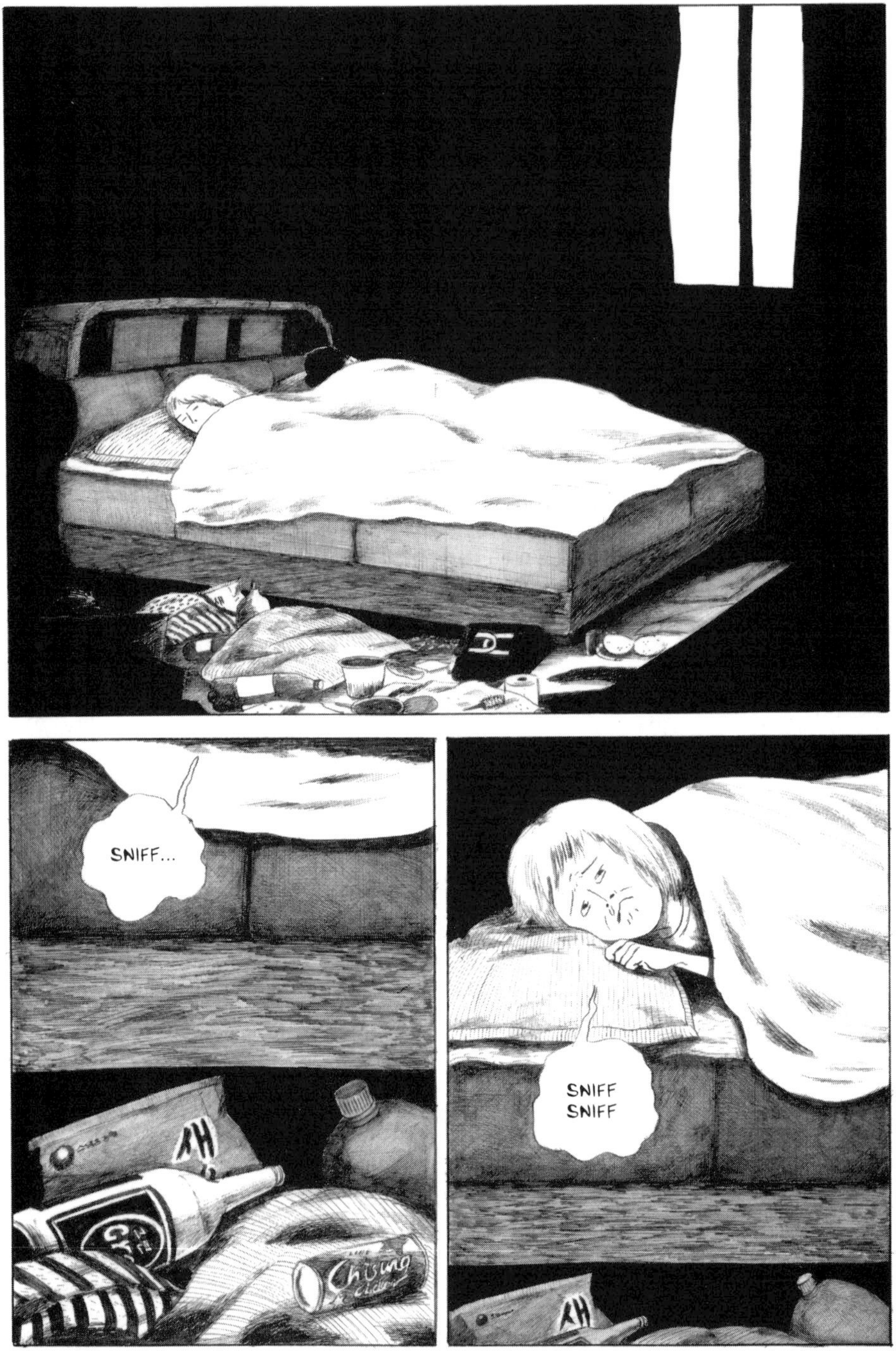
SNIFF...
SNIFF SNIFF

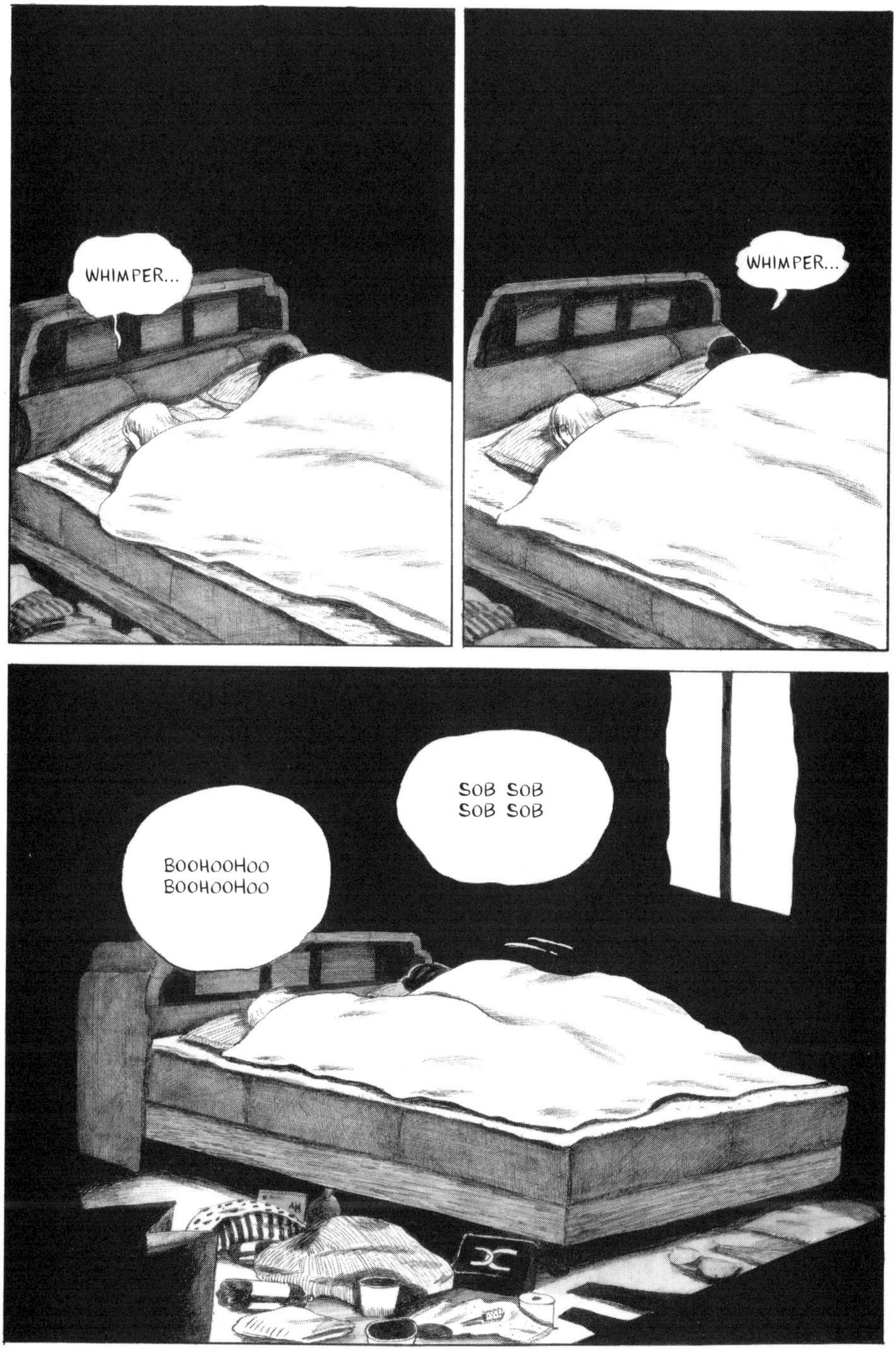
WHIMPER...
WHIMPER...
BOOHOOHOO BOOHOOHOO
SOB SOB SOB SOB

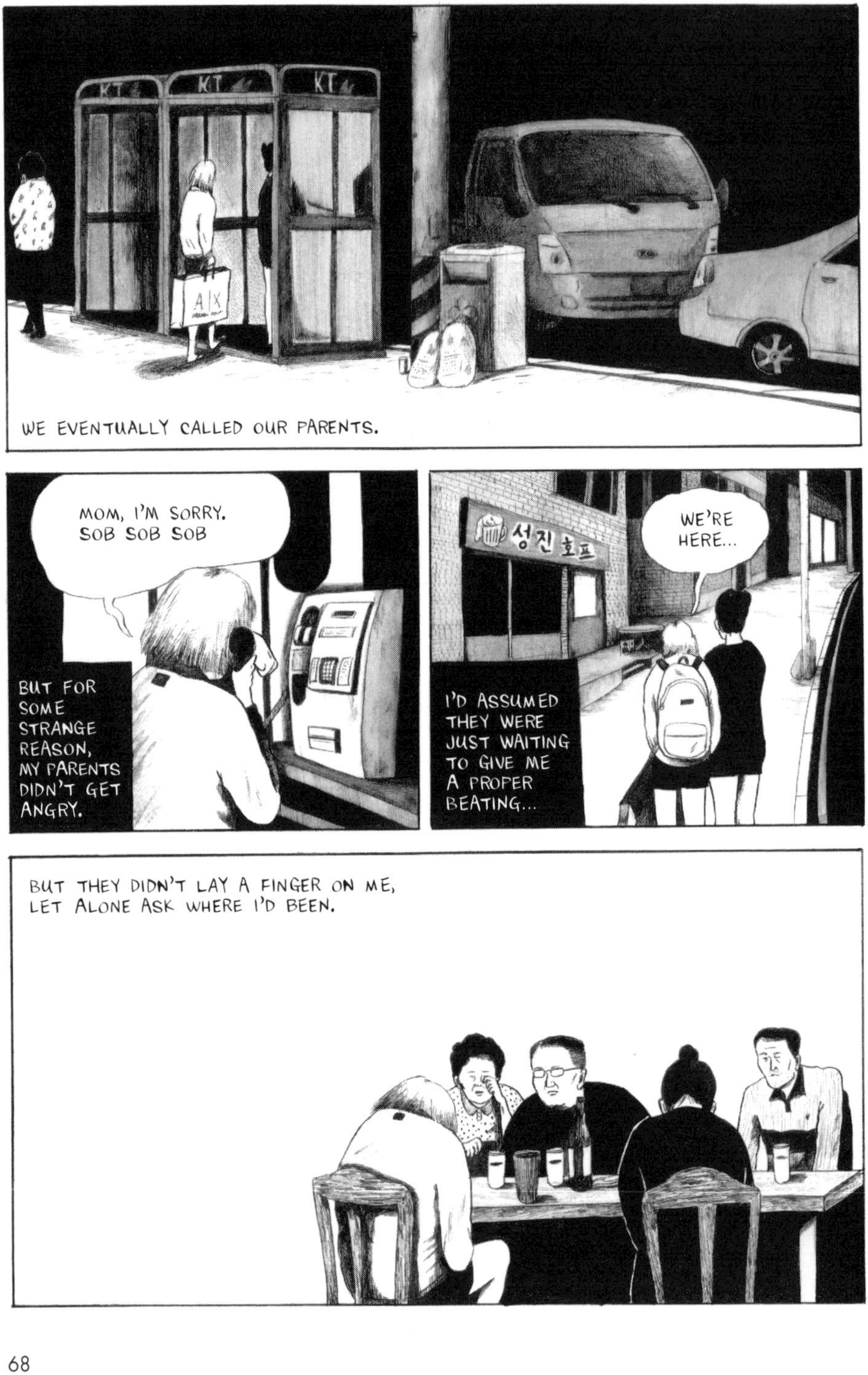
KT
KT
KT
A|X
WE EVENTUALLY CALLED OUR PARENTS.
MOM, I'M SORRY.
SOB SOB SOB
BUT FOR SOME STRANGE REASON, MY PARENTS DIDN'T GET ANGRY.
성진 호프
WE'RE HERE...
I'D ASSUMED THEY WERE JUST WAITING TO GIVE ME A PROPER BEATING...
BUT THEY DIDN'T LAY A FINGER ON ME, LET ALONE ASK WHERE I'D BEEN.

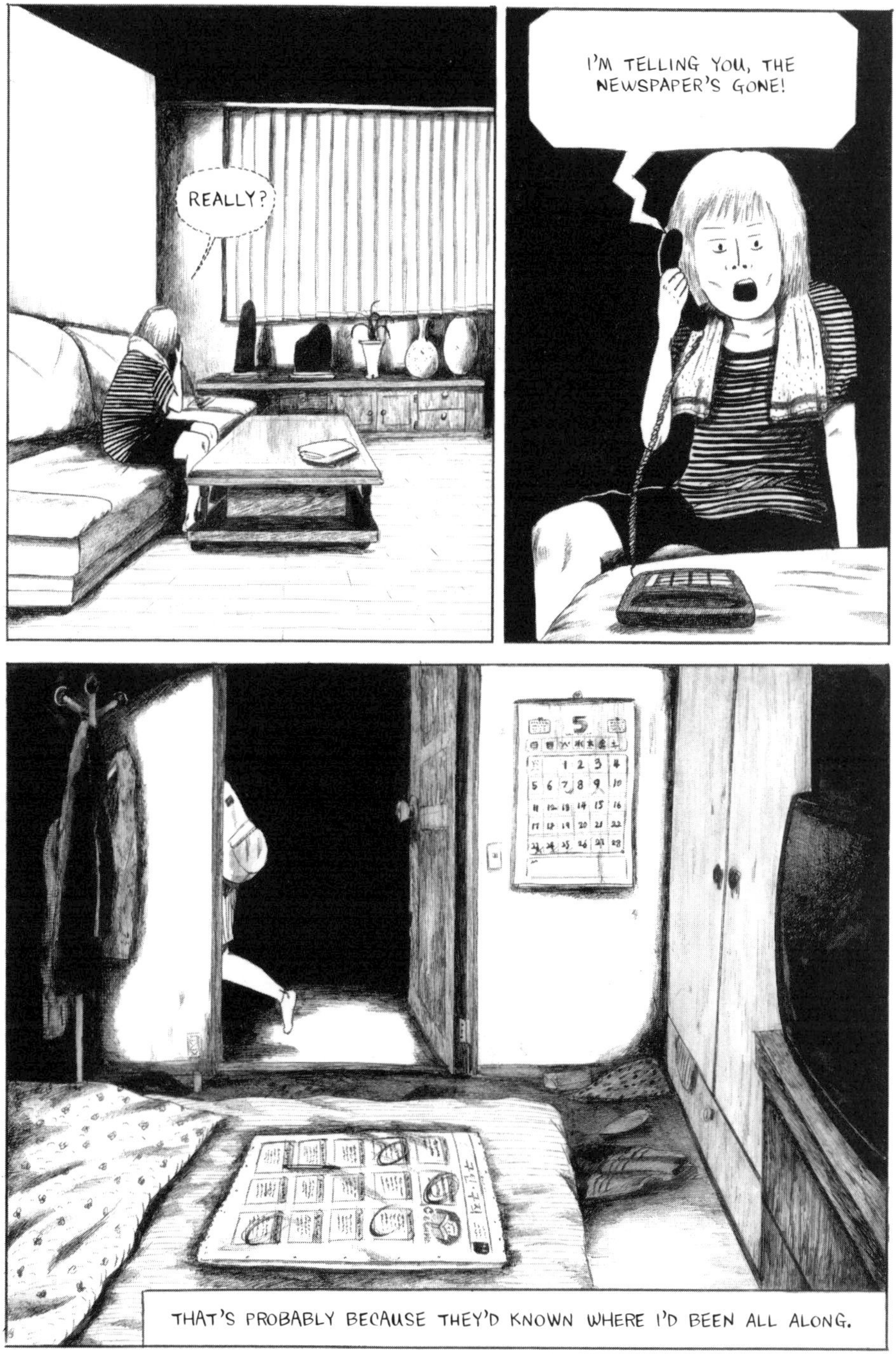
REALLY?
I'M TELLING YOU, THE NEWSPAPER'S GONE!
THAT'S PROBABLY BECAUSE THEY'D KNOWN WHERE I'D BEEN ALL ALONG.

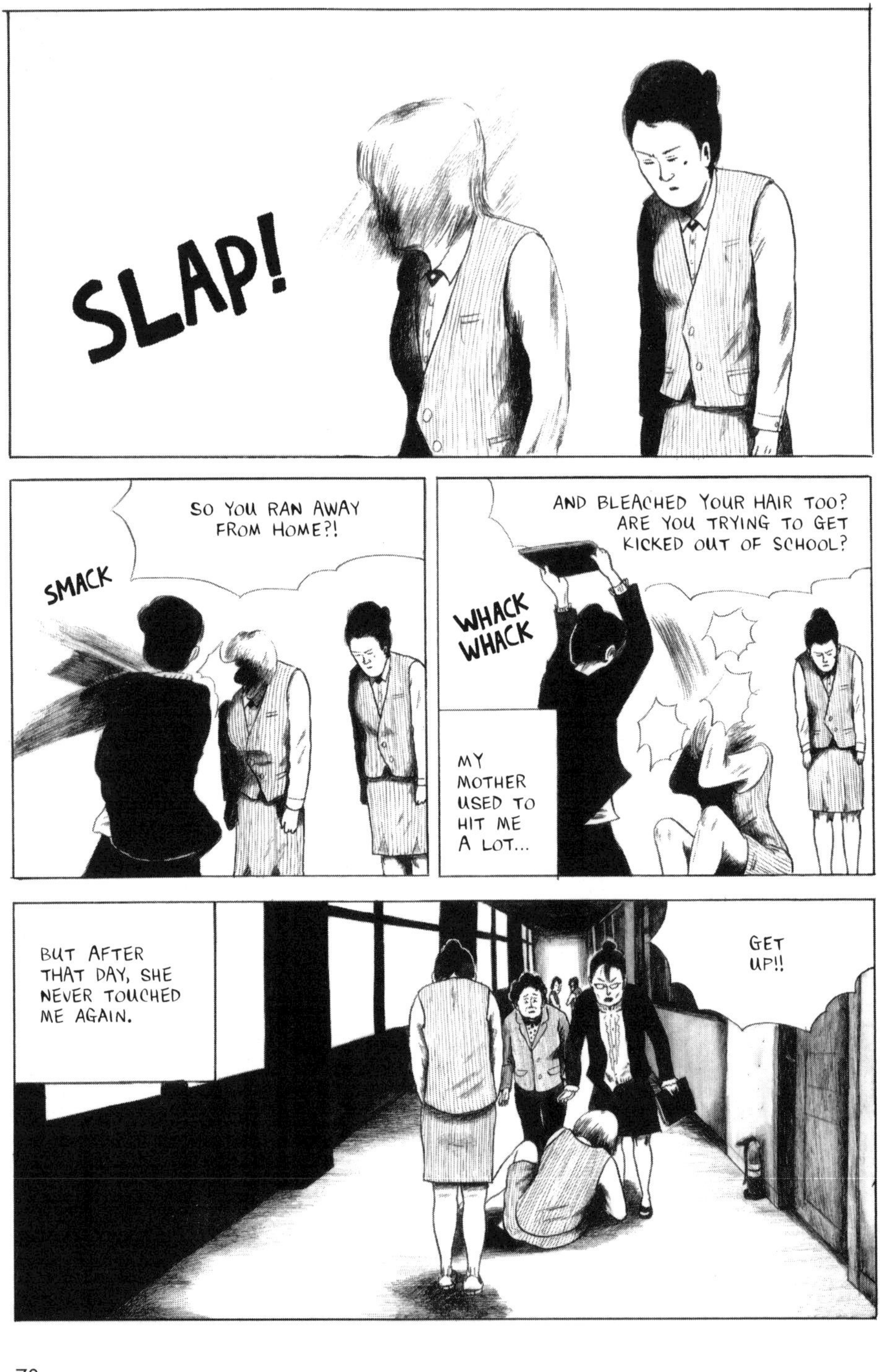
SLAP!
SO YOU RAN AWAY FROM HOME?!
SMACK
AND BLEACHED YOUR HAIR TOO? ARE YOU TRYING TO GET KICKED OUT OF SCHOOL?
WHACK WHACK
MY MOTHER USED TO HIT ME A LOT...
BUT AFTER THAT DAY, SHE NEVER TOUCHED ME AGAIN.
GET UP!!

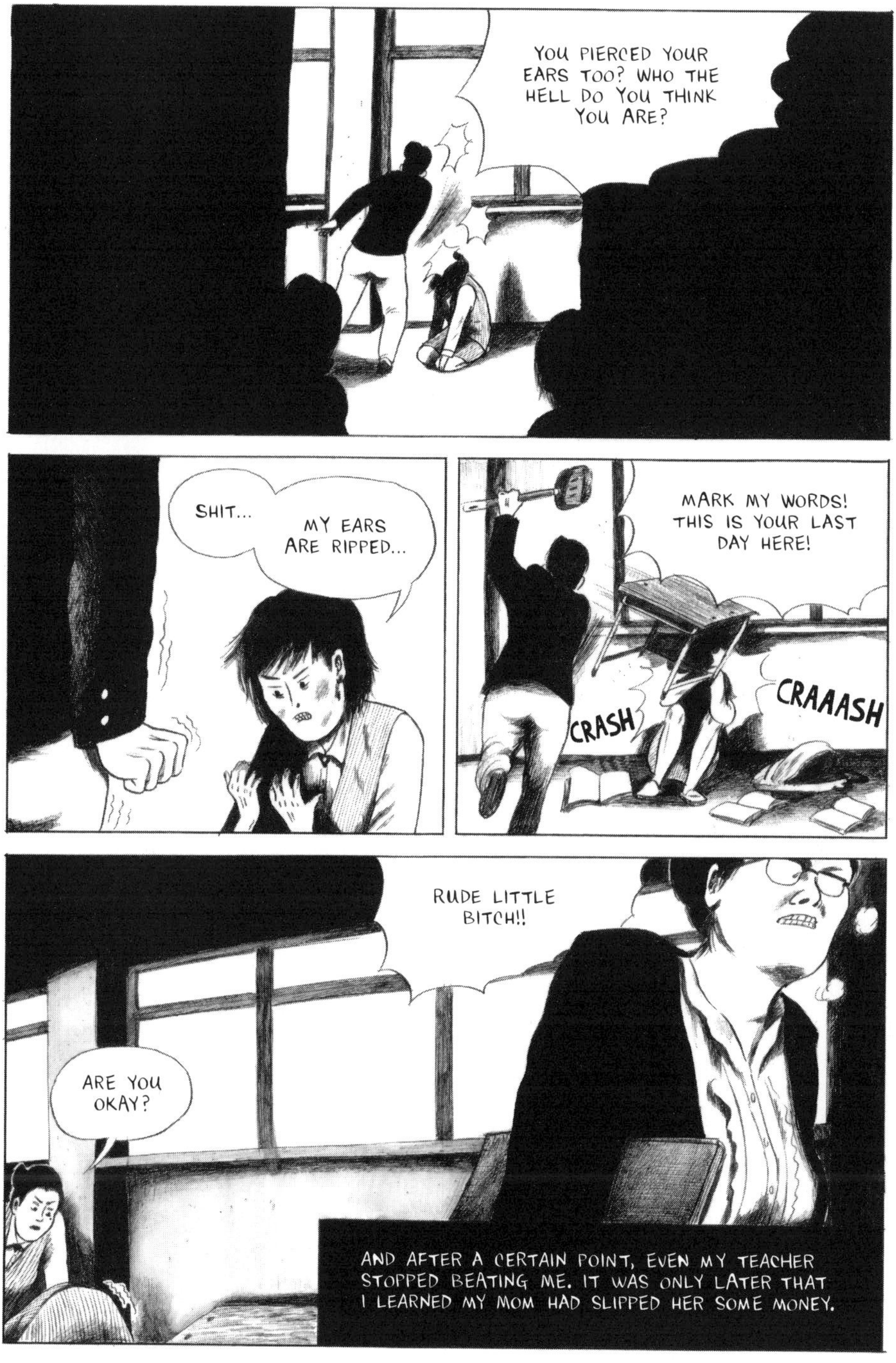

YOU PIERCED YOUR EARS TOO? WHO THE HELL DO YOU THINK YOU ARE?
SHIT...
MY EARS ARE RIPPED...
MARK MY WORDS! THIS IS YOUR LAST DAY HERE!
CRASH
CRAAASH
RUDE LITTLE BITCH!!
ARE YOU OKAY?
AND AFTER A CERTAIN POINT, EVEN MY TEACHER STOPPED BEATING ME. IT WAS ONLY LATER THAT I LEARNED MY MOM HAD SLIPPED HER SOME MONEY.

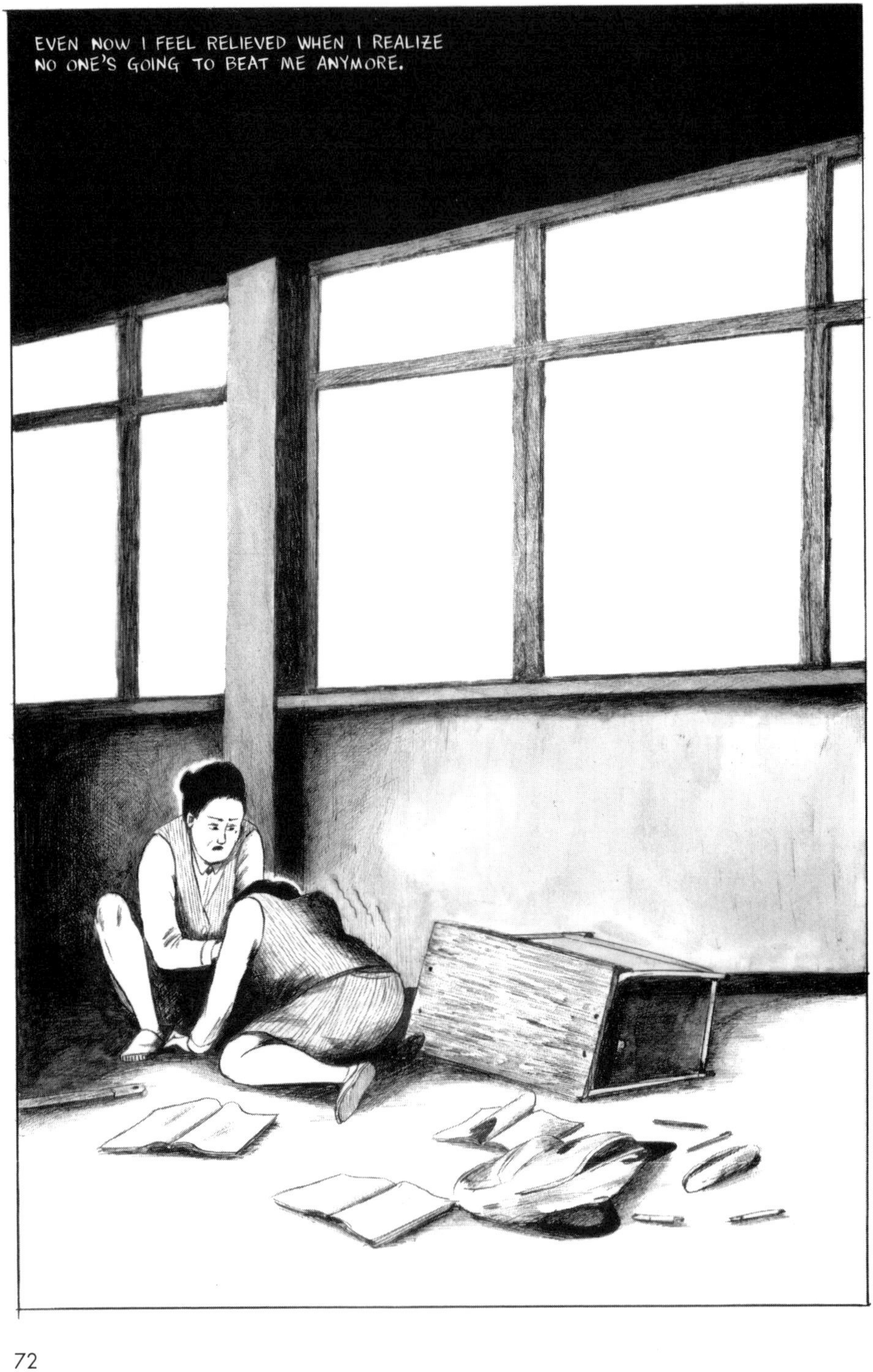
EVEN NOW I FEEL RELIEVED WHEN I REALIZE NO ONE'S GOING TO BEAT ME ANYMORE.

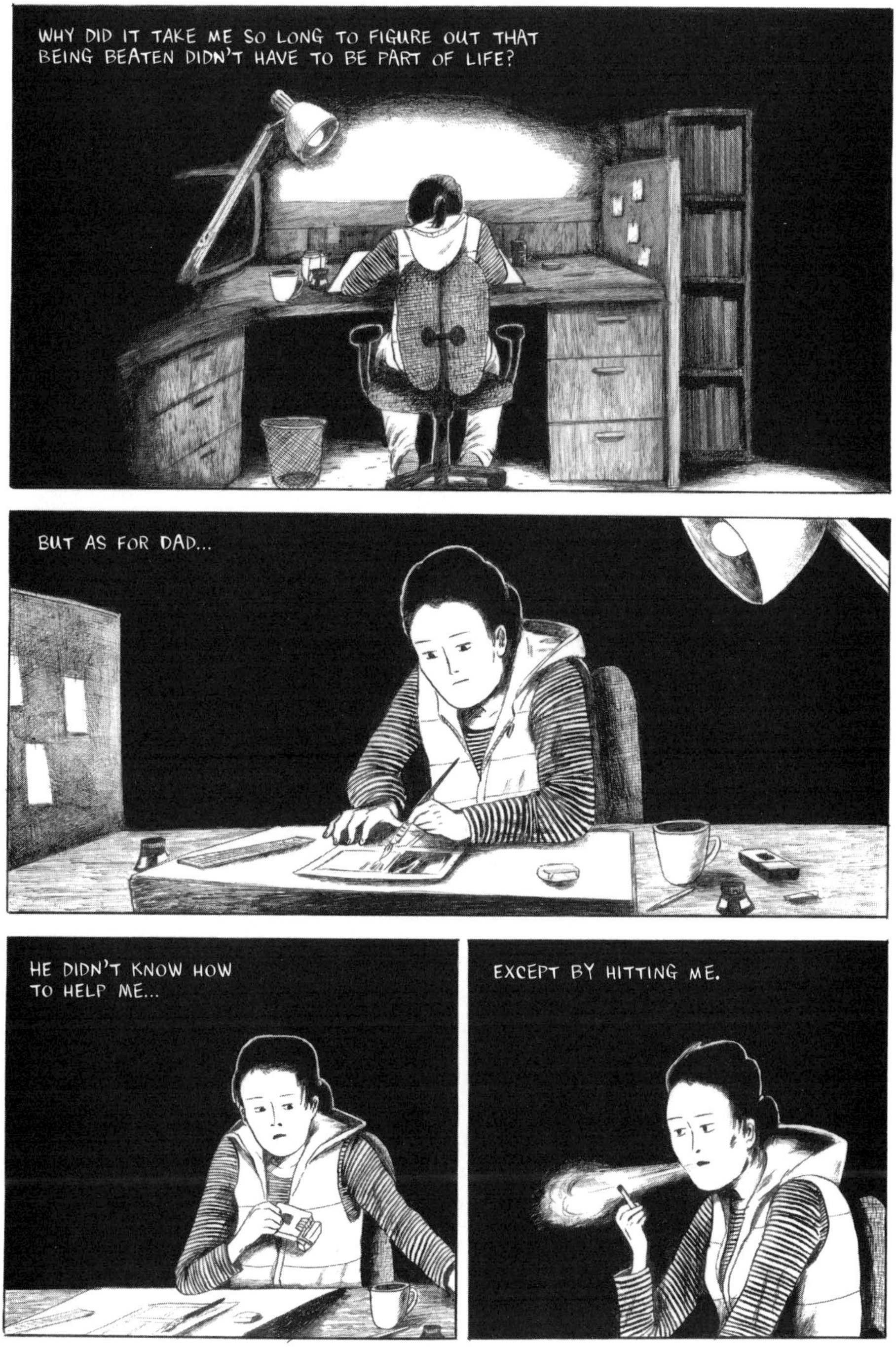
WHY DID IT TAKE ME SO LONG TO FIGURE OUT THAT BEING BEATEN DIDN'T HAVE TO BE PART OF LIFE?
BUT AS FOR DAD...
HE DIDN'T KNOW HOW TO HELP ME...
EXCEPT BY HITTING ME.

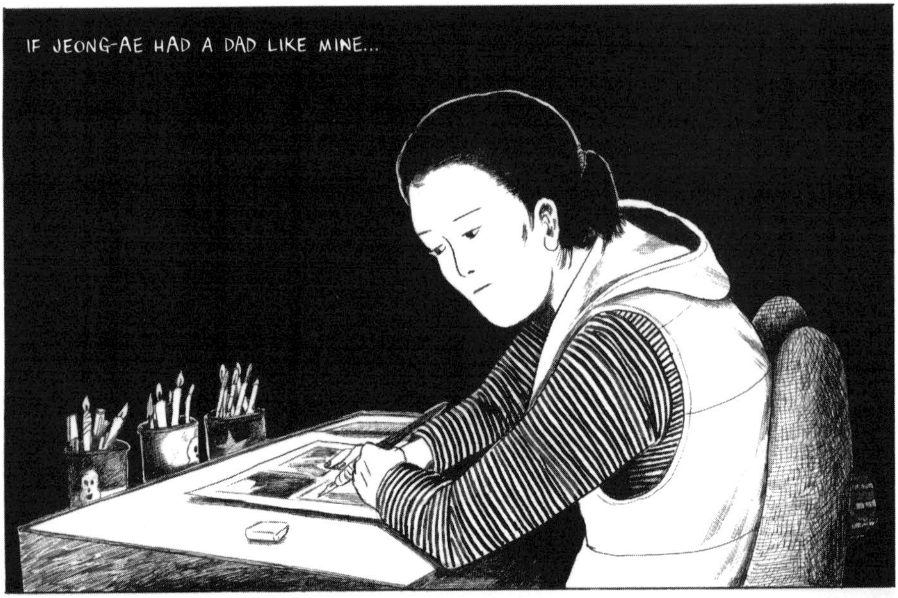
IF JEONG-AE HAD A DAD LIKE MINE...

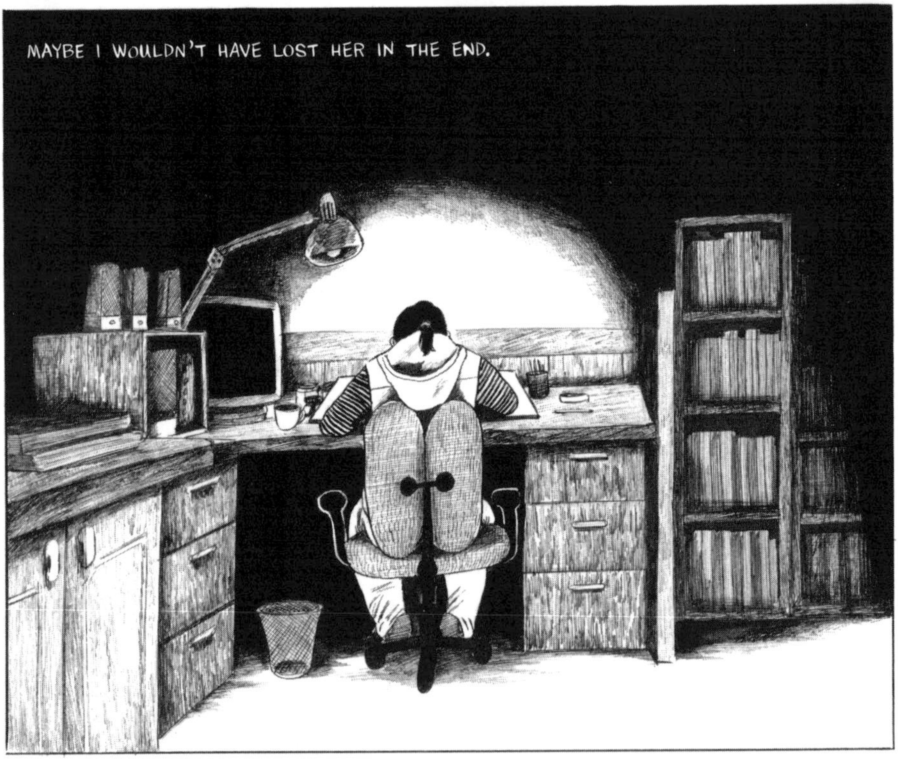
MAYBE I WOULDN'T HAVE LOST HER IN THE END.

jeong-ae

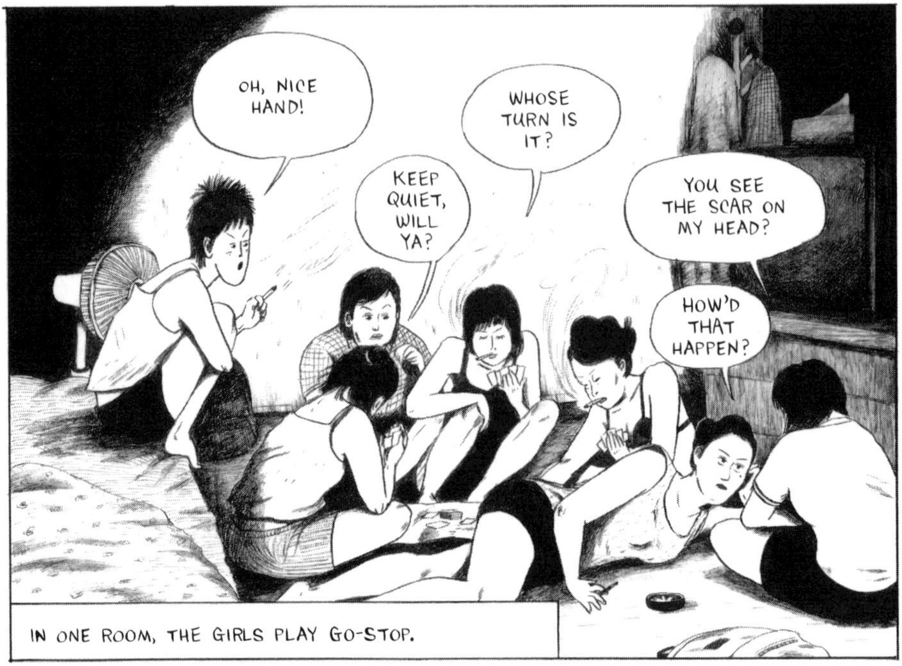
OH, NICE HAND!
KEEP QUIET, WILL YA?
WHOSE TURN IS IT?
YOU SEE THE SCAR ON MY HEAD?
HOW'D THAT HAPPEN?
IN ONE ROOM, THE GIRLS PLAY GO-STOP.

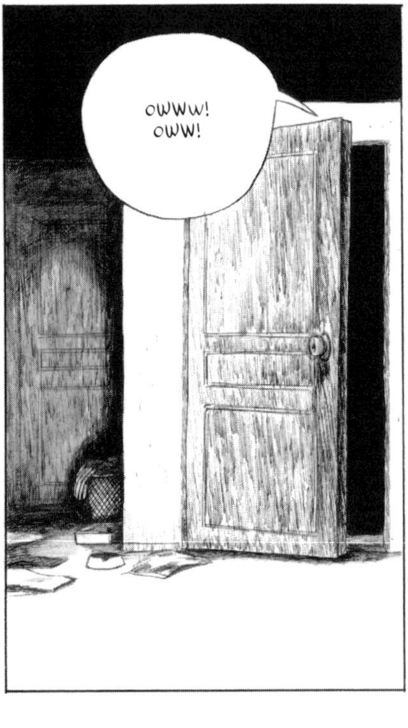
OWWW! OWW!

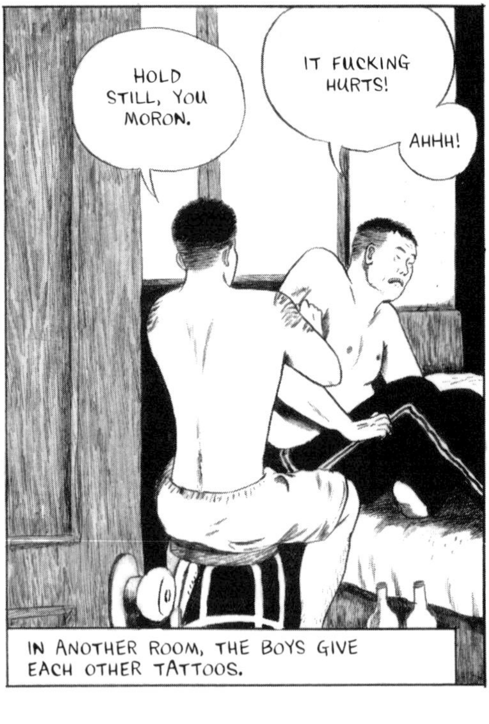
HOLD STILL, YOU MORON.
IT FUCKING HURTS!
AHHH!
IN ANOTHER ROOM, THE BOYS GIVE EACH OTHER TATTOOS.

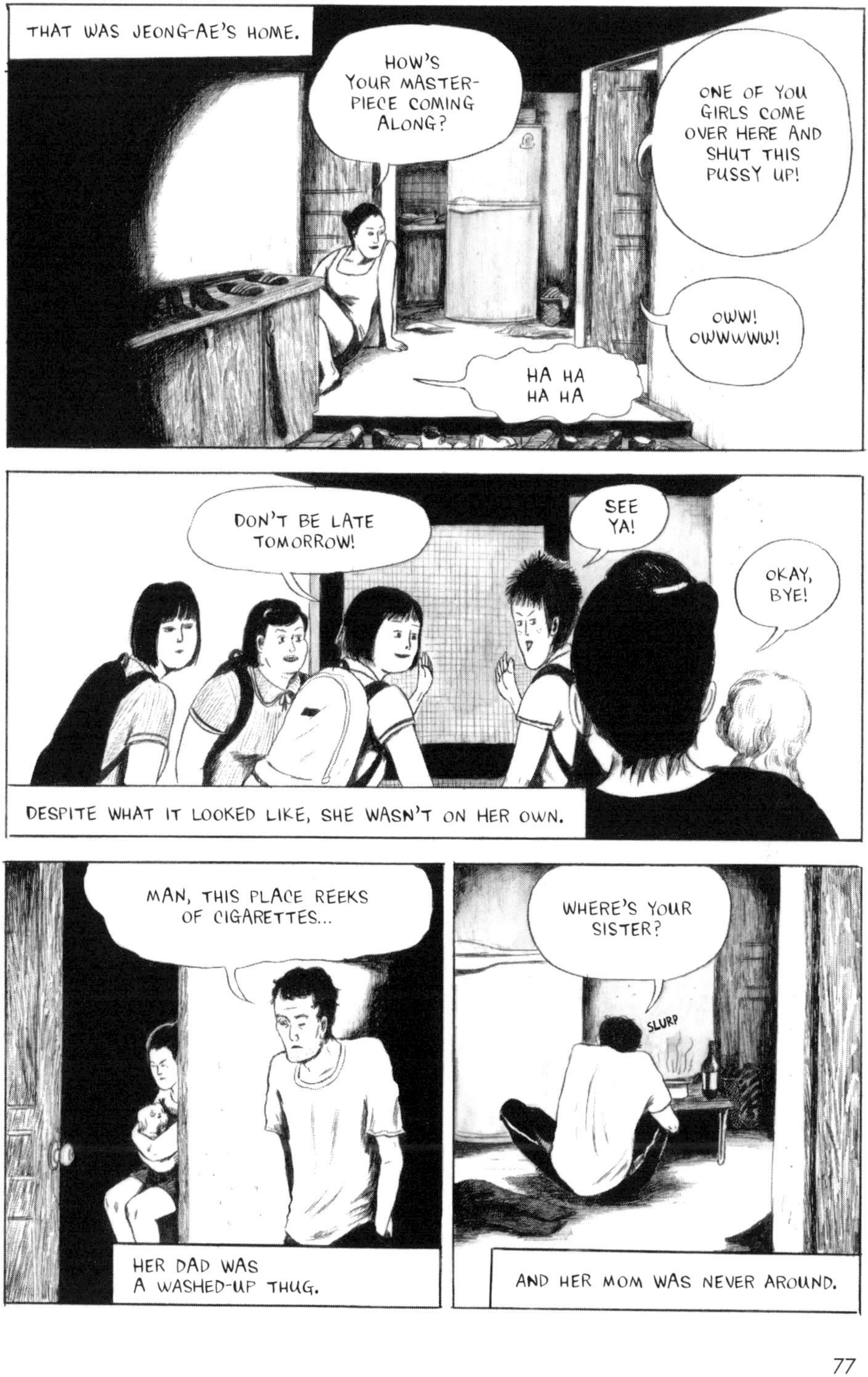
THAT WAS JEONG-AE'S HOME.
HOW'S YOUR MASTER-PIECE COMING ALONG?
ONE OF YOU GIRLS COME OVER HERE AND SHUT THIS PUSSY UP!
OWW! OWWWWW!
HA HA HA HA
DON'T BE LATE TOMORROW!
SEE YA!
OKAY, BYE!
DESPITE WHAT IT LOOKED LIKE, SHE WASN'T ON HER OWN.
MAN, THIS PLACE REEKS OF CIGARETTES...
HER DAD WAS A WASHED-UP THUG.
WHERE'S YOUR SISTER?
SLURP
AND HER MOM WAS NEVER AROUND.

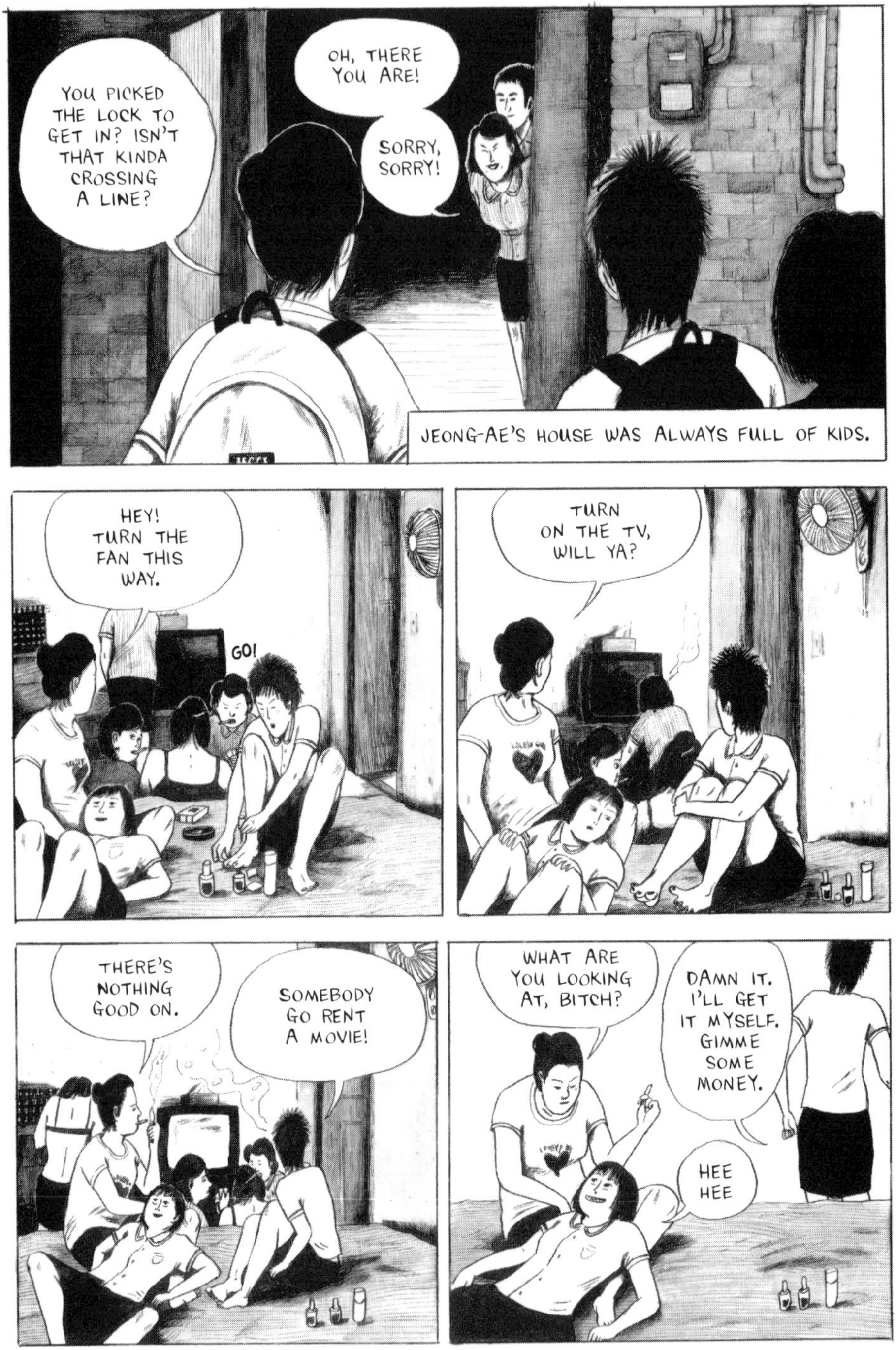
YOU PICKED THE LOCK TO GET IN? ISN'T THAT KINDA CROSSING A LINE?
OH, THERE YOU ARE!
SORRY, SORRY!
JEONG-AE'S HOUSE WAS ALWAYS FULL OF KIDS.
HEY! TURN THE FAN THIS WAY.
GO!
TURN ON THE TV, WILL YA?
THERE'S NOTHING GOOD ON.
SOMEBODY GO RENT A MOVIE!
WHAT ARE YOU LOOKING AT, BITCH?
DAMN IT. I'LL GET IT MYSELF. GIMME SOME MONEY.
HEE HEE

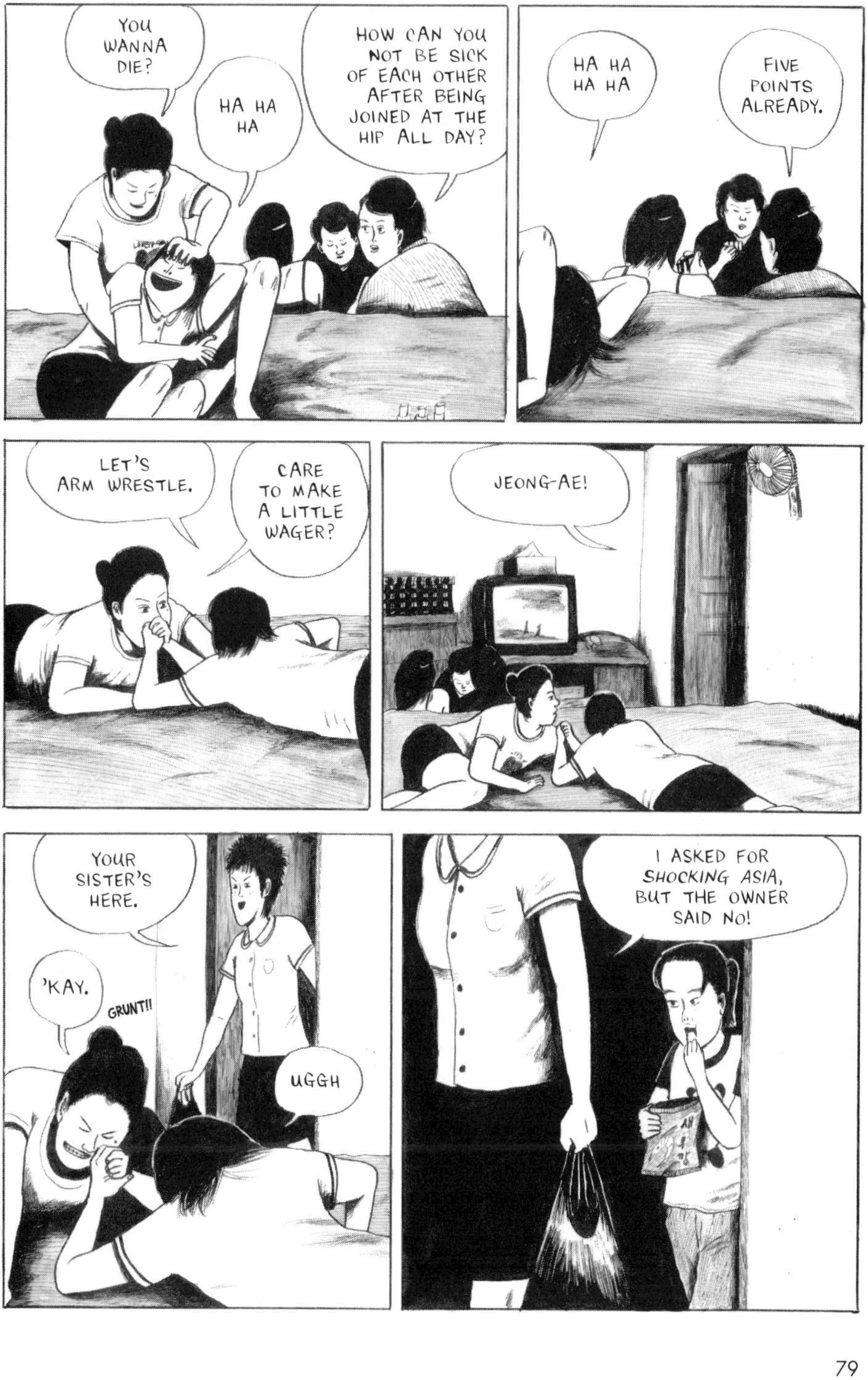

YOU WANNA DIE?
HA HA HA
HOW CAN YOU NOT BE SICK OF EACH OTHER AFTER BEING JOINED AT THE HIP ALL DAY?
HA HA HA HA
FIVE POINTS ALREADY.
LET'S ARM WRESTLE.
CARE TO MAKE A LITTLE WAGER?
JEONG-AE!
YOUR SISTER'S HERE.
'KAY.
GRUNT!!
UGGH
I ASKED FOR SHOCKING ASIA, BUT THE OWNER SAID NO!

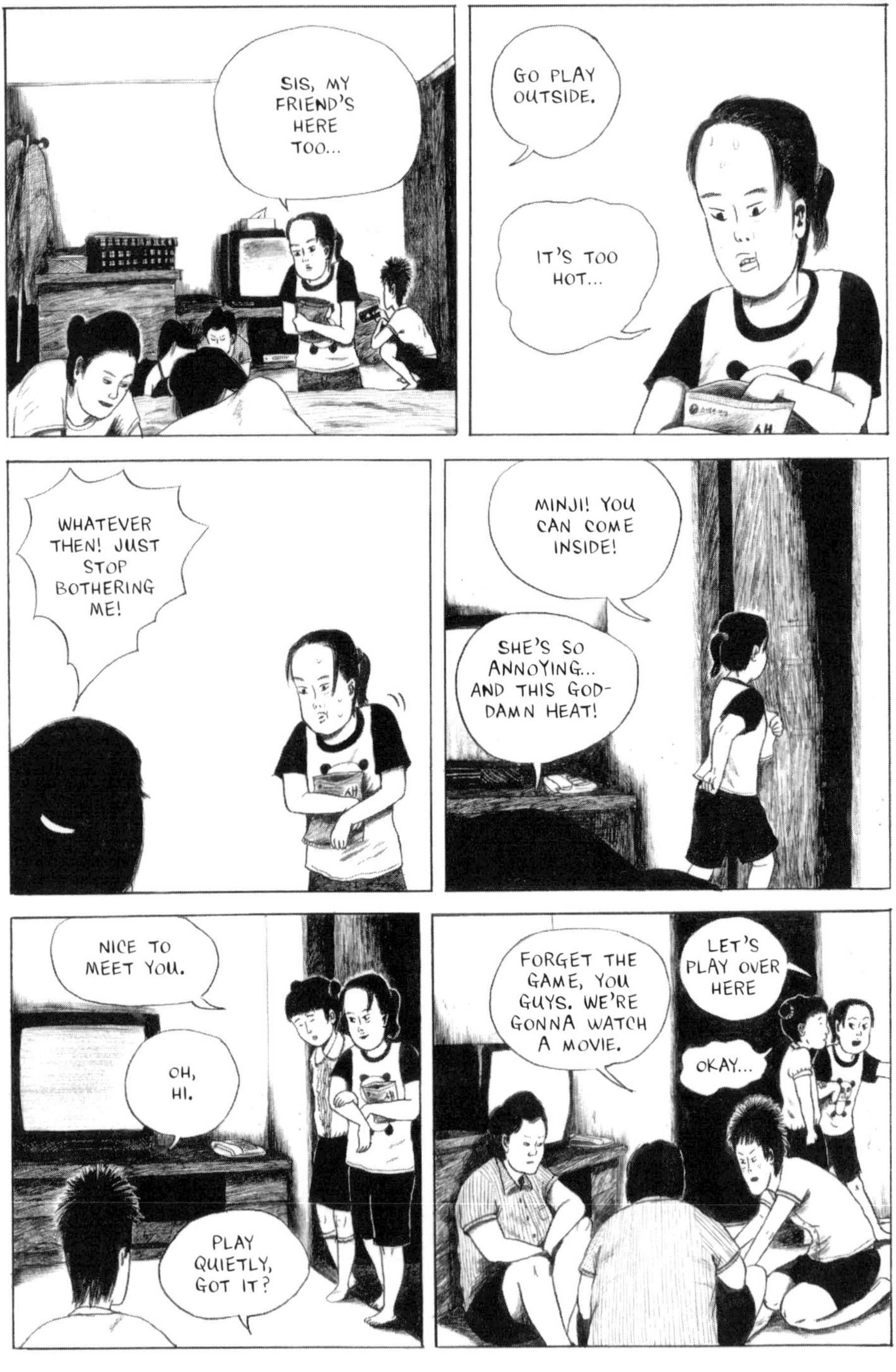
SIS, MY FRIEND'S HERE TOO...
GO PLAY OUTSIDE.
IT'S TOO HOT...
WHATEVER THEN! JUST STOP BOTHERING ME!
MINJI! YOU CAN COME INSIDE!
SHE'S SO ANNOYING... AND THIS GOD-DAMN HEAT!
NICE TO MEET YOU.
OH, HI.
PLAY QUIETLY, GOT IT?
FORGET THE GAME, YOU GUYS. WE'RE GONNA WATCH A MOVIE.
LET'S PLAY OVER HERE
OKAY...

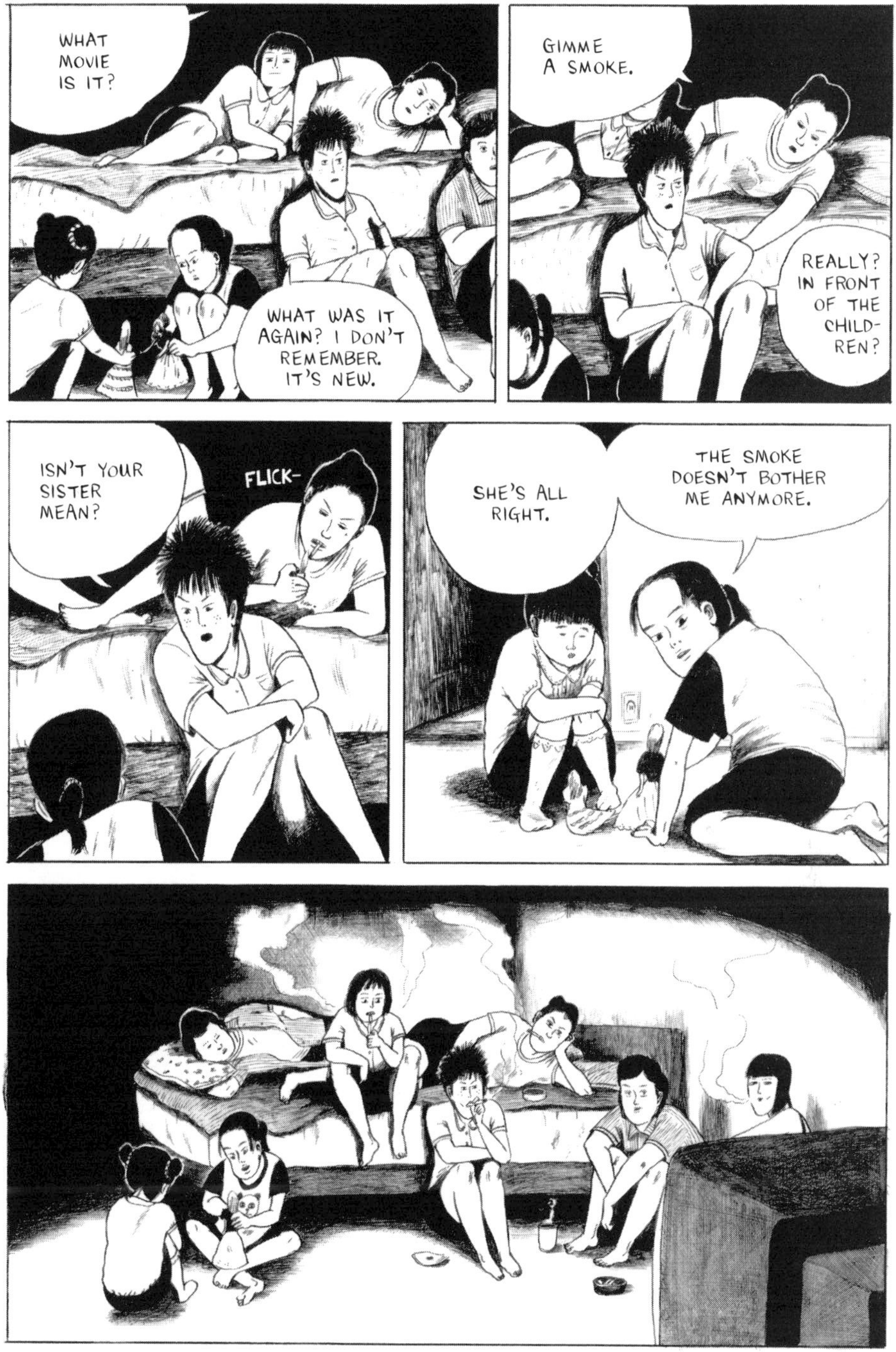
WHAT MOVIE IS IT?
WHAT WAS IT AGAIN? I DON'T REMEMBER. IT'S NEW.
GIMME A SMOKE.
REALLY? IN FRONT OF THE CHILD-REN?
ISN'T YOUR SISTER MEAN?
FLICK-
SHE'S ALL RIGHT.
THE SMOKE DOESN'T BOTHER ME ANYMORE.

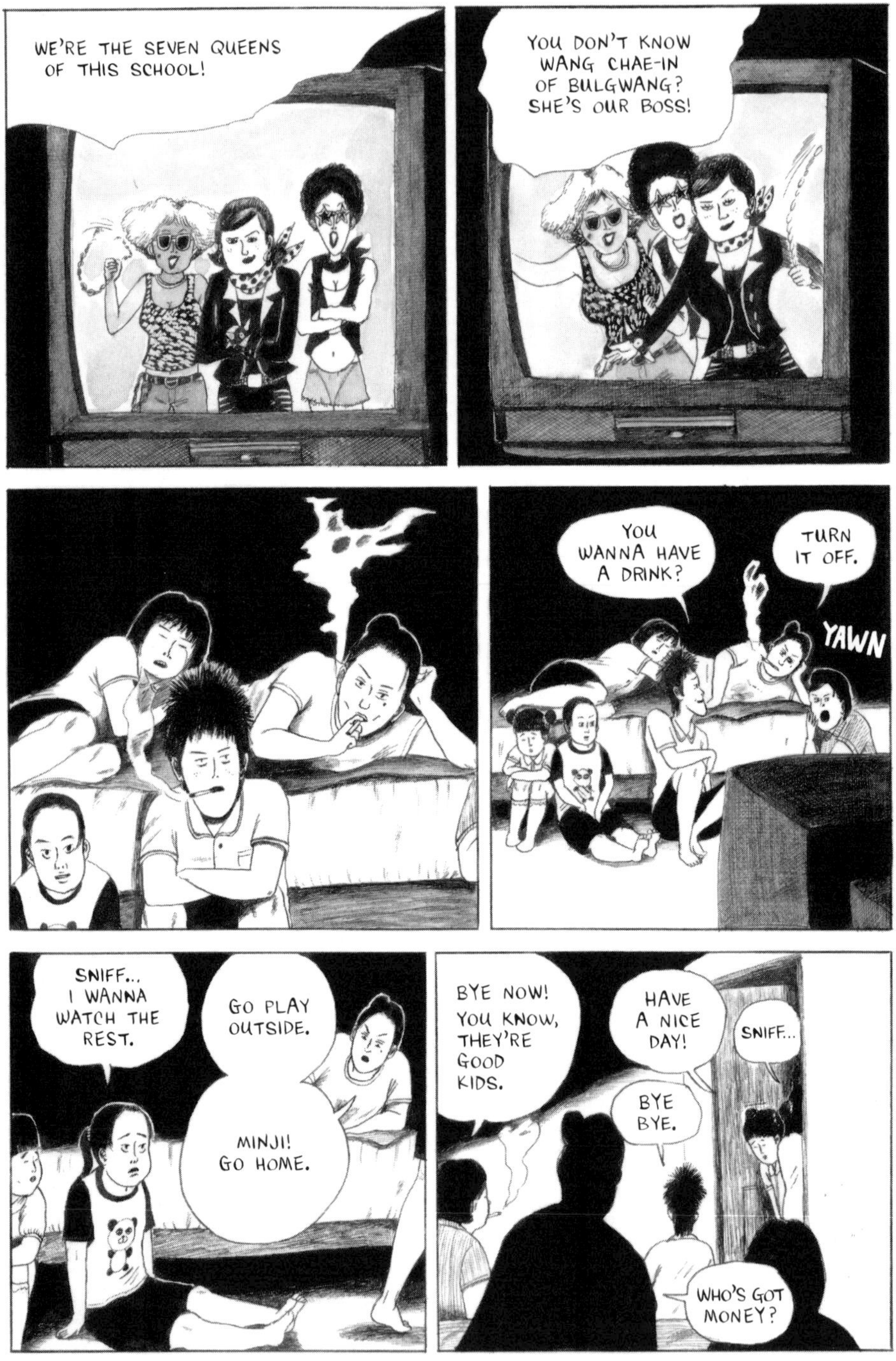
WE'RE THE SEVEN QUEENS OF THIS SCHOOL!
YOU DON'T KNOW WANG CHAE-IN OF BULGWANG? SHE'S OUR BOSS!
YOU WANNA HAVE A DRINK?
TURN IT OFF.
YAWN
SNIFF... I WANNA WATCH THE REST.
GO PLAY OUTSIDE.
MINJI! GO HOME.
BYE NOW! YOU KNOW, THEY'RE GOOD KIDS.
HAVE A NICE DAY!
SNIFF...
BYE BYE.
WHO'S GOT MONEY?

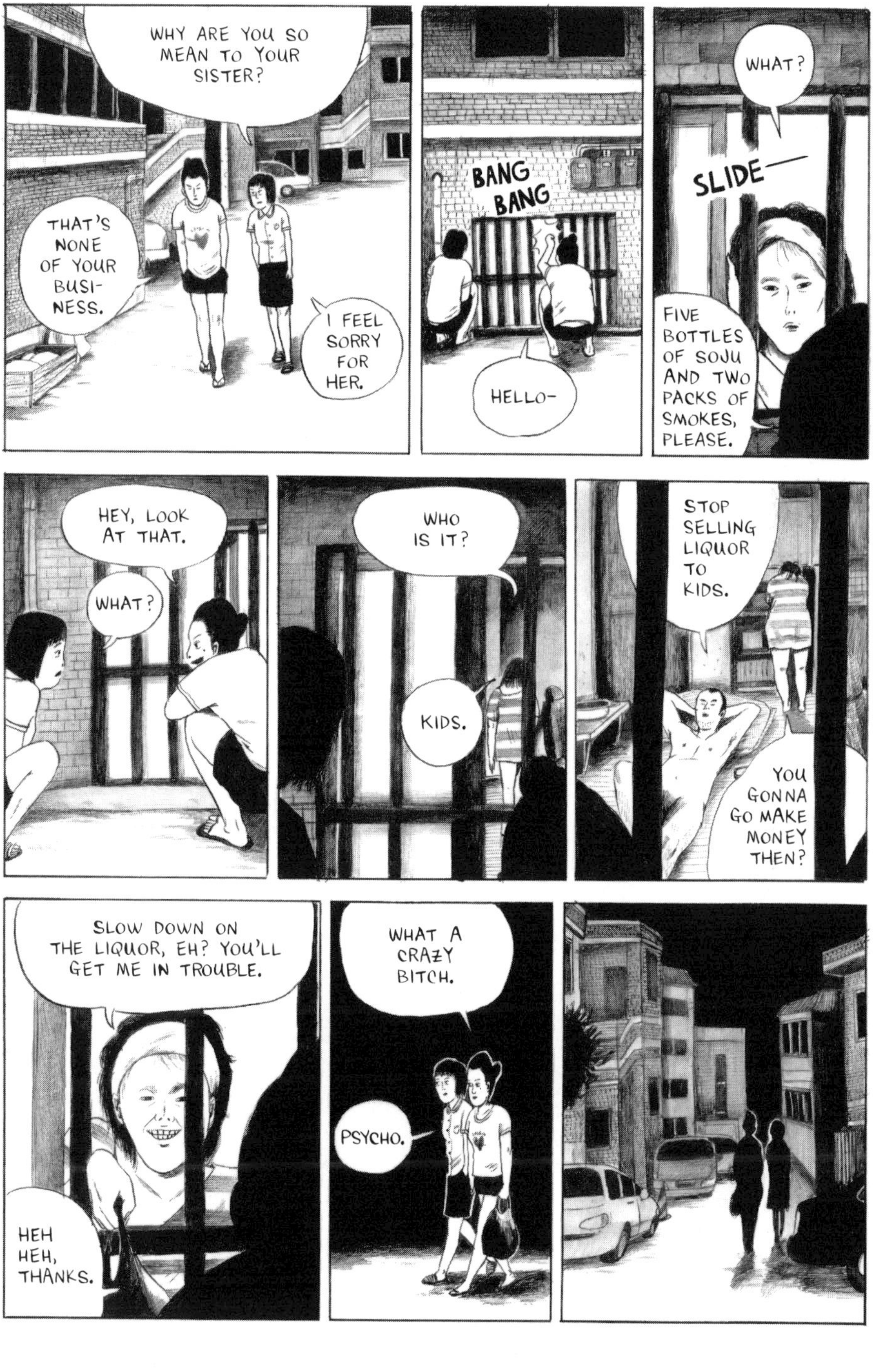
WHY ARE YOU SO MEAN TO YOUR SISTER?
THAT'S NONE OF YOUR BUSI-NESS.
I FEEL SORRY FOR HER.
BANG BANG
HELLO-
WHAT?
SLIDE—
FIVE BOTTLES OF SOJU AND TWO PACKS OF SMOKES, PLEASE.
HEY, LOOK AT THAT.
WHAT?
WHO IS IT?
KIDS.
STOP SELLING LIQUOR TO KIDS.
YOU GONNA GO MAKE MONEY THEN?
SLOW DOWN ON THE LIQUOR, EH? YOU'LL GET ME IN TROUBLE.
HEH HEH, THANKS.
WHAT A CRAZY BITCH.
PSYCHO.

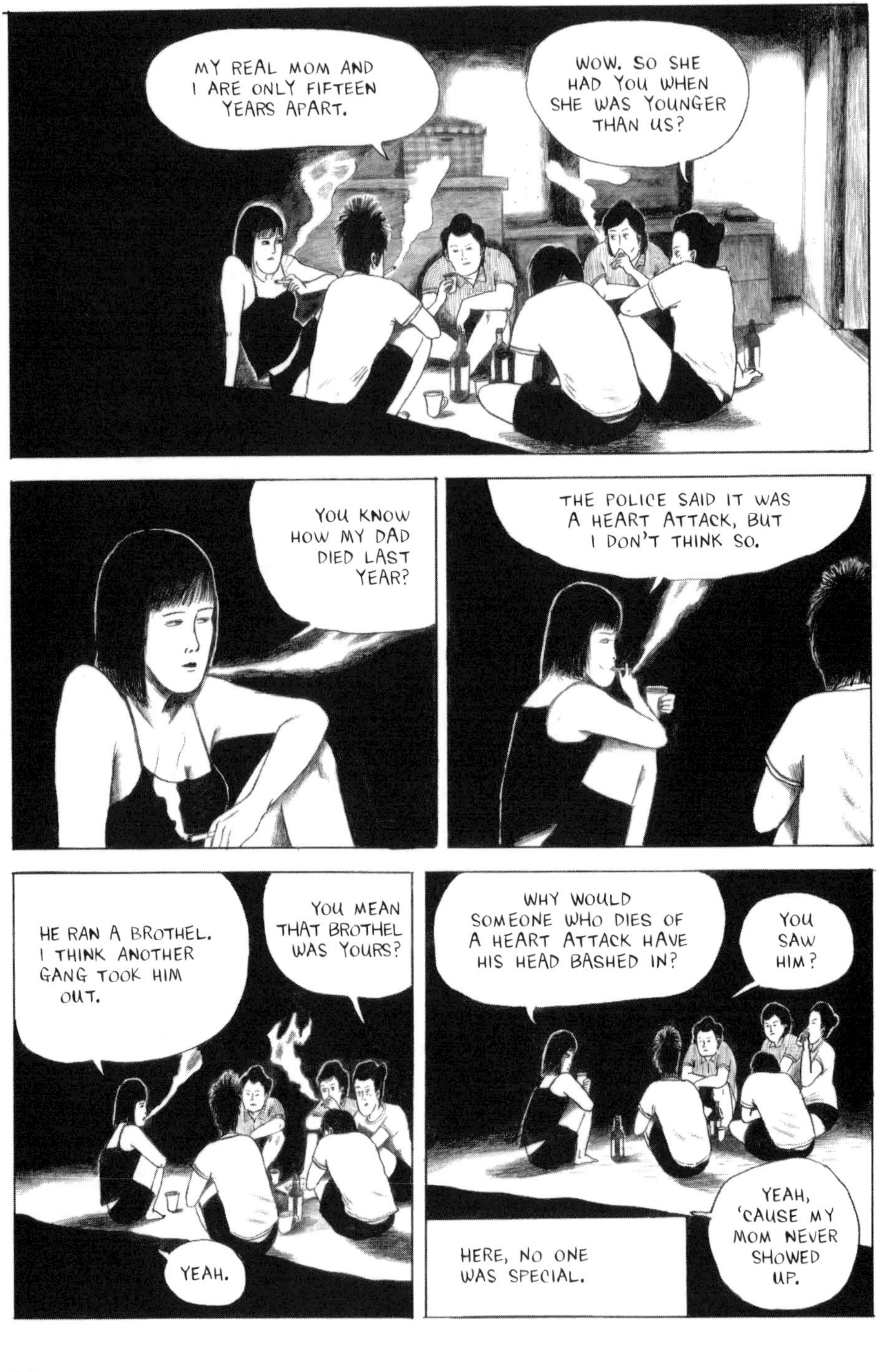
MY REAL MOM AND I ARE ONLY FIFTEEN YEARS APART.
WOW. SO SHE HAD YOU WHEN SHE WAS YOUNGER THAN US?
YOU KNOW HOW MY DAD DIED LAST YEAR?
THE POLICE SAID IT WAS A HEART ATTACK, BUT I DON'T THINK SO.
HE RAN A BROTHEL. I THINK ANOTHER GANG TOOK HIM OUT.
YOU MEAN THAT BROTHEL WAS YOURS?
YEAH.
WHY WOULD SOMEONE WHO DIES OF A HEART ATTACK HAVE HIS HEAD BASHED IN?
YOU SAW HIM?
HERE, NO ONE WAS SPECIAL.
YEAH, 'CAUSE MY MOM NEVER SHOWED UP.

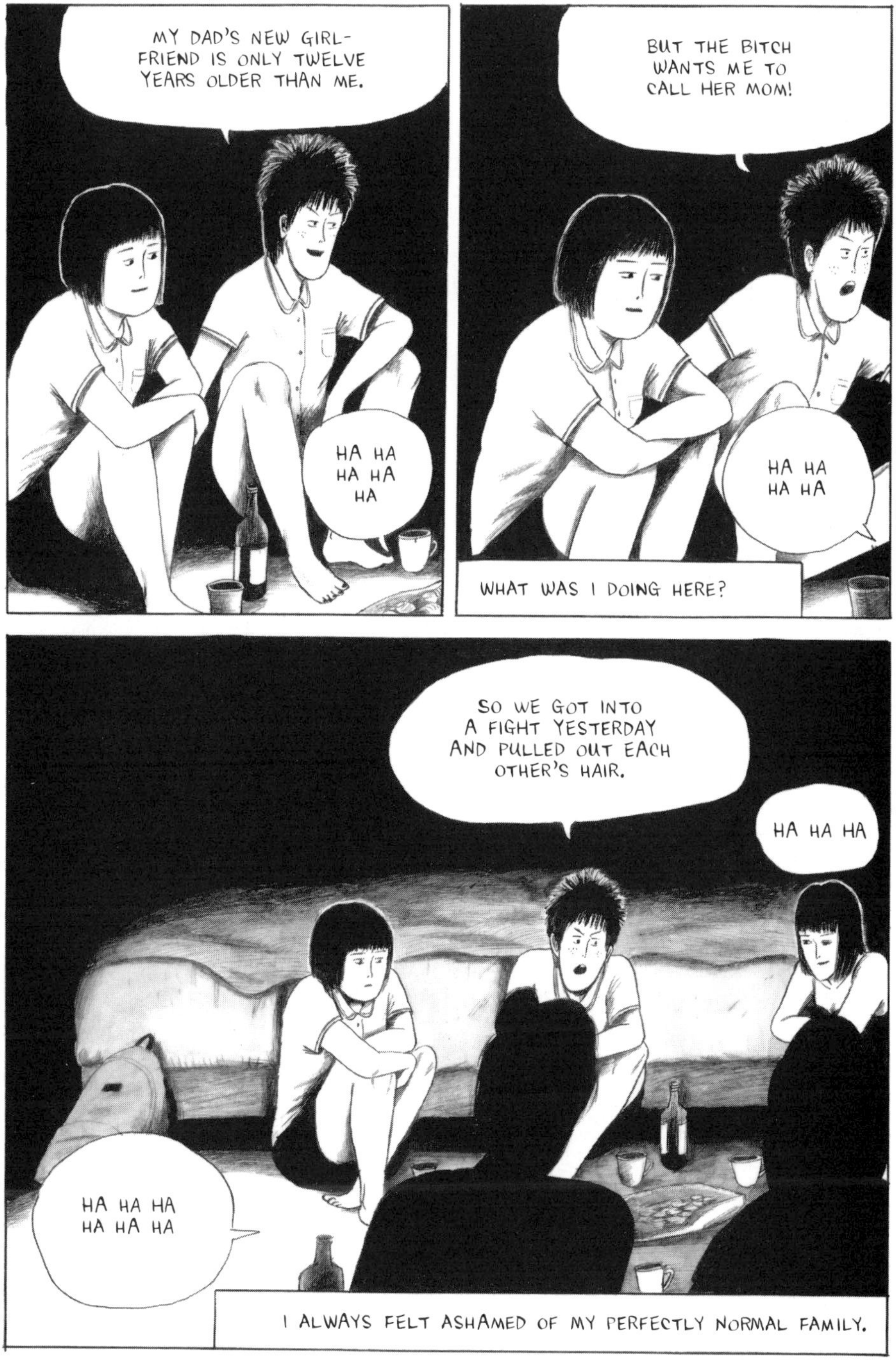
MY DAD'S NEW GIRLFRIEND IS ONLY TWELVE YEARS OLDER THAN ME.
HA HA HA HA HA
BUT THE BITCH WANTS ME TO CALL HER MOM!
HA HA HA HA
WHAT WAS I DOING HERE?
SO WE GOT INTO A FIGHT YESTERDAY AND PULLED OUT EACH OTHER'S HAIR.
HA HA HA
HA HA HA HA HA HA
I ALWAYS FELT ASHAMED OF MY PERFECTLY NORMAL FAMILY.

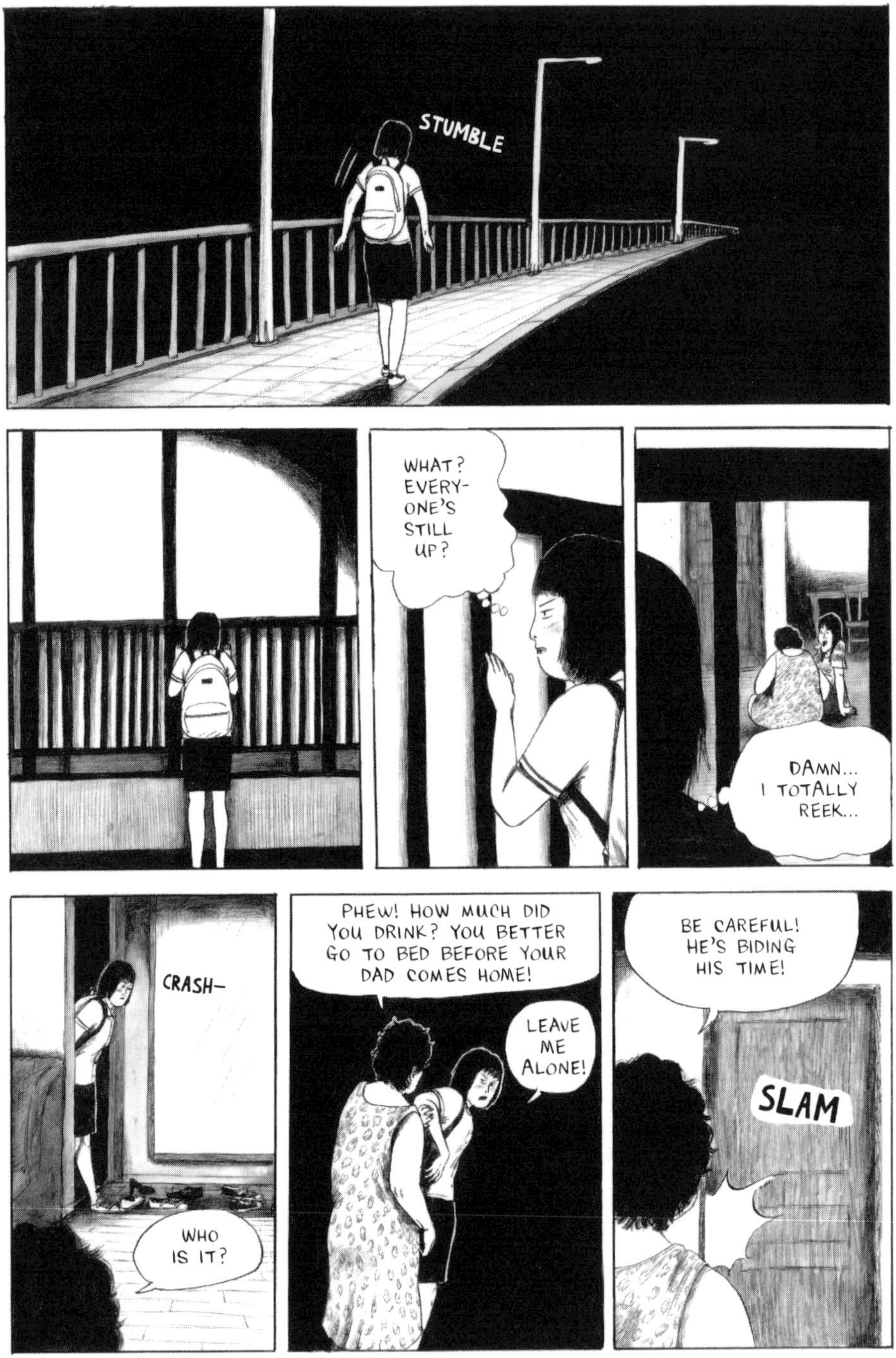
STUMBLE
WHAT? EVERY-ONE'S STILL UP?
DAMN... I TOTALLY REEK...
CRASH-
WHO IS IT?
PHEW! HOW MUCH DID YOU DRINK? YOU BETTER GO TO BED BEFORE YOUR DAD COMES HOME!
LEAVE ME ALONE!
BE CAREFUL! HE'S BIDING HIS TIME!
SLAM

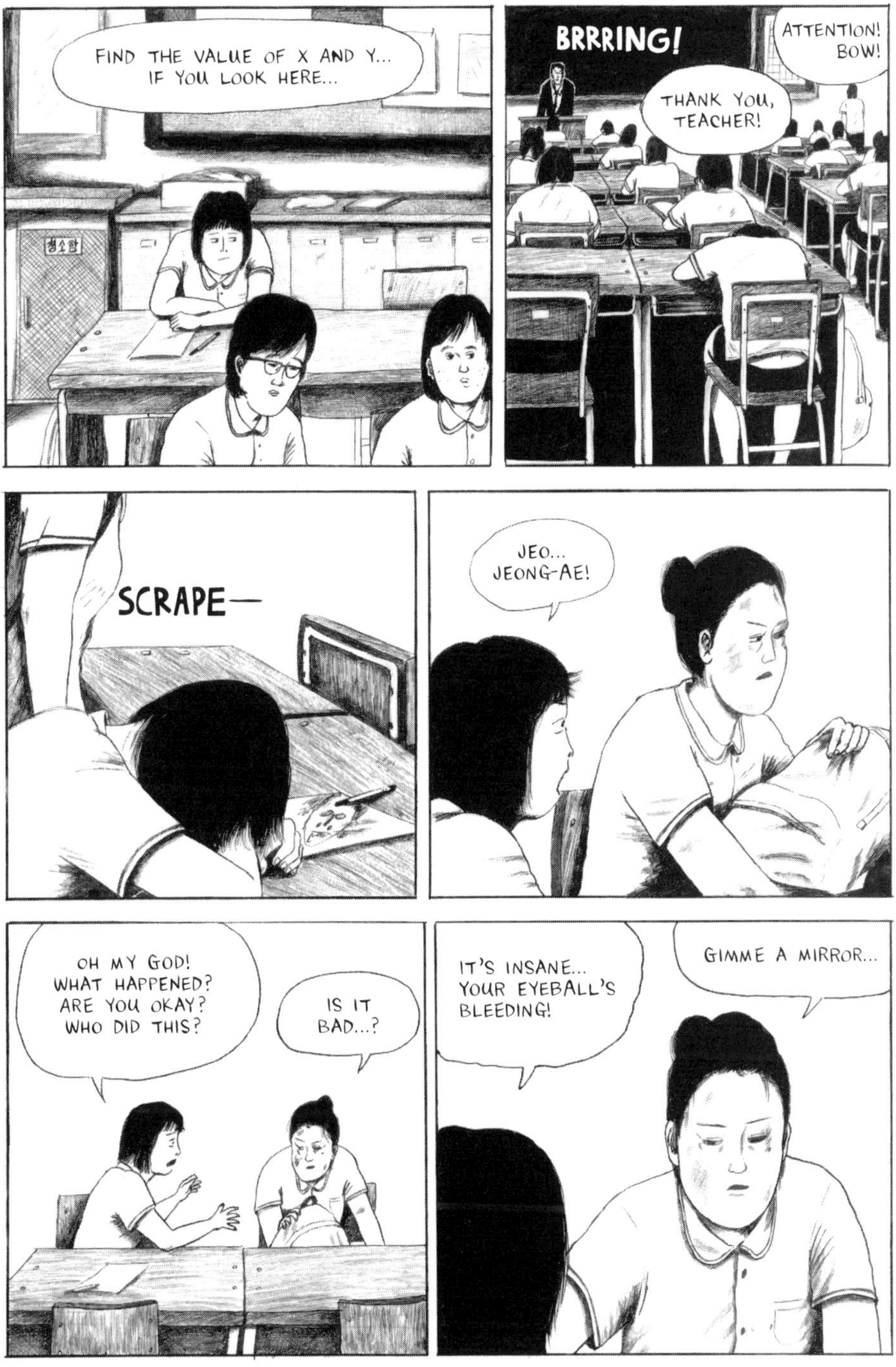
FIND THE VALUE OF X AND Y... IF YOU LOOK HERE...
BRRRING!
ATTENTION! BOW!
THANK YOU, TEACHER!
SCRAPE—
JEO... JEONG-AE!
OH MY GOD! WHAT HAPPENED? ARE YOU OKAY? WHO DID THIS?
IS IT BAD...?
IT'S INSANE... YOUR EYEBALL'S BLEEDING!
GIMME A MIRROR...

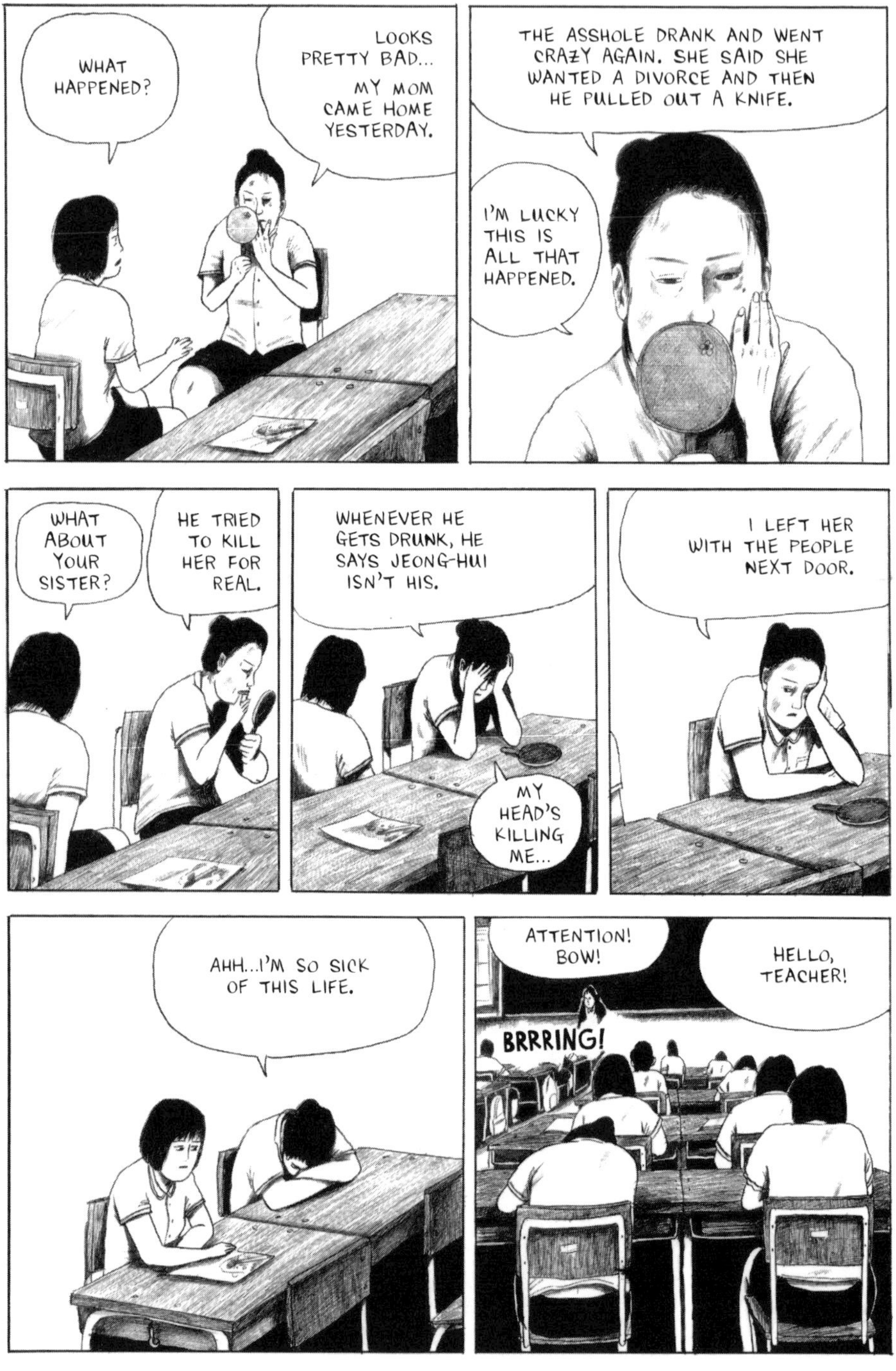
WHAT HAPPENED?
LOOKS PRETTY BAD... MY MOM CAME HOME YESTERDAY.
THE ASSHOLE DRANK AND WENT CRAZY AGAIN. SHE SAID SHE WANTED A DIVORCE AND THEN HE PULLED OUT A KNIFE.
I'M LUCKY THIS IS ALL THAT HAPPENED.
WHAT ABOUT YOUR SISTER?
HE TRIED TO KILL HER FOR REAL.
WHENEVER HE GETS DRUNK, HE SAYS JEONG-HUI ISN'T HIS.
MY HEAD'S KILLING ME...
I LEFT HER WITH THE PEOPLE NEXT DOOR.
AHH...I'M SO SICK OF THIS LIFE.
BRRRING!
ATTENTION! BOW!
HELLO, TEACHER!

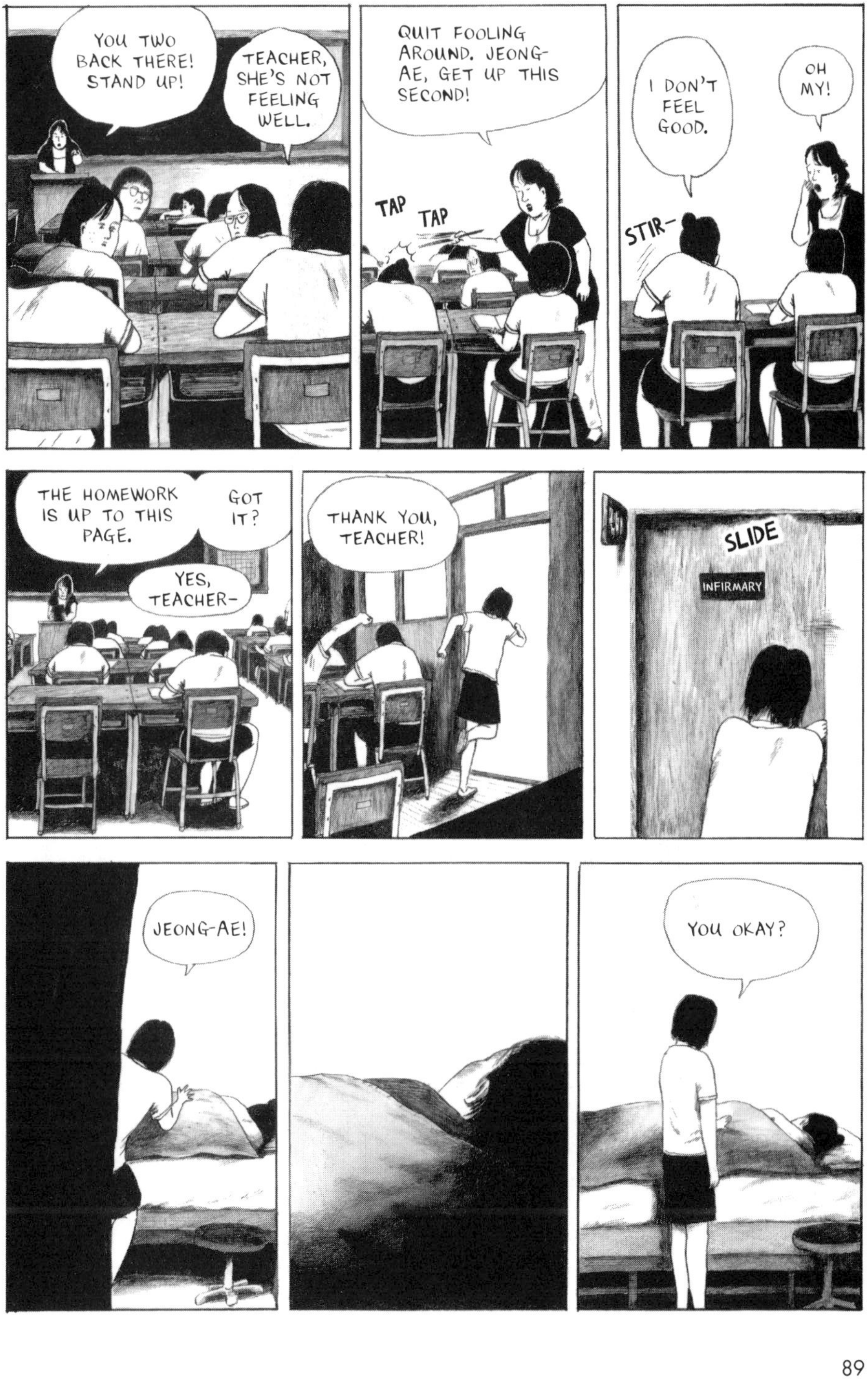
YOU TWO BACK THERE! STAND UP!
TEACHER, SHE'S NOT FEELING WELL.
QUIT FOOLING AROUND. JEONG-AE, GET UP THIS SECOND!
TAP TAP
I DON'T FEEL GOOD.
OH MY!
STIR-
THE HOMEWORK IS UP TO THIS PAGE.
GOT IT?
YES, TEACHER-
THANK YOU, TEACHER!
SLIDE
INFIRMARY
JEONG-AE!
YOU OKAY?

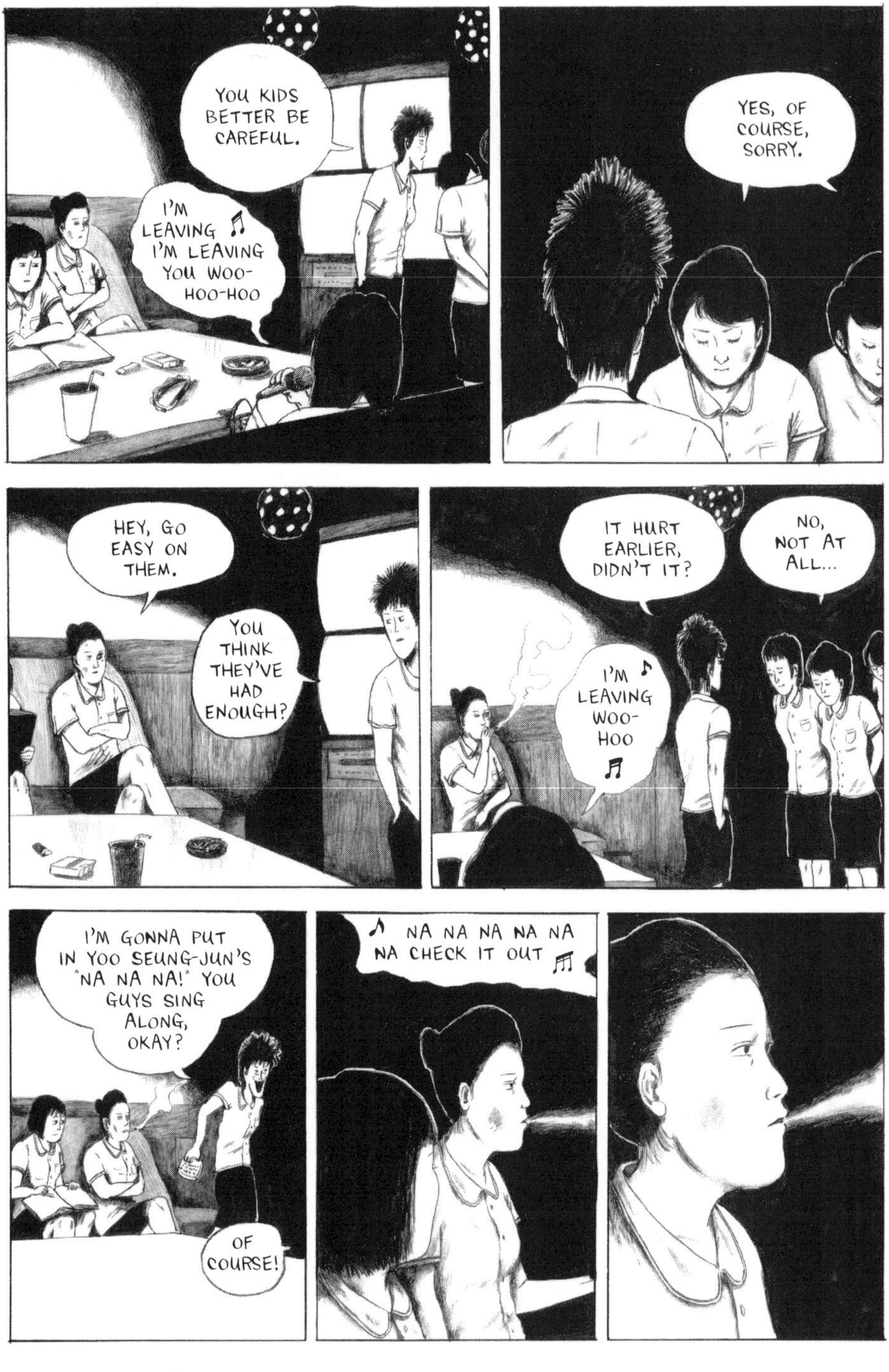
YOU KIDS BETTER BE CAREFUL.
I'M LEAVING ♫ I'M LEAVING YOU WOO-HOO-HOO
YES, OF COURSE, SORRY.
HEY, GO EASY ON THEM.
YOU THINK THEY'VE HAD ENOUGH?
IT HURT EARLIER, DIDN'T IT?
NO, NOT AT ALL...
I'M ♪ LEAVING WOO-HOO ♬
I'M GONNA PUT IN YOO SEUNG-JUN'S "NA NA NA!" YOU GUYS SING ALONG, OKAY?
OF COURSE!
♪ NA NA NA NA NA NA CHECK IT OUT ♬

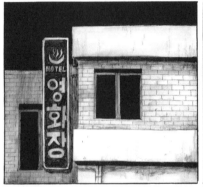

HEY! THAT'S WHERE WE STAYED!

OH YAH!

HEY—

WHAT??

NEVER MIND...

WHAT? WHAT IS IT?

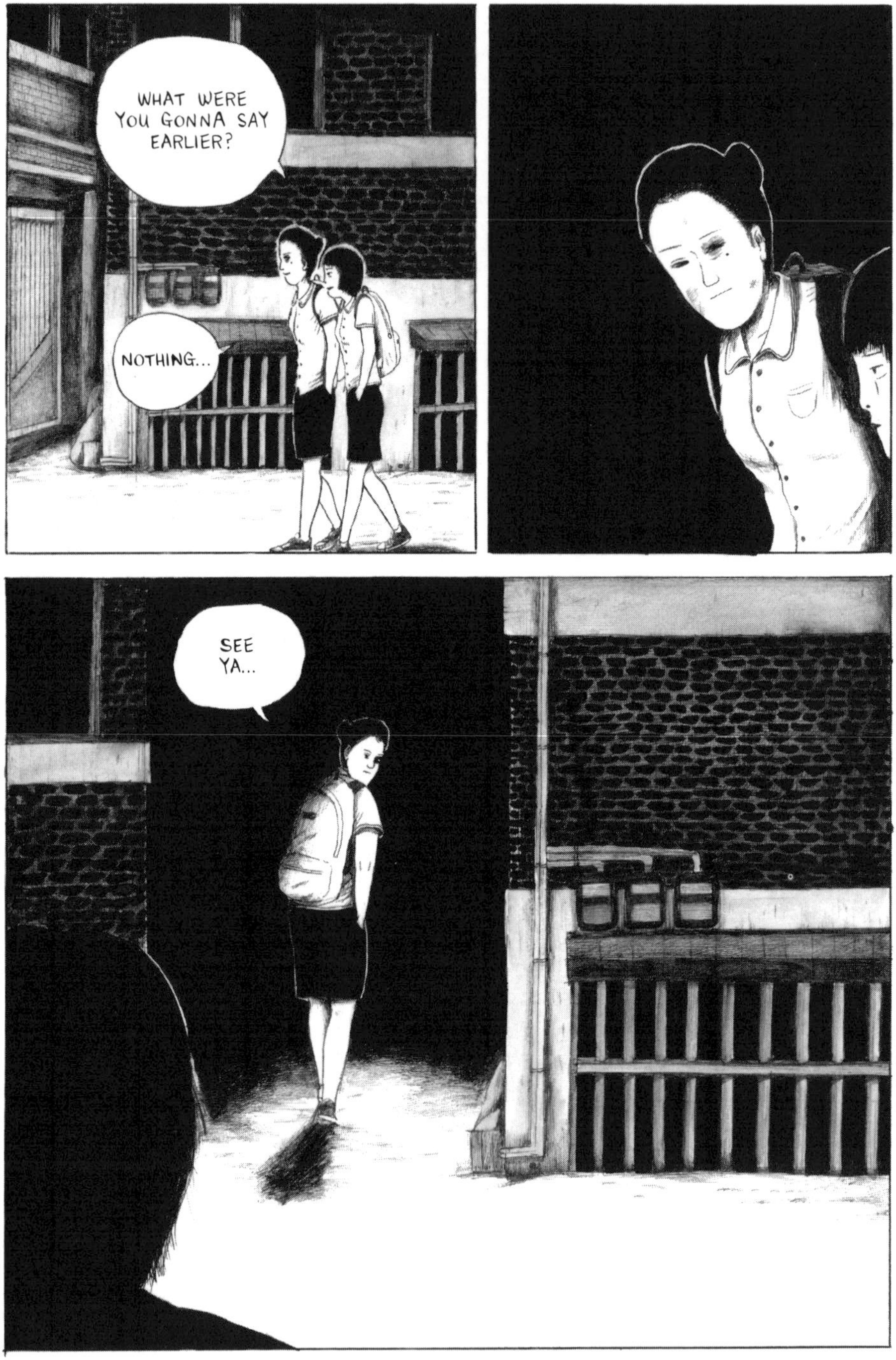
WHAT WERE YOU GONNA SAY EARLIER?
NOTHING...
SEE YA...

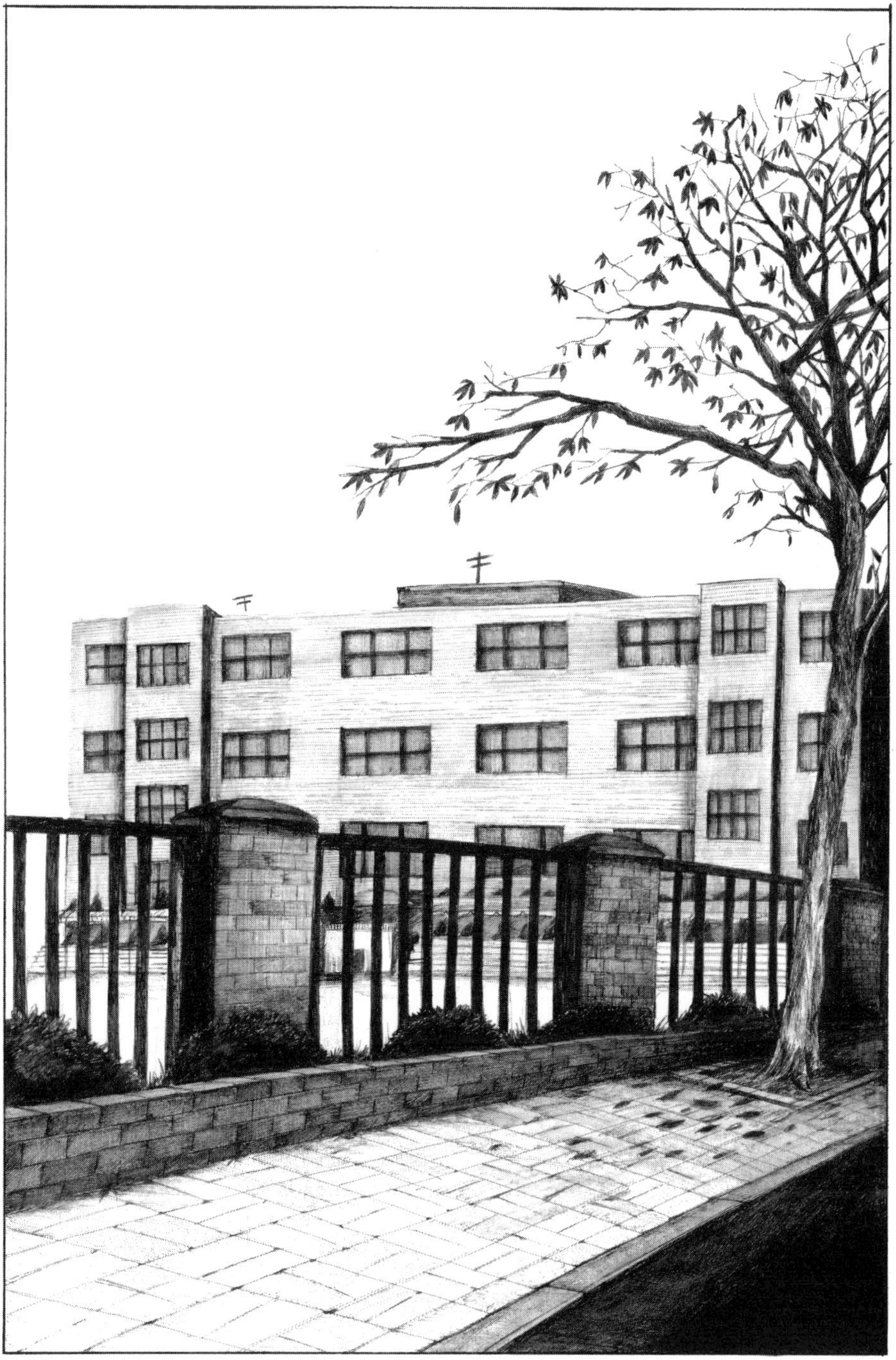

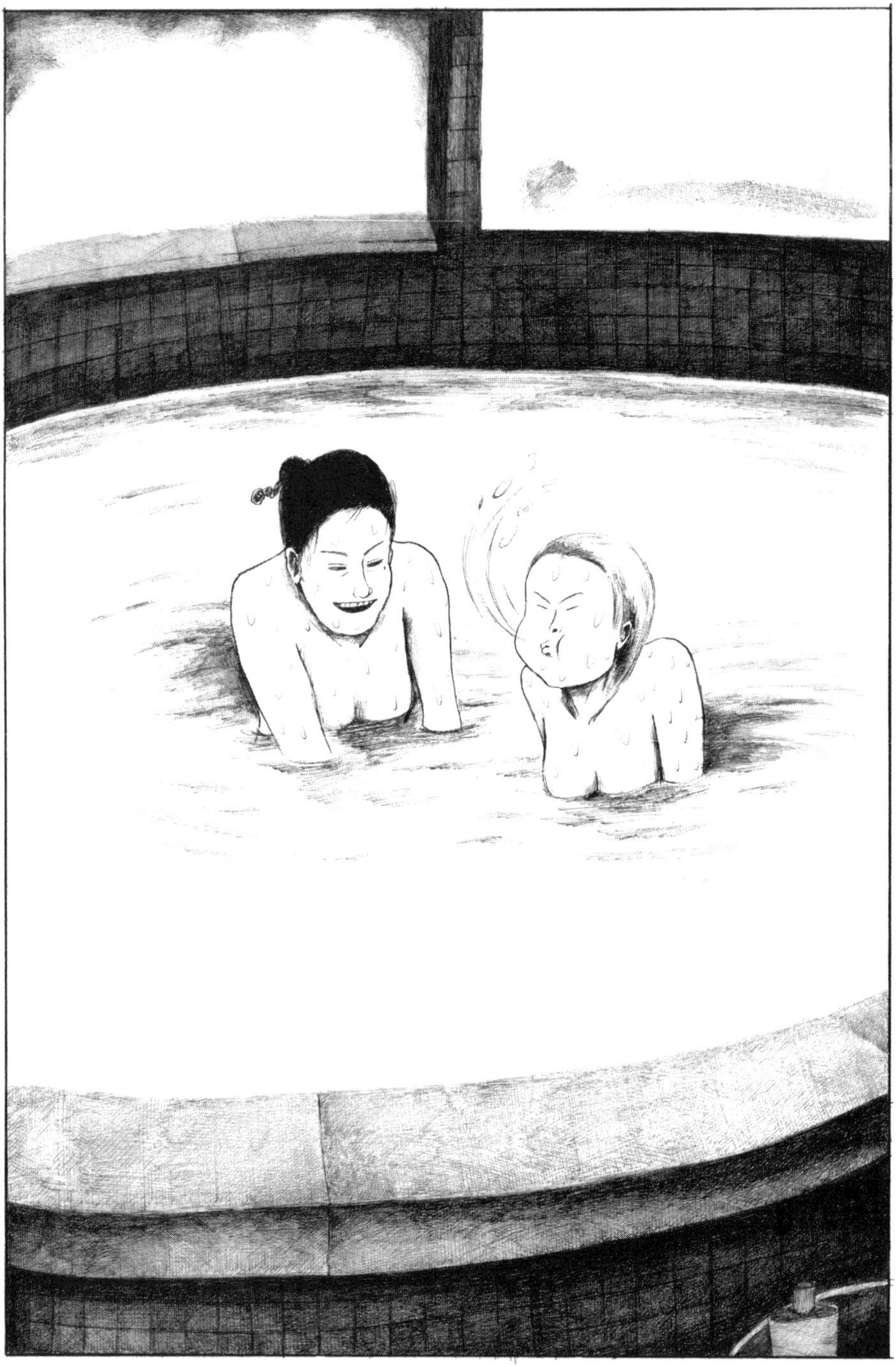

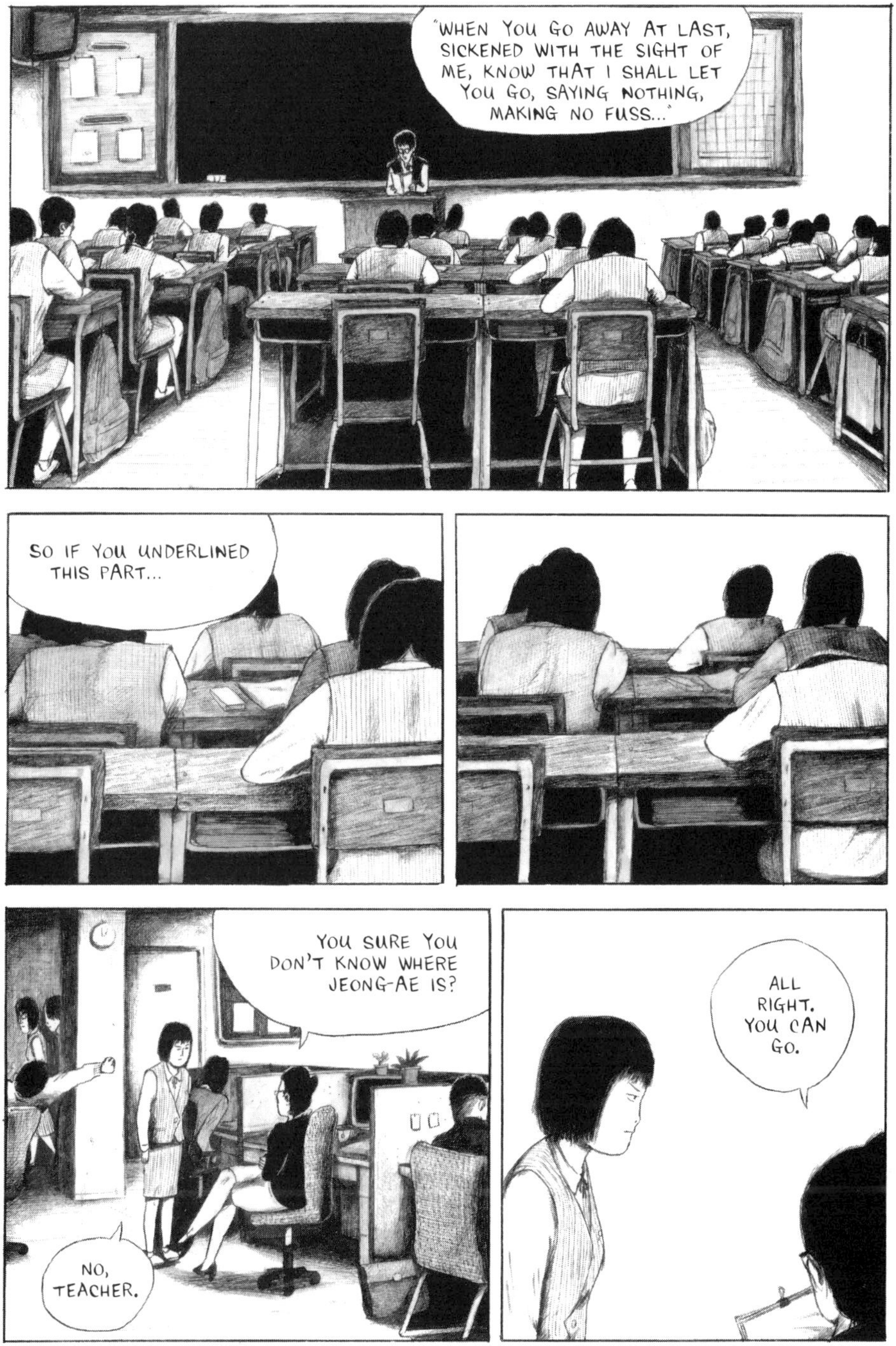
"WHEN YOU GO AWAY AT LAST, SICKENED WITH THE SIGHT OF ME, KNOW THAT I SHALL LET YOU GO, SAYING NOTHING, MAKING NO FUSS..."
SO IF YOU UNDERLINED THIS PART...
YOU SURE YOU DON'T KNOW WHERE JEONG-AE IS?
NO, TEACHER.
ALL RIGHT. YOU CAN GO.

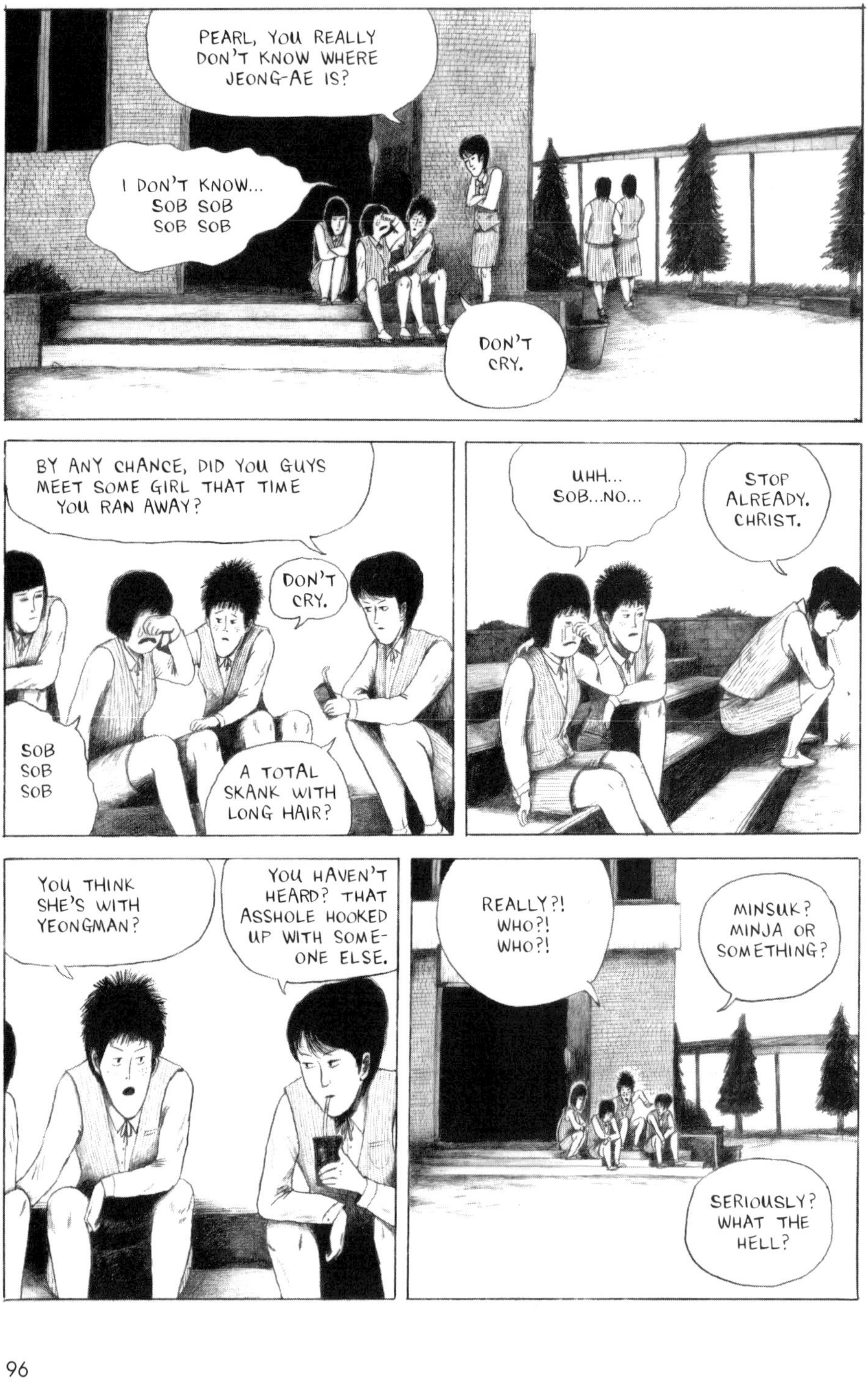
PEARL, YOU REALLY DON'T KNOW WHERE JEONG-AE IS?
I DON'T KNOW... SOB SOB SOB SOB
DON'T CRY.
BY ANY CHANCE, DID YOU GUYS MEET SOME GIRL THAT TIME YOU RAN AWAY?
DON'T CRY.
SOB SOB SOB
A TOTAL SKANK WITH LONG HAIR?
UHH... SOB...NO...
STOP ALREADY. CHRIST.
YOU THINK SHE'S WITH YEONGMAN?
YOU HAVEN'T HEARD? THAT ASSHOLE HOOKED UP WITH SOME-ONE ELSE.
REALLY?! WHO?! WHO?!
MINSUK? MINJA OR SOMETHING?
SERIOUSLY? WHAT THE HELL?

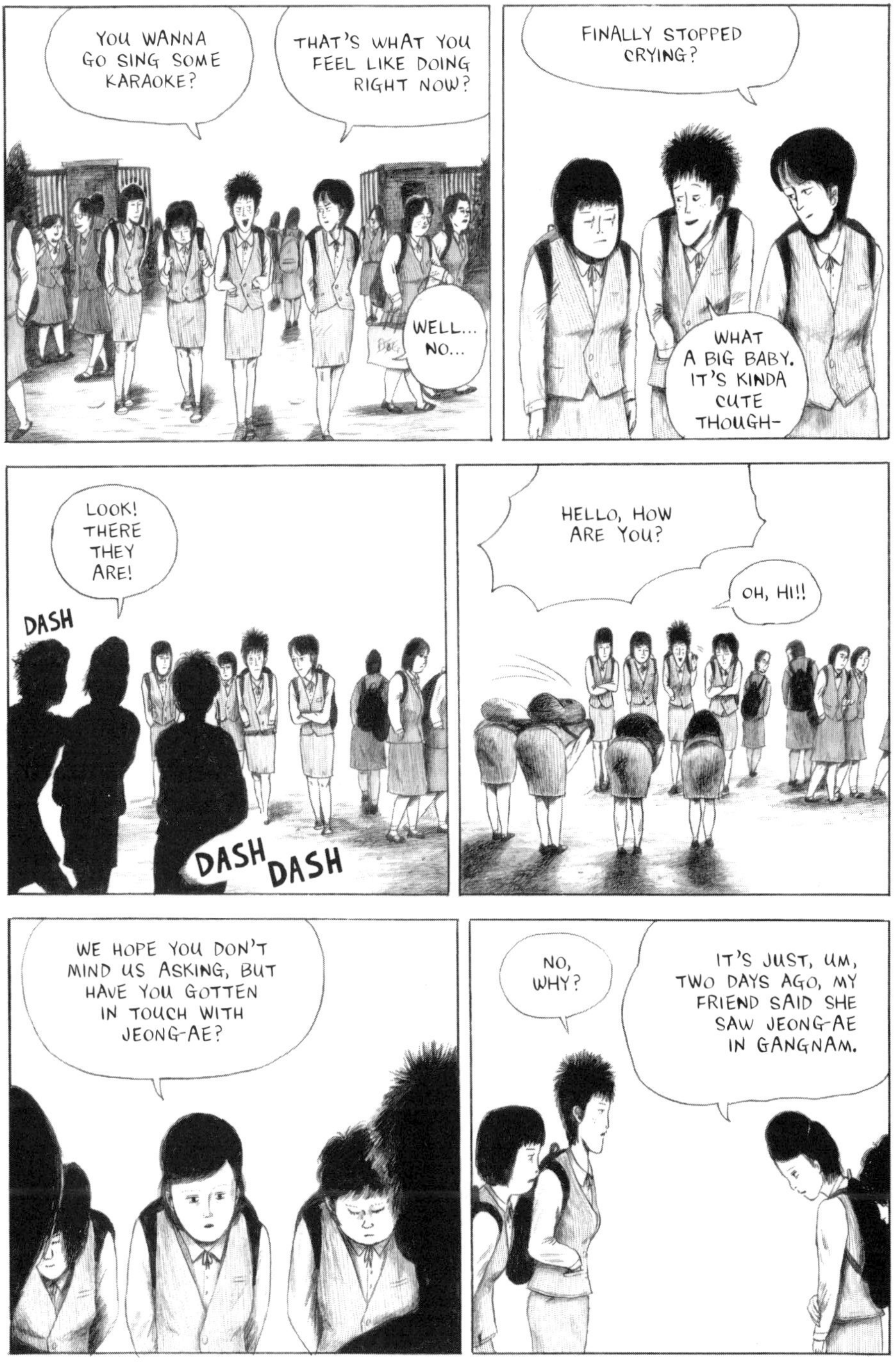

YOU WANNA GO SING SOME KARAOKE?
THAT'S WHAT YOU FEEL LIKE DOING RIGHT NOW?
WELL... NO...
FINALLY STOPPED CRYING?
WHAT A BIG BABY. IT'S KINDA CUTE THOUGH-
LOOK! THERE THEY ARE!
DASH
DASH DASH
HELLO, HOW ARE YOU?
OH, HI!!
WE HOPE YOU DON'T MIND US ASKING, BUT HAVE YOU GOTTEN IN TOUCH WITH JEONG-AE?
NO, WHY?
IT'S JUST, UM, TWO DAYS AGO, MY FRIEND SAID SHE SAW JEONG-AE IN GANGNAM.

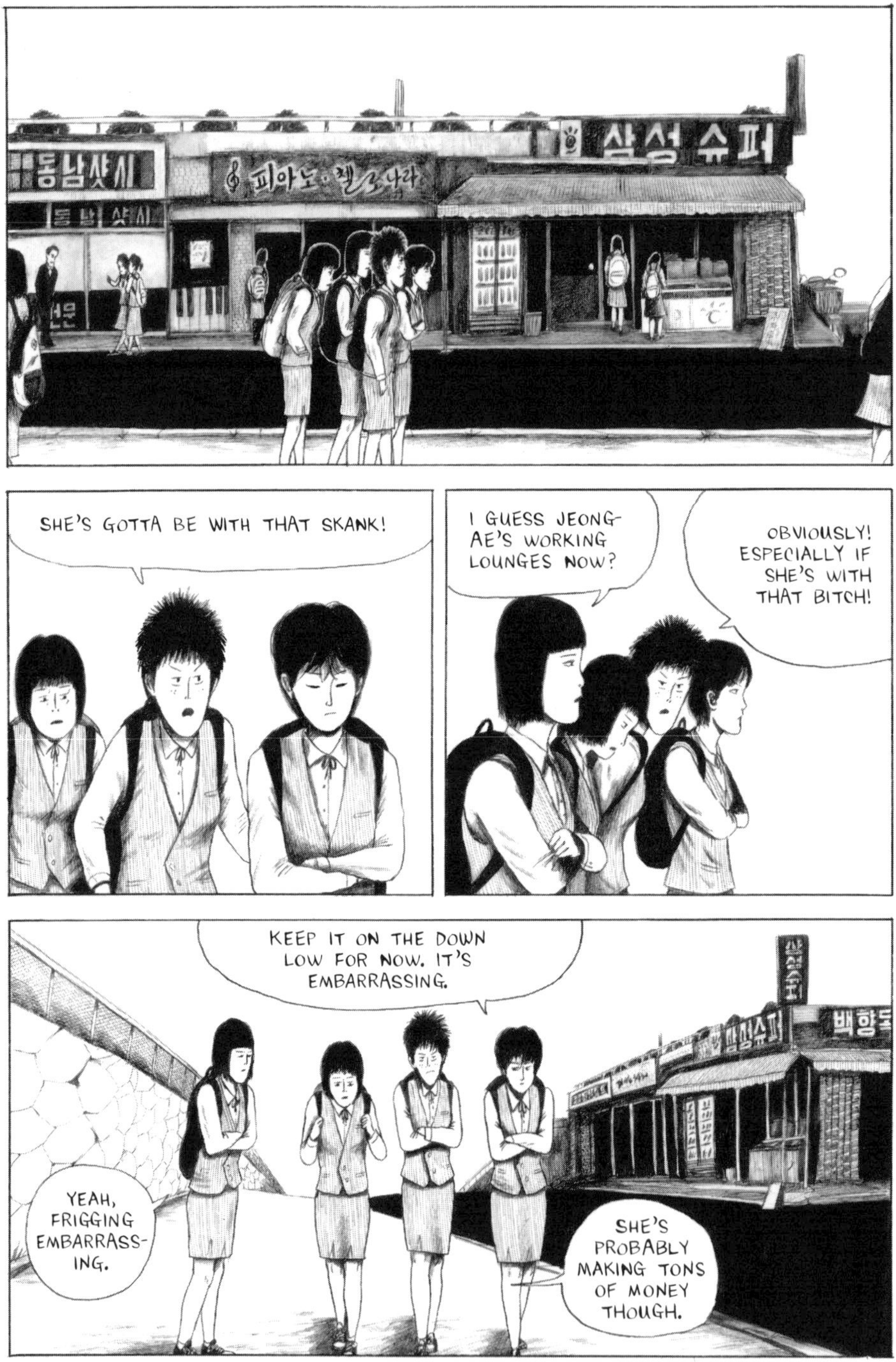

동남샷시
삼성 슈퍼
SHE'S GOTTA BE WITH THAT SKANK!
I GUESS JEONG-AE'S WORKING LOUNGES NOW?
OBVIOUSLY! ESPECIALLY IF SHE'S WITH THAT BITCH!
KEEP IT ON THE DOWN LOW FOR NOW. IT'S EMBARRASSING.
YEAH, FRIGGING EMBARRASS-ING.
SHE'S PROBABLY MAKING TONS OF MONEY THOUGH.

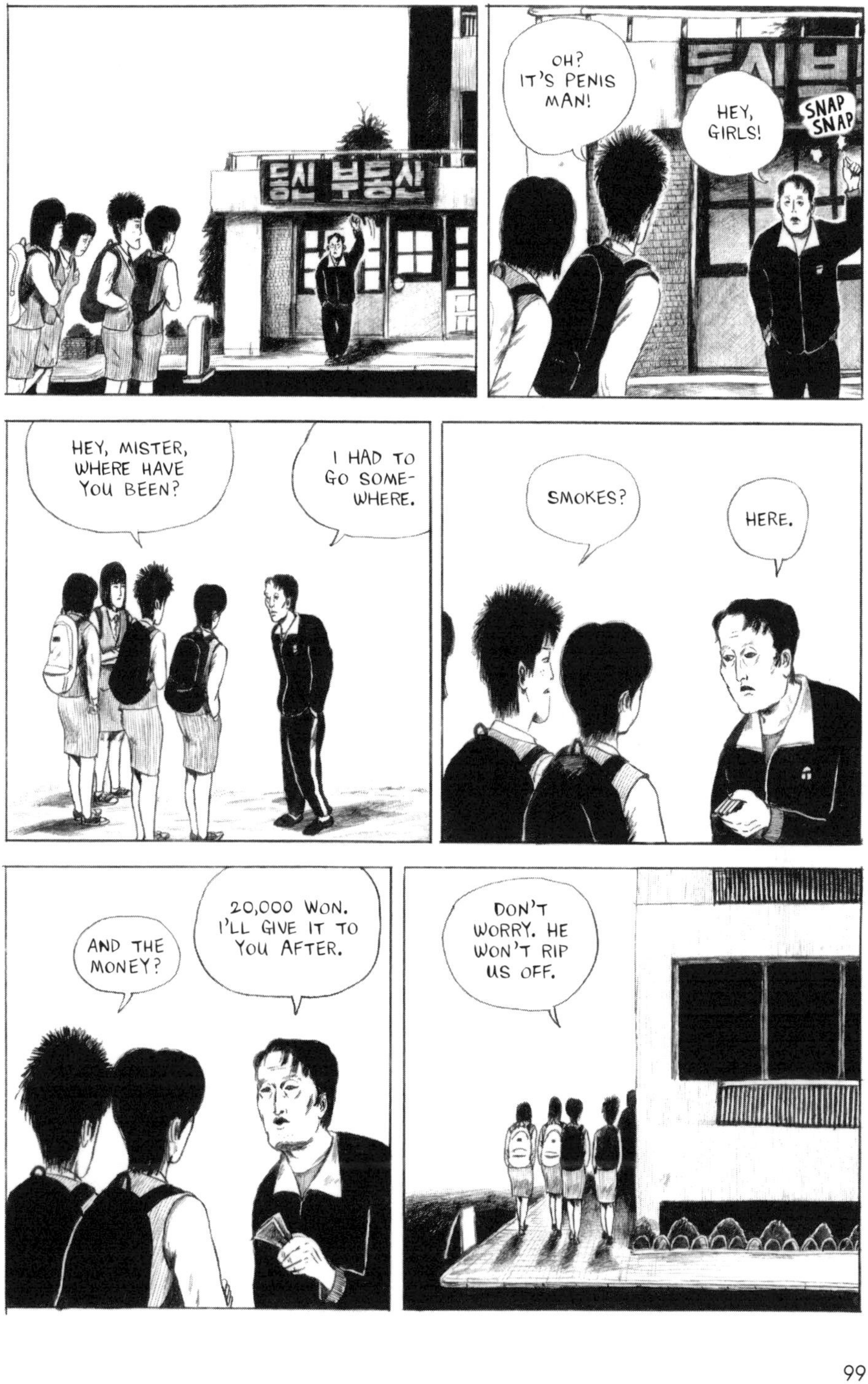

동신 부동산
OH? IT'S PENIS MAN!
HEY, GIRLS!
SNAP SNAP
HEY, MISTER, WHERE HAVE YOU BEEN?
I HAD TO GO SOME-WHERE.
SMOKES?
HERE.
AND THE MONEY?
20,000 WON. I'LL GIVE IT TO YOU AFTER.
DON'T WORRY. HE WON'T RIP US OFF.

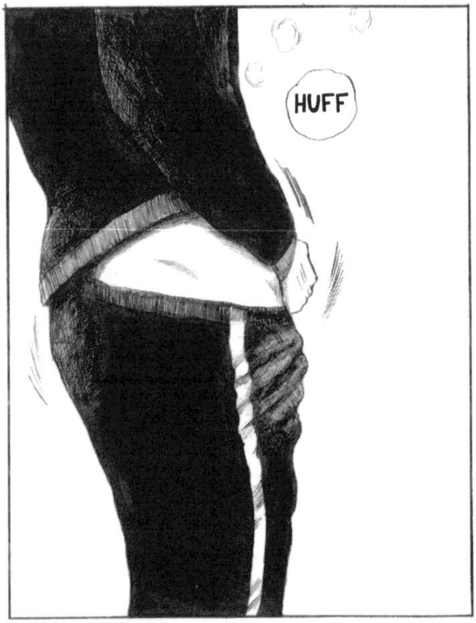
HUFF

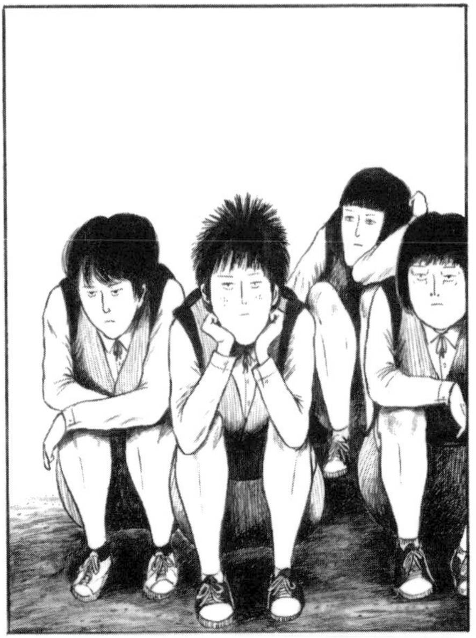

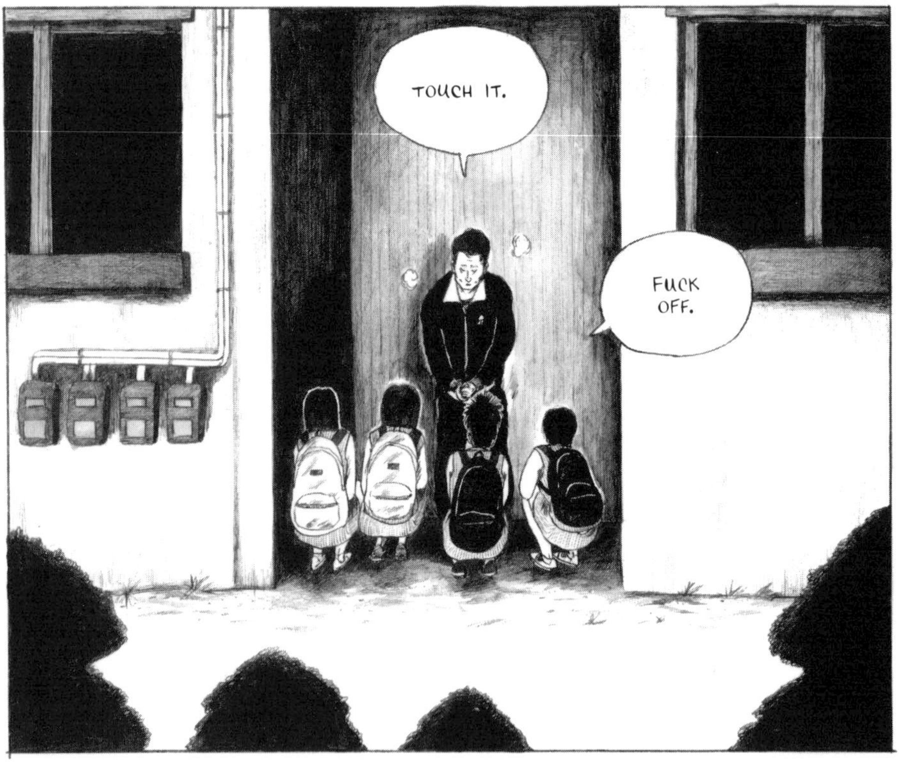
TOUCH IT.
FUCK OFF.

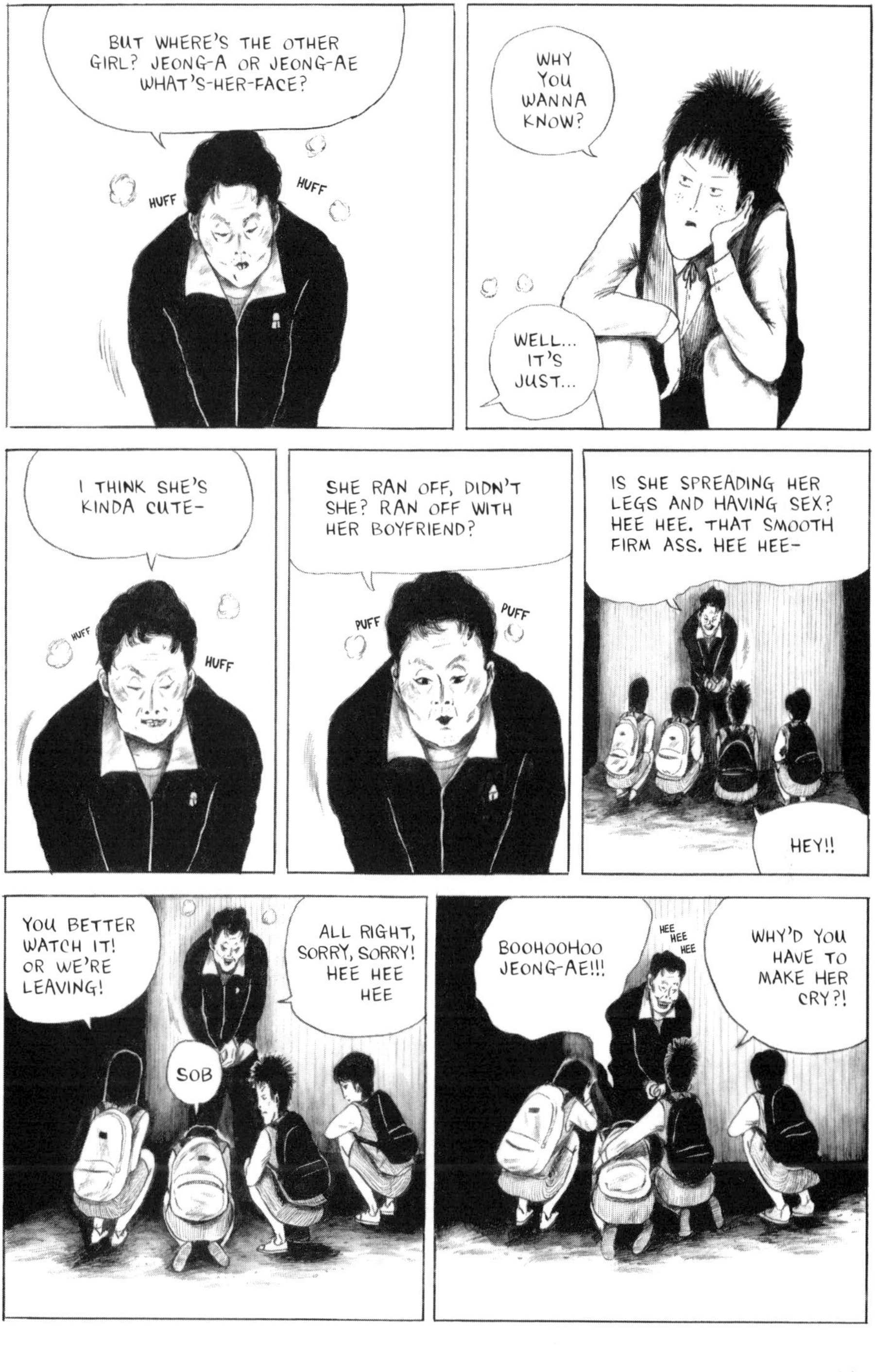
BUT WHERE'S THE OTHER GIRL? JEONG-A OR JEONG-AE WHAT'S-HER-FACE?
HUFF
HUFF
WHY YOU WANNA KNOW?
WELL... IT'S JUST...
I THINK SHE'S KINDA CUTE-
HUFF
HUFF
SHE RAN OFF, DIDN'T SHE? RAN OFF WITH HER BOYFRIEND?
PUFF
PUFF
IS SHE SPREADING HER LEGS AND HAVING SEX? HEE HEE. THAT SMOOTH FIRM ASS. HEE HEE-
HEY!!
YOU BETTER WATCH IT! OR WE'RE LEAVING!
ALL RIGHT, SORRY, SORRY! HEE HEE HEE
SOB
BOOHOOHOO JEONG-AE!!!
HEE HEE HEE
WHY'D YOU HAVE TO MAKE HER CRY?!

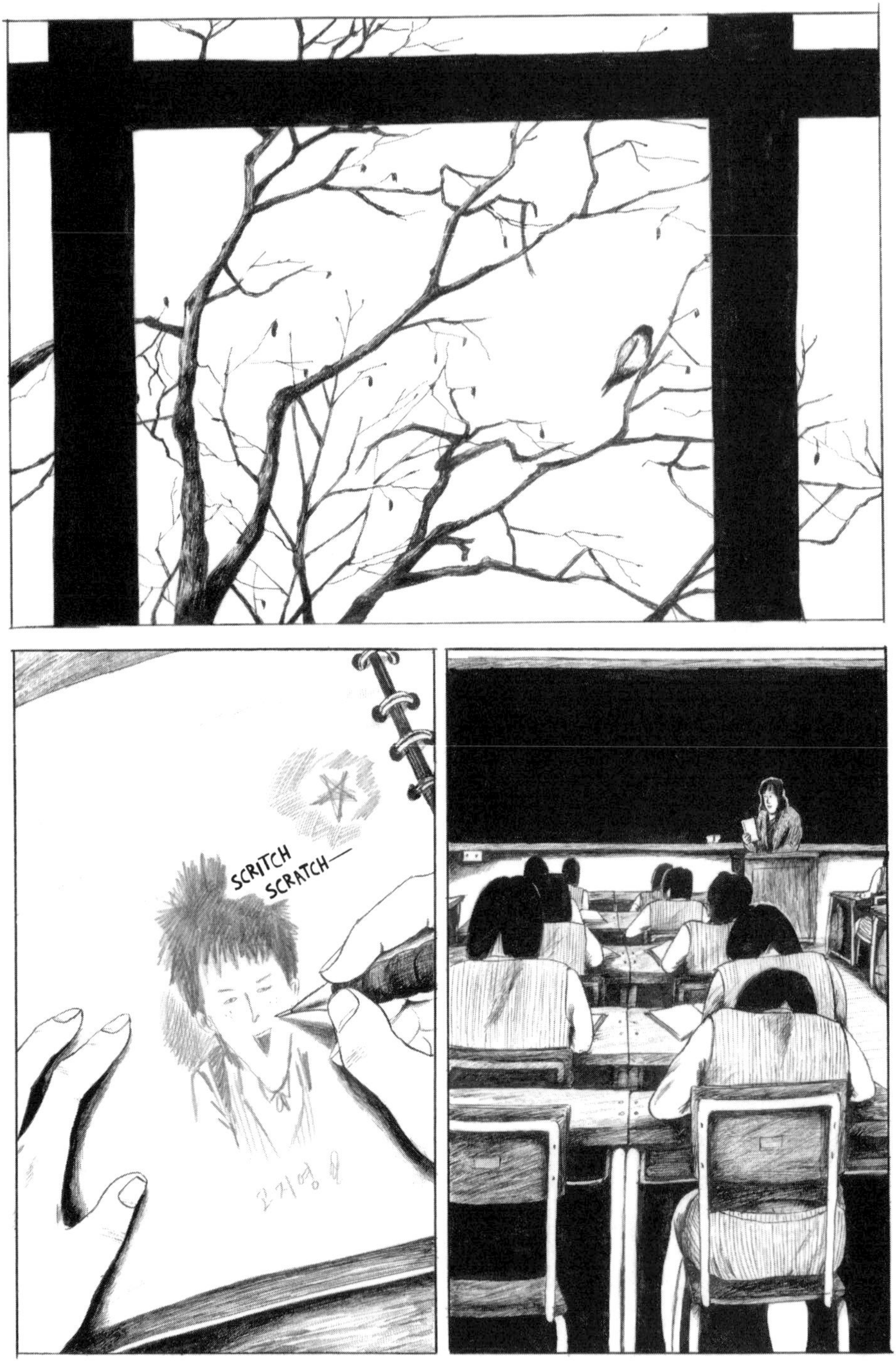
SCRITCH
SCRATCH—

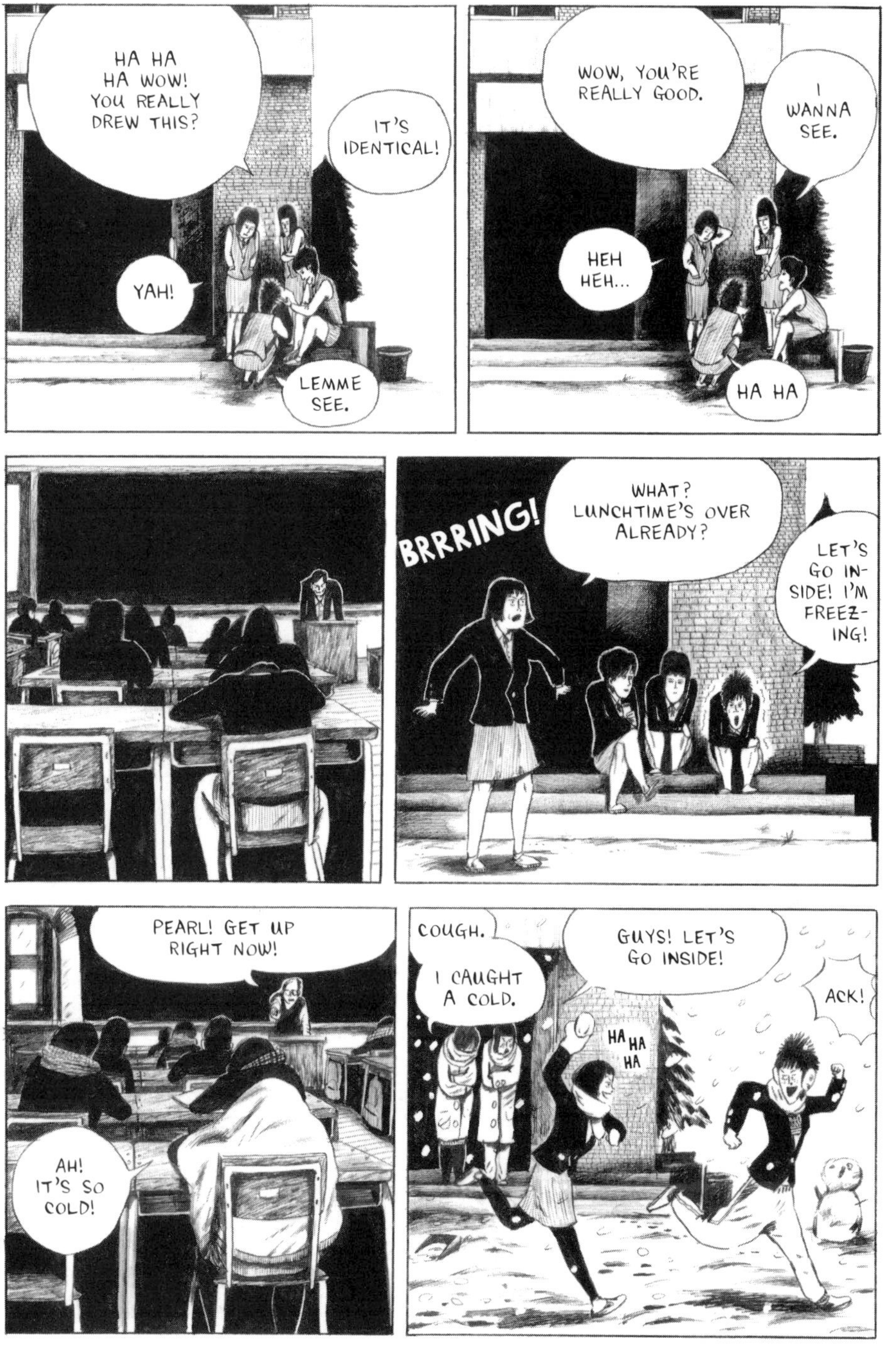
HA HA HA WOW! YOU REALLY DREW THIS?
IT'S IDENTICAL!
YAH!
LEMME SEE.
WOW, YOU'RE REALLY GOOD.
I WANNA SEE.
HEH HEH...
HA HA
BRRRING!
WHAT? LUNCHTIME'S OVER ALREADY?
LET'S GO IN-SIDE! I'M FREEZ-ING!
PEARL! GET UP RIGHT NOW!
AH! IT'S SO COLD!
COUGH.
I CAUGHT A COLD.
GUYS! LET'S GO INSIDE!
HA HA HA
ACK!

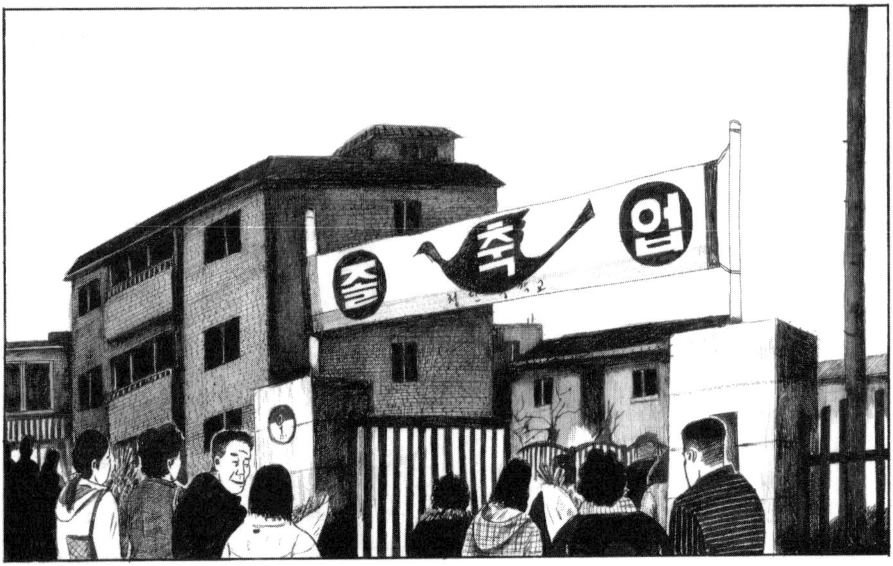
졸 축 업

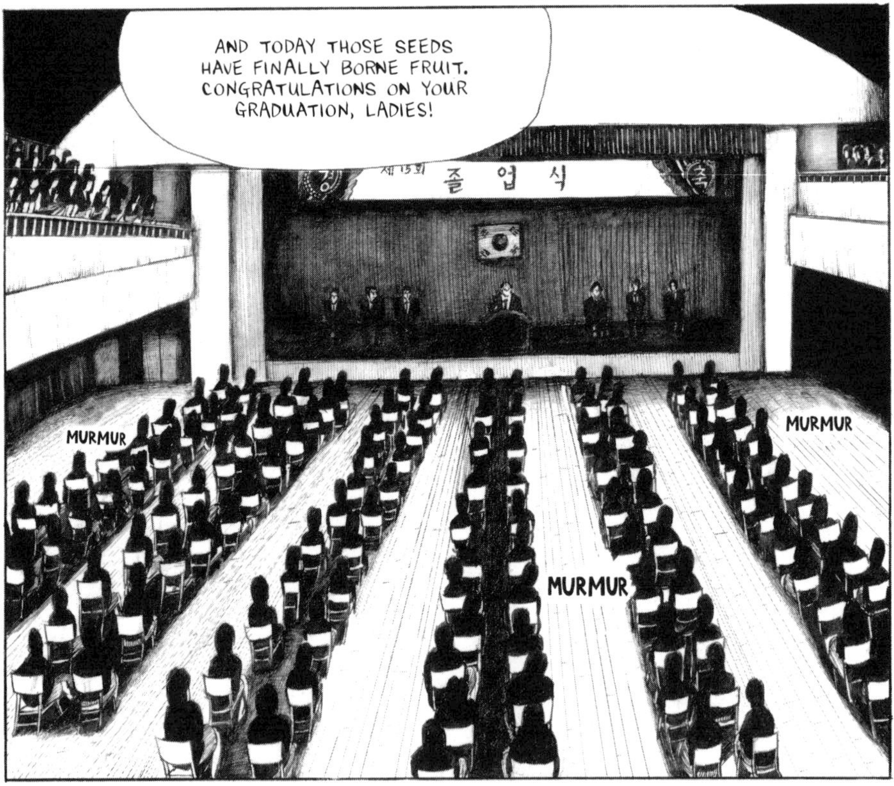
AND TODAY THOSE SEEDS HAVE FINALLY BORNE FRUIT. CONGRATULATIONS ON YOUR GRADUATION, LADIES!
제15회 졸업식
MURMUR
MURMUR
MURMUR

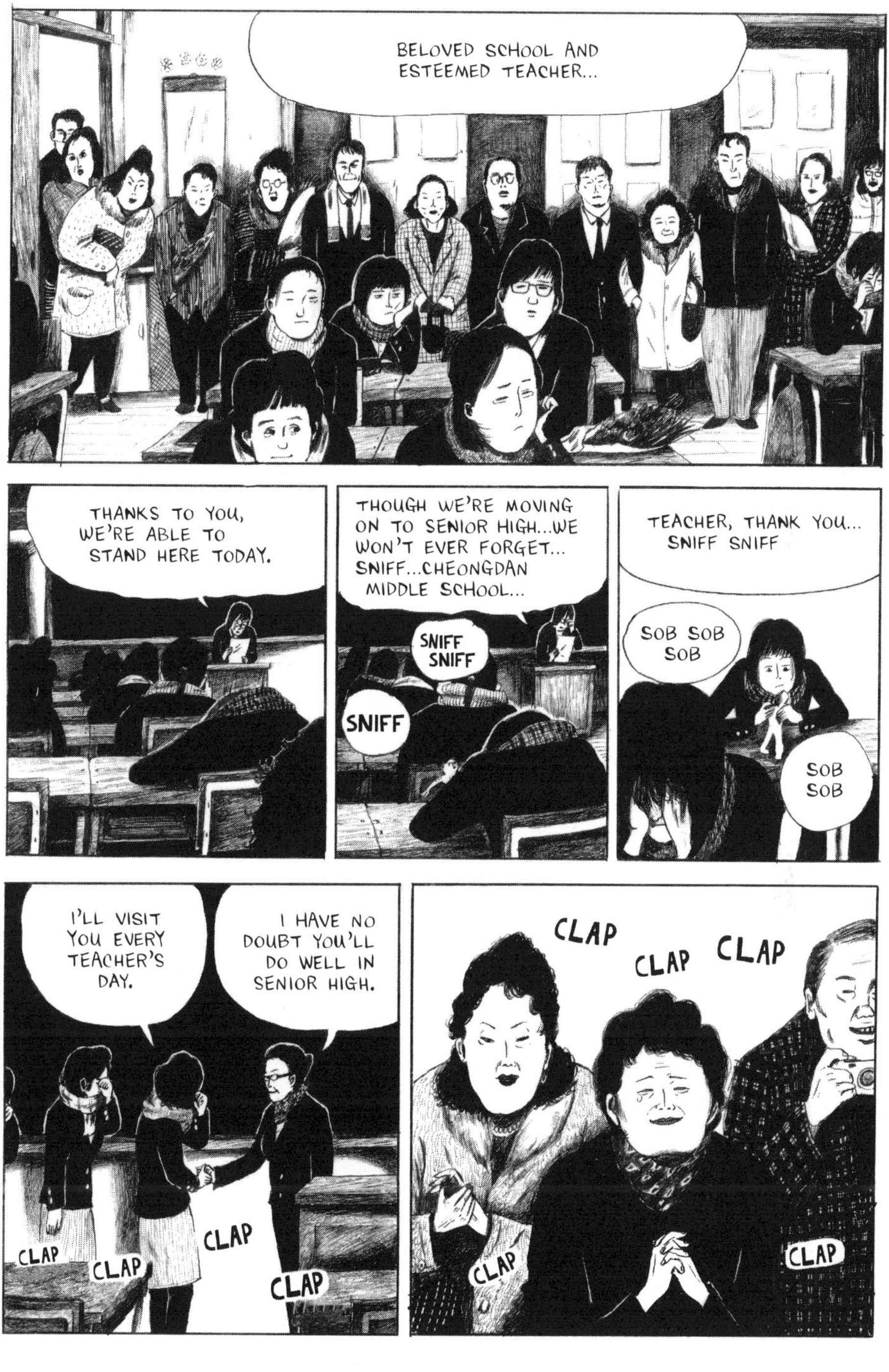
BELOVED SCHOOL AND ESTEEMED TEACHER...
THANKS TO YOU, WE'RE ABLE TO STAND HERE TODAY.
THOUGH WE'RE MOVING ON TO SENIOR HIGH...WE WON'T EVER FORGET... SNIFF...CHEONGDAN MIDDLE SCHOOL...
SNIFF SNIFF
SNIFF
TEACHER, THANK YOU... SNIFF SNIFF
SOB SOB SOB
SOB SOB
I'LL VISIT YOU EVERY TEACHER'S DAY.
I HAVE NO DOUBT YOU'LL DO WELL IN SENIOR HIGH.
CLAP
CLAP
CLAP
CLAP
CLAP
CLAP CLAP
CLAP
CLAP

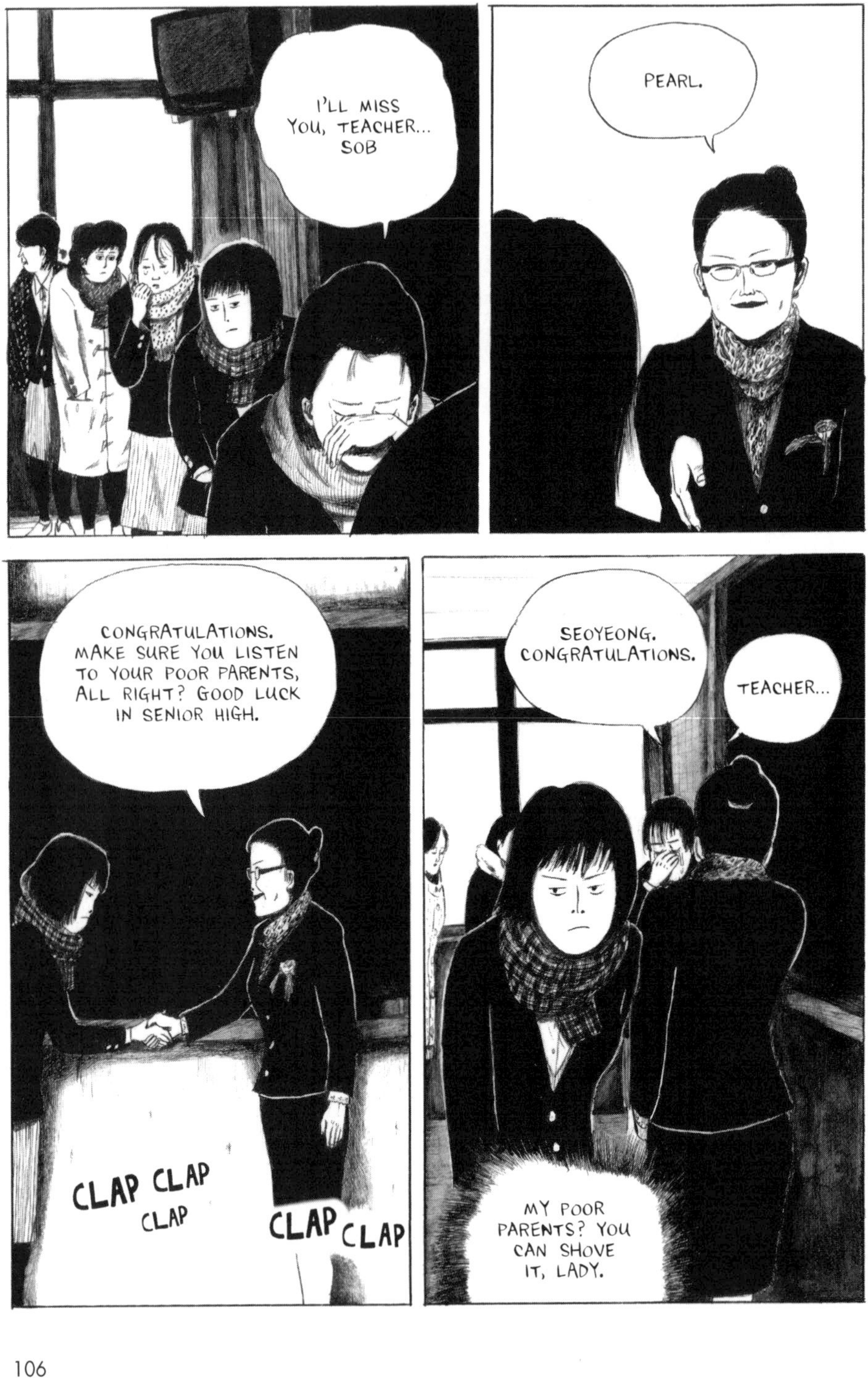
I'LL MISS YOU, TEACHER... SOB
PEARL.
CONGRATULATIONS. MAKE SURE YOU LISTEN TO YOUR POOR PARENTS, ALL RIGHT? GOOD LUCK IN SENIOR HIGH.
CLAP CLAP CLAP
CLAP CLAP
SEOYEONG. CONGRATULATIONS.
TEACHER...
MY POOR PARENTS? YOU CAN SHOVE IT, LADY.

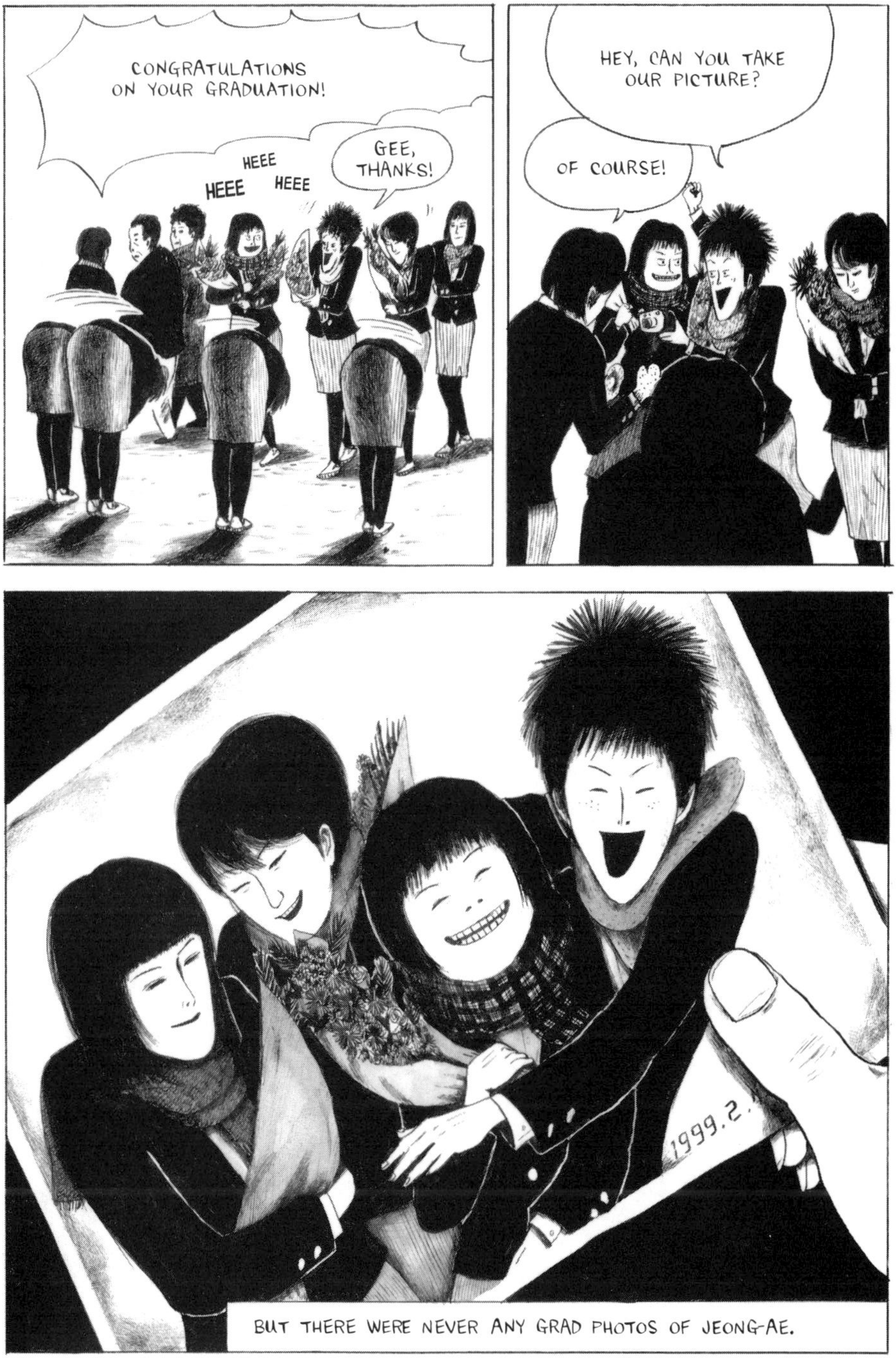
CONGRATULATIONS ON YOUR GRADUATION!
HEEE HEEE HEEE
GEE, THANKS!
HEY, CAN YOU TAKE OUR PICTURE?
OF COURSE!
1999.2.
BUT THERE WERE NEVER ANY GRAD PHOTOS OF JEONG-AE.

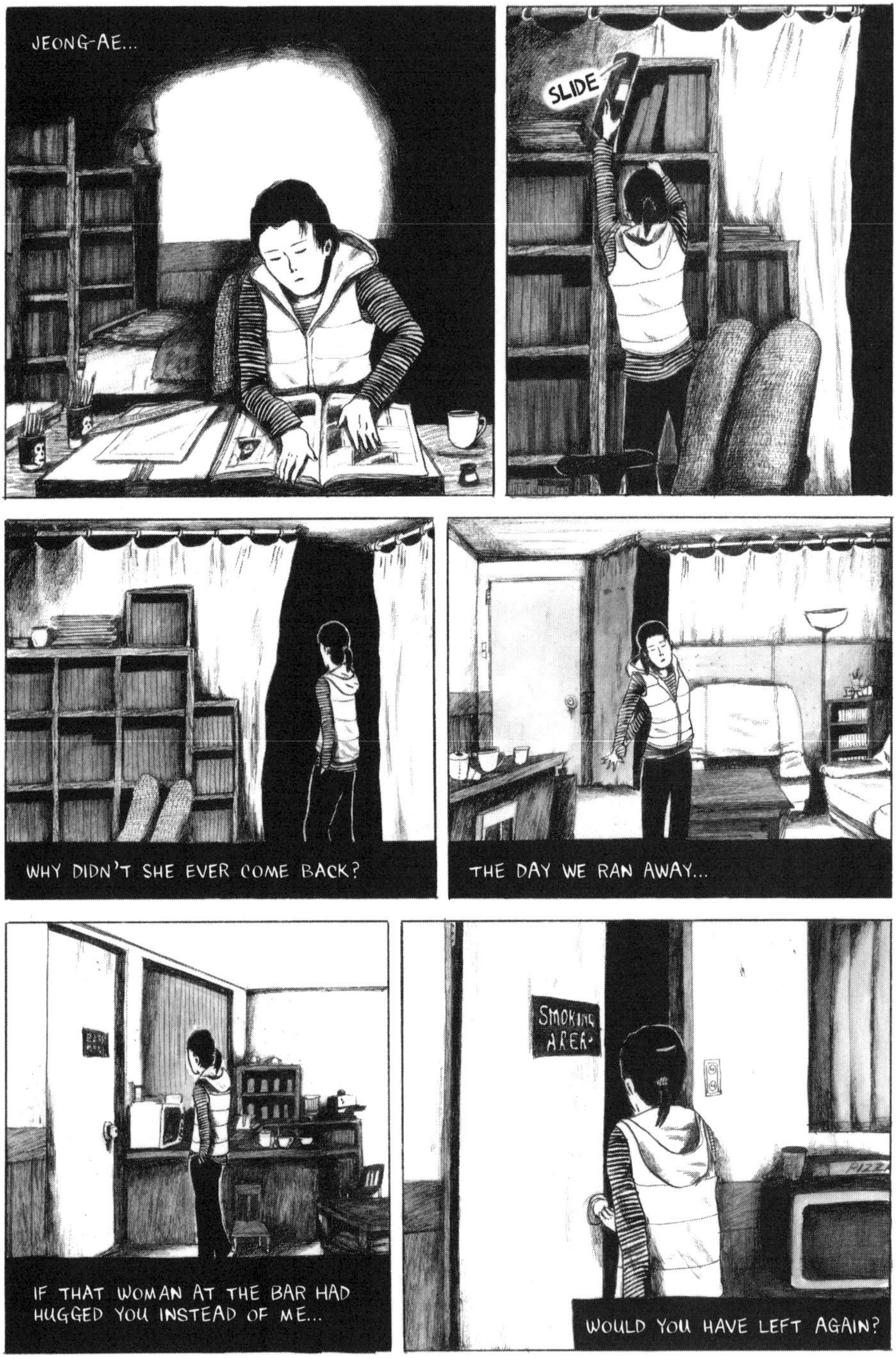
JEONG-AE...
SLIDE
WHY DIDN'T SHE EVER COME BACK?
THE DAY WE RAN AWAY...
IF THAT WOMAN AT THE BAR HAD
HUGGED YOU INSTEAD OF ME...
SMOKING AREA
WOULD YOU HAVE LEFT AGAIN?

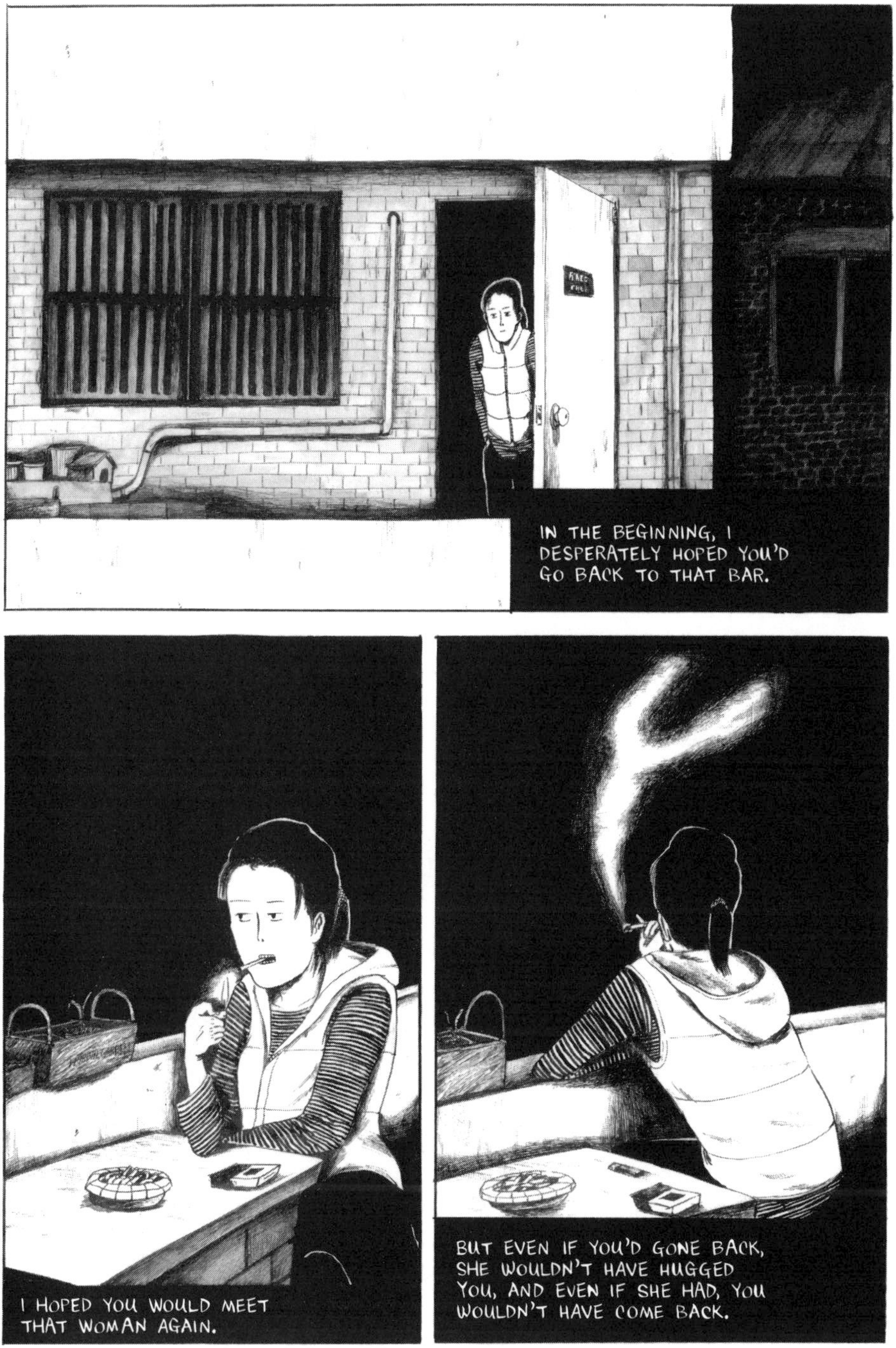
IN THE BEGINNING, I DESPERATELY HOPED YOU'D GO BACK TO THAT BAR.
I HOPED YOU WOULD MEET THAT WOMAN AGAIN.
BUT EVEN IF YOU'D GONE BACK, SHE WOULDN'T HAVE HUGGED YOU, AND EVEN IF SHE HAD, YOU WOULDN'T HAVE COME BACK.

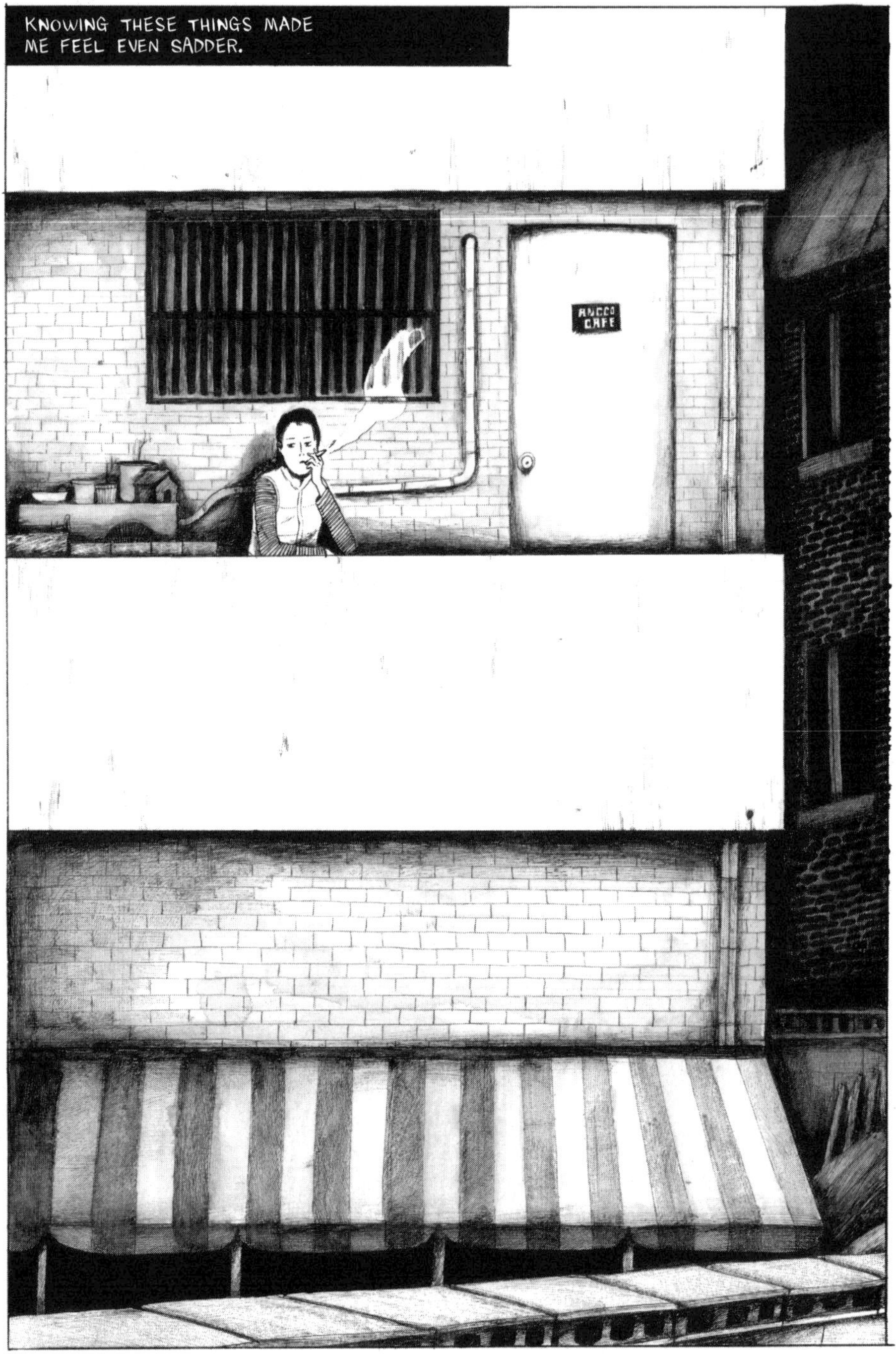
KNOWING THESE THINGS MADE ME FEEL EVEN SADDER.

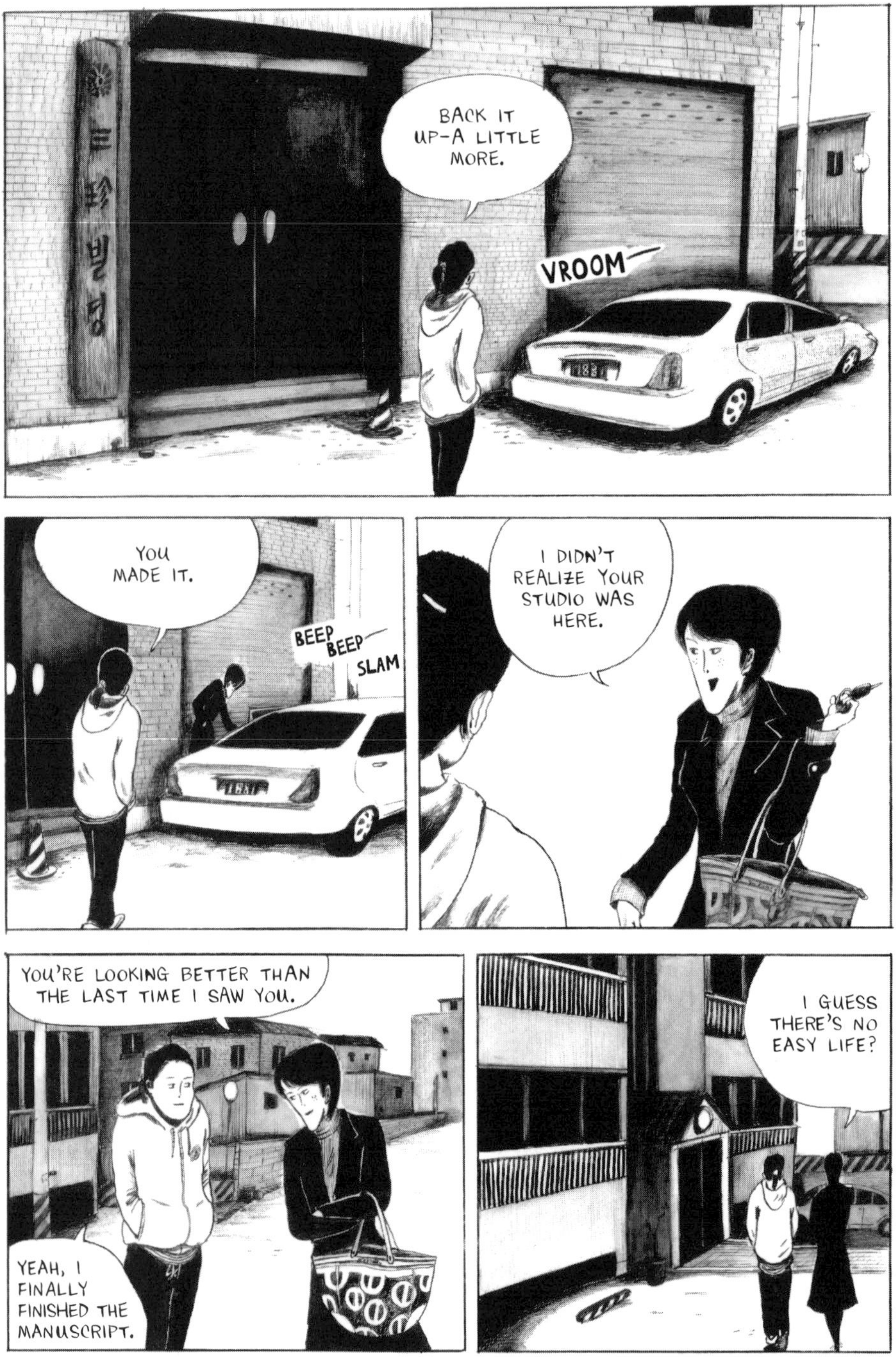
BACK IT UP–A LITTLE MORE.
VROOM
YOU MADE IT.
BEEP BEEP
SLAM
I DIDN'T REALIZE YOUR STUDIO WAS HERE.
YOU'RE LOOKING BETTER THAN THE LAST TIME I SAW YOU.
YEAH, I FINALLY FINISHED THE MANUSCRIPT.
I GUESS THERE'S NO EASY LIFE?

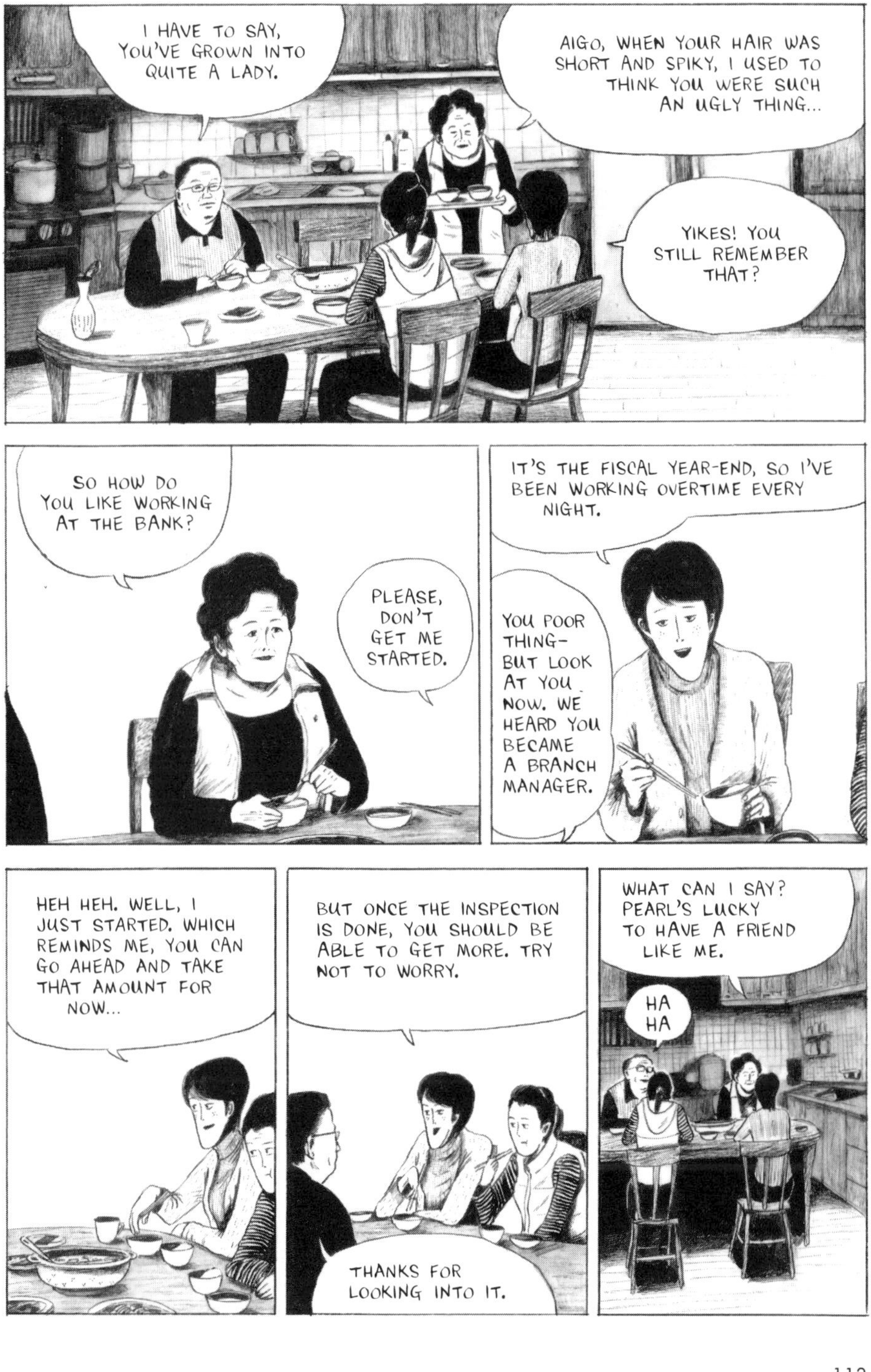
I HAVE TO SAY, YOU'VE GROWN INTO QUITE A LADY.
AIGO, WHEN YOUR HAIR WAS SHORT AND SPIKY, I USED TO THINK YOU WERE SUCH AN UGLY THING...
YIKES! YOU STILL REMEMBER THAT?
SO HOW DO YOU LIKE WORKING AT THE BANK?
PLEASE, DON'T GET ME STARTED.
IT'S THE FISCAL YEAR-END, SO I'VE BEEN WORKING OVERTIME EVERY NIGHT.
YOU POOR THING- BUT LOOK AT YOU NOW. WE HEARD YOU BECAME A BRANCH MANAGER.
HEH HEH. WELL, I JUST STARTED. WHICH REMINDS ME, YOU CAN GO AHEAD AND TAKE THAT AMOUNT FOR NOW...
BUT ONCE THE INSPECTION IS DONE, YOU SHOULD BE ABLE TO GET MORE. TRY NOT TO WORRY.
THANKS FOR LOOKING INTO IT.
WHAT CAN I SAY? PEARL'S LUCKY TO HAVE A FRIEND LIKE ME.
HA HA

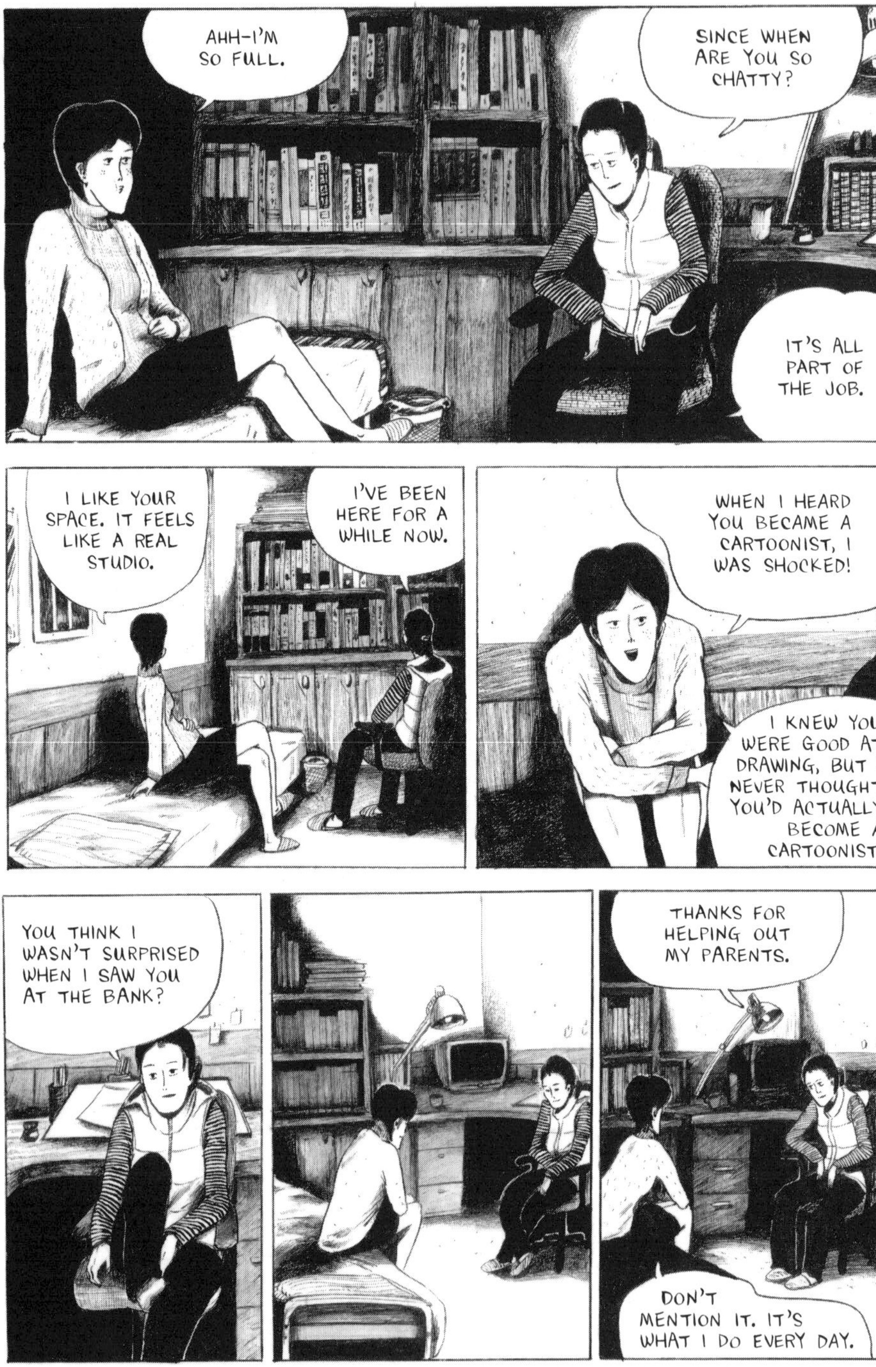
AHH-I'M SO FULL.
SINCE WHEN ARE YOU SO CHATTY?
IT'S ALL PART OF THE JOB.
I LIKE YOUR SPACE. IT FEELS LIKE A REAL STUDIO.
I'VE BEEN HERE FOR A WHILE NOW.
WHEN I HEARD YOU BECAME A CARTOONIST, I WAS SHOCKED!
I KNEW YOU WERE GOOD AT DRAWING, BUT I NEVER THOUGHT YOU'D ACTUALLY BECOME A CARTOONIST.
YOU THINK I WASN'T SURPRISED WHEN I SAW YOU AT THE BANK?
THANKS FOR HELPING OUT MY PARENTS.
DON'T MENTION IT. IT'S WHAT I DO EVERY DAY.

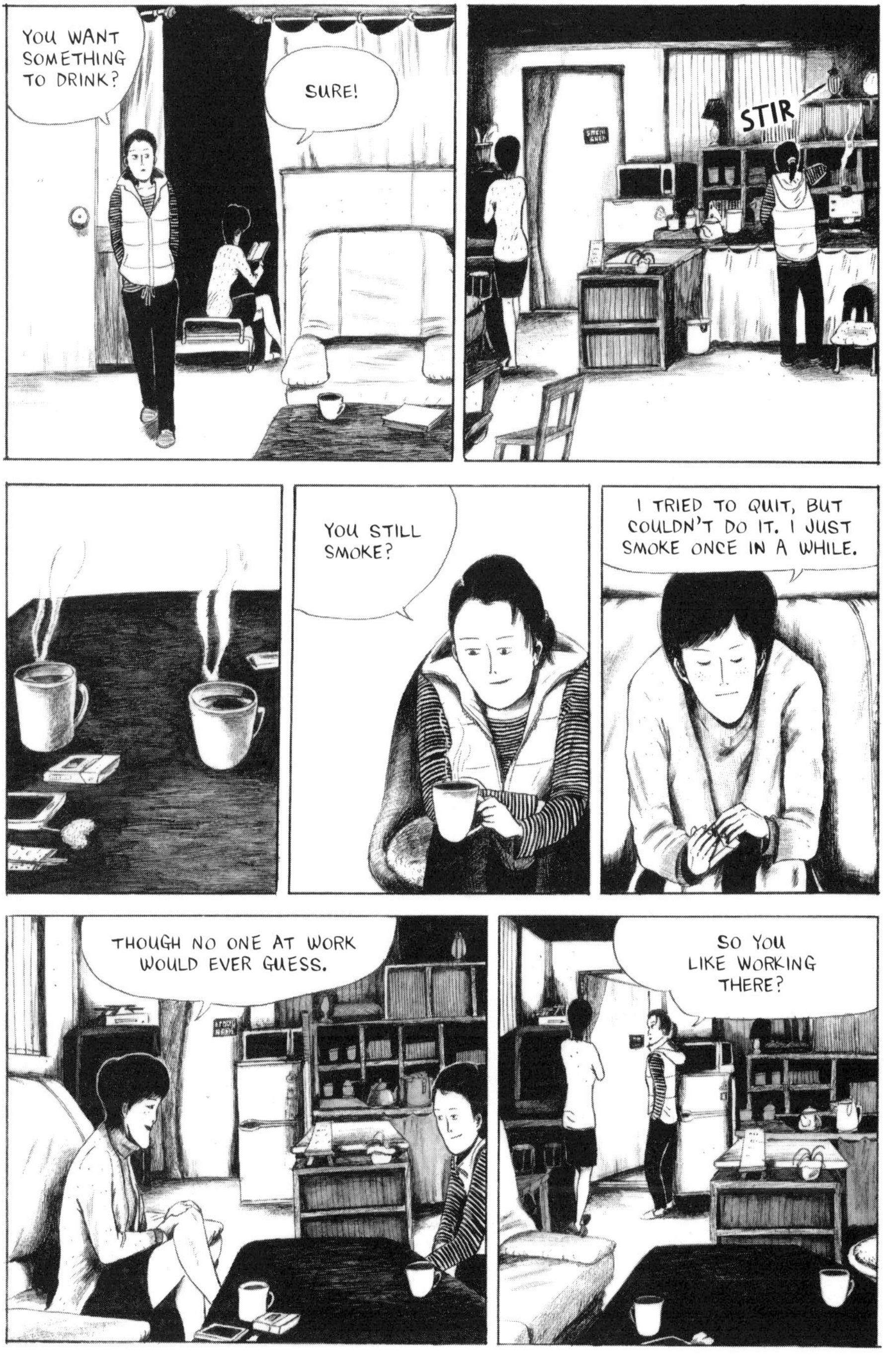
YOU WANT SOMETHING TO DRINK?
SURE!
STIR
YOU STILL SMOKE?
I TRIED TO QUIT, BUT COULDN'T DO IT. I JUST SMOKE ONCE IN A WHILE.
THOUGH NO ONE AT WORK WOULD EVER GUESS.
SO YOU LIKE WORKING THERE?

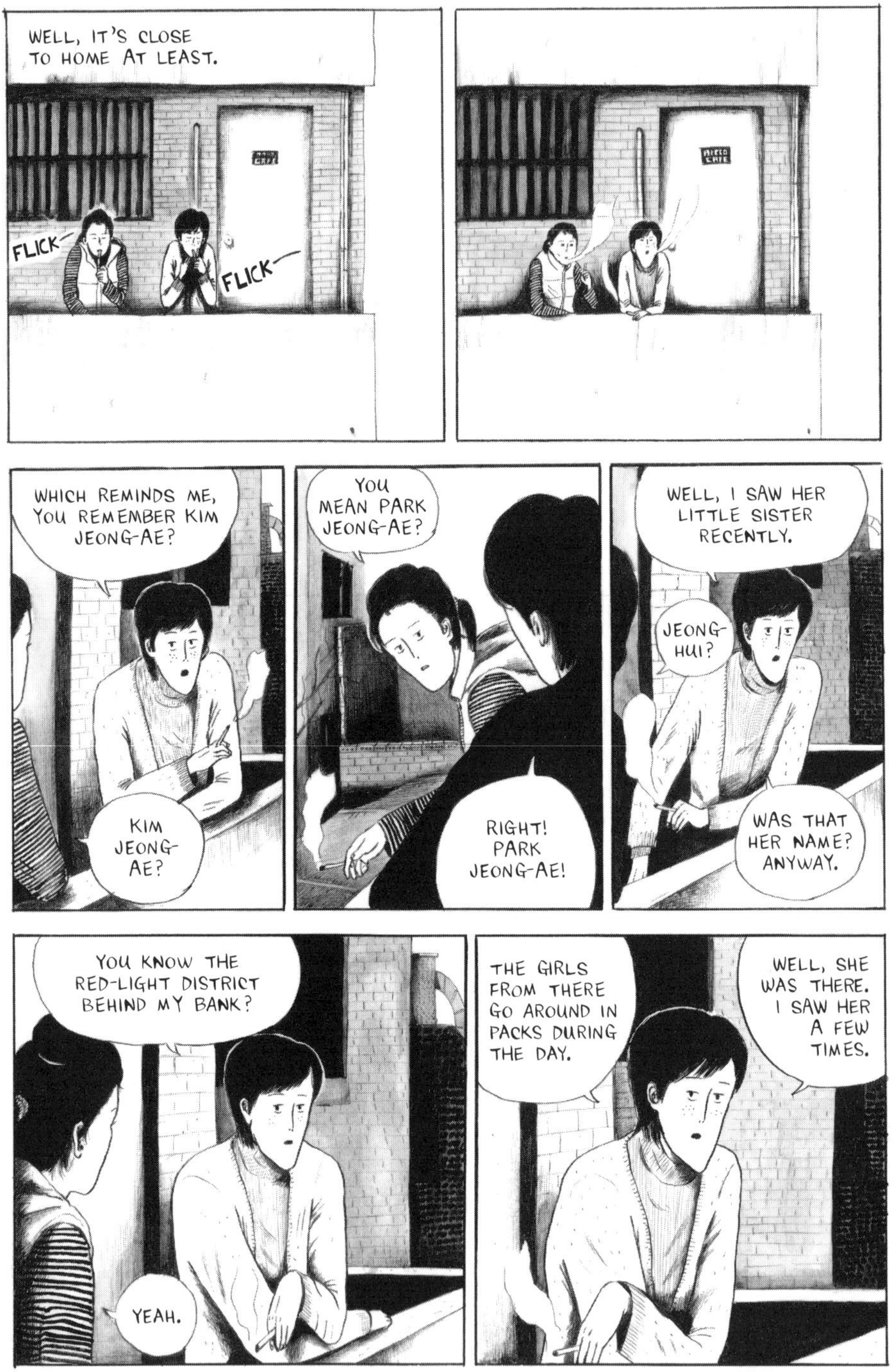
WELL, IT'S CLOSE TO HOME AT LEAST.
FLICK
FLICK
WHICH REMINDS ME, YOU REMEMBER KIM JEONG-AE?
KIM JEONG-AE?
YOU MEAN PARK JEONG-AE?
RIGHT! PARK JEONG-AE!
WELL, I SAW HER LITTLE SISTER RECENTLY.
JEONG-HUI?
WAS THAT HER NAME? ANYWAY.
YOU KNOW THE RED-LIGHT DISTRICT BEHIND MY BANK?
YEAH.
THE GIRLS FROM THERE GO AROUND IN PACKS DURING THE DAY.
WELL, SHE WAS THERE. I SAW HER A FEW TIMES.

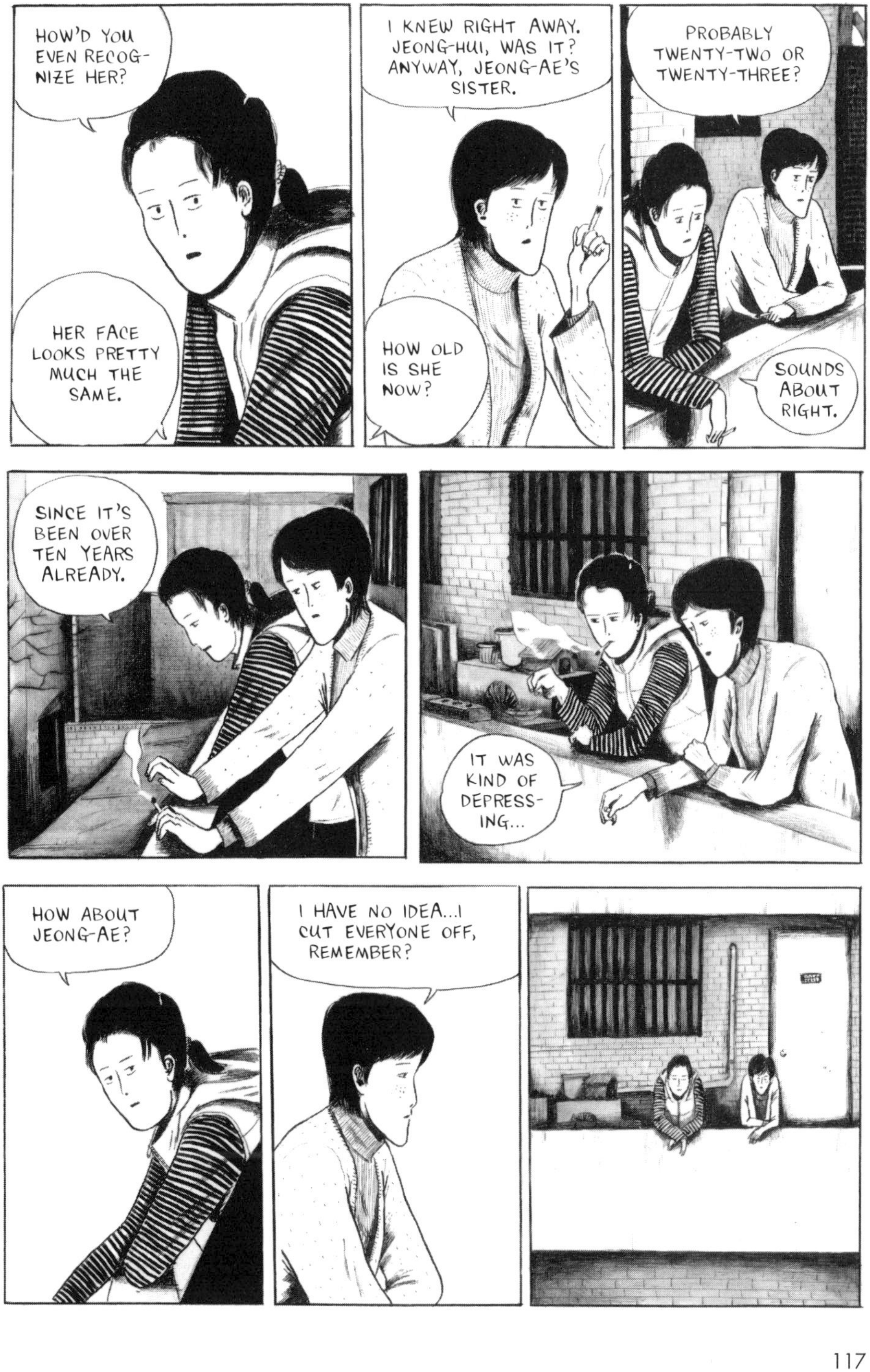
HOW'D YOU EVEN RECOG-NIZE HER?
HER FACE LOOKS PRETTY MUCH THE SAME.
I KNEW RIGHT AWAY. JEONG-HUI, WAS IT? ANYWAY, JEONG-AE'S SISTER.
HOW OLD IS SHE NOW?
PROBABLY TWENTY-TWO OR TWENTY-THREE?
SOUNDS ABOUT RIGHT.
SINCE IT'S BEEN OVER TEN YEARS ALREADY.
IT WAS KIND OF DEPRESS-ING...
HOW ABOUT JEONG-AE?
I HAVE NO IDEA...I CUT EVERYONE OFF, REMEMBER?

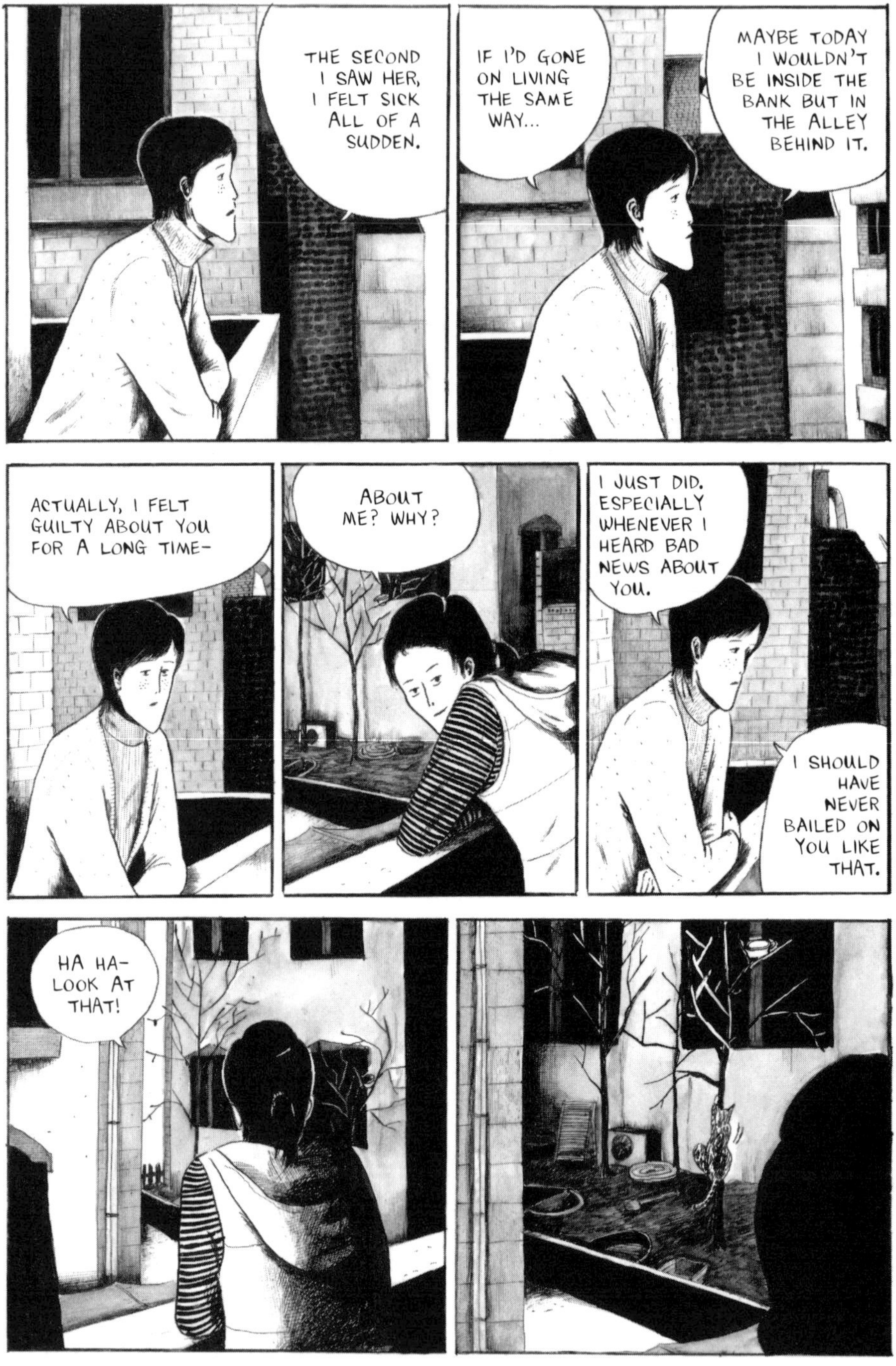
THE SECOND I SAW HER, I FELT SICK ALL OF A SUDDEN.
IF I'D GONE ON LIVING THE SAME WAY...
MAYBE TODAY I WOULDN'T BE INSIDE THE BANK BUT IN THE ALLEY BEHIND IT.
ACTUALLY, I FELT GUILTY ABOUT YOU FOR A LONG TIME-
ABOUT ME? WHY?
I JUST DID. ESPECIALLY WHENEVER I HEARD BAD NEWS ABOUT YOU.
I SHOULD HAVE NEVER BAILED ON YOU LIKE THAT.
HA HA- LOOK AT THAT!

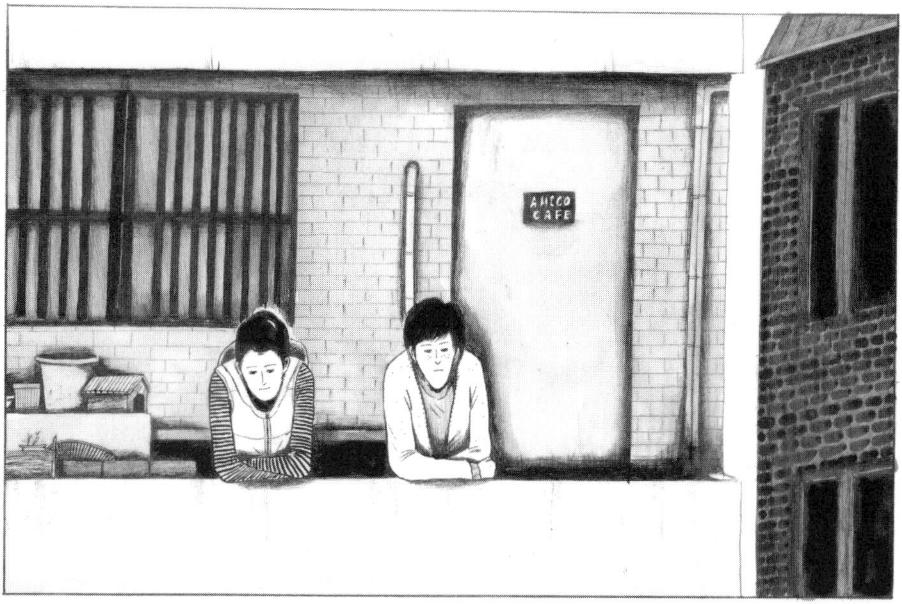
CAFE

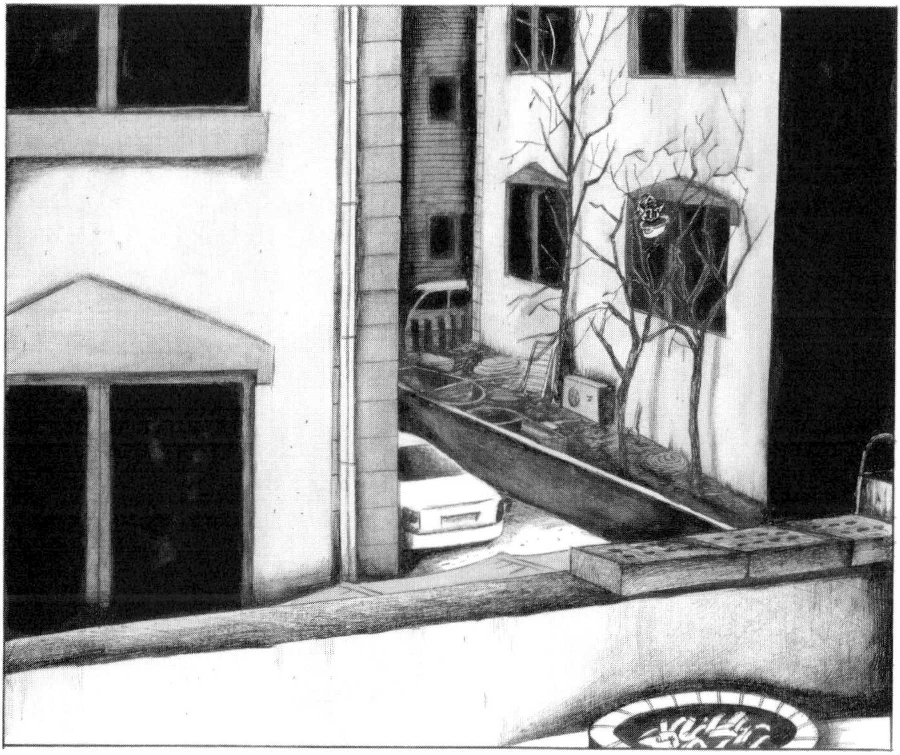

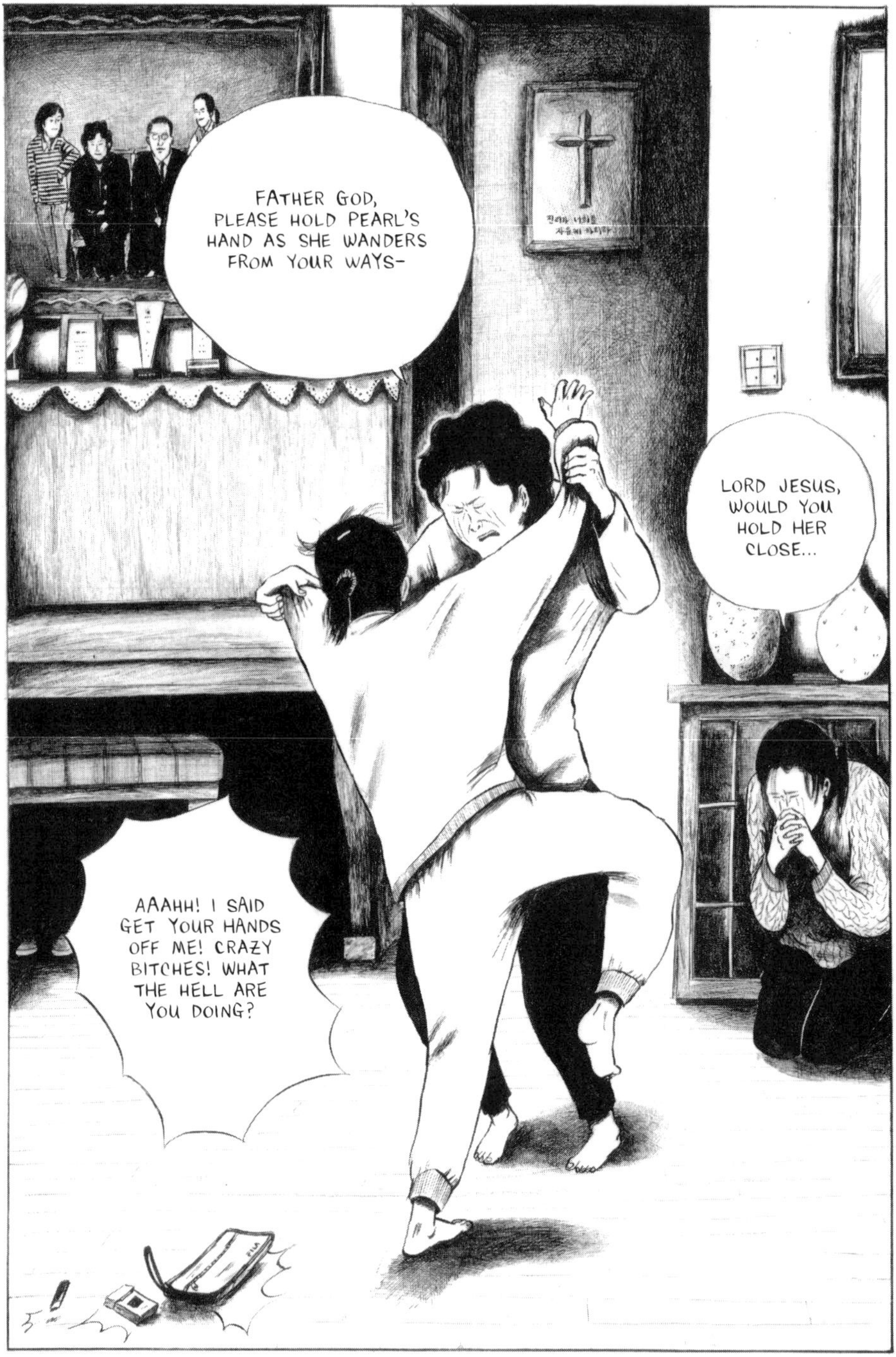
FATHER GOD, PLEASE HOLD PEARL'S HAND AS SHE WANDERS FROM YOUR WAYS-
LORD JESUS, WOULD YOU HOLD HER CLOSE...
AAAHH! I SAID GET YOUR HANDS OFF ME! CRAZY BITCHES! WHAT THE HELL ARE YOU DOING?

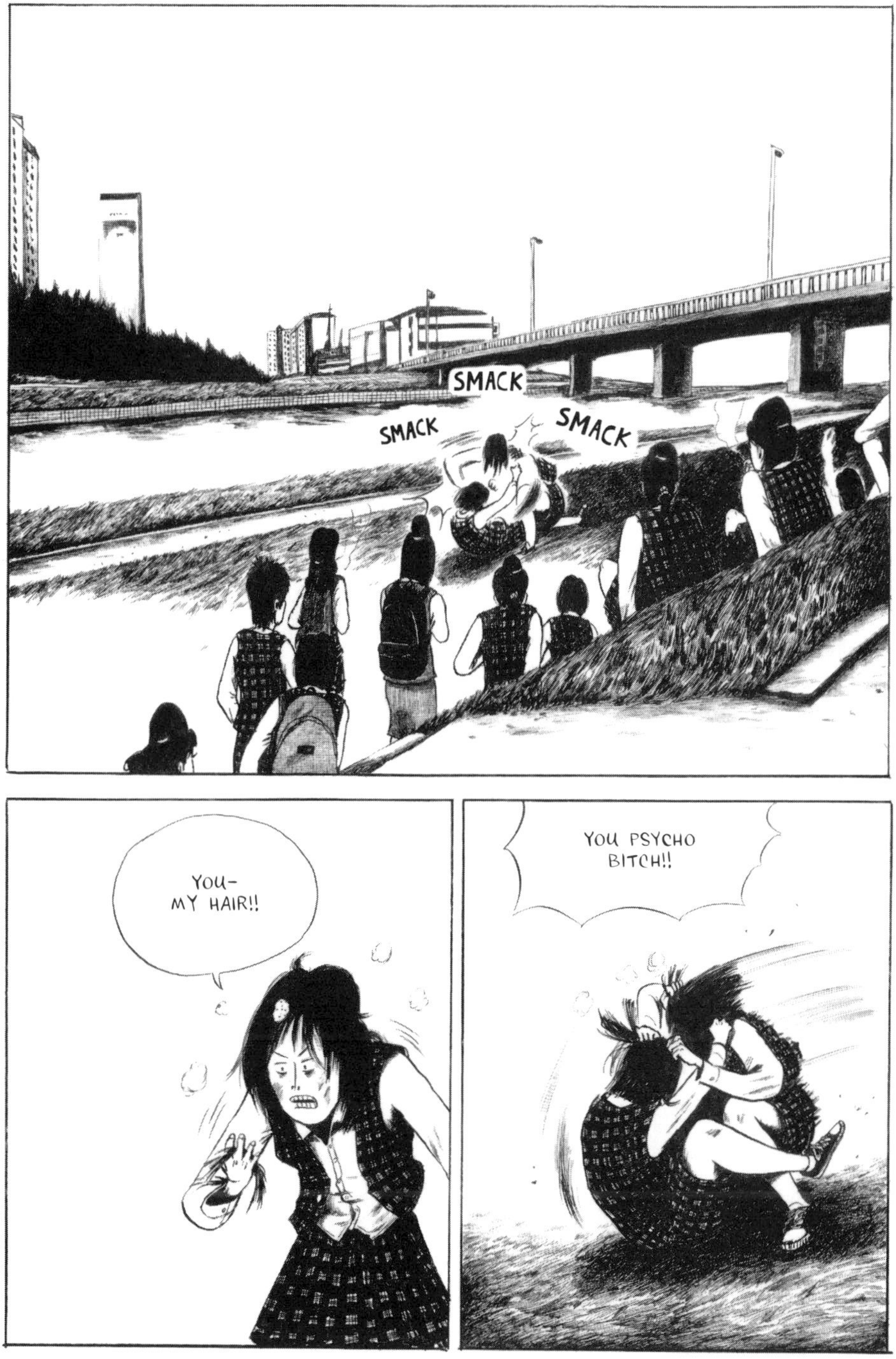
SMACK
SMACK
SMACK
YOU-
MY HAIR!!
YOU PSYCHO
BITCH!!

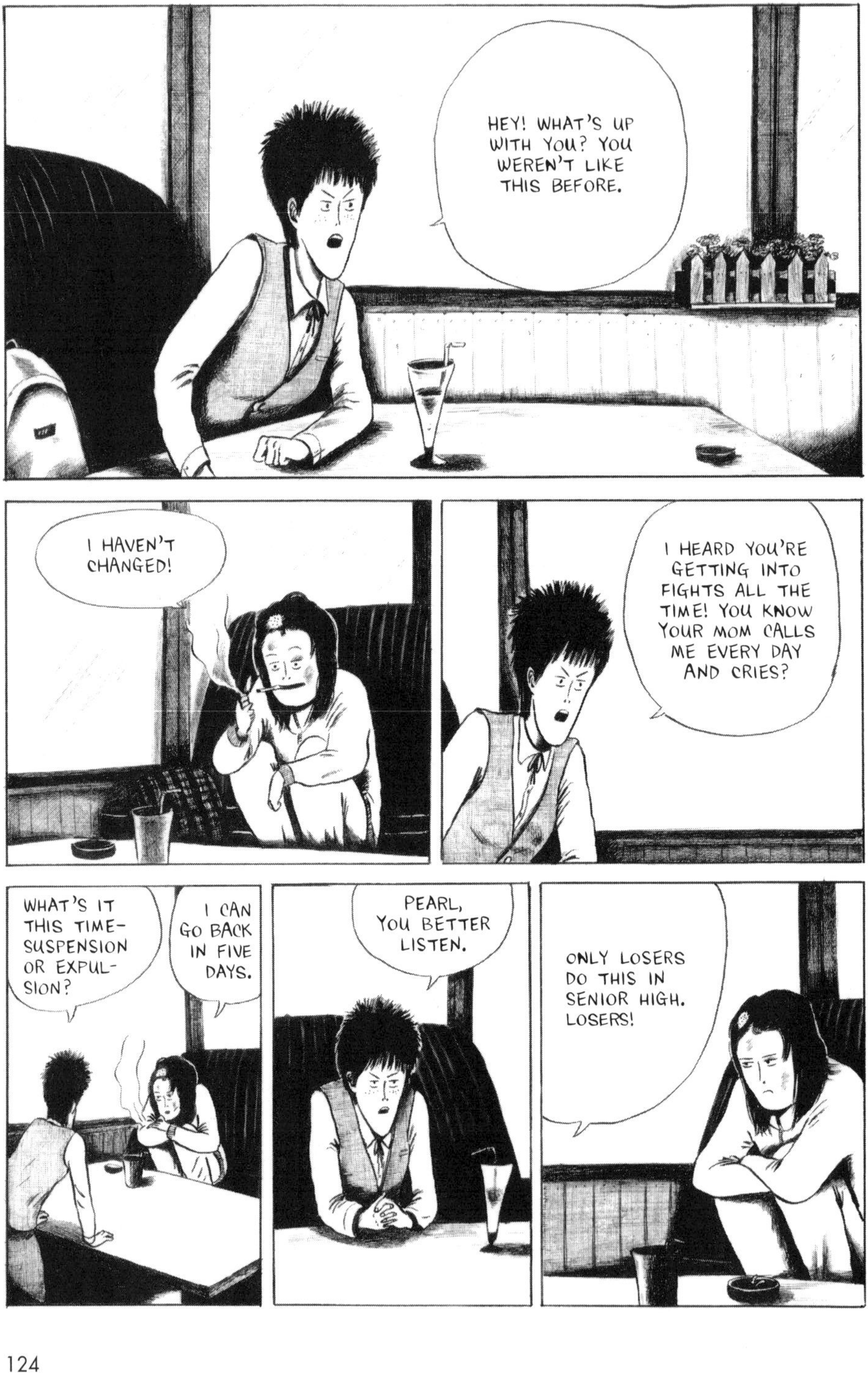
HEY! WHAT'S UP WITH YOU? YOU WEREN'T LIKE THIS BEFORE.
I HAVEN'T CHANGED!
I HEARD YOU'RE GETTING INTO FIGHTS ALL THE TIME! YOU KNOW YOUR MOM CALLS ME EVERY DAY AND CRIES?
WHAT'S IT THIS TIME- SUSPENSION OR EXPUL- SION?
I CAN GO BACK IN FIVE DAYS.
PEARL, YOU BETTER LISTEN.
ONLY LOSERS DO THIS IN SENIOR HIGH. LOSERS!

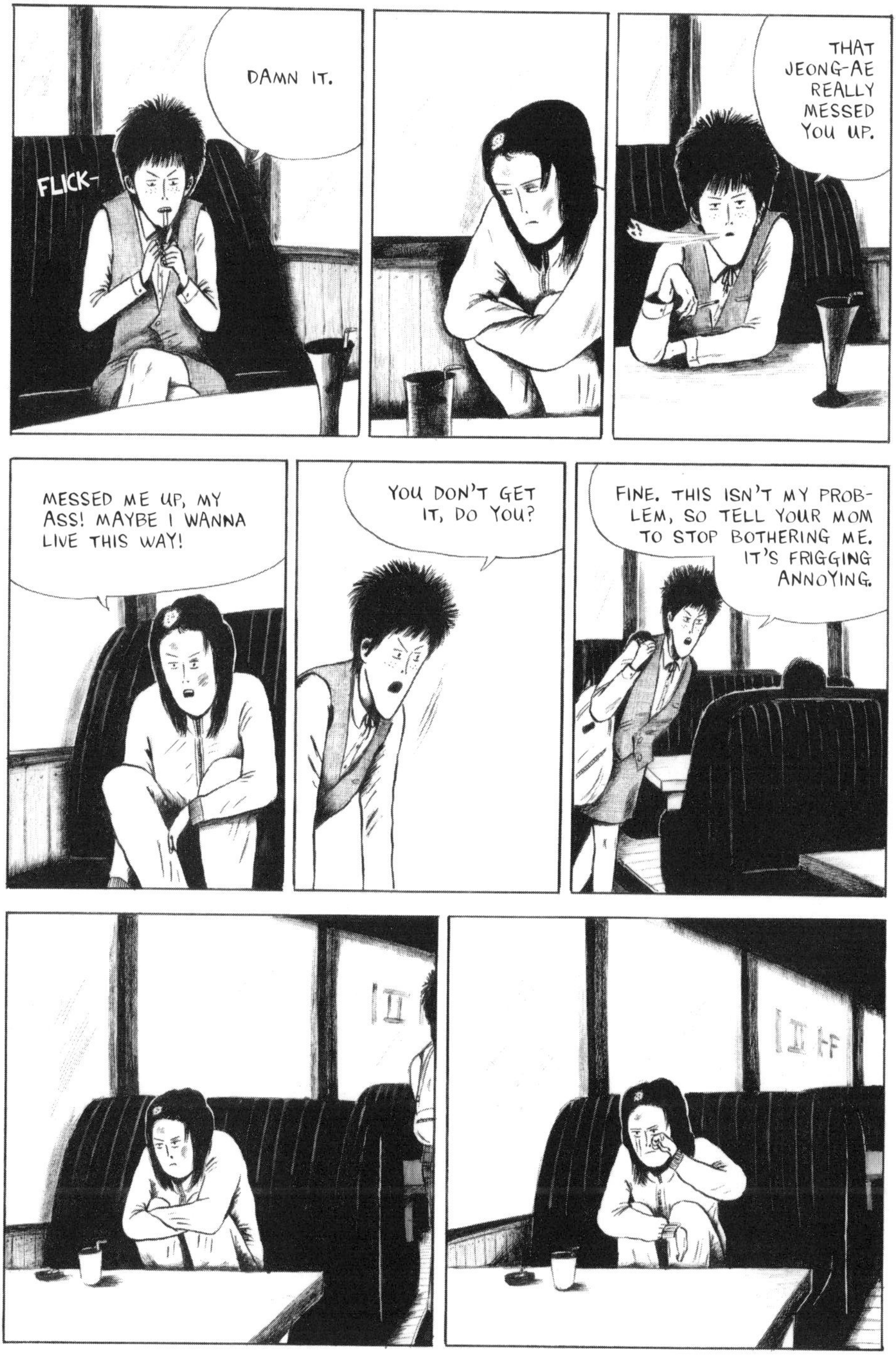
DAMN IT.
FLICK-
THAT JEONG-AE REALLY MESSED YOU UP.
MESSED ME UP, MY ASS! MAYBE I WANNA LIVE THIS WAY!
YOU DON'T GET IT, DO YOU?
FINE. THIS ISN'T MY PROB-LEM, SO TELL YOUR MOM TO STOP BOTHERING ME. IT'S FRIGGING ANNOYING.

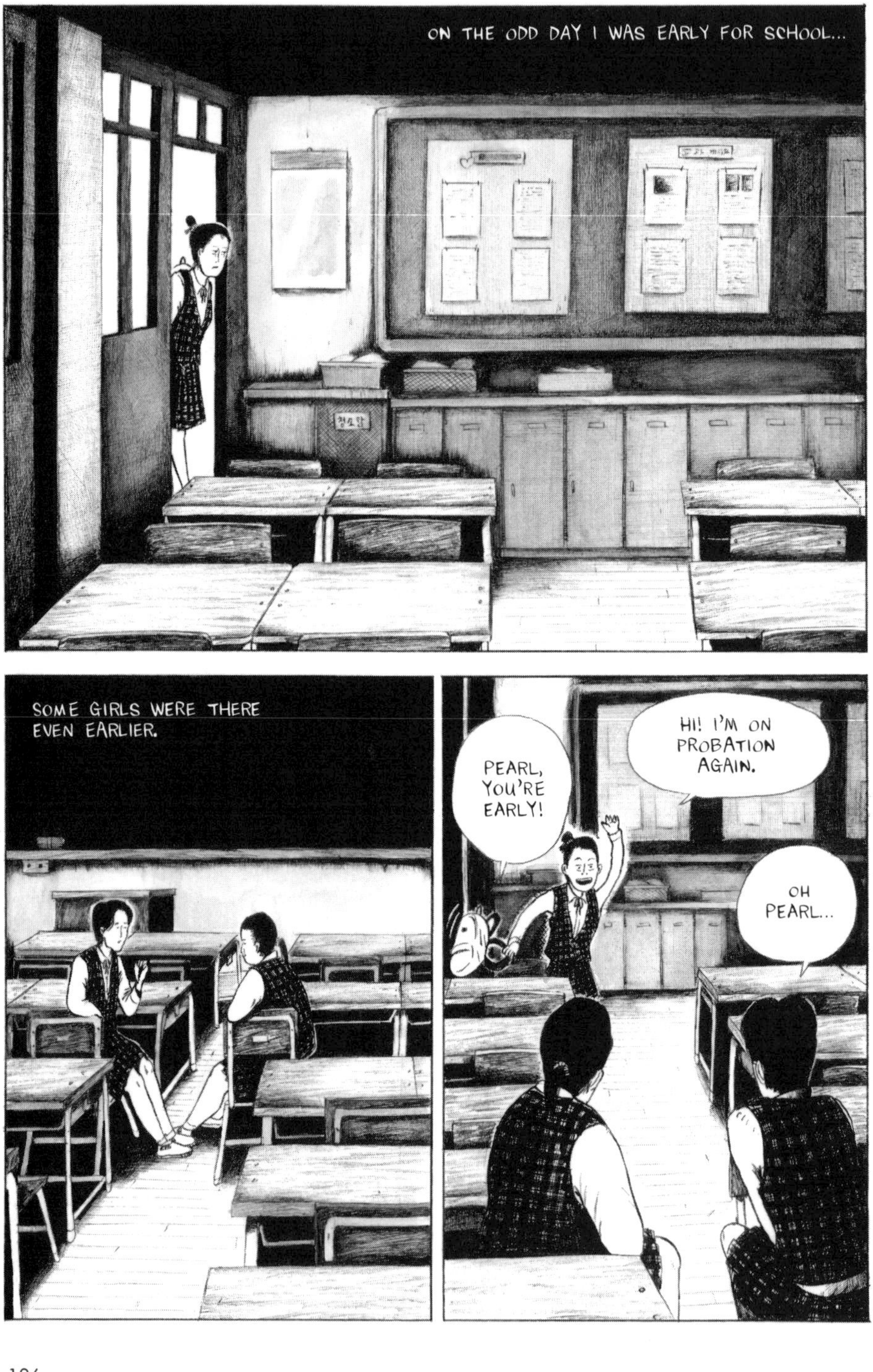
ON THE ODD DAY I WAS EARLY FOR SCHOOL...
SOME GIRLS WERE THERE EVEN EARLIER.
PEARL, YOU'RE EARLY!
HI! I'M ON PROBATION AGAIN.
OH PEARL...

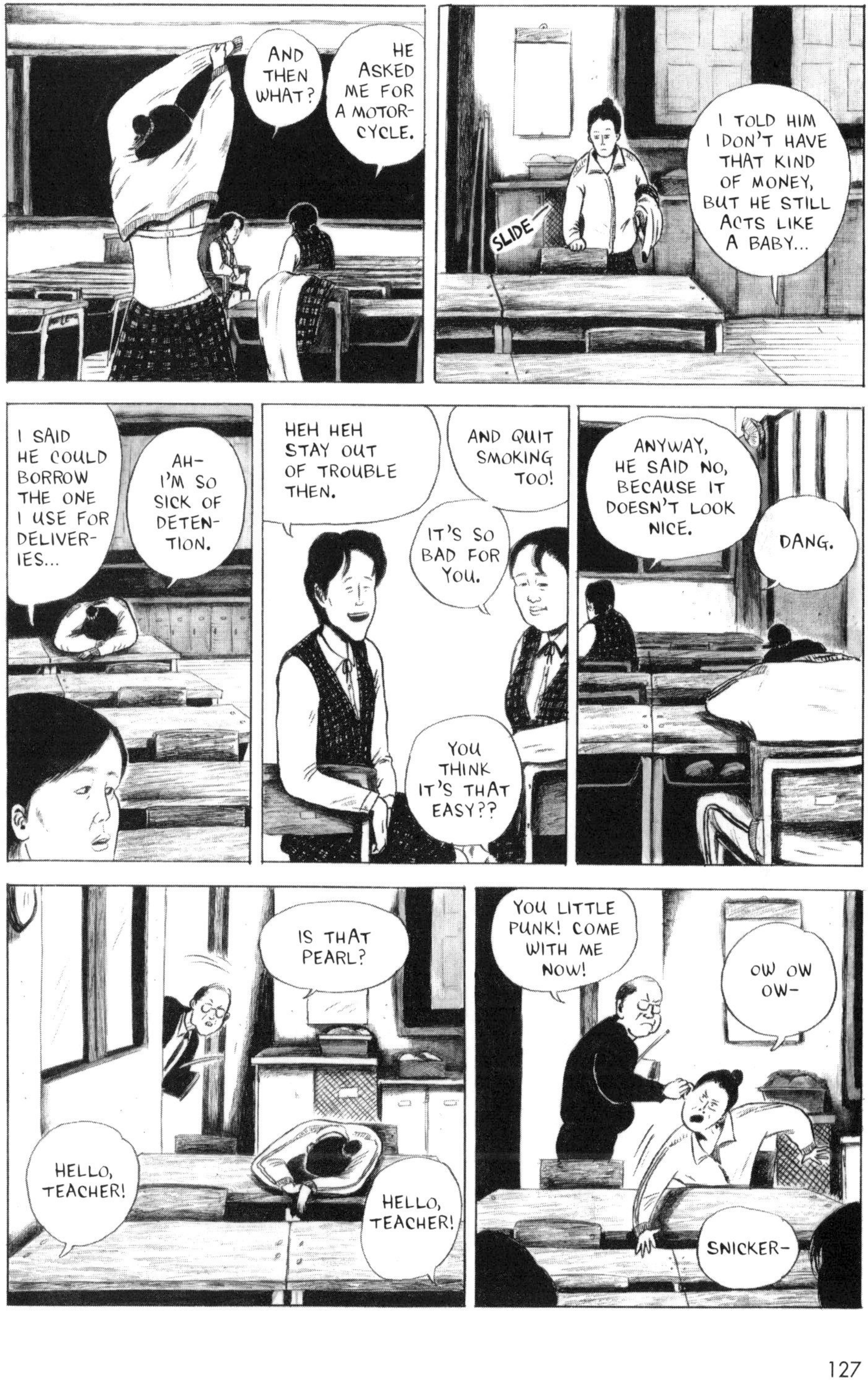
HE ASKED ME FOR A MOTORCYCLE.
AND THEN WHAT?
SLIDE
I TOLD HIM I DON'T HAVE THAT KIND OF MONEY, BUT HE STILL ACTS LIKE A BABY...
I SAID HE COULD BORROW THE ONE I USE FOR DELIVERIES...
AH- I'M SO SICK OF DETENTION.
HEH HEH STAY OUT OF TROUBLE THEN.
AND QUIT SMOKING TOO!
IT'S SO BAD FOR YOU.
YOU THINK IT'S THAT EASY??
ANYWAY, HE SAID NO, BECAUSE IT DOESN'T LOOK NICE.
DANG.
IS THAT PEARL?
HELLO, TEACHER!
HELLO, TEACHER!
YOU LITTLE PUNK! COME WITH ME NOW!
OW OW OW-
SNICKER-

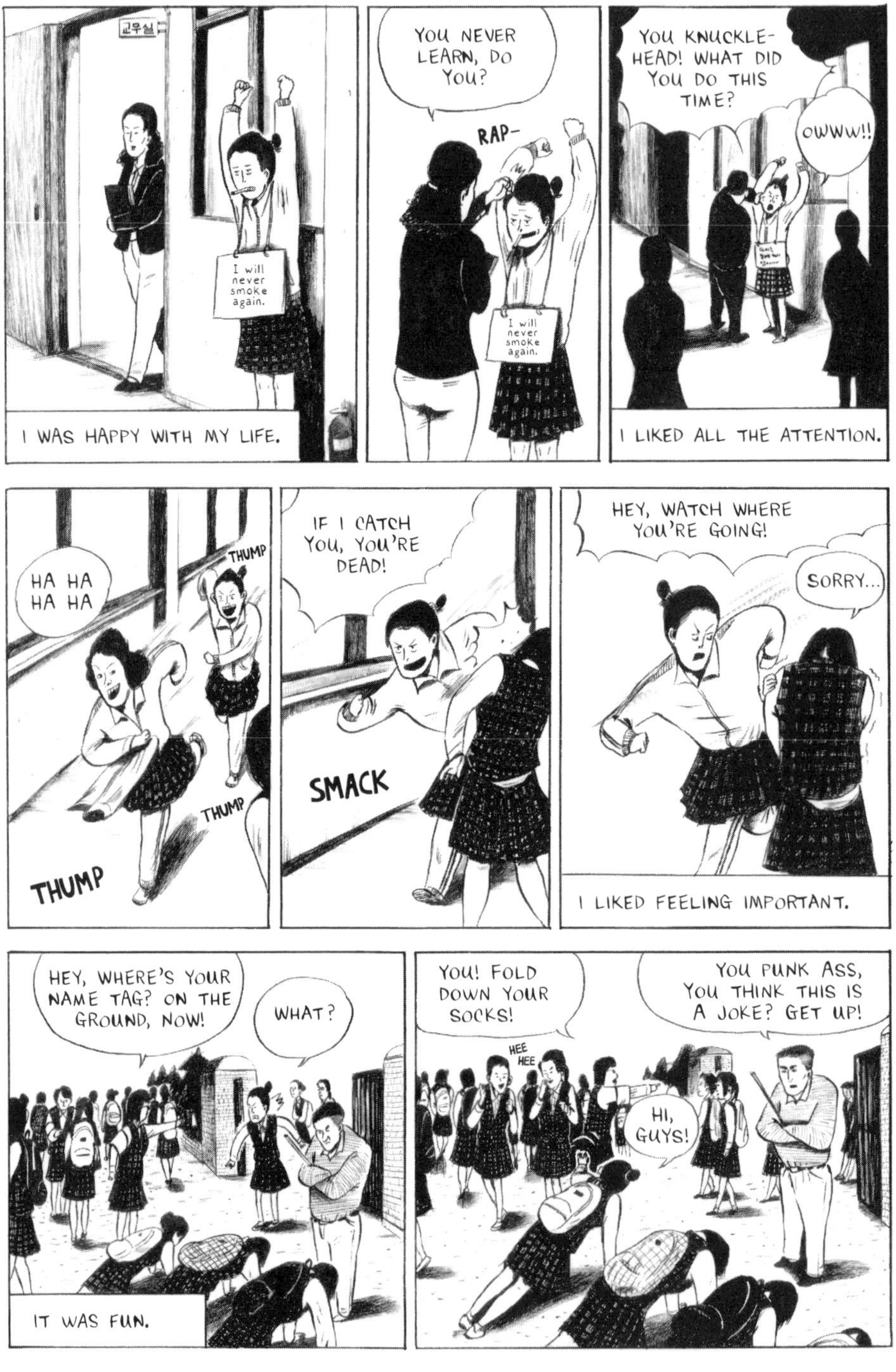
교무실
I will never smoke again.
I WAS HAPPY WITH MY LIFE.
YOU NEVER LEARN, DO YOU?
RAP-
I will never smoke again.
YOU KNUCKLE-HEAD! WHAT DID YOU DO THIS TIME?
OWWW!!
I LIKED ALL THE ATTENTION.
HA HA HA HA
THUMP
THUMP
THUMP
IF I CATCH YOU, YOU'RE DEAD!
SMACK
HEY, WATCH WHERE YOU'RE GOING!
SORRY...
I LIKED FEELING IMPORTANT.
HEY, WHERE'S YOUR NAME TAG? ON THE GROUND, NOW!
WHAT?
IT WAS FUN.
YOU! FOLD DOWN YOUR SOCKS!
HEE HEE
YOU PUNK ASS, YOU THINK THIS IS A JOKE? GET UP!
HI, GUYS!

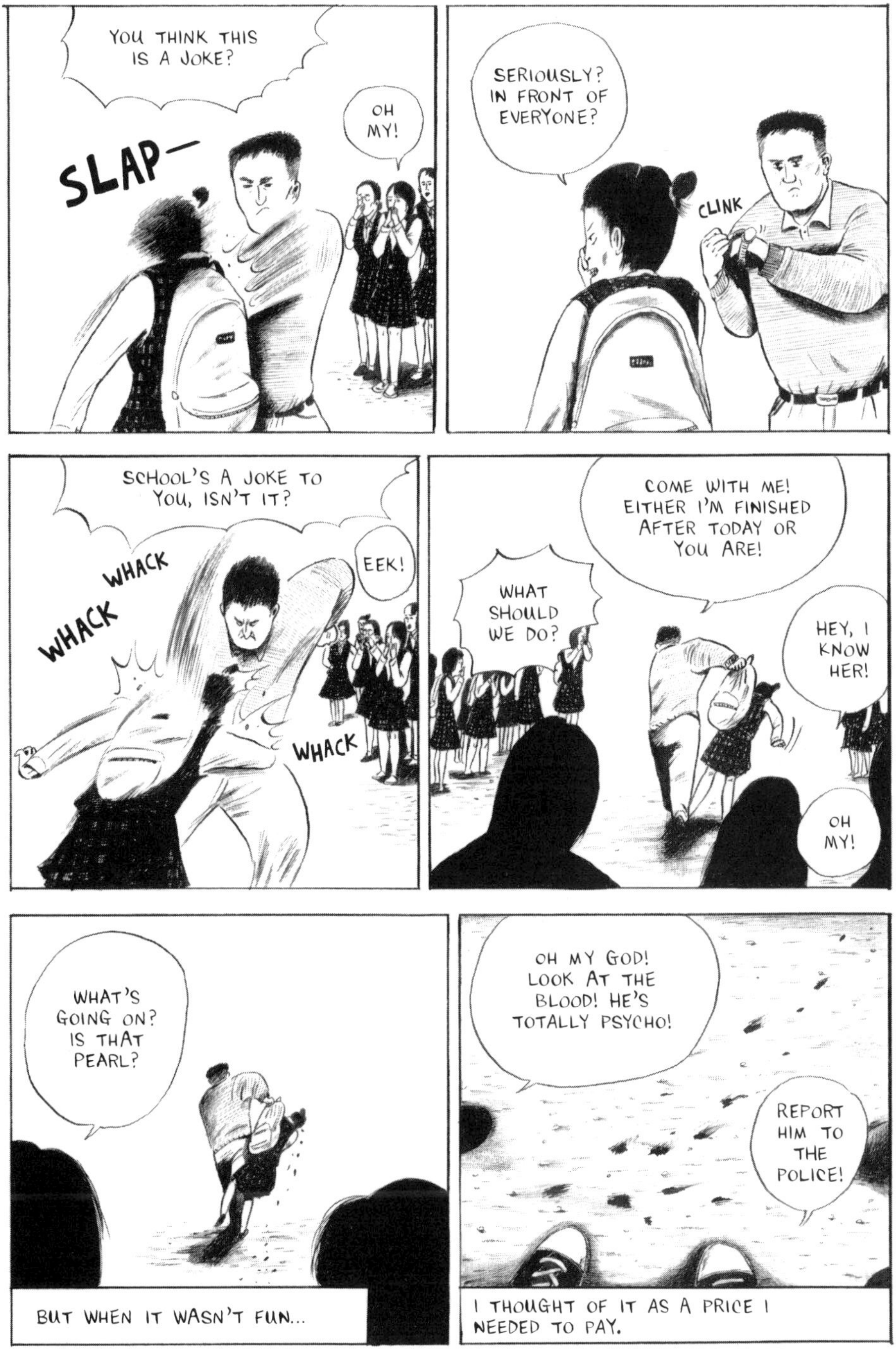
YOU THINK THIS IS A JOKE?
OH MY!
SLAP—
SERIOUSLY? IN FRONT OF EVERYONE?
CLINK
SCHOOL'S A JOKE TO YOU, ISN'T IT?
EEK!
WHACK
WHACK
WHACK
COME WITH ME! EITHER I'M FINISHED AFTER TODAY OR YOU ARE!
WHAT SHOULD WE DO?
HEY, I KNOW HER!
OH MY!
WHAT'S GOING ON? IS THAT PEARL?
BUT WHEN IT WASN'T FUN...
OH MY GOD! LOOK AT THE BLOOD! HE'S TOTALLY PSYCHO!
REPORT HIM TO THE POLICE!
I THOUGHT OF IT AS A PRICE I NEEDED TO PAY.

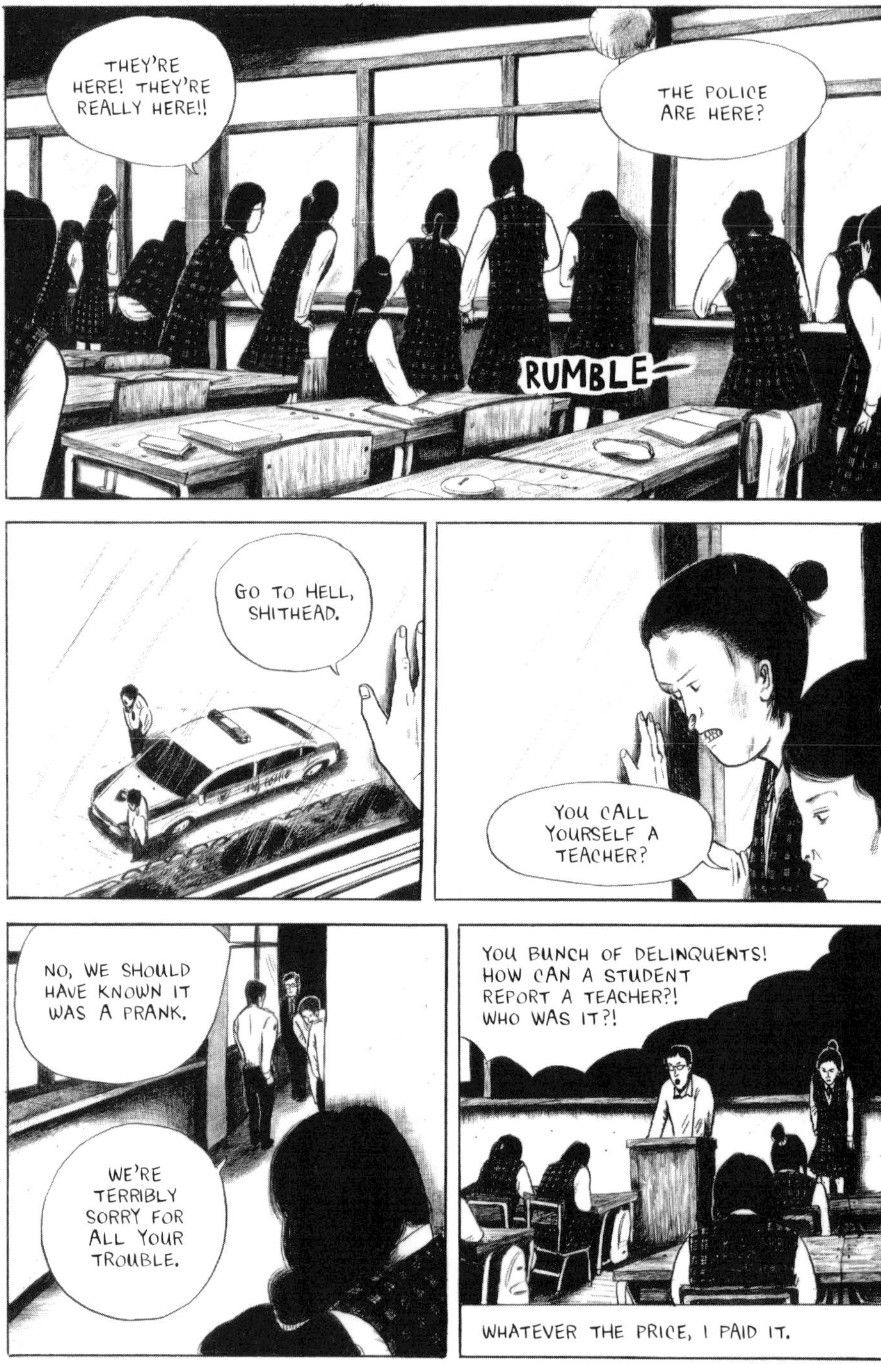
THEY'RE HERE! THEY'RE REALLY HERE!!
THE POLICE ARE HERE?
RUMBLE
GO TO HELL, SHITHEAD.
YOU CALL YOURSELF A TEACHER?
NO, WE SHOULD HAVE KNOWN IT WAS A PRANK.
WE'RE TERRIBLY SORRY FOR ALL YOUR TROUBLE.
YOU BUNCH OF DELINQUENTS! HOW CAN A STUDENT REPORT A TEACHER?! WHO WAS IT?!
WHATEVER THE PRICE, I PAID IT.

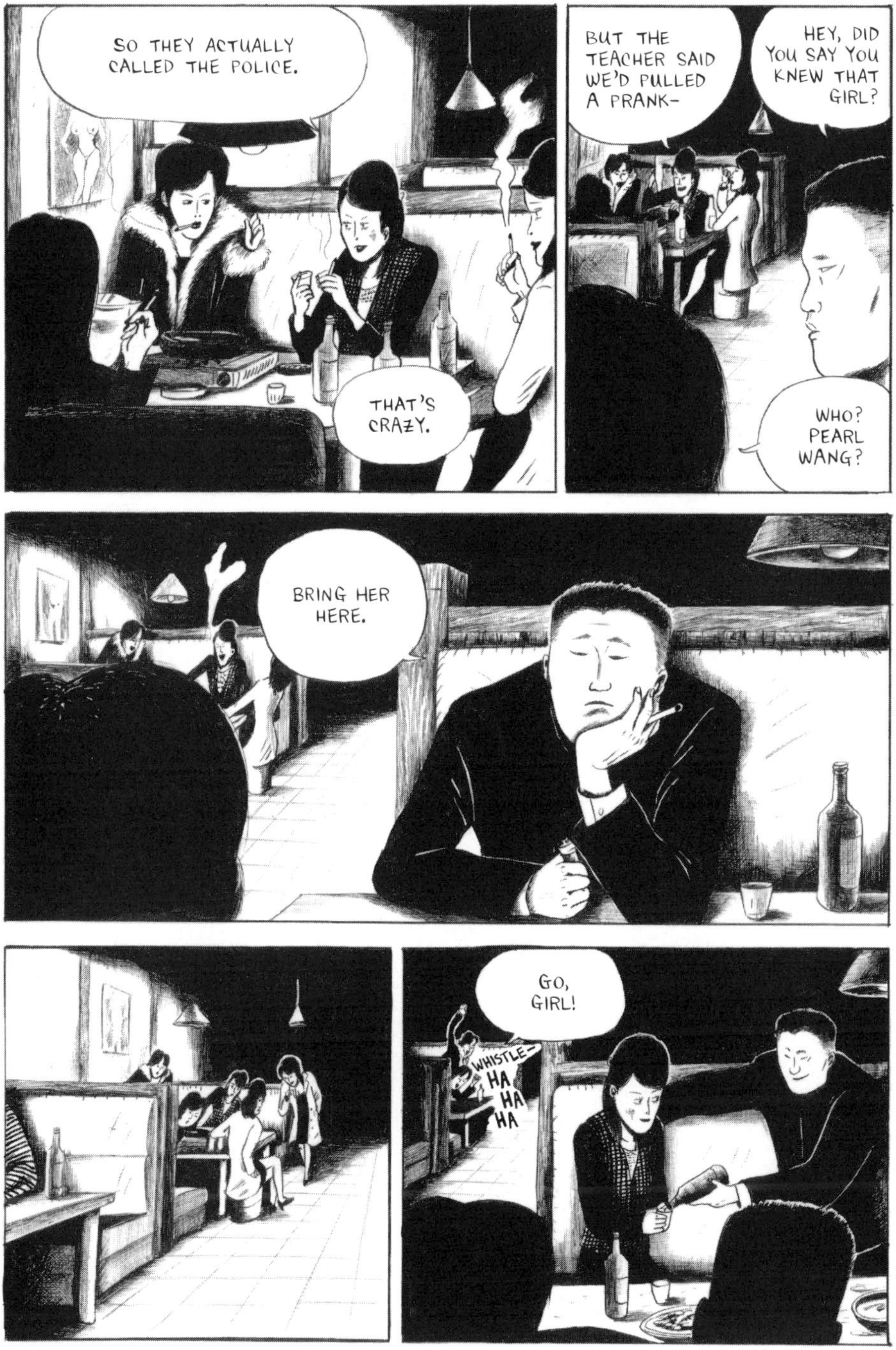
SO THEY ACTUALLY CALLED THE POLICE.
THAT'S CRAZY.
HEY, DID YOU SAY YOU KNEW THAT GIRL?
BUT THE TEACHER SAID WE'D PULLED A PRANK-
WHO? PEARL WANG?
BRING HER HERE.
GO, GIRL!
WHISTLE-
HA HA HA

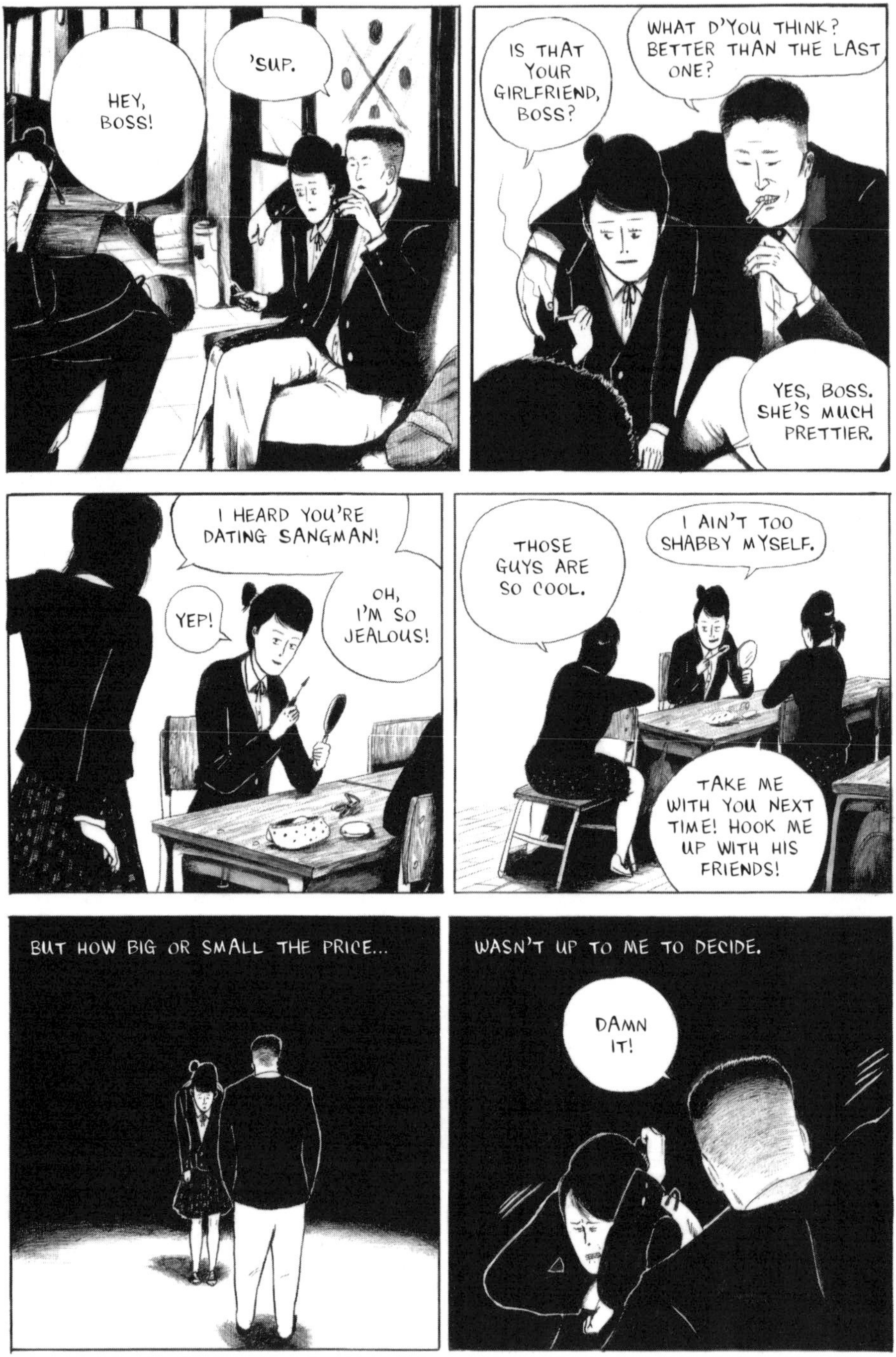
HEY, BOSS!
'SUP.
IS THAT YOUR GIRLFRIEND, BOSS?
WHAT D'YOU THINK? BETTER THAN THE LAST ONE?
YES, BOSS. SHE'S MUCH PRETTIER.
I HEARD YOU'RE DATING SANGMAN!
YEP!
OH, I'M SO JEALOUS!
THOSE GUYS ARE SO COOL.
I AIN'T TOO SHABBY MYSELF.
TAKE ME WITH YOU NEXT TIME! HOOK ME UP WITH HIS FRIENDS!
BUT HOW BIG OR SMALL THE PRICE...
WASN'T UP TO ME TO DECIDE.
DAMN IT!

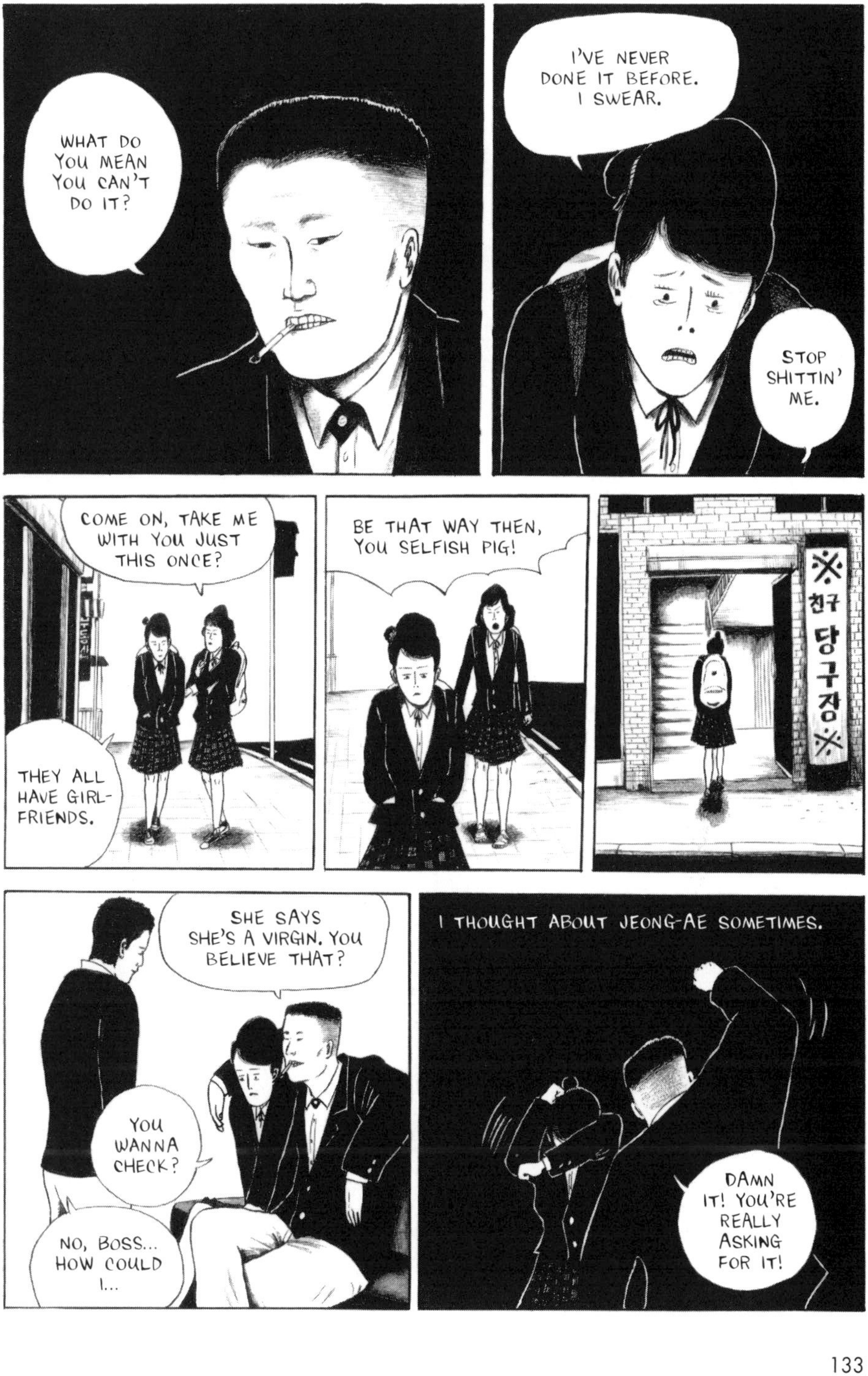
WHAT DO YOU MEAN YOU CAN'T DO IT?
I'VE NEVER DONE IT BEFORE. I SWEAR.
STOP SHITTIN' ME.
COME ON, TAKE ME WITH YOU JUST THIS ONCE?
THEY ALL HAVE GIRL-FRIENDS.
BE THAT WAY THEN, YOU SELFISH PIG!
※ 친구 당구장 ※
SHE SAYS SHE'S A VIRGIN. YOU BELIEVE THAT?
YOU WANNA CHECK?
NO, BOSS... HOW COULD I...
I THOUGHT ABOUT JEONG-AE SOMETIMES.
DAMN IT! YOU'RE REALLY ASKING FOR IT!

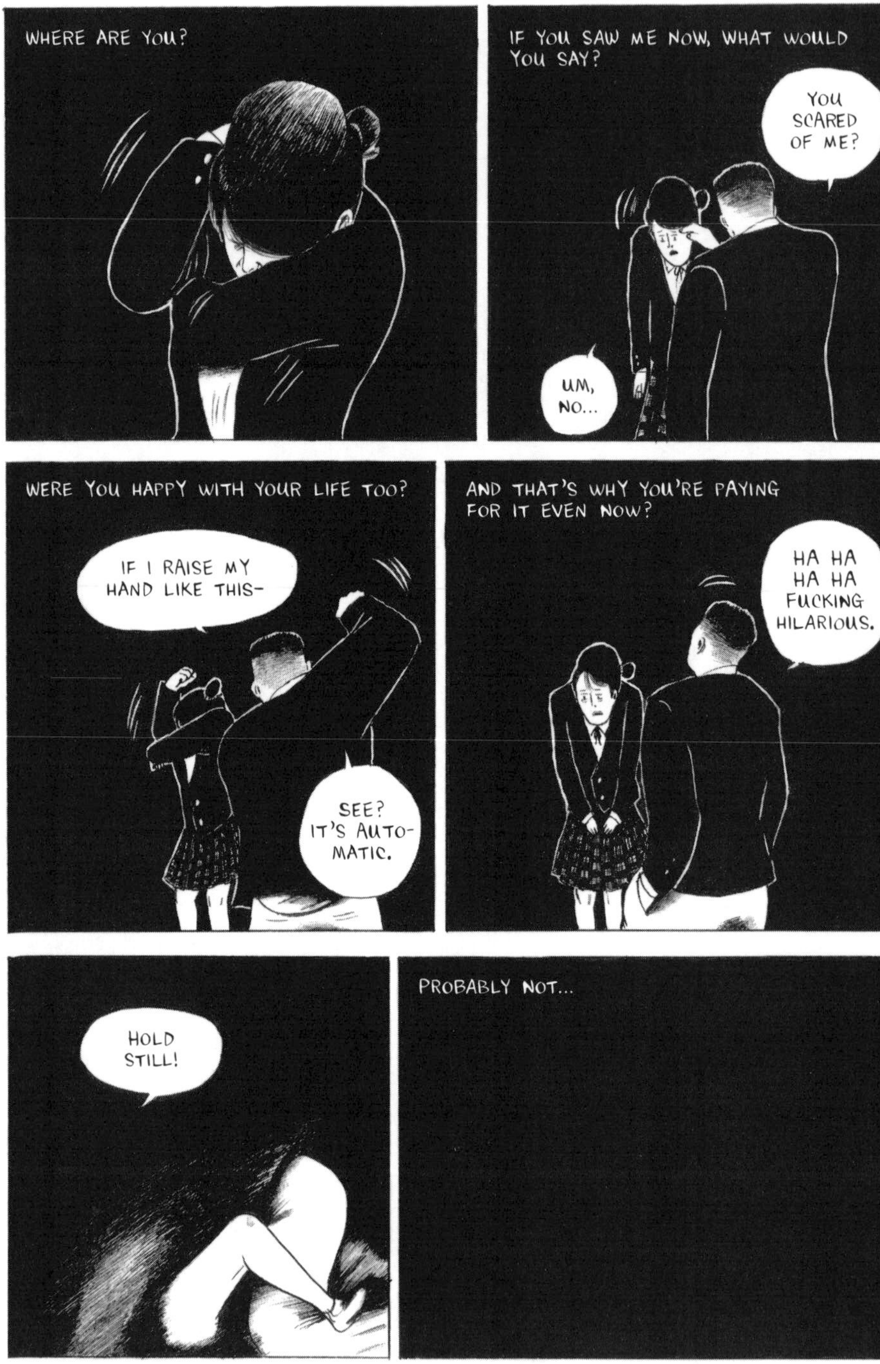
WHERE ARE YOU?
IF YOU SAW ME NOW, WHAT WOULD YOU SAY?
YOU SCARED OF ME?
UM, NO...
WERE YOU HAPPY WITH YOUR LIFE TOO?
IF I RAISE MY HAND LIKE THIS-
SEE? IT'S AUTO-MATIC.
AND THAT'S WHY YOU'RE PAYING FOR IT EVEN NOW?
HA HA HA HA FUCKING HILARIOUS.
HOLD STILL!
PROBABLY NOT...

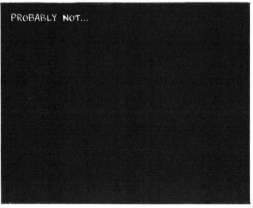

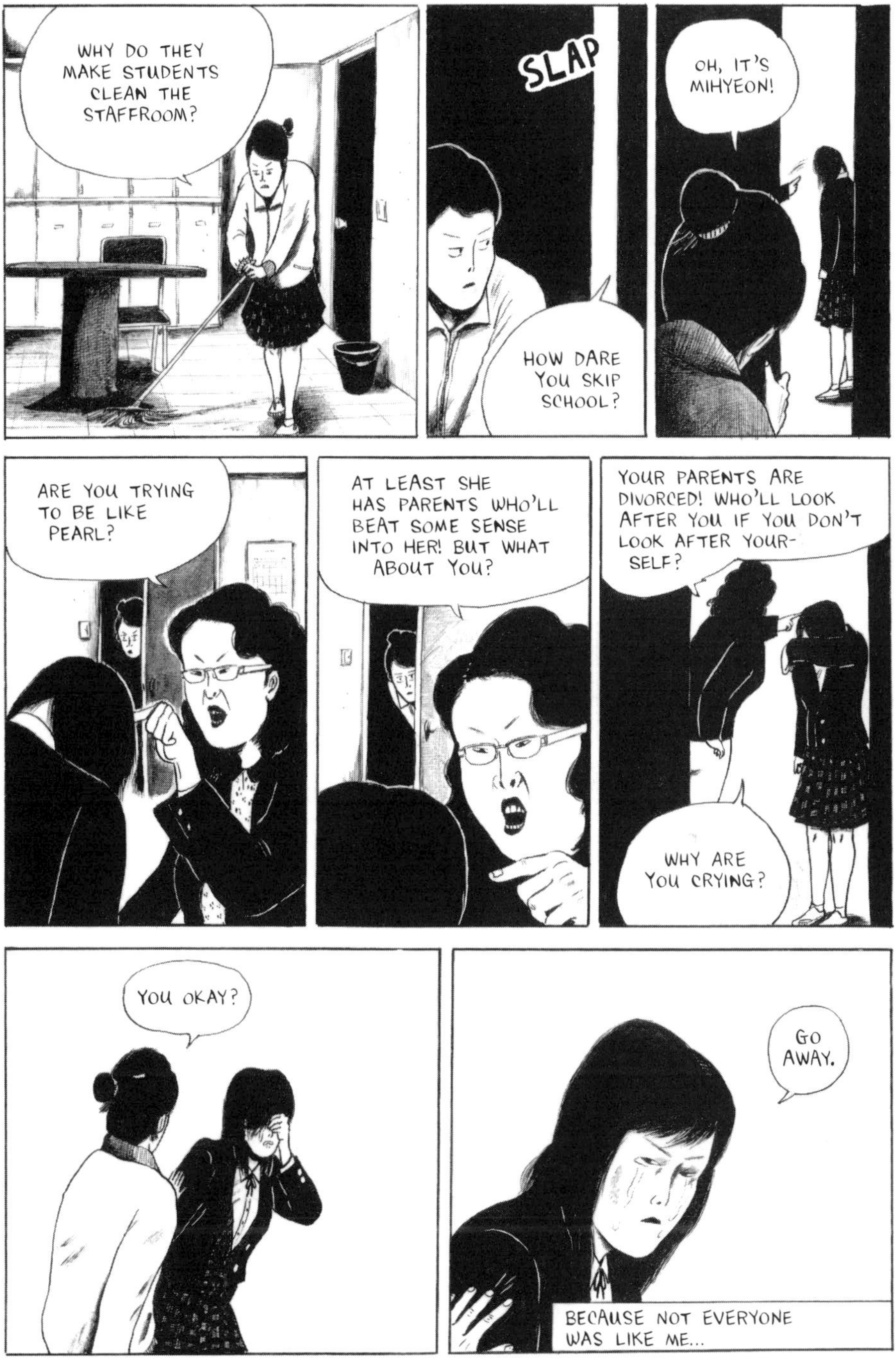
WHY DO THEY MAKE STUDENTS CLEAN THE STAFFROOM?
SLAP
HOW DARE YOU SKIP SCHOOL?
OH, IT'S MIHYEON!
ARE YOU TRYING TO BE LIKE PEARL?
AT LEAST SHE HAS PARENTS WHO'LL BEAT SOME SENSE INTO HER! BUT WHAT ABOUT YOU?
YOUR PARENTS ARE DIVORCED! WHO'LL LOOK AFTER YOU IF YOU DON'T LOOK AFTER YOURSELF?
WHY ARE YOU CRYING?
YOU OKAY?
GO AWAY.
BECAUSE NOT EVERYONE WAS LIKE ME...

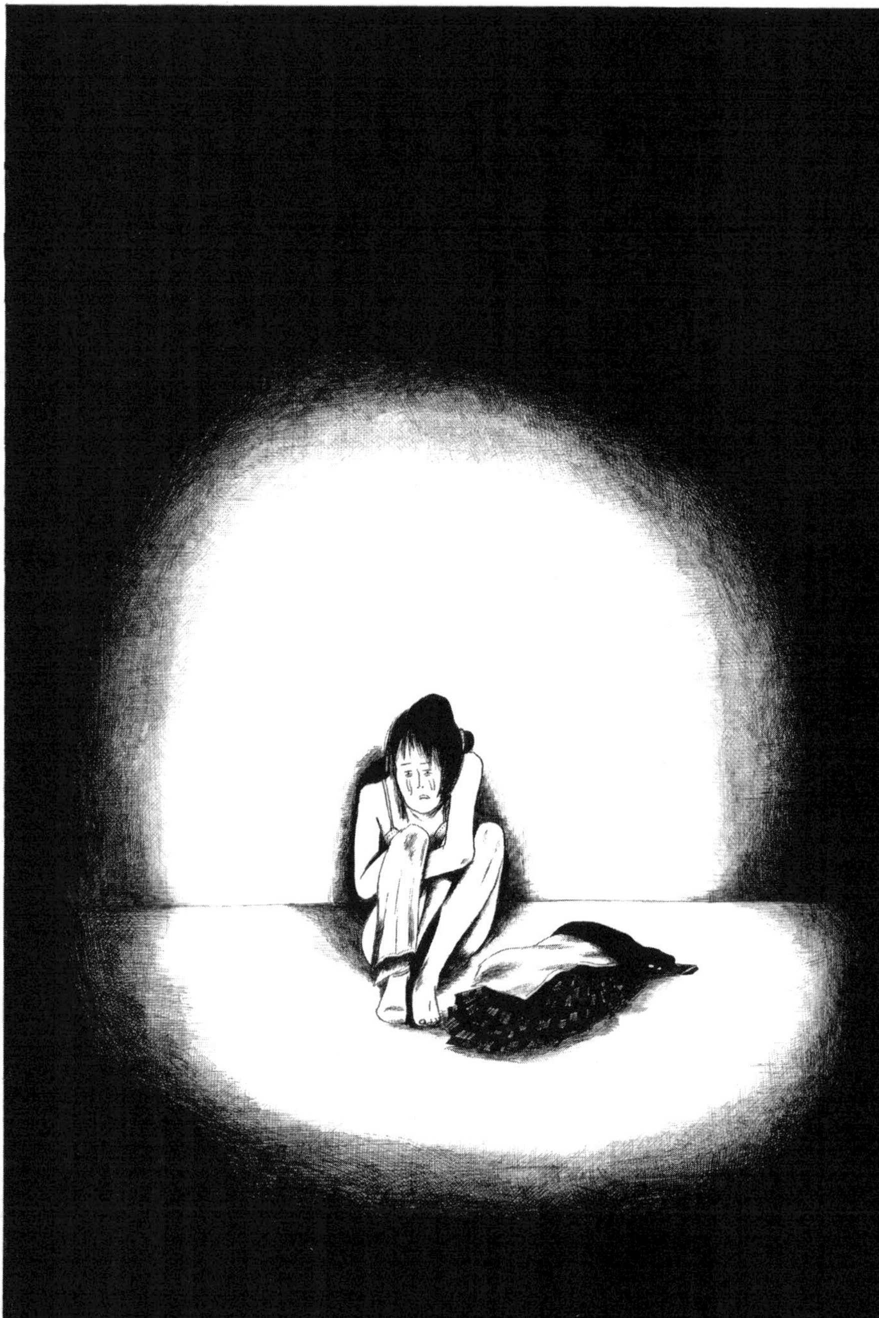

jeong-ae and me

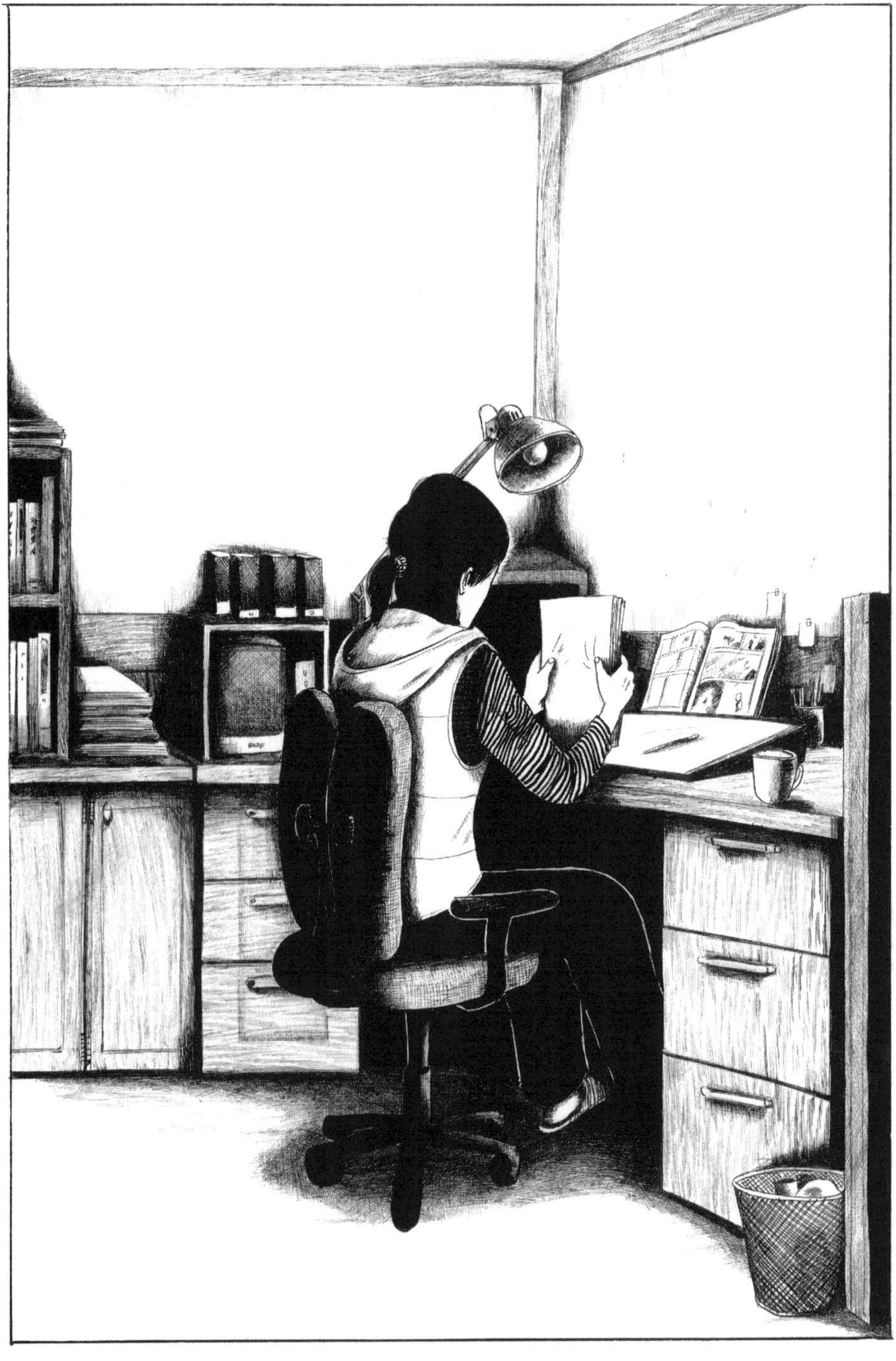

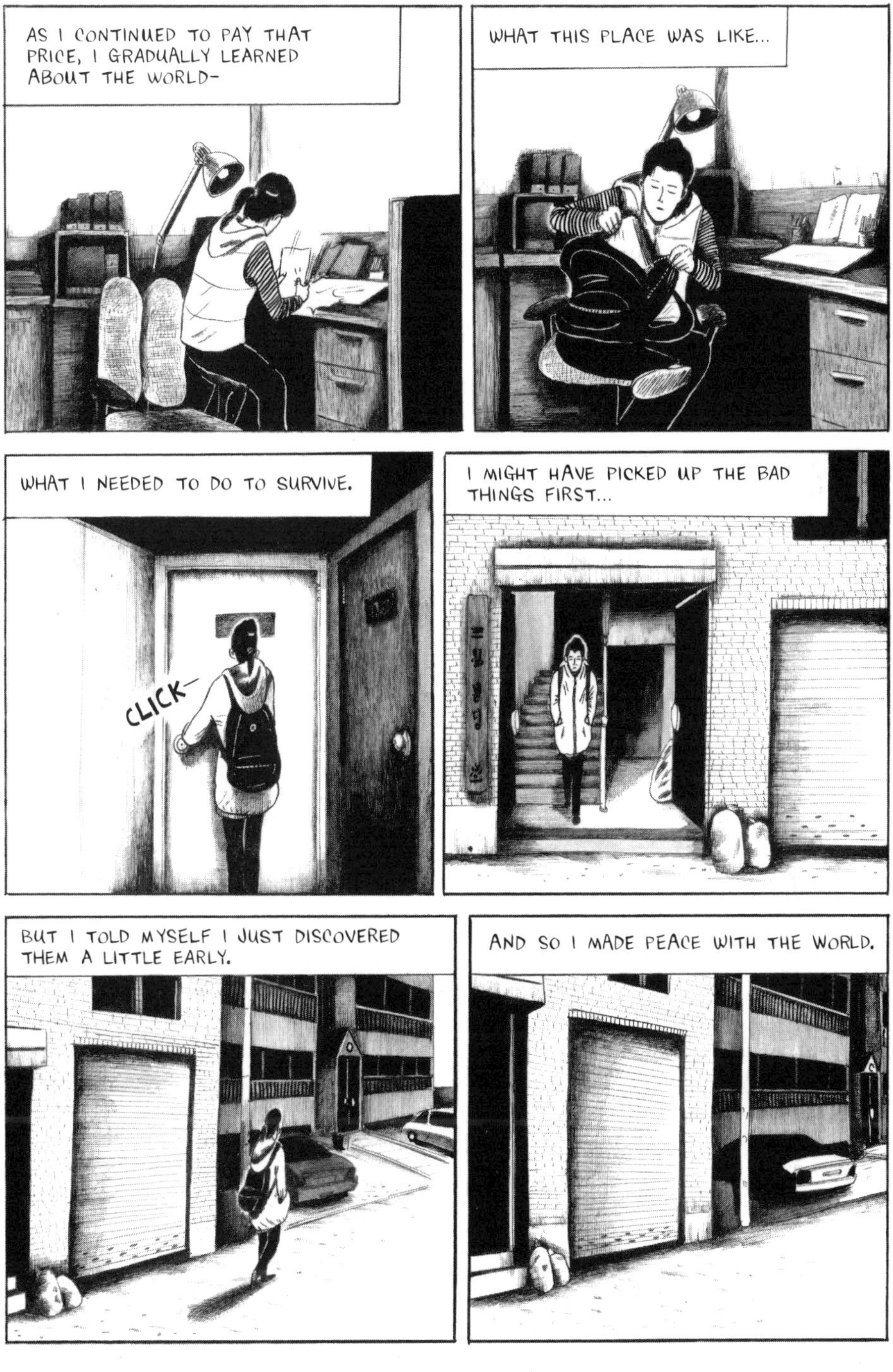
AS I CONTINUED TO PAY THAT PRICE, I GRADUALLY LEARNED ABOUT THE WORLD-
WHAT THIS PLACE WAS LIKE...
WHAT I NEEDED TO DO TO SURVIVE.
CLICK-
I MIGHT HAVE PICKED UP THE BAD THINGS FIRST...
BUT I TOLD MYSELF I JUST DISCOVERED THEM A LITTLE EARLY.
AND SO I MADE PEACE WITH THE WORLD.

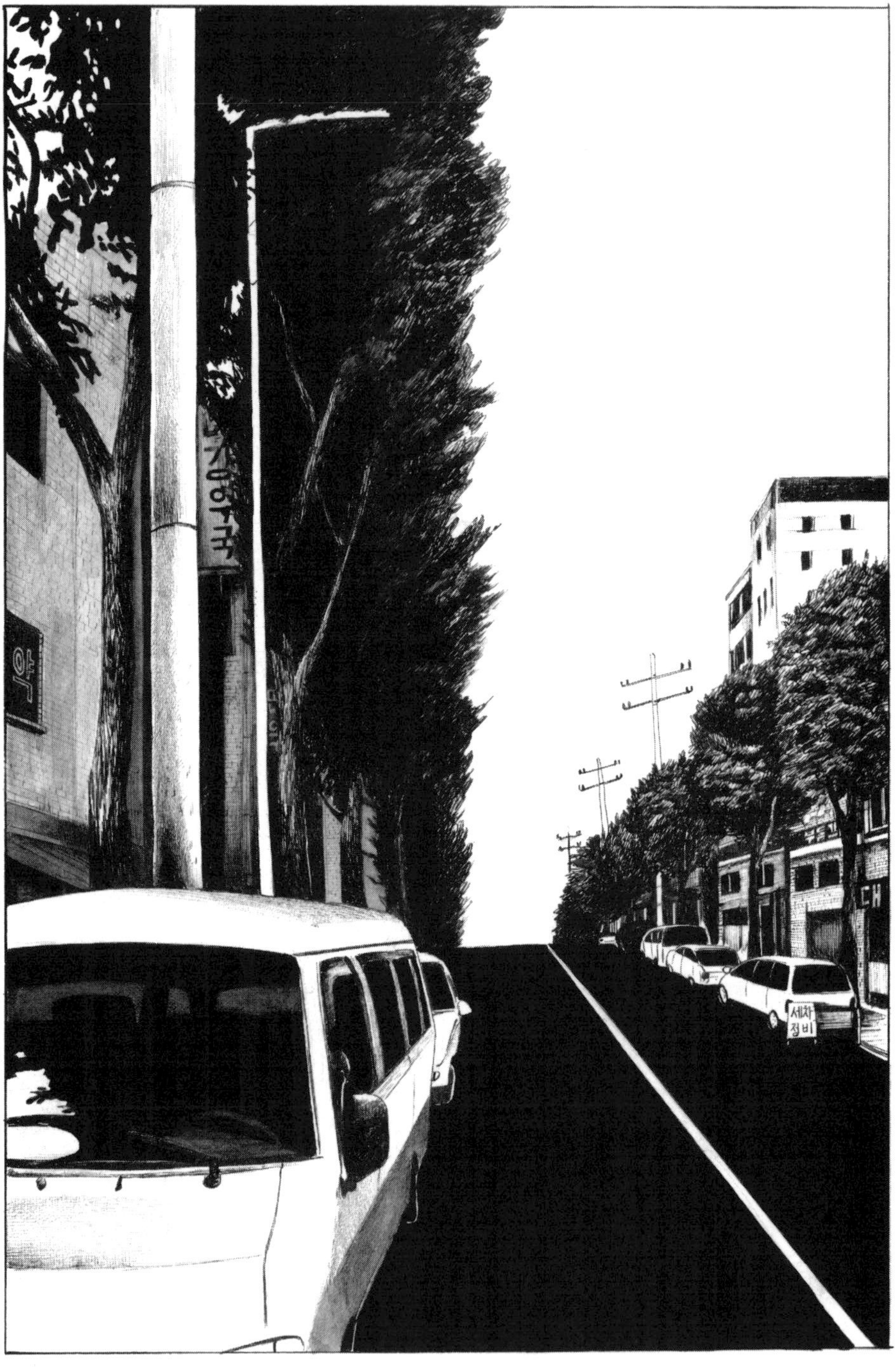
약
세차
정비

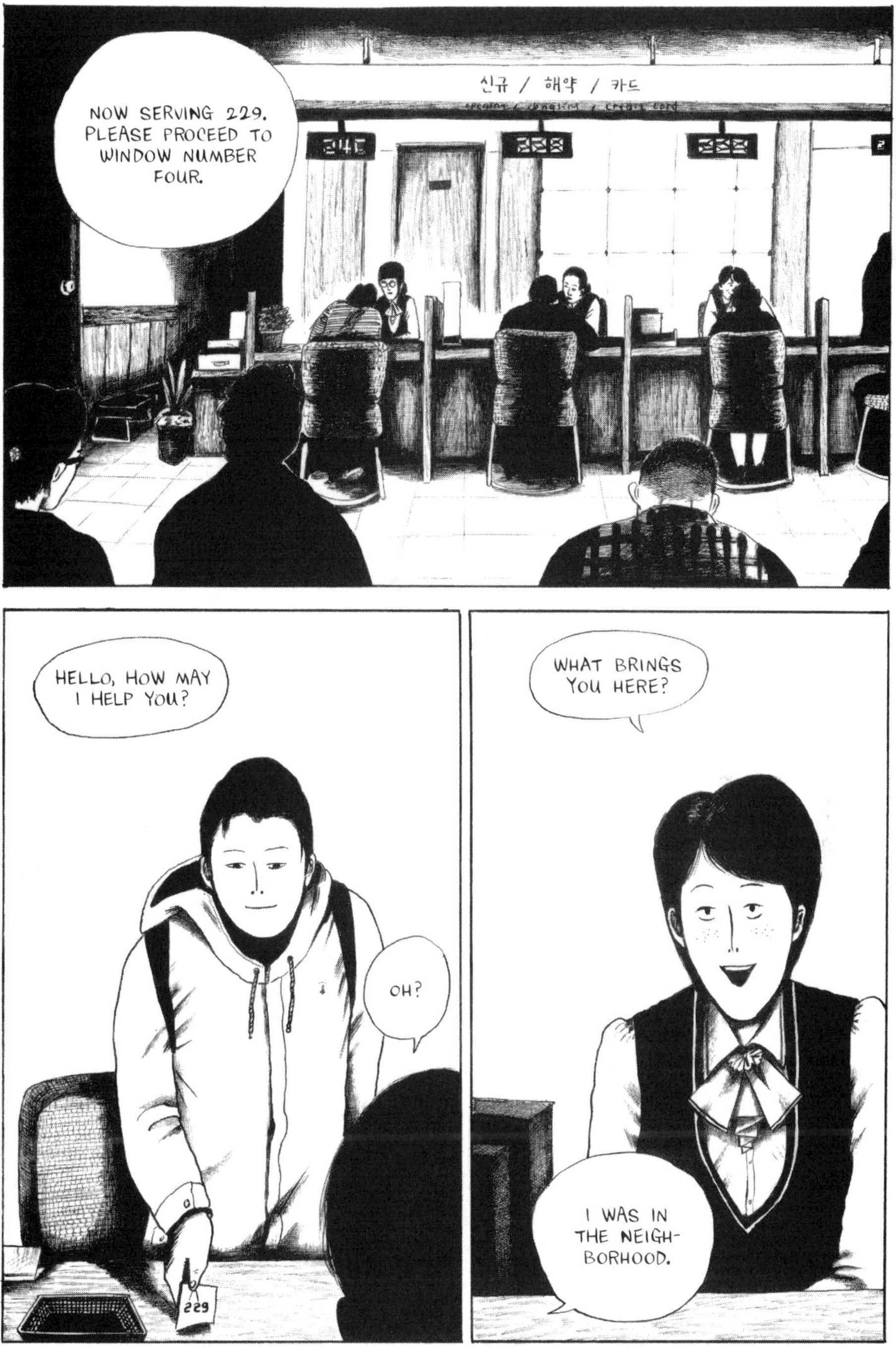
신규 / 해약 / 카드
NOW SERVING 229. PLEASE PROCEED TO WINDOW NUMBER FOUR.
HELLO, HOW MAY I HELP YOU?
OH?
229
WHAT BRINGS YOU HERE?
I WAS IN THE NEIGH-BORHOOD.

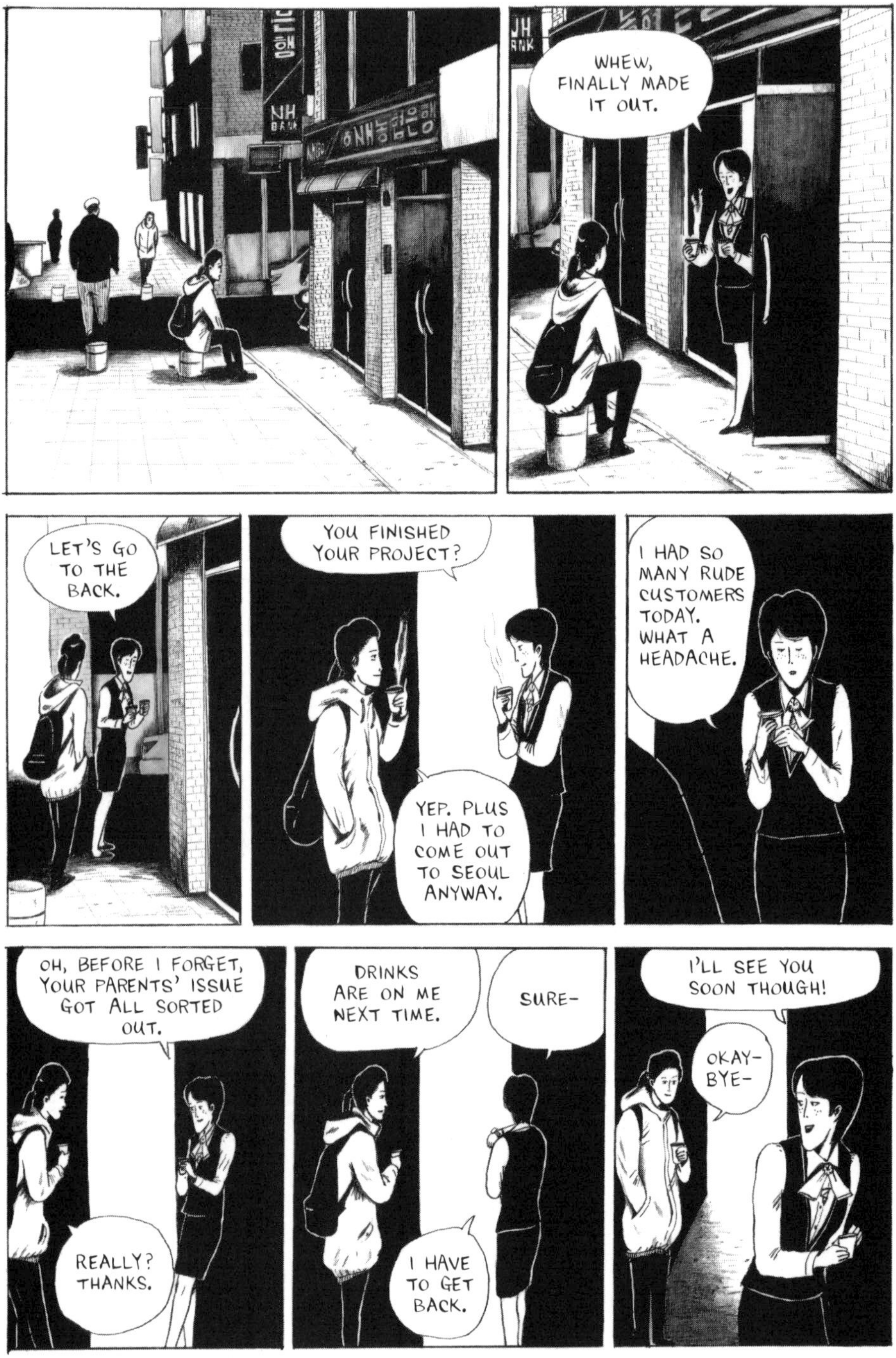
WHEW, FINALLY MADE IT OUT.
LET'S GO TO THE BACK.
YOU FINISHED YOUR PROJECT?
YEP. PLUS I HAD TO COME OUT TO SEOUL ANYWAY.
I HAD SO MANY RUDE CUSTOMERS TODAY. WHAT A HEADACHE.
OH, BEFORE I FORGET, YOUR PARENTS' ISSUE GOT ALL SORTED OUT.
REALLY? THANKS.
DRINKS ARE ON ME NEXT TIME.
SURE-
I HAVE TO GET BACK.
I'LL SEE YOU SOON THOUGH!
OKAY-BYE-

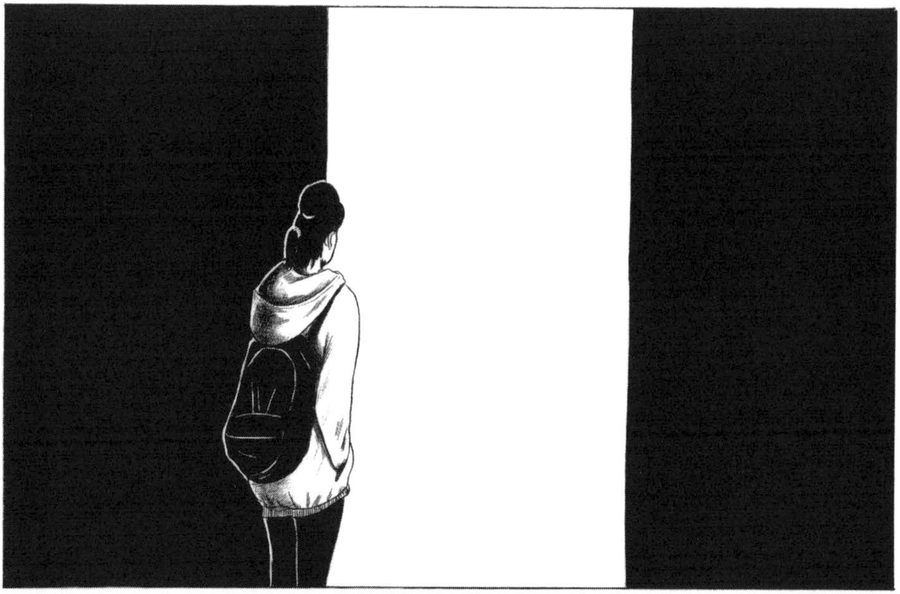

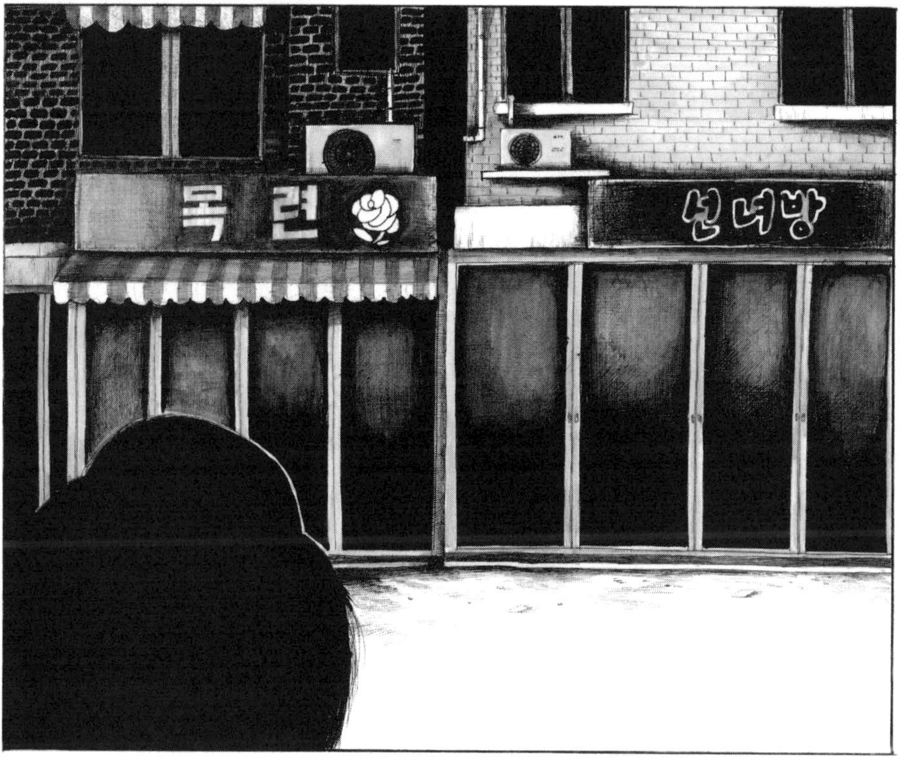
목련
선녀방

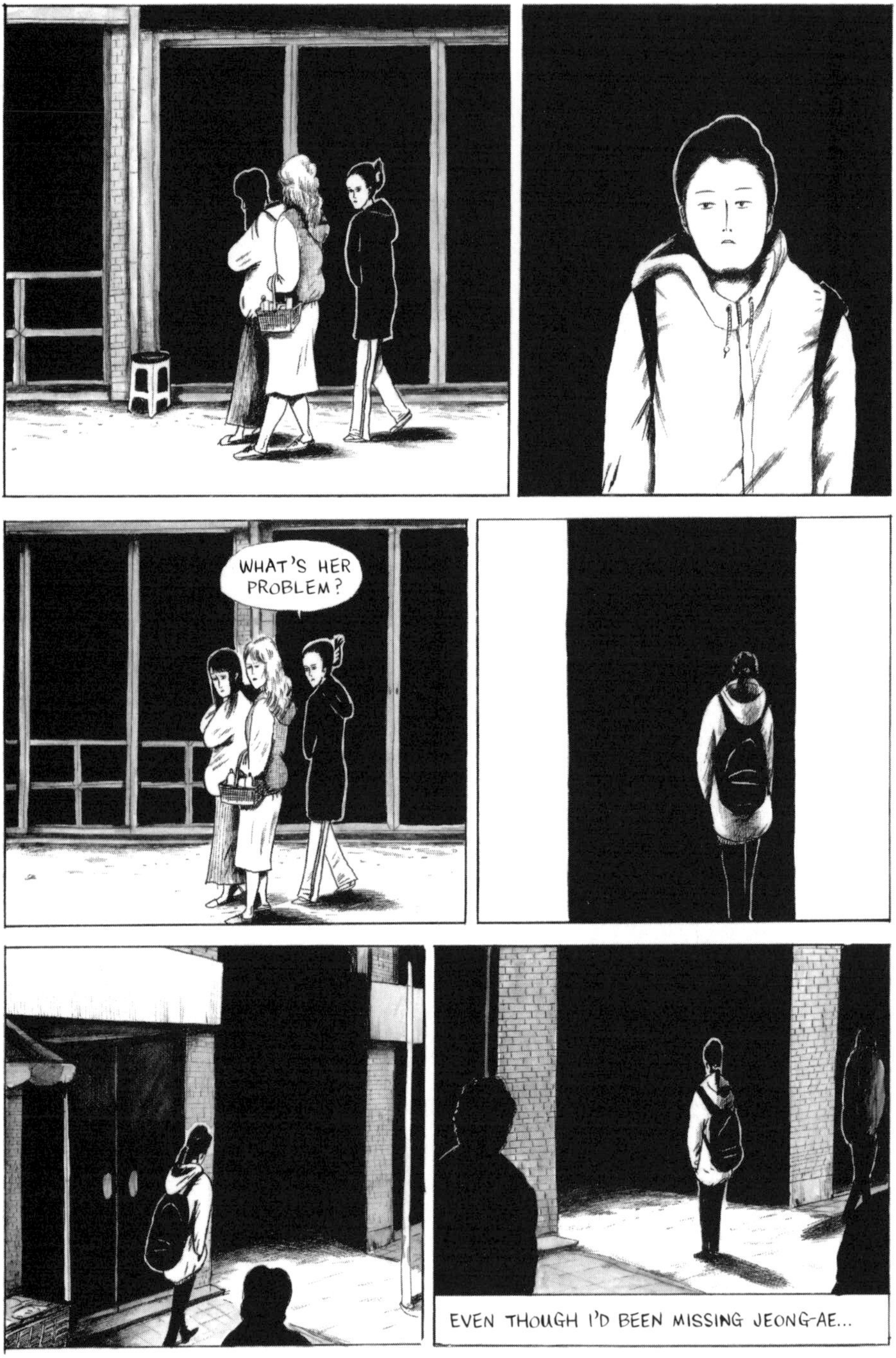
WHAT'S HER PROBLEM?
EVEN THOUGH I'D BEEN MISSING JEONG-AE...

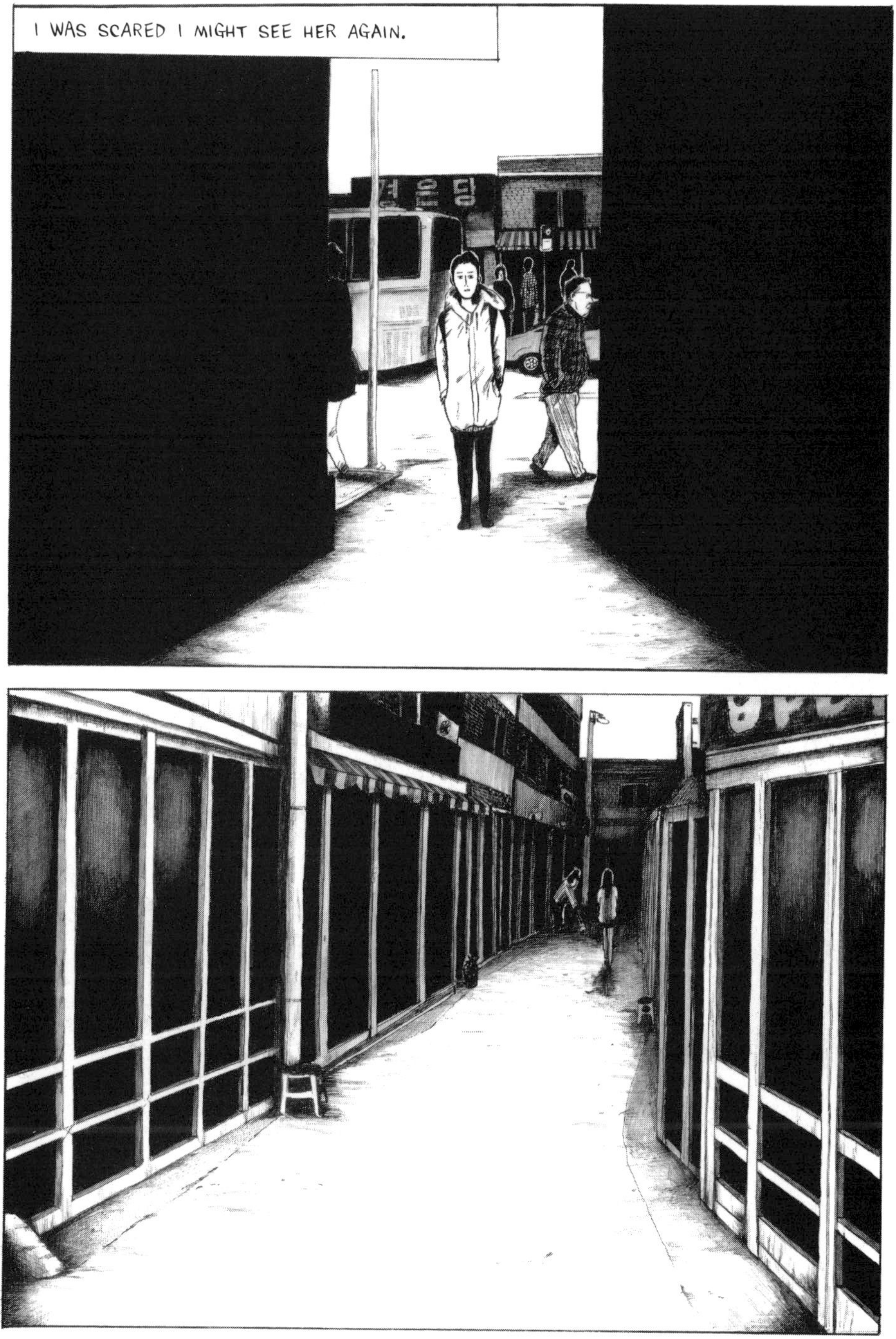
I WAS SCARED I MIGHT SEE HER AGAIN.

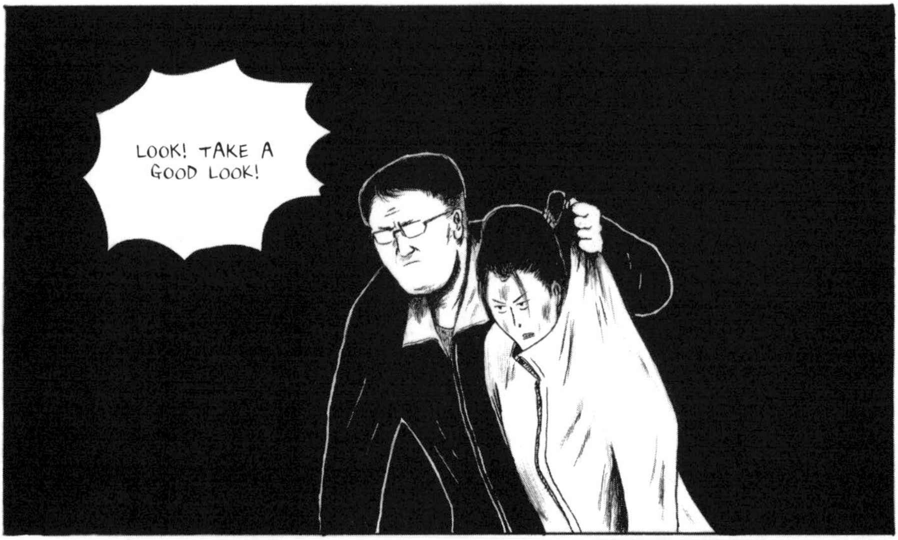
LOOK! TAKE A GOOD LOOK!

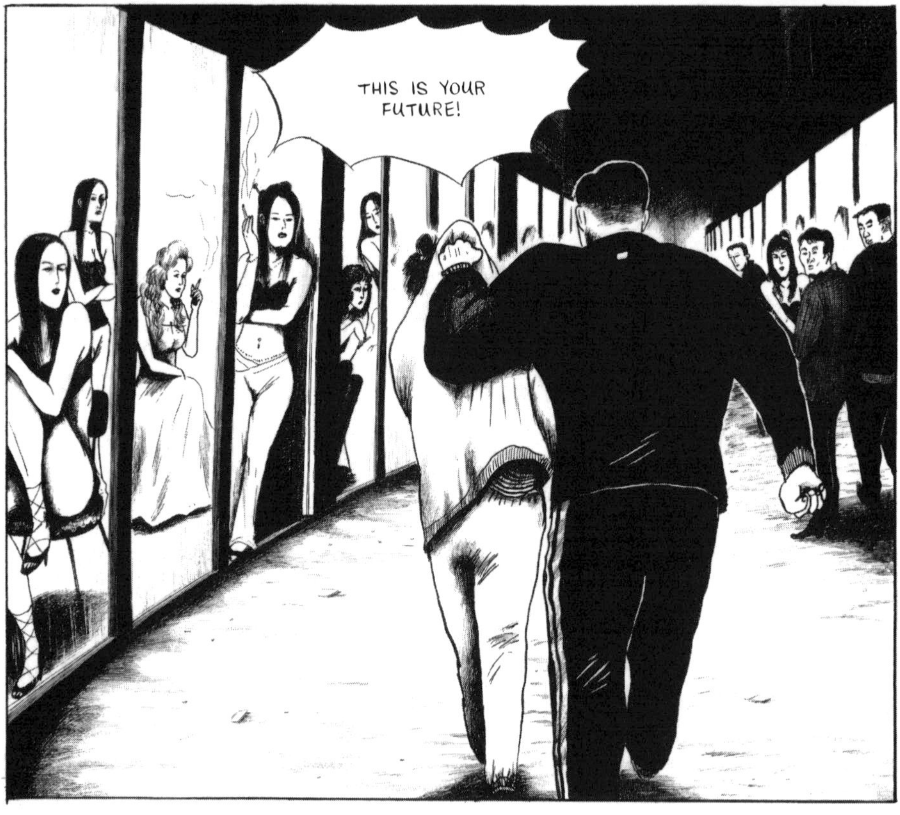
THIS IS YOUR FUTURE!

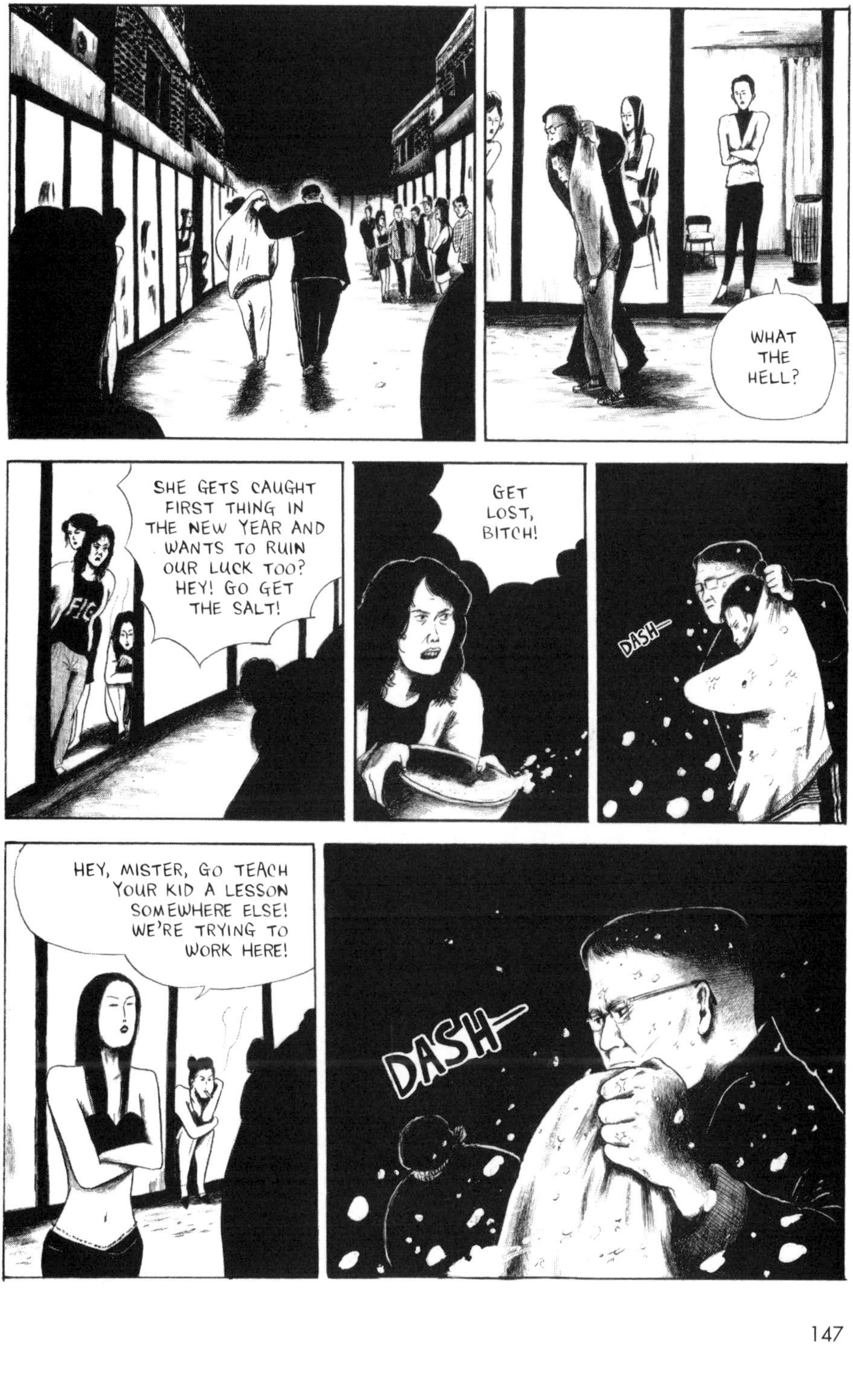
WHAT THE HELL?
SHE GETS CAUGHT FIRST THING IN THE NEW YEAR AND WANTS TO RUIN OUR LUCK TOO? HEY! GO GET THE SALT!
GET LOST, BITCH!
DASH—
HEY, MISTER, GO TEACH YOUR KID A LESSON SOMEWHERE ELSE! WE'RE TRYING TO WORK HERE!
DASH—

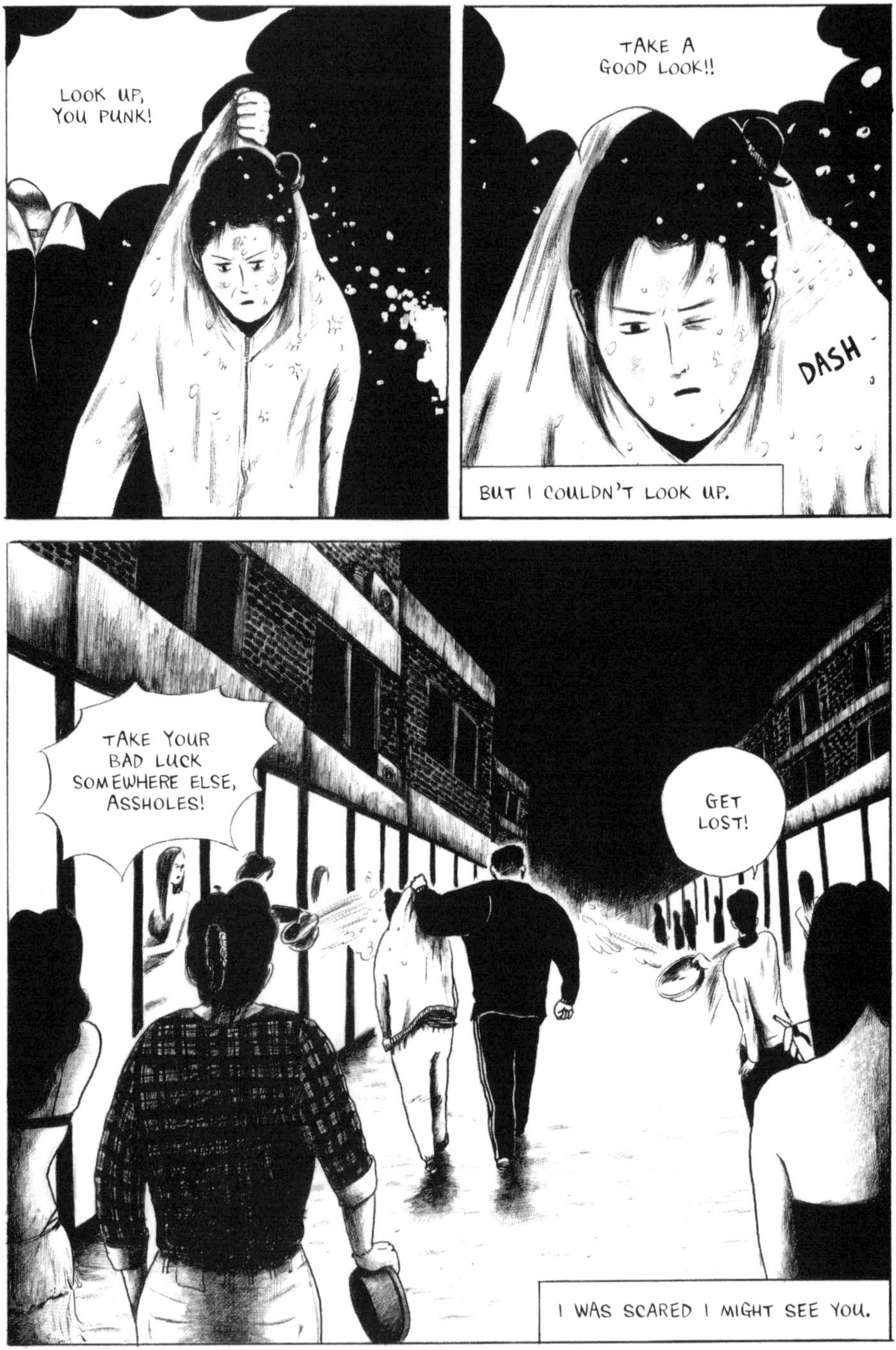
LOOK UP, YOU PUNK!
TAKE A GOOD LOOK!!
DASH
BUT I COULDN'T LOOK UP.
TAKE YOUR BAD LUCK SOMEWHERE ELSE, ASSHOLES!
GET LOST!
I WAS SCARED I MIGHT SEE YOU.

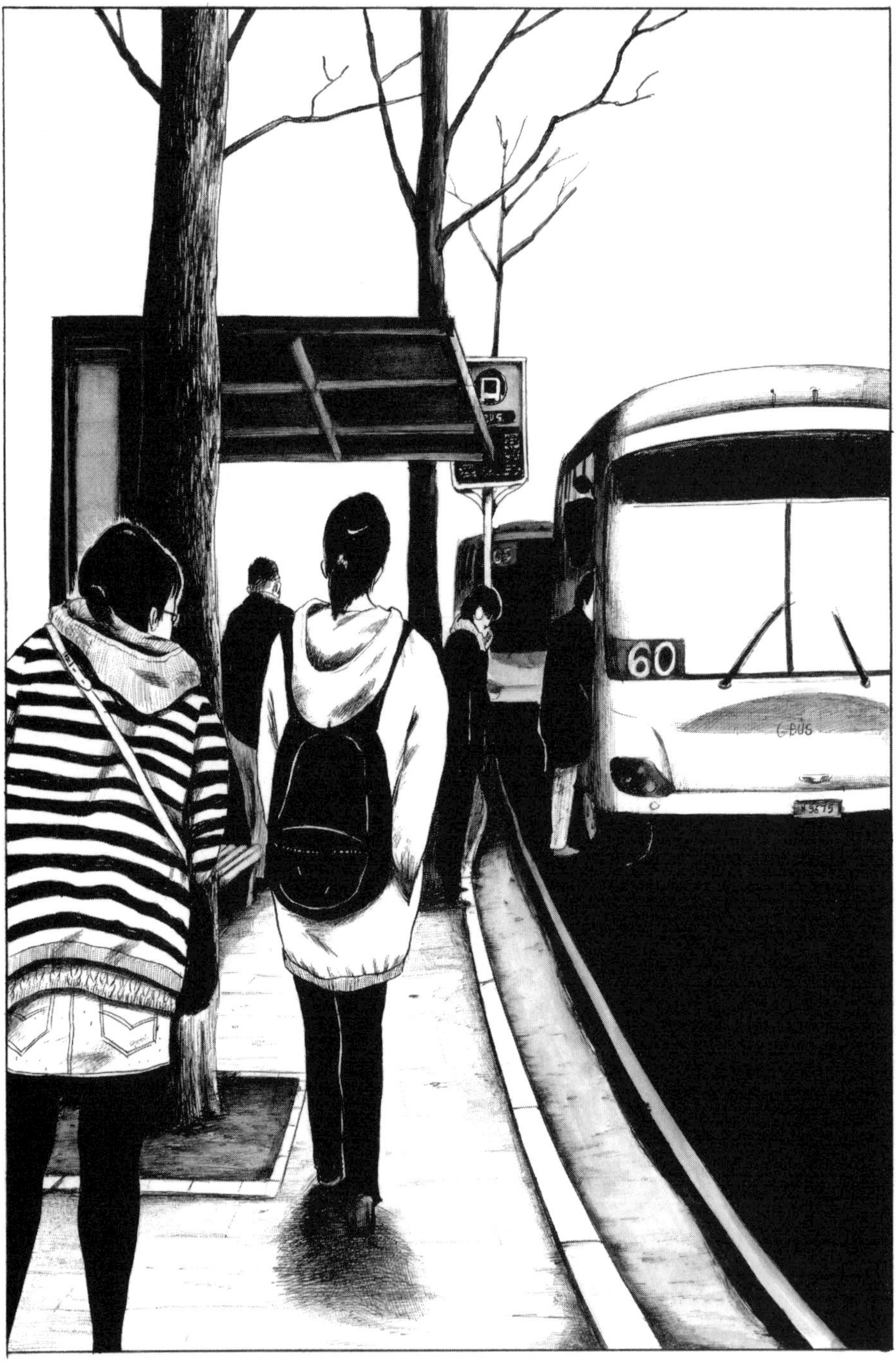
60

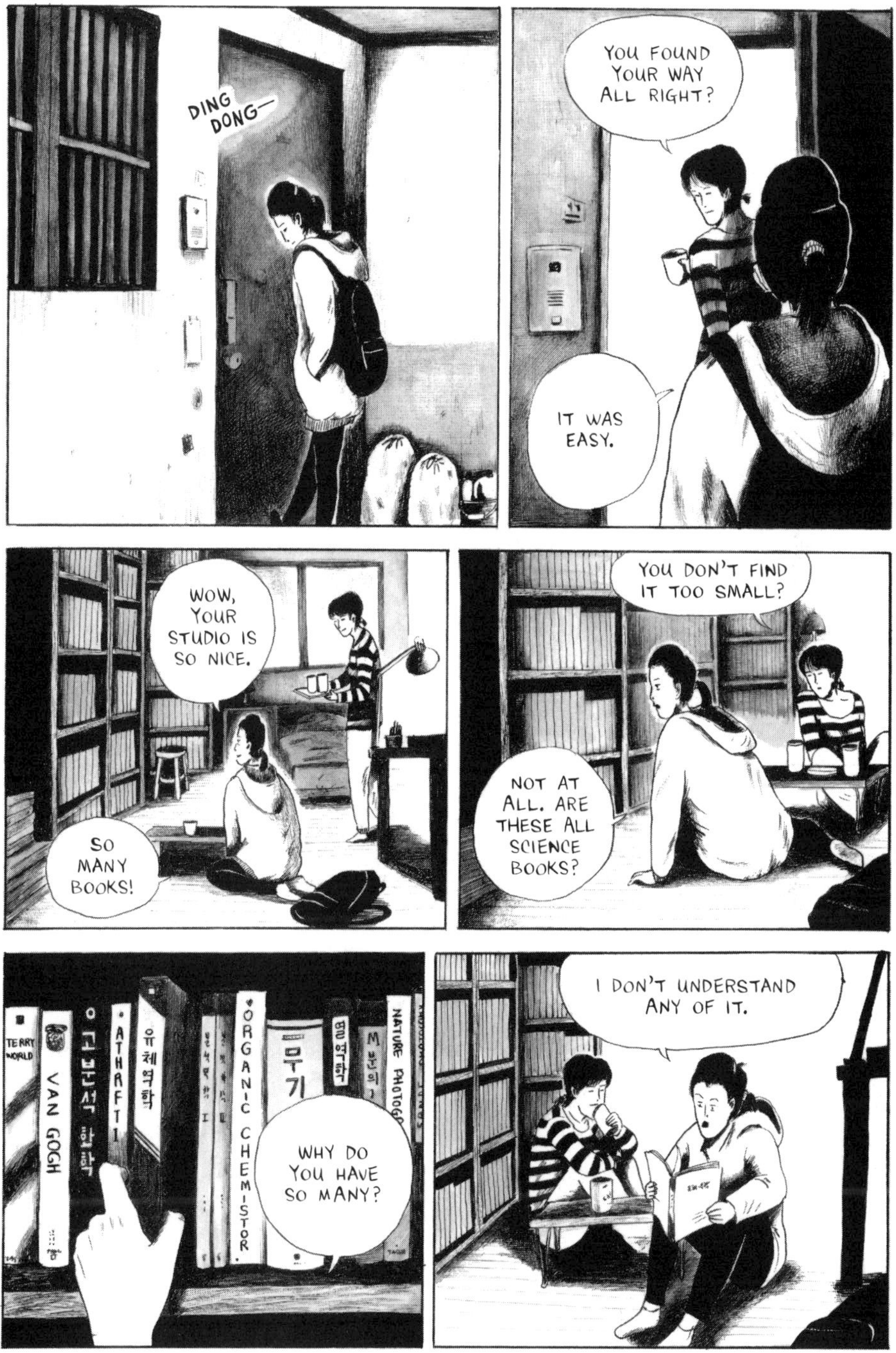
DING DONG—
YOU FOUND YOUR WAY ALL RIGHT?
IT WAS EASY.
WOW, YOUR STUDIO IS SO NICE.
SO MANY BOOKS!
YOU DON'T FIND IT TOO SMALL?
NOT AT ALL. ARE THESE ALL SCIENCE BOOKS?
VAN GOGH
유체역학
ORGANIC CHEMISTOR
무기
WHY DO YOU HAVE SO MANY?
I DON'T UNDERSTAND ANY OF IT.

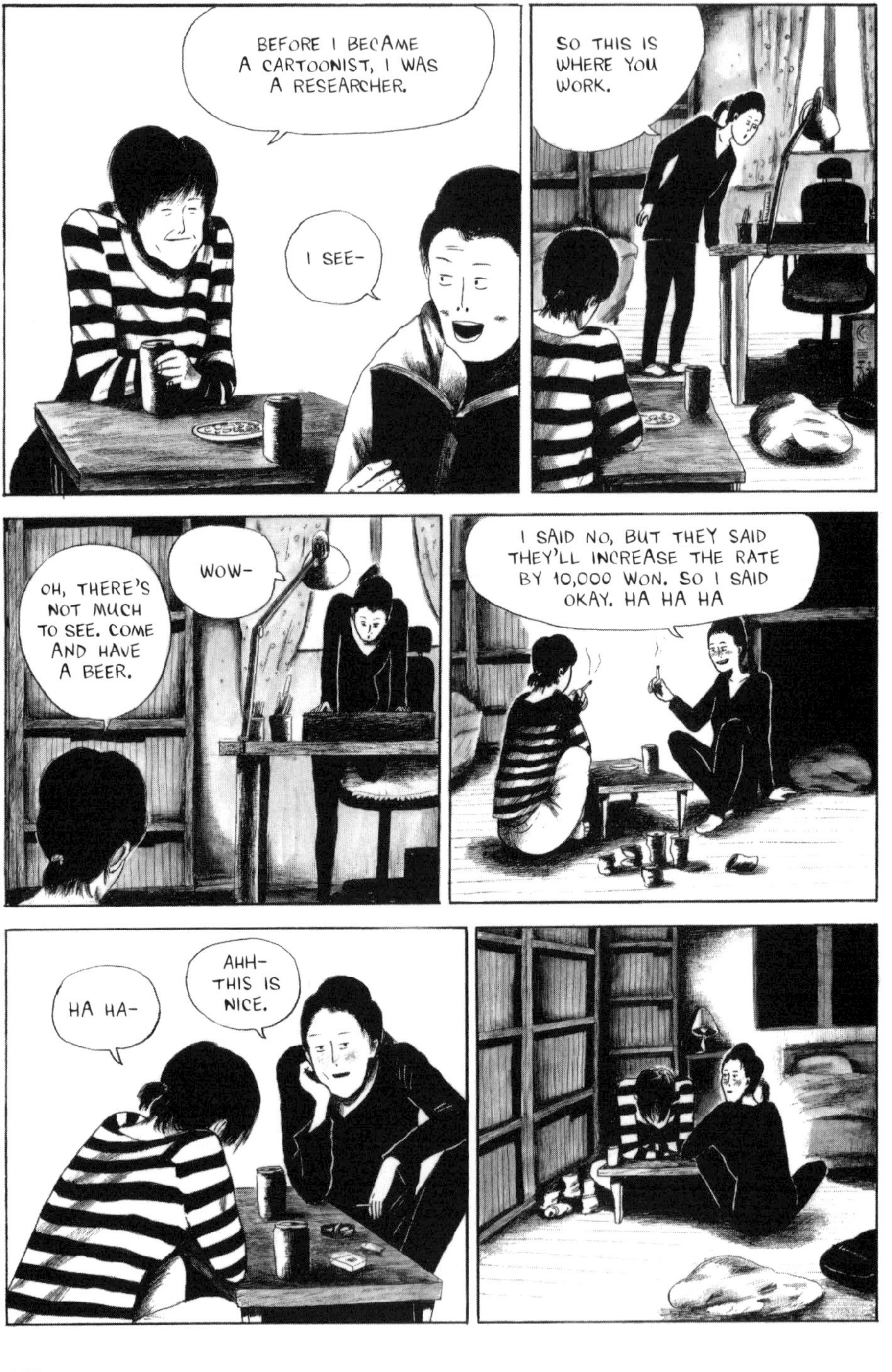
BEFORE I BECAME A CARTOONIST, I WAS A RESEARCHER.
I SEE-
SO THIS IS WHERE YOU WORK.
WOW-
OH, THERE'S NOT MUCH TO SEE. COME AND HAVE A BEER.
I SAID NO, BUT THEY SAID THEY'LL INCREASE THE RATE BY 10,000 WON. SO I SAID OKAY. HA HA HA
AHH- THIS IS NICE.
HA HA-

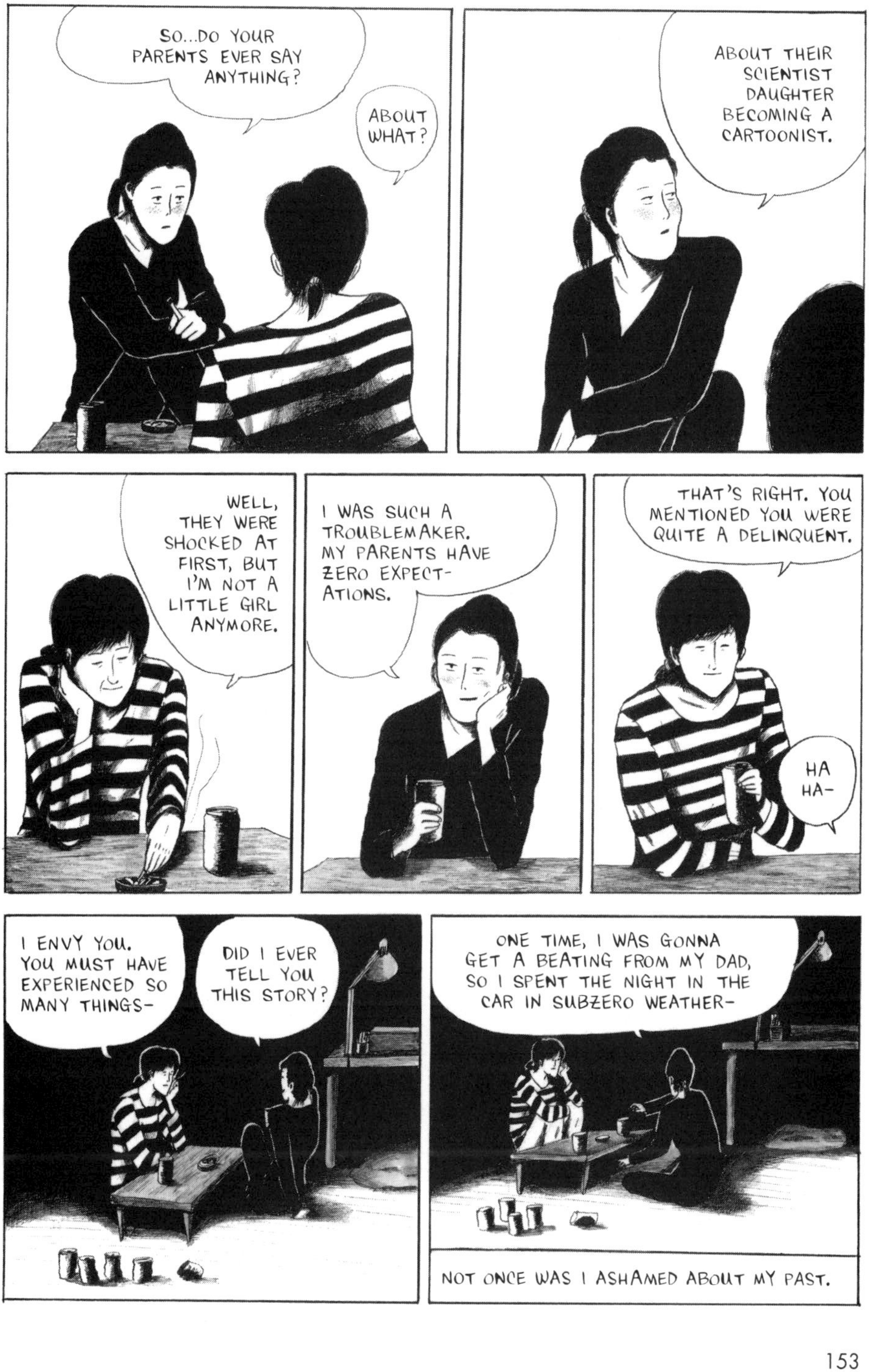
SO...DO YOUR PARENTS EVER SAY ANYTHING?
ABOUT WHAT?
ABOUT THEIR SCIENTIST DAUGHTER BECOMING A CARTOONIST.
WELL, THEY WERE SHOCKED AT FIRST, BUT I'M NOT A LITTLE GIRL ANYMORE.
I WAS SUCH A TROUBLEMAKER. MY PARENTS HAVE ZERO EXPECT-ATIONS.
THAT'S RIGHT. YOU MENTIONED YOU WERE QUITE A DELINQUENT.
HA HA-
I ENVY YOU. YOU MUST HAVE EXPERIENCED SO MANY THINGS-
DID I EVER TELL YOU THIS STORY?
ONE TIME, I WAS GONNA GET A BEATING FROM MY DAD, SO I SPENT THE NIGHT IN THE CAR IN SUBZERO WEATHER-
NOT ONCE WAS I ASHAMED ABOUT MY PAST.

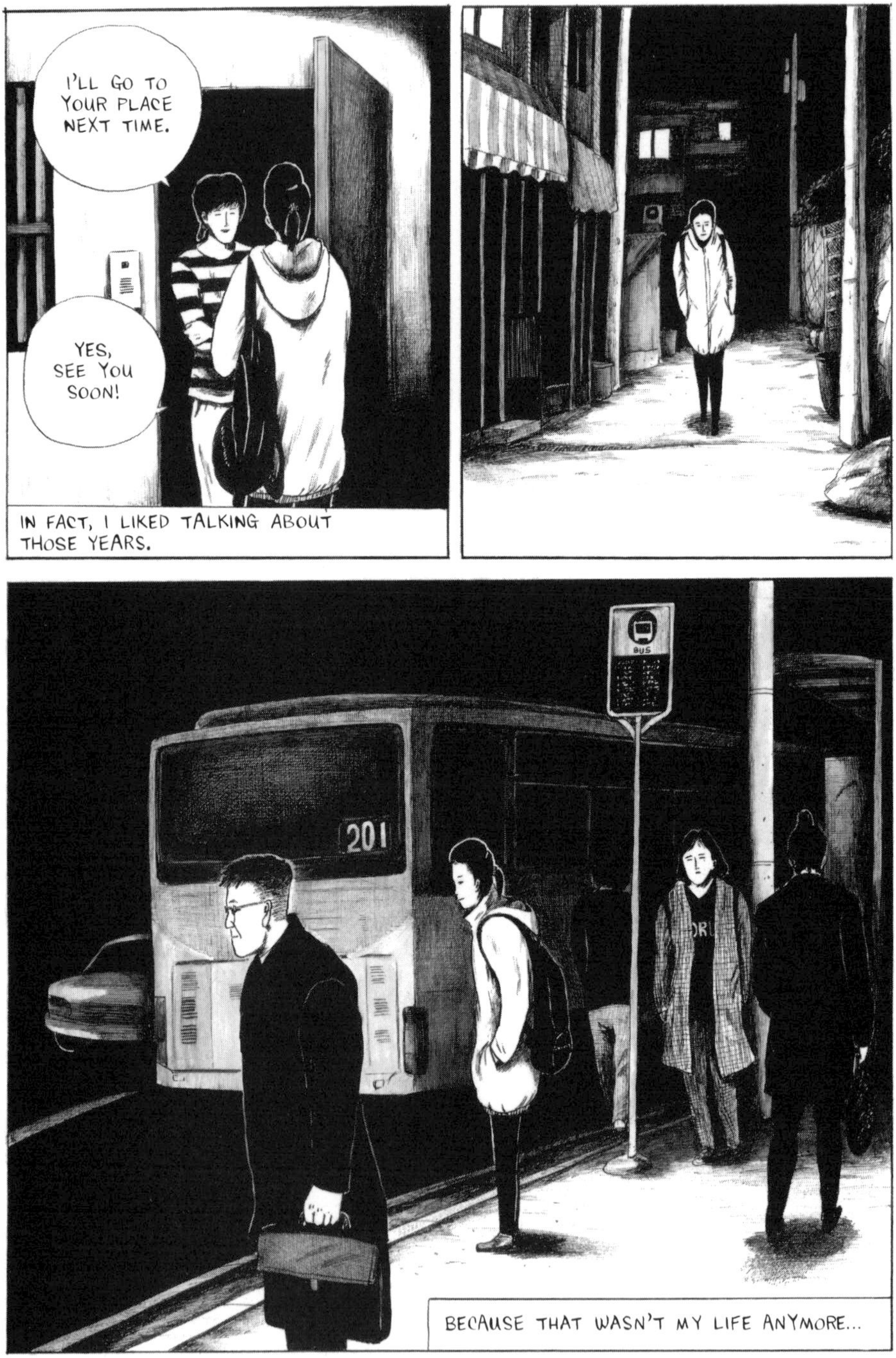
I'LL GO TO YOUR PLACE NEXT TIME.
YES, SEE YOU SOON!
IN FACT, I LIKED TALKING ABOUT THOSE YEARS.
201
BECAUSE THAT WASN'T MY LIFE ANYMORE...

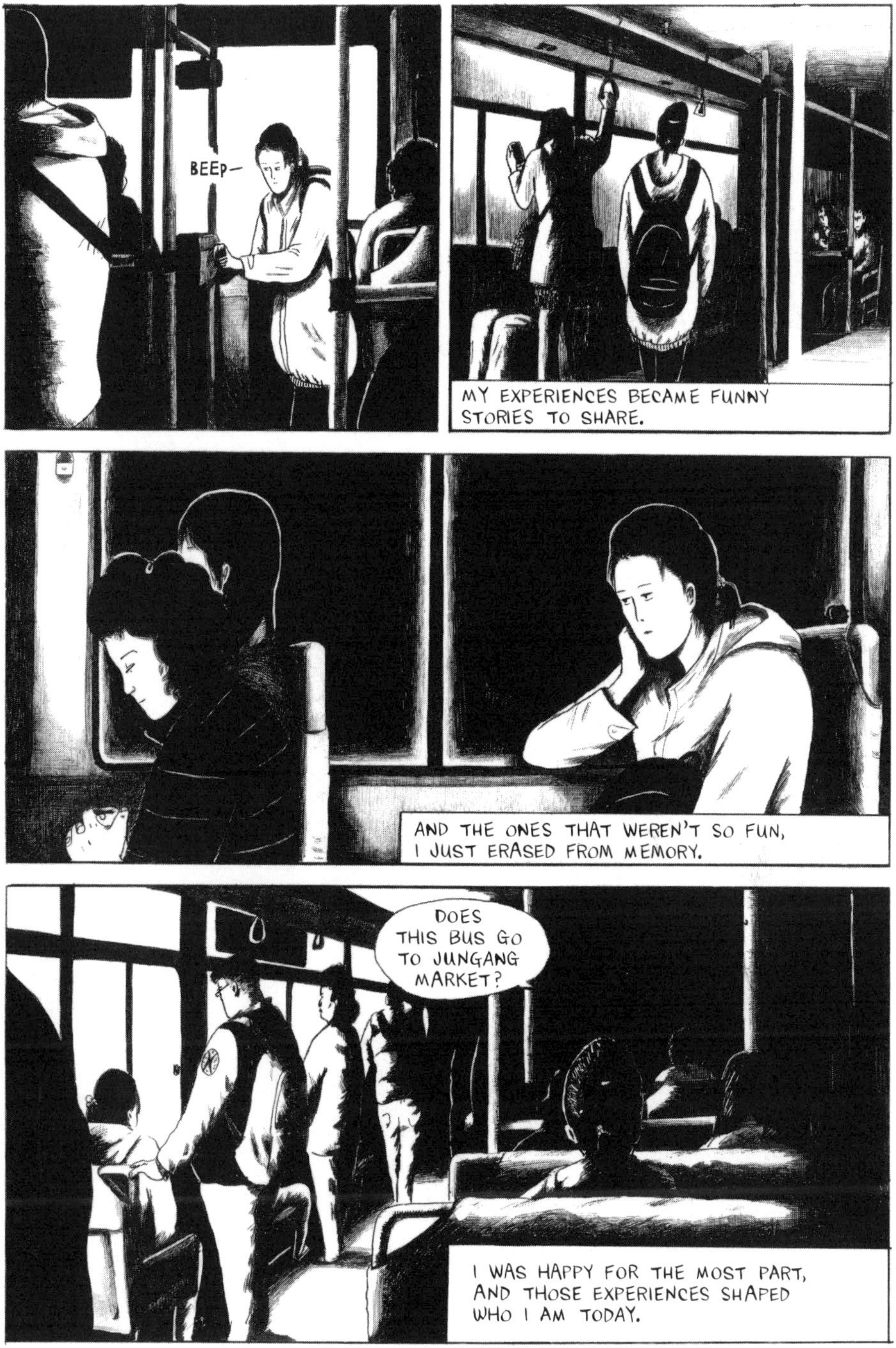
BEEP—
MY EXPERIENCES BECAME FUNNY STORIES TO SHARE.
AND THE ONES THAT WEREN'T SO FUN, I JUST ERASED FROM MEMORY.
DOES THIS BUS GO TO JUNGANG MARKET?
I WAS HAPPY FOR THE MOST PART, AND THOSE EXPERIENCES SHAPED WHO I AM TODAY.

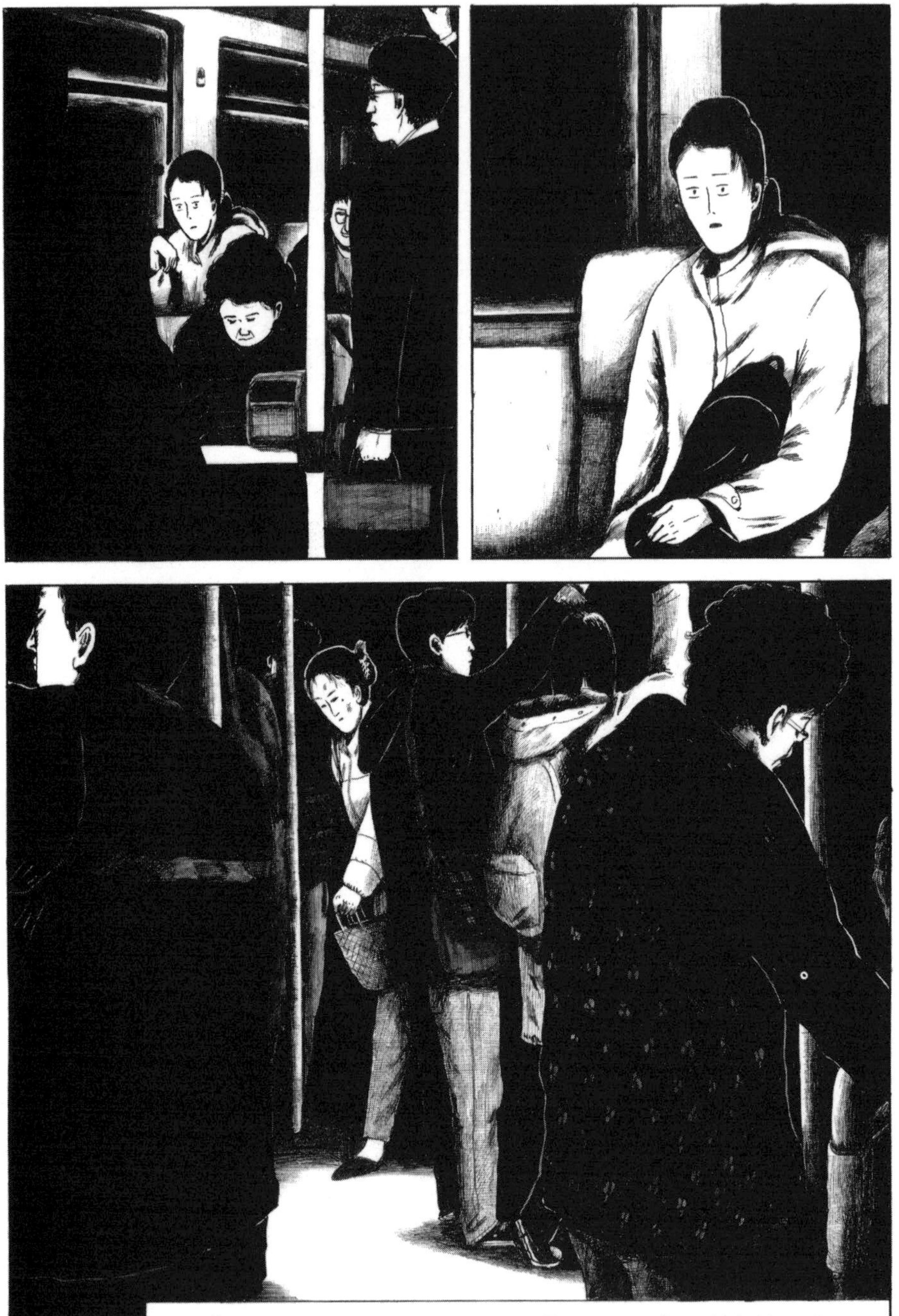
THAT'S WHY WHEN I SAW YOU THAT DAY, I COULDN'T SAY ANYTHING.

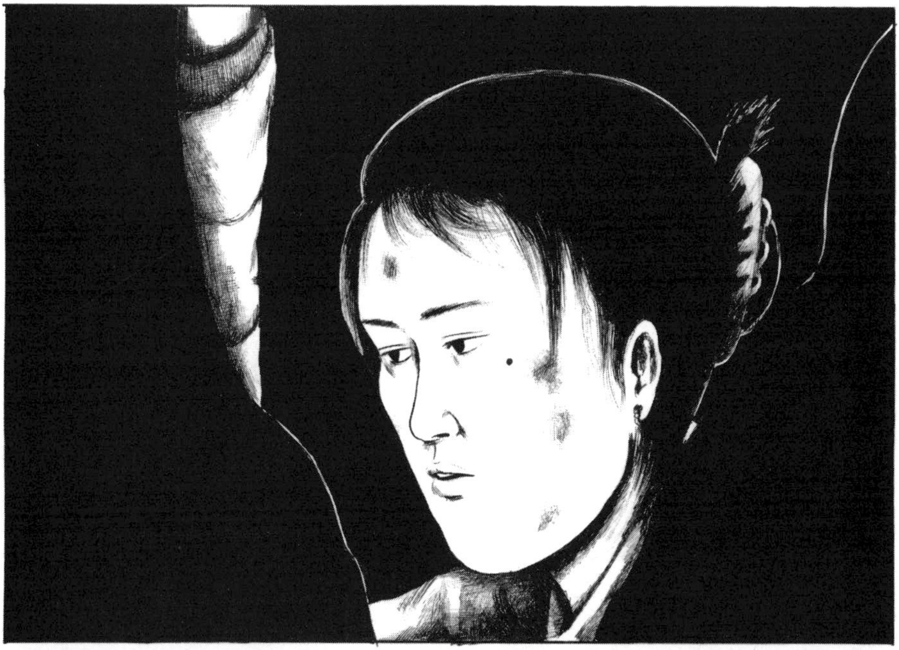

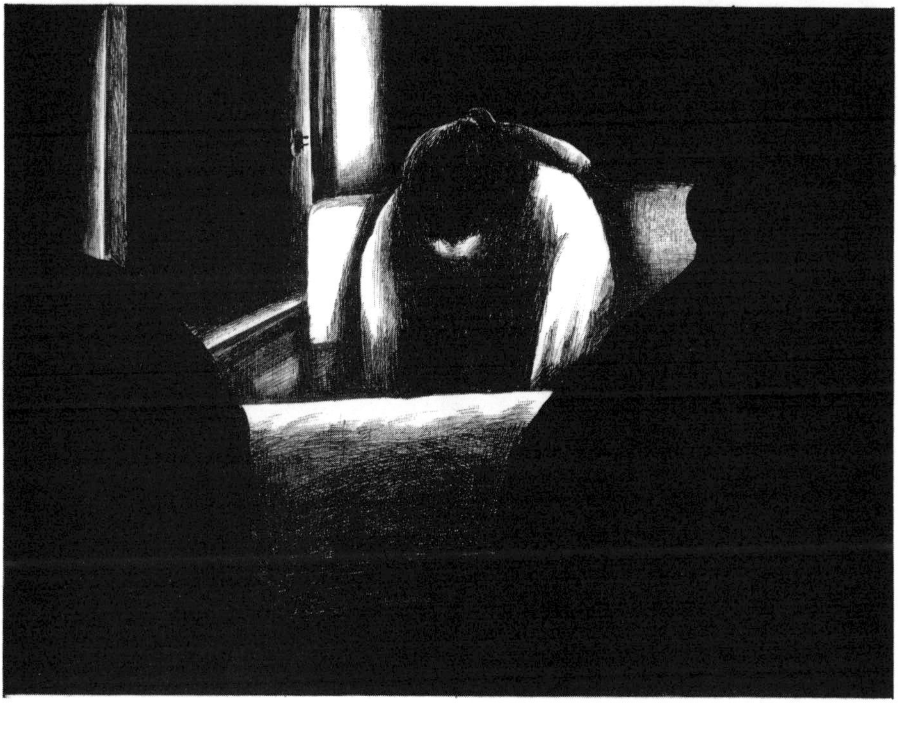

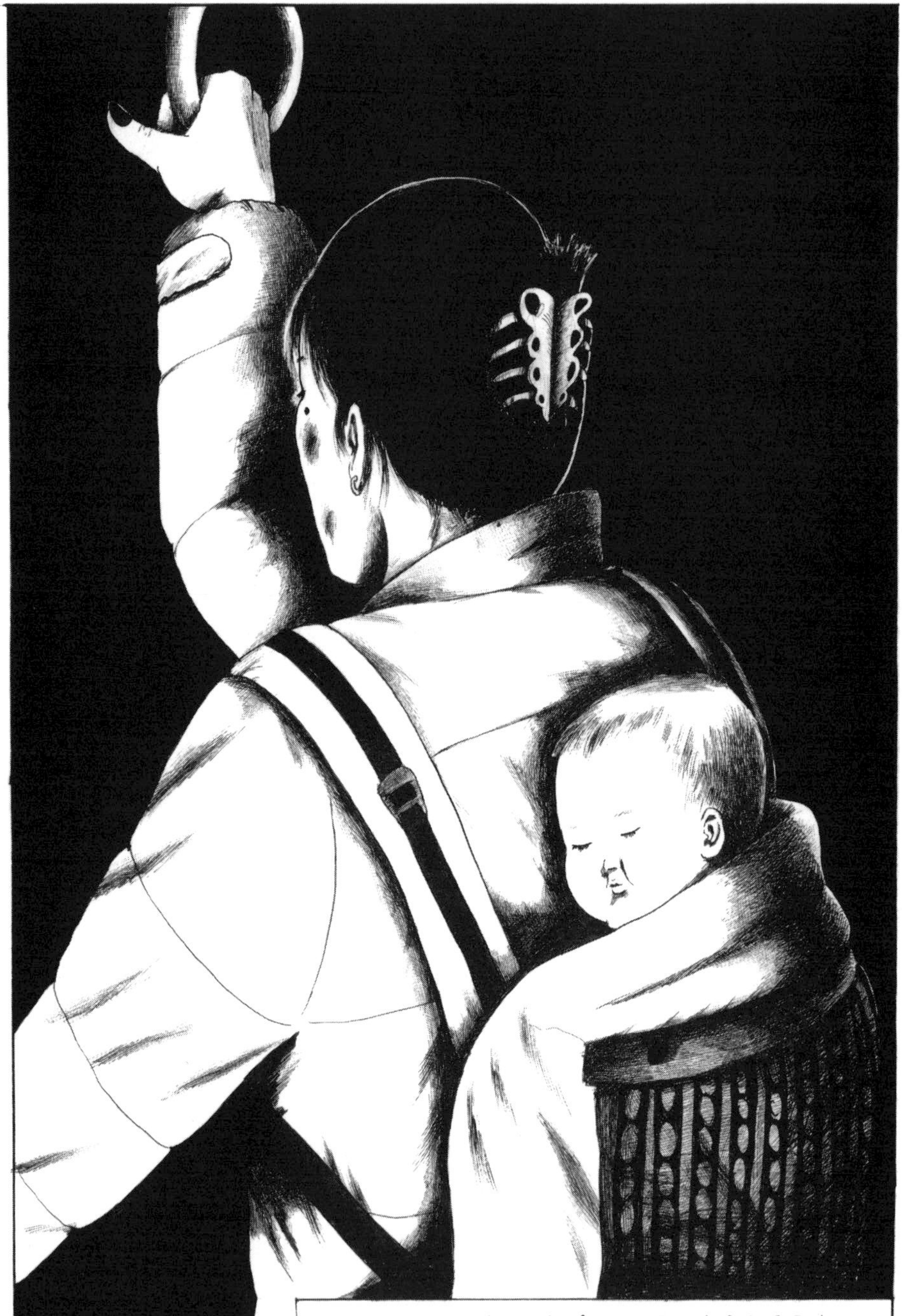
I FELT SICK TO SEE LIFE HAD NEVER CHANGED FOR YOU.

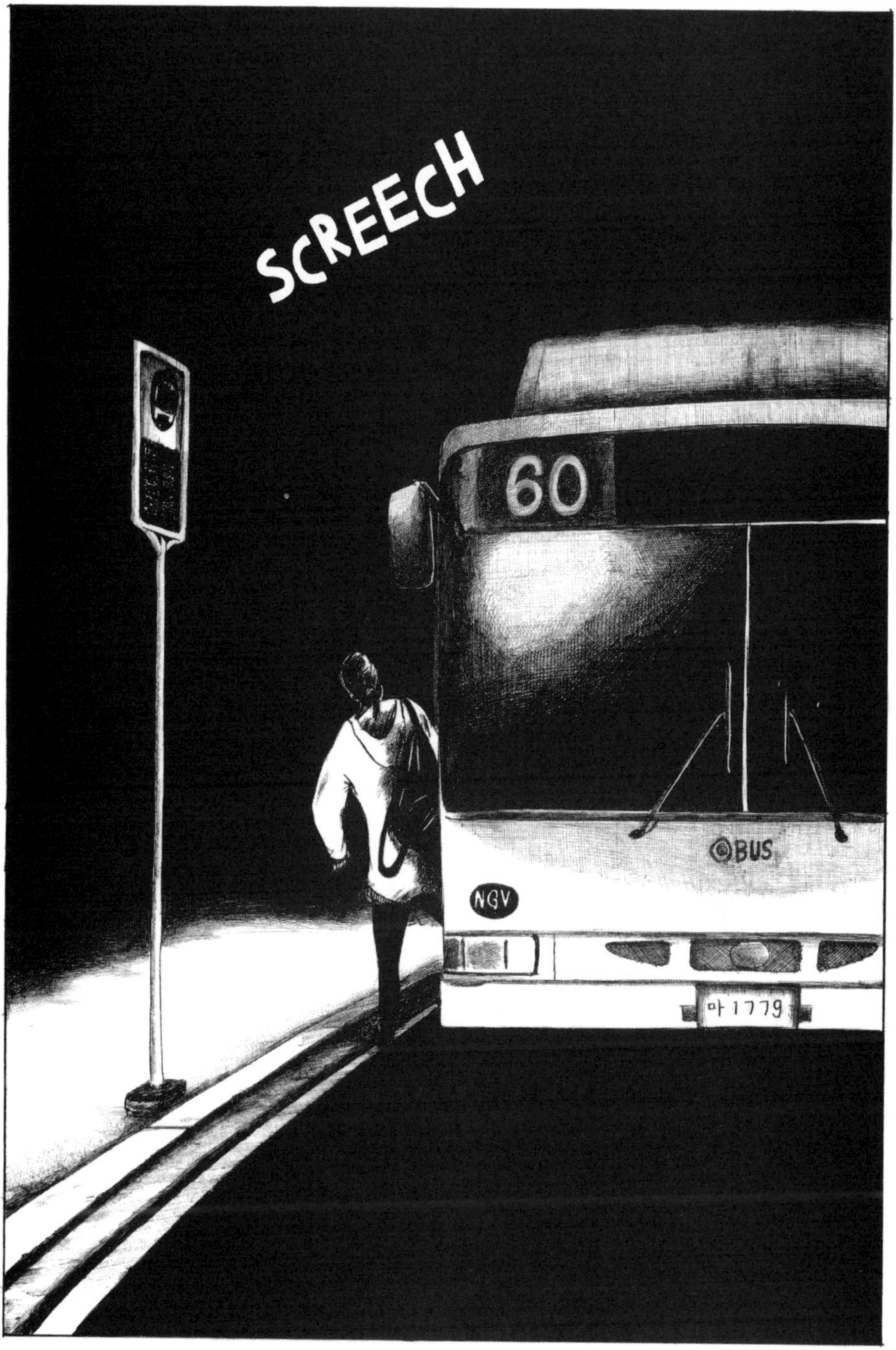
SCREECH
60
BUS
NGV
마 1779

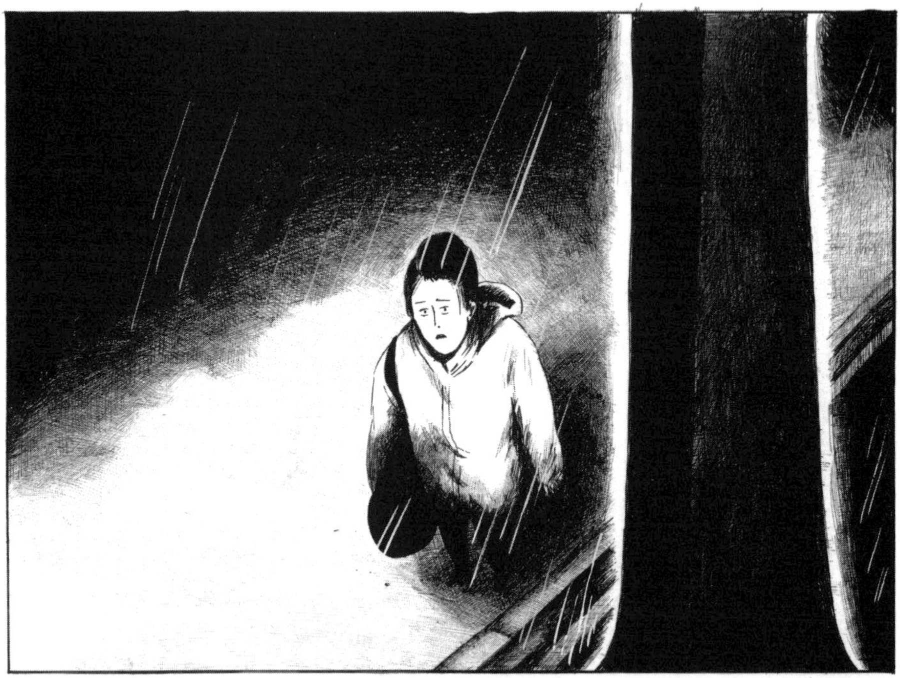

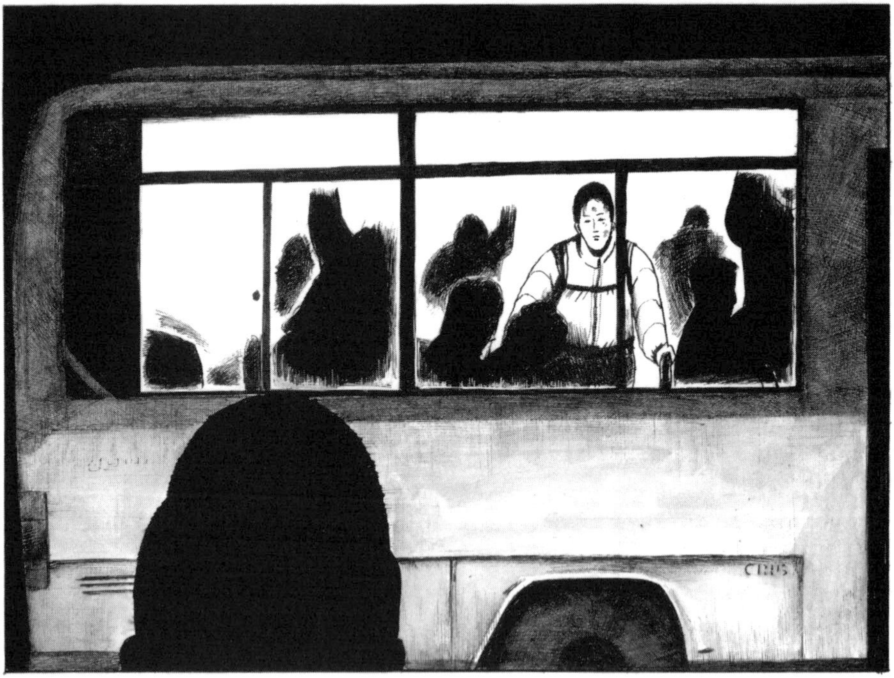

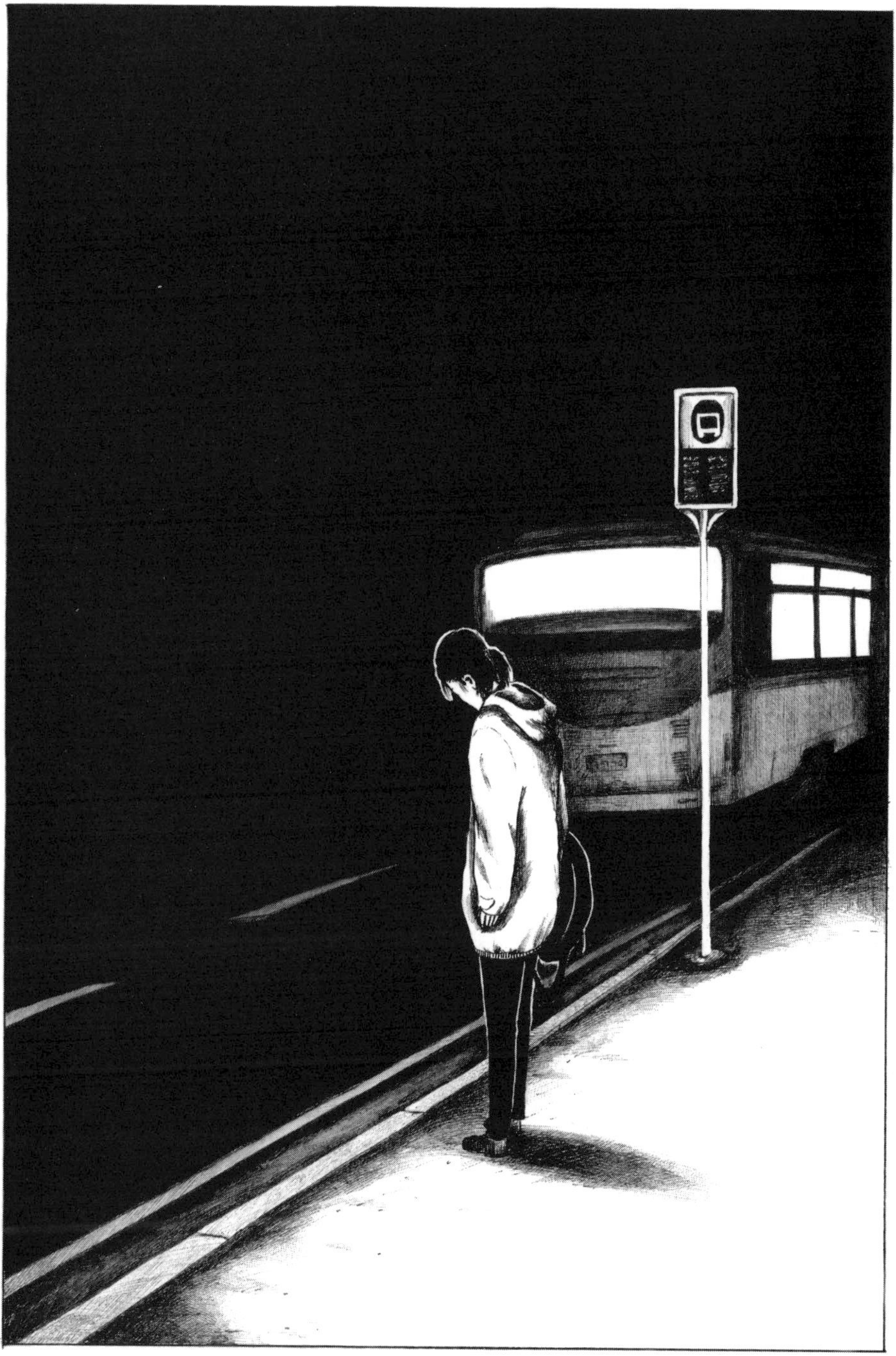

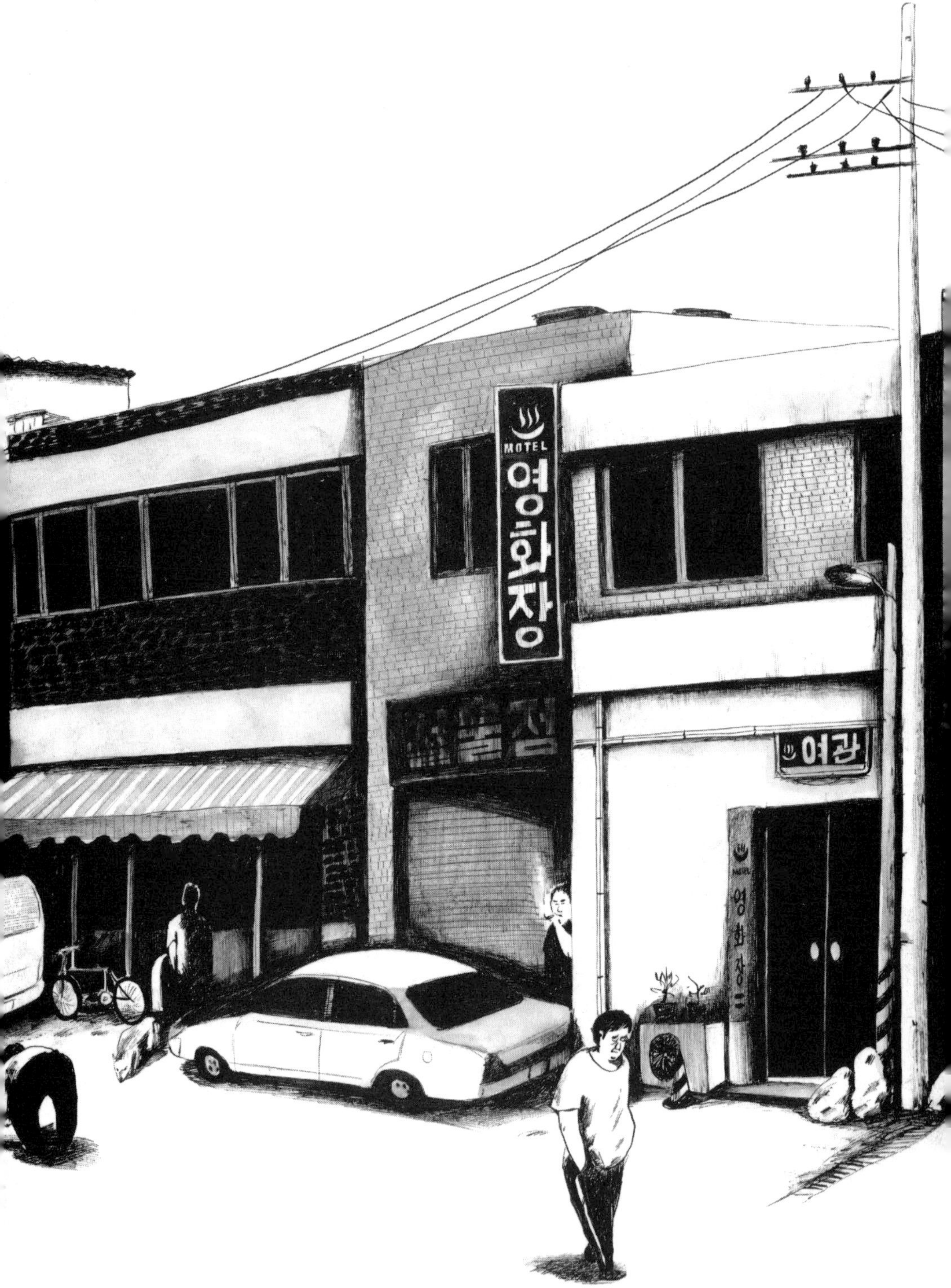
MOTEL
영화장
여관
영화장

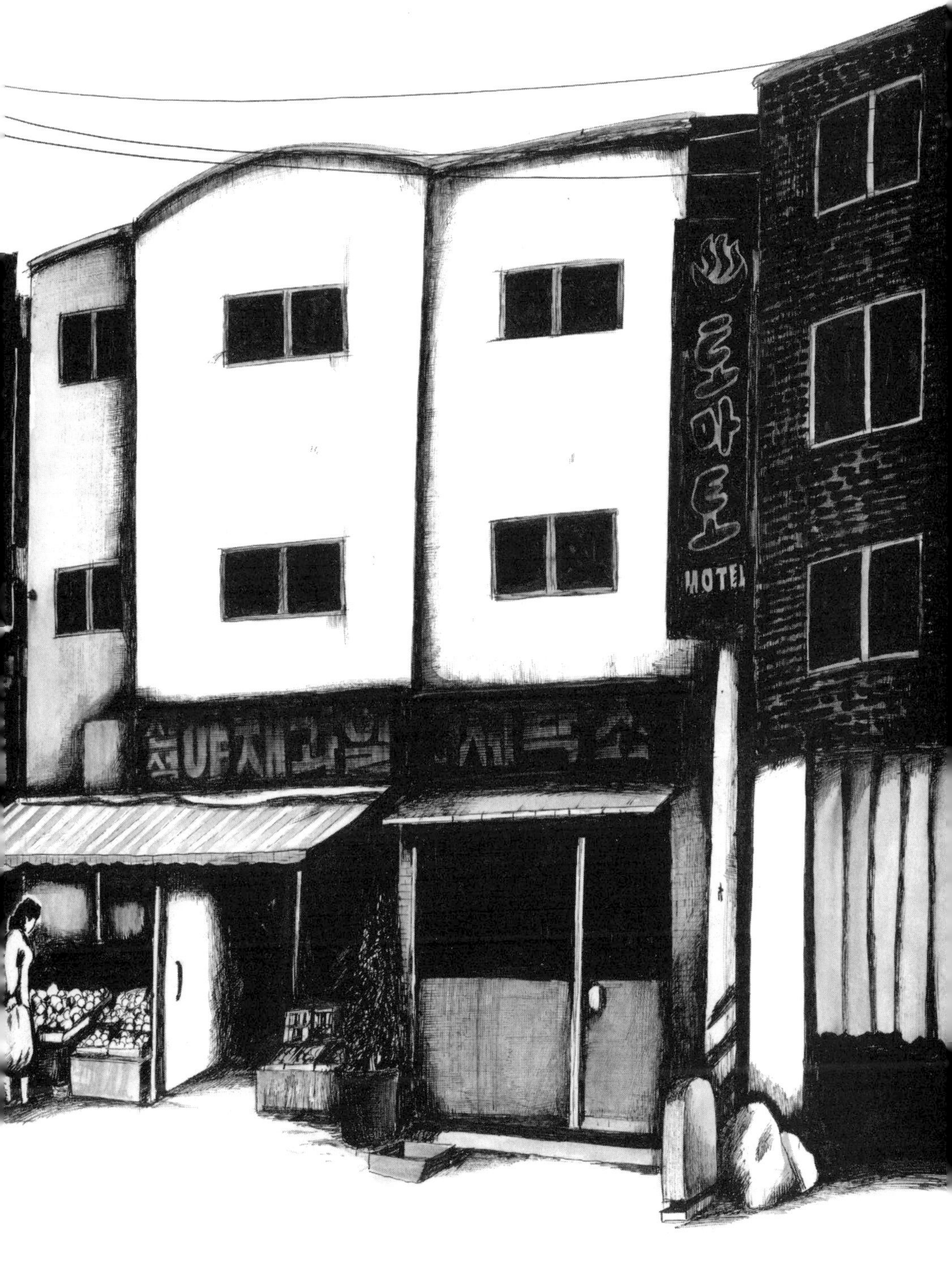
MOTEL

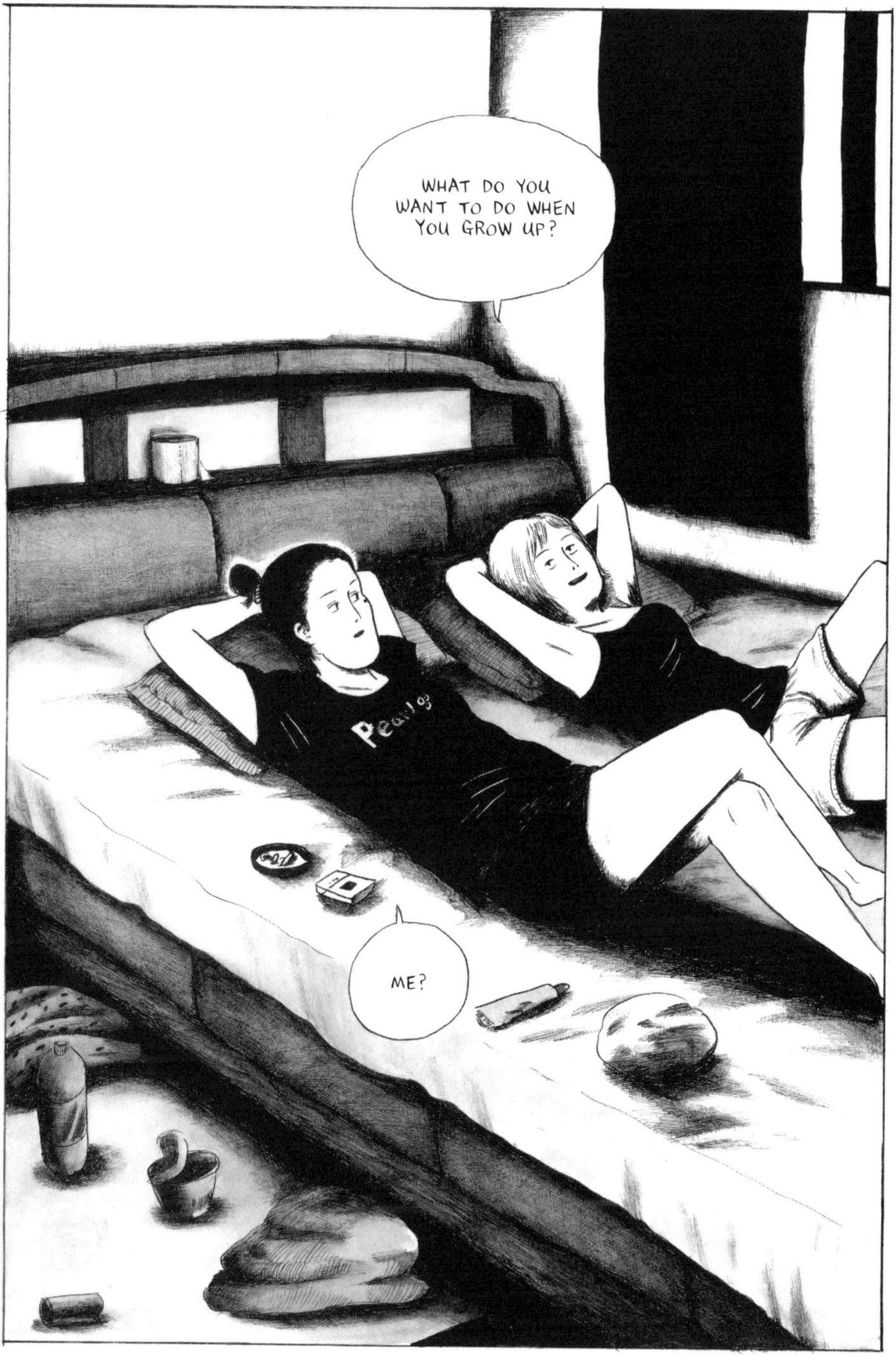
WHAT DO YOU WANT TO DO WHEN YOU GROW UP?
ME?

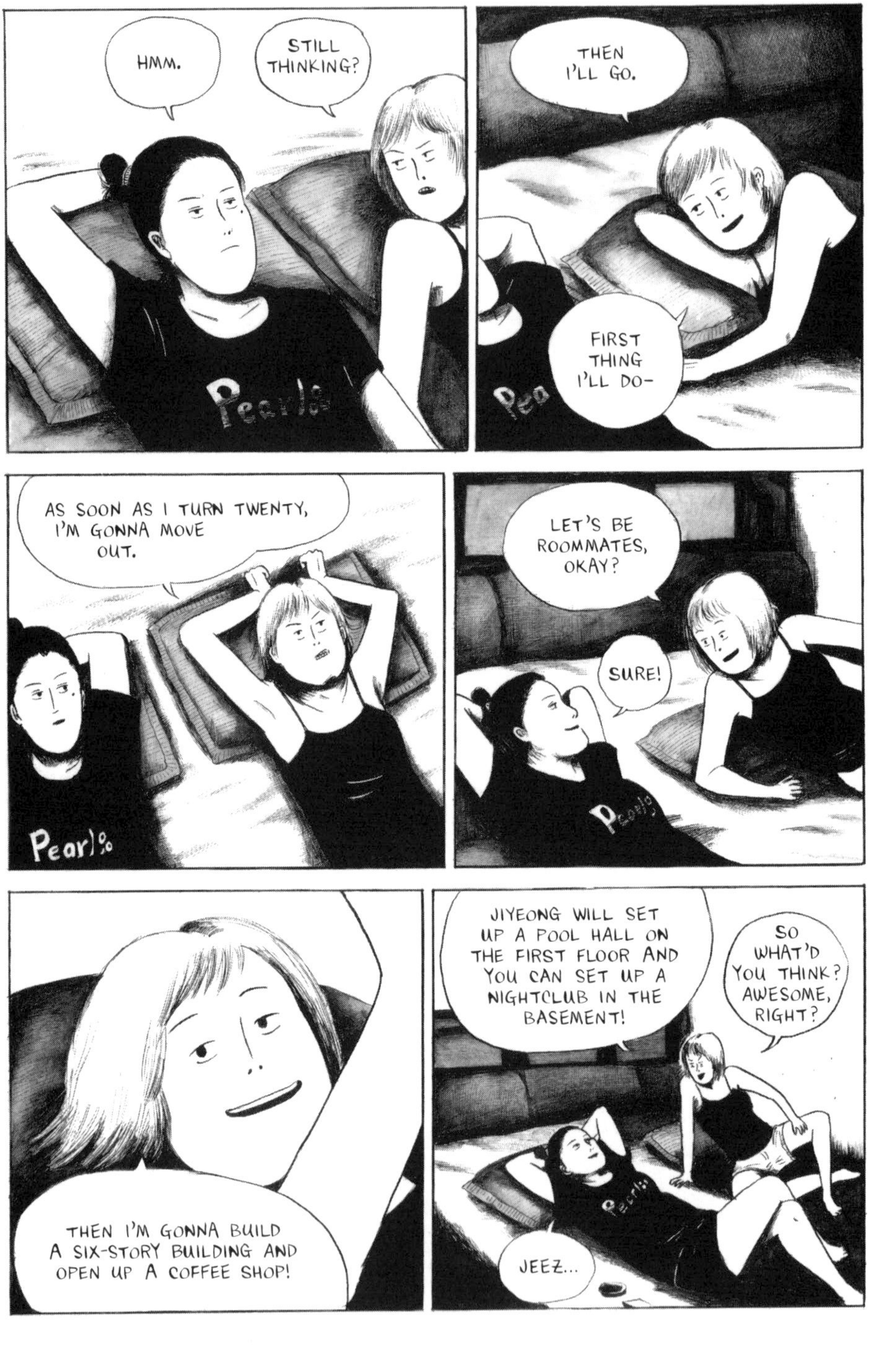

HMM.
STILL THINKING?
THEN I'LL GO.
FIRST THING I'LL DO-
AS SOON AS I TURN TWENTY, I'M GONNA MOVE OUT.
LET'S BE ROOMMATES, OKAY?
SURE!
THEN I'M GONNA BUILD A SIX-STORY BUILDING AND OPEN UP A COFFEE SHOP!
JIYEONG WILL SET UP A POOL HALL ON THE FIRST FLOOR AND YOU CAN SET UP A NIGHTCLUB IN THE BASEMENT!
SO WHAT'D YOU THINK? AWESOME, RIGHT?
JEEZ...

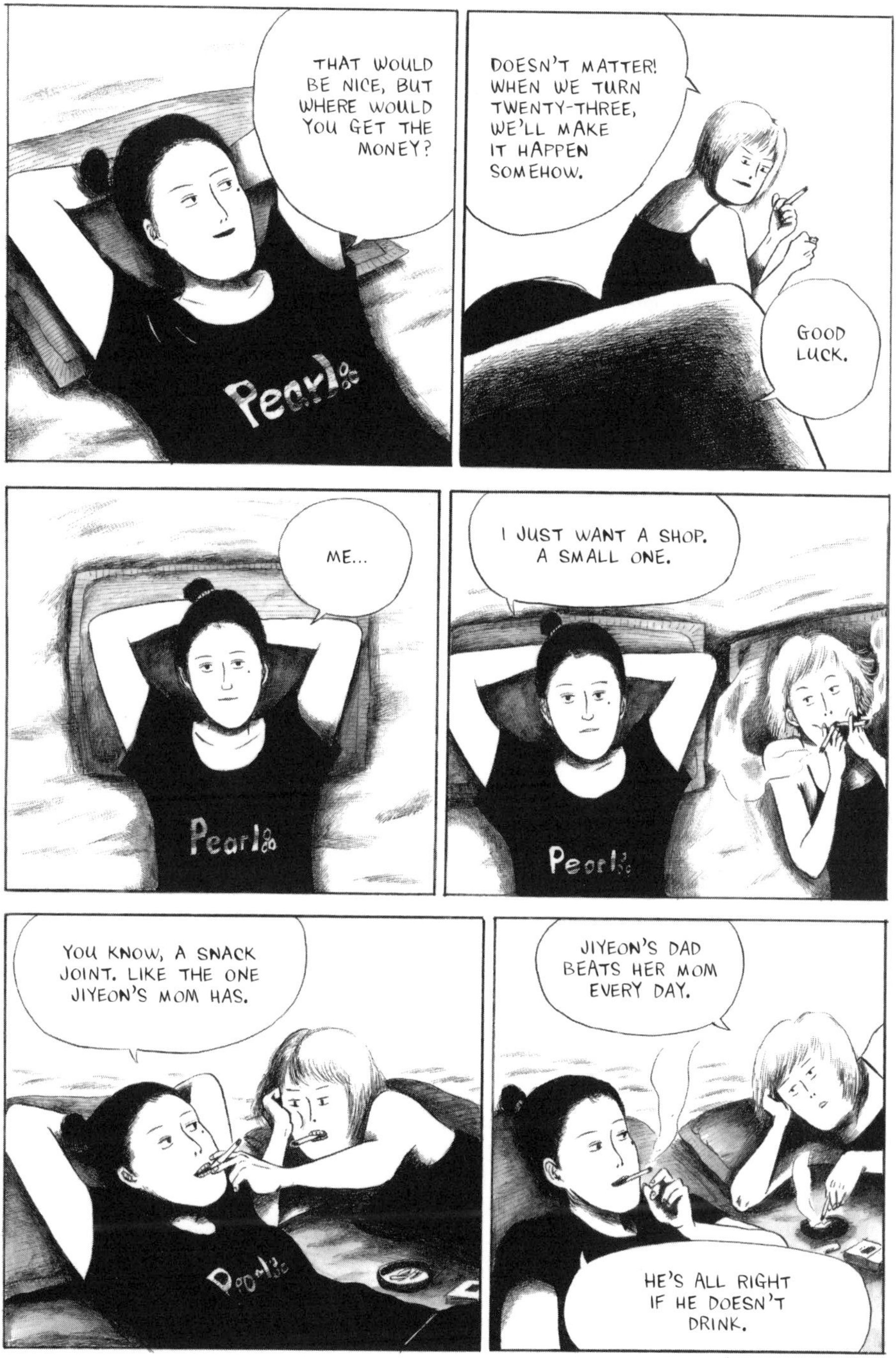
THAT WOULD BE NICE, BUT WHERE WOULD YOU GET THE MONEY?
DOESN'T MATTER! WHEN WE TURN TWENTY-THREE, WE'LL MAKE IT HAPPEN SOMEHOW.
GOOD LUCK.
ME...
I JUST WANT A SHOP. A SMALL ONE.
YOU KNOW, A SNACK JOINT. LIKE THE ONE JIYEON'S MOM HAS.
JIYEON'S DAD BEATS HER MOM EVERY DAY.
HE'S ALL RIGHT IF HE DOESN'T DRINK.

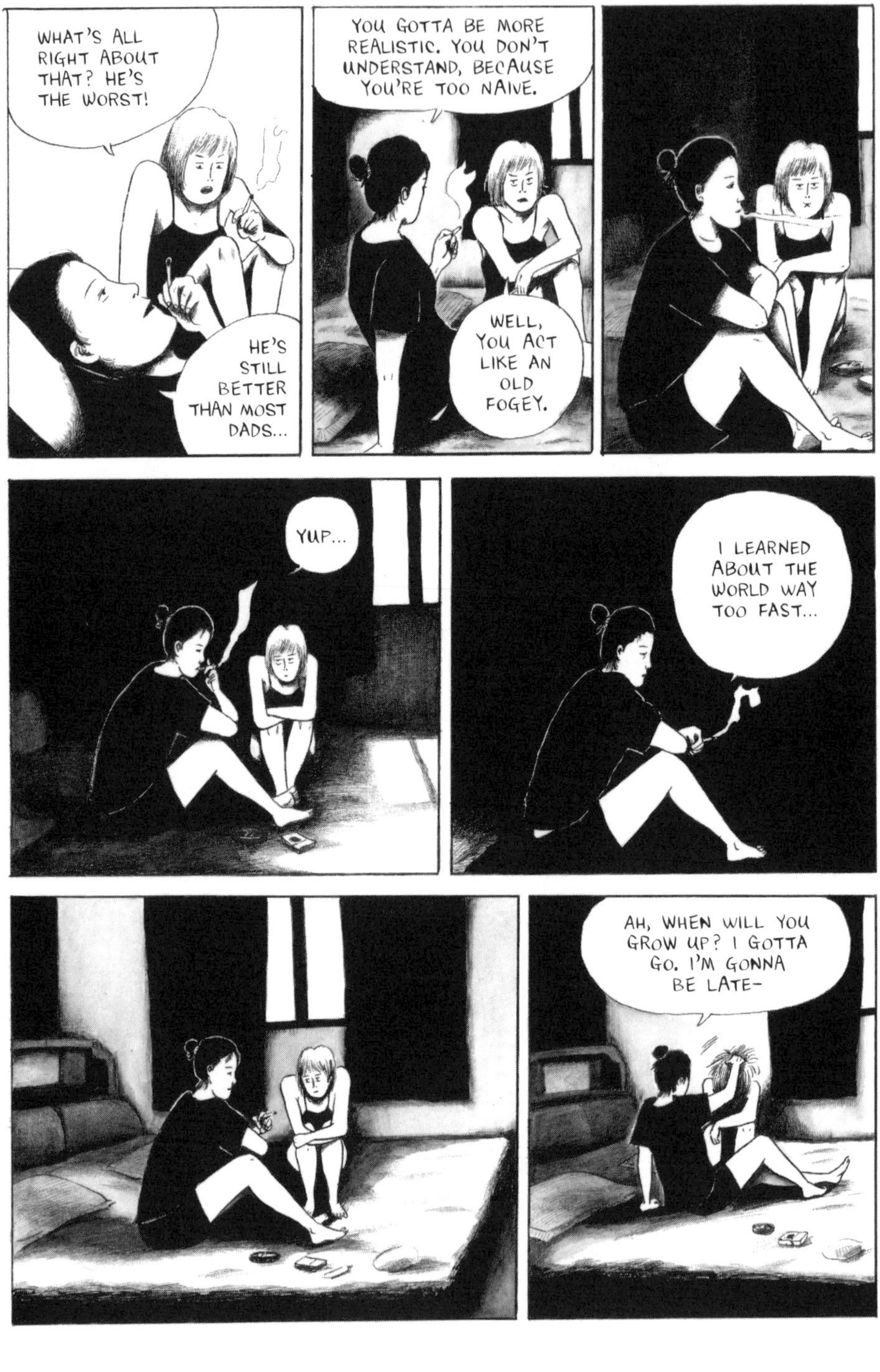
WHAT'S ALL RIGHT ABOUT THAT? HE'S THE WORST!
HE'S STILL BETTER THAN MOST DADS...
YOU GOTTA BE MORE REALISTIC. YOU DON'T UNDERSTAND, BECAUSE YOU'RE TOO NAIVE.
WELL, YOU ACT LIKE AN OLD FOGEY.
YUP...
I LEARNED ABOUT THE WORLD WAY TOO FAST...
AH, WHEN WILL YOU GROW UP? I GOTTA GO. I'M GONNA BE LATE-

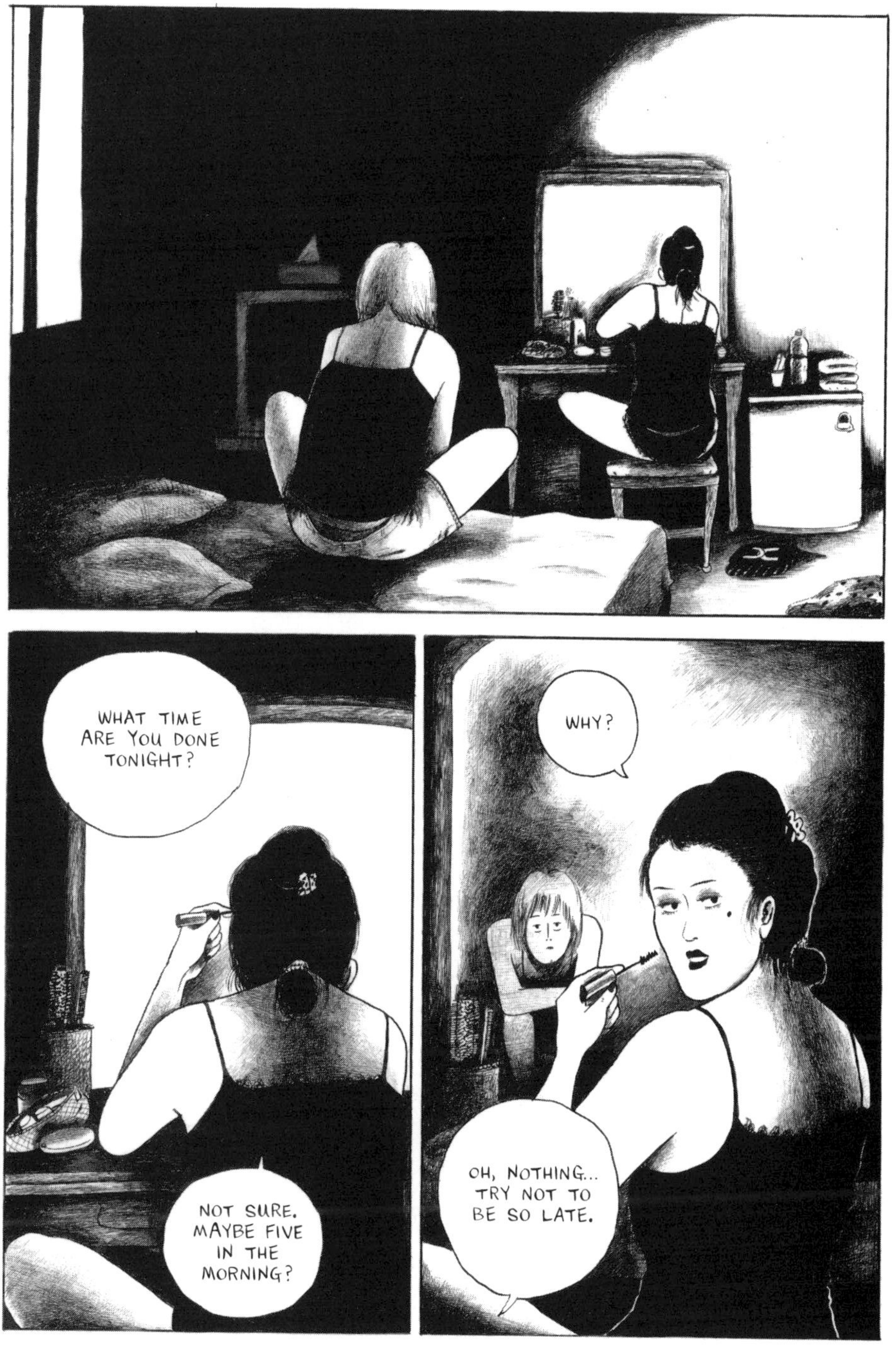
WHAT TIME ARE YOU DONE TONIGHT?
NOT SURE. MAYBE FIVE IN THE MORNING?
WHY?
OH, NOTHING... TRY NOT TO BE SO LATE.

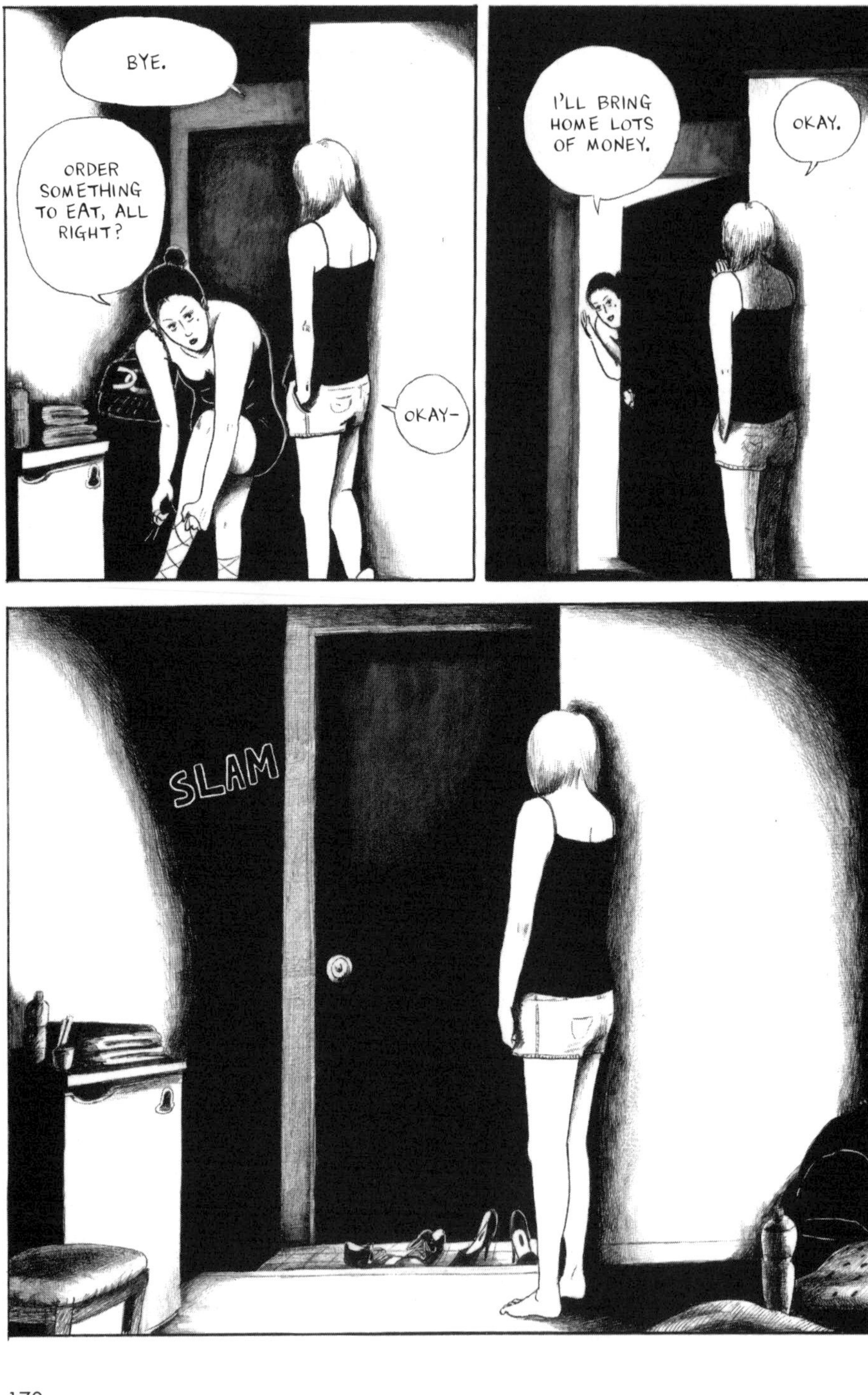
BYE.
ORDER SOMETHING TO EAT, ALL RIGHT?
OKAY-
I'LL BRING HOME LOTS OF MONEY.
OKAY.
SLAM

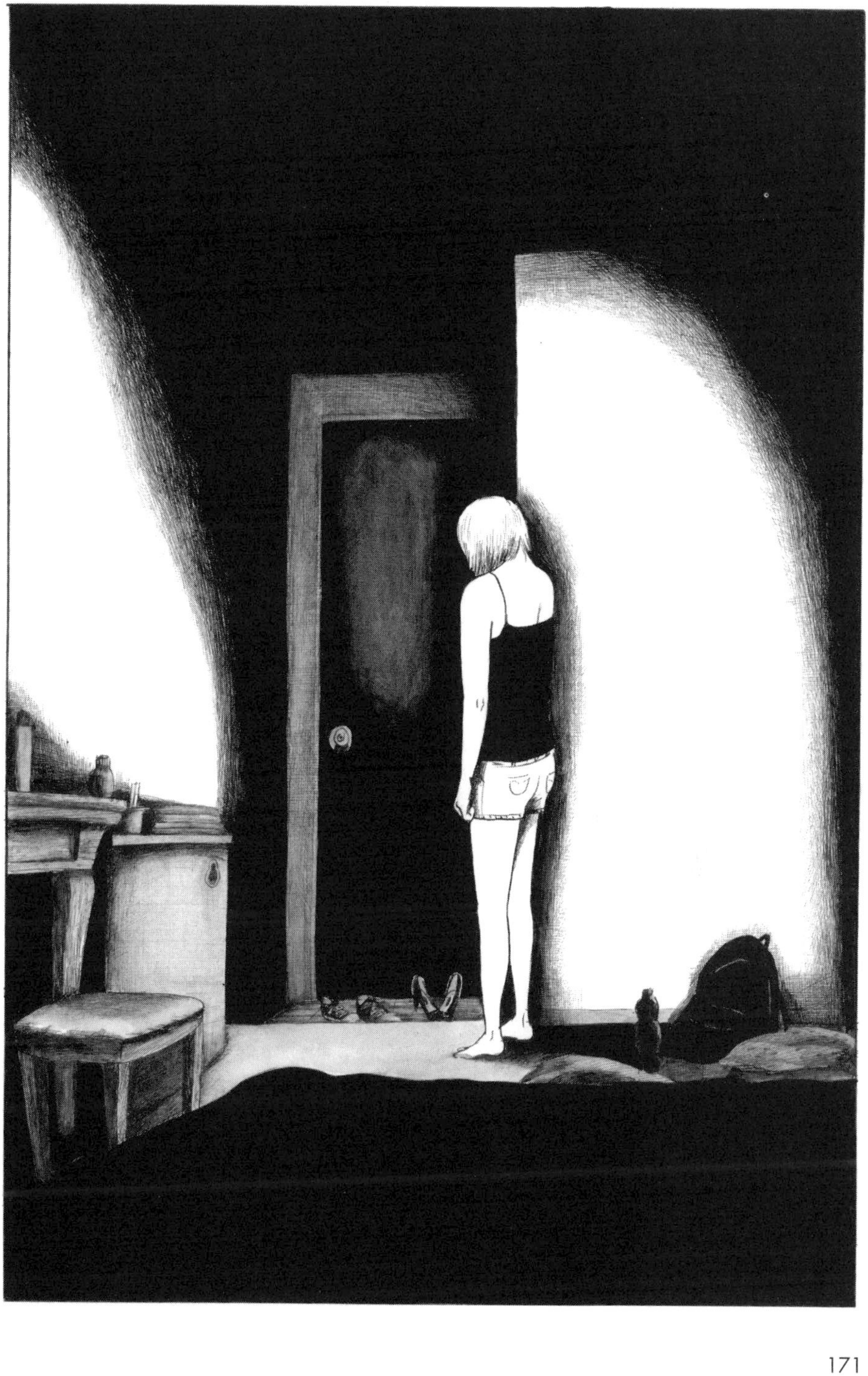

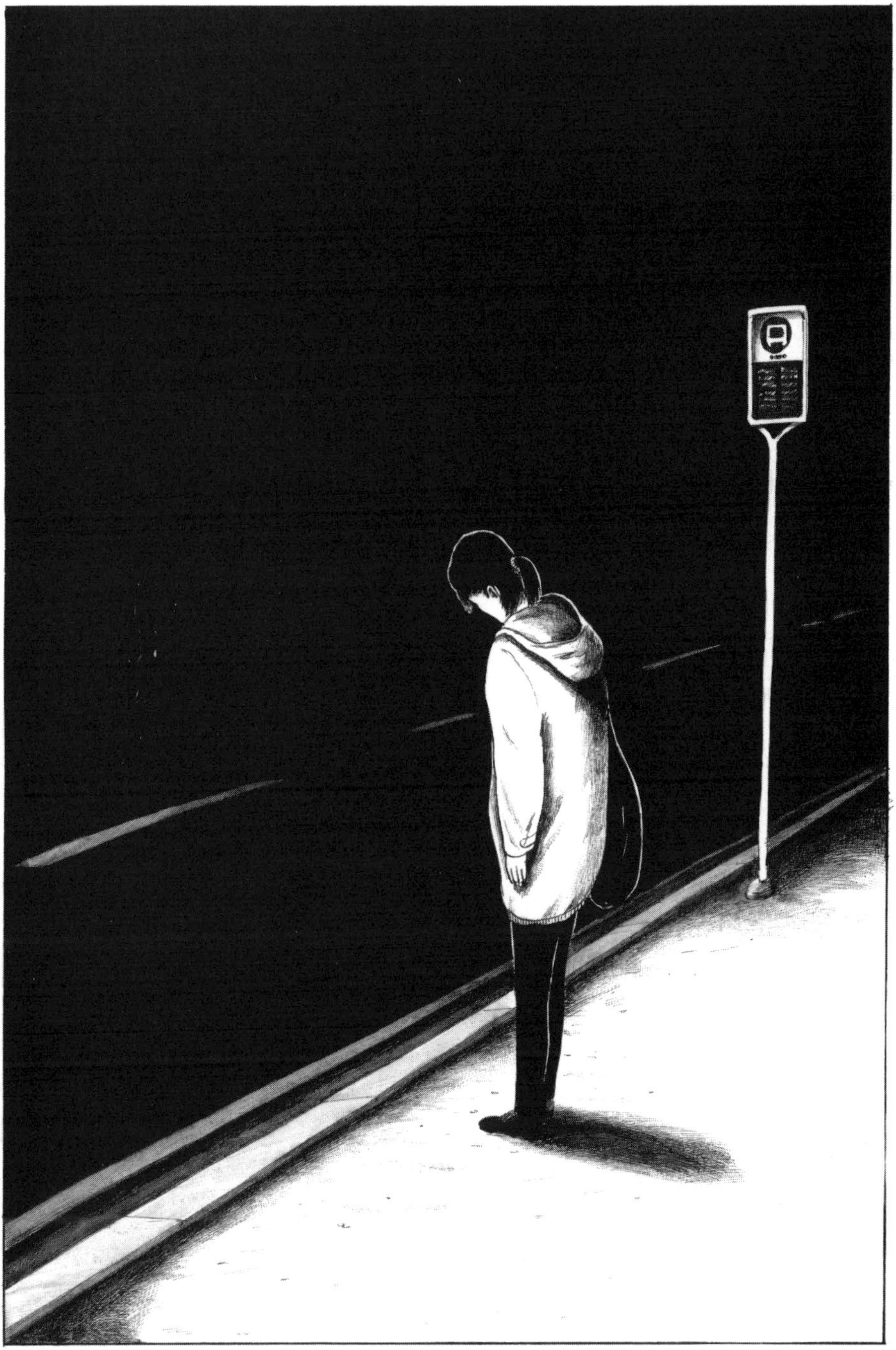